Memristors for Neuromorphic Circuits and Artificial Intelligence Applications

Memristors for Neuromorphic Circuits and Artificial Intelligence Applications

Special Issue Editor

Jordi Suñé

MDPI • Basel • Beijing • Wuhan • Barcelona • Belgrade

Special Issue Editor
Jordi Suñé
Universitat Autònoma de
Barcelona, Departament
d'Enginyeria Electrònica
Spain

Editorial Office
MDPI
St. Alban-Anlage 66
4052 Basel, Switzerland

This is a reprint of articles from the Special Issue published online in the open access journal *Materials* (ISSN 1996-1944) from 2018 to 2020 (available at: https://www.mdpi.com/journal/materials/special_issues/memristors).

For citation purposes, cite each article independently as indicated on the article page online and as indicated below:

LastName, A.A.; LastName, B.B.; LastName, C.C. Article Title. *Journal Name* **Year**, *Article Number*, Page Range.

ISBN 978-3-03928-576-1 (Pbk)
ISBN 978-3-03928-577-8 (PDF)

Cover image courtesy of Jaime Moroldo, Italian-Venezuelan plastic artist based in Spain, who is a long-lasting friend of Jordi Suñé, editor of this book.

Contents

About the Special Issue Editor

Jordi Suñé is a full professor of Electronics at the Universitat Autònoma de Barcelona (UAB). He is the coordinator of the NANOCOMP research group, dedicated to the modeling and simulation of electron devices with a multi-scale approach. His main contributions are in the area of gate oxide reliability for CMOS technology. In terms of research achievements in this field, he was upgraded to IEEE Fellow for contributions to the understanding of gate oxide failure and reliability methodology. In 2008, he received the IBM Faculty award for a long-lasting collaboration with IBM Microelectronics in this field. Since 2008, he has worked in the area of memristive devices and their application to neuromorphic circuits. In 2010, he received the ICREA ACADEMIA award and, in 2012 and 2013, he was awarded the Chinese Academy of Sciences Professorship for Senior International Scientists, for a collaboration with IMECAS (Beijing, China). Recently, he launched a new research group/network (neuromimeTICs.org) dedicated to the application of neuromorphic electronics to artificial intelligence and to dissemination activities. He has (co)authored more than 400 papers (h-index = 44) in international journals and relevant conferences, including 14 IEDM papers, several invited papers, and five tutorials on oxide reliability at the IEEE-IRPS. At present, he's the local UAB coordinator of a European project (EU2020-ECSEL-WAKeMeUP) on emerging non-volatile memories embedded in microprocessors for automotive, secure, and general electronics applications. His present research interests are: transition metal oxide-based filamentary RRAM memristors; complex perovskite oxide based memristors; bio-realistic compact modeling of memristors for neuromorphic applications; RRAM fabrication, characterization and modelling; biomimetic electrical circuit simulation with SPICE; analog circuits based on the combination of CMOS and memristors; and, in general, artificial neural networks for artificial intelligence applications. Jordi Suñé was funded by the WAKeMeUP 783176 project, co-funded by grants from the Spanish Ministerio de Ciencia, Innovación y Universidades (PCI2018-093107 grant) and the ECSEL EU Joint Undertaking.

Preface to "Memristors for Neuromorphic Circuits and Artificial Intelligence Applications"

The applications of artificial intelligence (AI) and their impacts on global society are currently growing at an exponential pace. Image and speech recognition and processing, business optimization, medical diagnosis, autonomous cars, and science discovery are only some of these applications. Although the term AI was coined in the late 1950s, it is only in the past decade that due to the impressive improvements in computing power, AI has found applications in many areas, even exceeding humans in some tasks. It is convenient to distinguish between conventional (narrow) AI applications designed for one specific task, and artificial general intelligence (AGI), which aims at emulating humans in the most general situations. All big AI industrial players are committed to achieving AGI with the idea that once you solve intelligence, you can use it to solve everything else. AI is heralded as a revolutionary technology for the 21st century; it has many applications for the good but, in its AGI version, it has also been signaled as one of the significant risks for the future of humanity. Artificial neural networks (ANNs) are inspired by the structure of the brain and are formed by artificial neurons interconnected by artificial synapses exhibiting plasticity effects. During the training of an ANN, large amounts of data are provided through the input neurons and the strength of the synaptic interconnections are progressively modified until the network learns how to classify not only the training data but also unforeseen data of a similar kind. Most AI algorithms have been implemented by software programs run on conventional computing systems with a Von Neumann architecture, such as central processing units, graphical processing units, and field programmable gate arrays. Recently, specially designed integrated circuits, such as the tensor processing unit (TPU), have been introduced to optimize the type of operations (vector-matrix multiplication) required for training and inference. In these computing systems, the memory and processing units are physically separated so that significant amounts of data need to be shuttled back and forth during computation. This creates a performance bottleneck both in processing speed due to the memory latency and in power consumption due to the energy requirements for data retrieval, transportation, and storage. The problem is aggravated by deep learning systems growing significantly in complexity for better recognition accuracy; as a consequence, training time, cost, and energy consumption significantly increase. This trend has the drawback that the over-the-air distribution required by edge applications becomes more difficult, if not impossible. Given the required complexity of computing resources and the huge amounts of energy consumed, alternative approaches to software-based AI tools are urgently needed. In this regard, the hardware realization of AI applications and, in particular, the use of memristors to implement ANNs might be the next step in the way toward fast, compact, and energy efficient AI systems with a performance much closer to that of the human brain.

In this book, various reputed authors cover different aspects of the implementation of these memristive neuromorphic systems. The book starts with an editorial and two invited contributions that review the state-of-the-art ANNs implemented in hardware and present the basic concepts of neuromorphics. After this, different papers cover the whole field by focusing on advanced memristor devices for synaptic applications, including modelling for device improvement and circuit simulation; on some issues related to the organization of memristors in dense crossbar arrays, and finally on the application of these circuits to AI problems. The device-related papers cover promising three-terminal structures based on complex perovskite oxides, devices based on binary oxides and new training protocols to achieve improved synaptic properties, and new vertical resistive random-access resistive memories for 3D crossbar stacking and improved integration density. Then, the contributions addres memristor modelling, including a multiscale physics-based approach, a time-series and quantum point contact model, and a behavioral model for the realistic simulation of non-volatile memory and neuromorphic applications. The organization of the memristors crossbar arrays is also considered, dealing with non-idealities at the device (variability) and the interconnection (series resistance) levels. Finally, several papers focus on the application of memristors to neuromorphic applications, including a memristor emulator able to reproduce simple association behavior, self-organizing unsupervised spiking networks for pattern classification, and the application of CMOS-memristor neuromorphic circuits to emulate brain functions such as the coupling between sensory and hippocampal responses of cortical neurons. In summary, this book provides an updated general overview of the hardware implementation of neuromorphic systems for AI applications from the device to the system level.

I dedicate this book to my children. To my big boys, Cristian and Quim, who are living their independent lifes, always fighting against adversity. To my beautiful daughters, Alma and Guiomar, who are the light of my life. For better times, after several years of conflict and personal growth.

Jordi Suñé
Special Issue Editor

materials

MDPI

Editorial

Memristors for Neuromorphic Circuits and Artificial Intelligence Applications

Enrique Miranda and Jordi Suñé *

Departament d'Enginyeria Electrònica, Universitat Autònoma de Barcelona, 08193 Bellaterra, Spain; enrique.miranda@uab.cat

* Correspondence: jordi.sune@uab.cat; Tel.: +34 935 813 527

Received: 18 January 2020; Accepted: 30 January 2020; Published: 20 February 2020

Abstract: Artificial Intelligence has found many applications in the last decade due to increased computing power. Artificial Neural Networks are inspired in the brain structure and consist in the interconnection of artificial neurons through artificial synapses in the so-called Deep Neural Networks (DNNs). Training these systems requires huge amounts of data and, after the network is trained, it can recognize unforeseen data and provide useful information. As far as the training is concerned, we can distinguish between supervised and unsupervised learning. The former requires labelled data and is based on the iterative minimization of the output error using the stochastic gradient descent method followed by the recalculation of the strength of the synaptic connections (weights) with the backpropagation algorithm. On the other hand, unsupervised learning does not require data labeling and it is not based on explicit output error minimization. Conventional ANNs can function with supervised learning algorithms (perceptrons, multi-layer perceptrons, convolutional networks, etc.) but also with unsupervised learning rules (Kohonen networks, self-organizing maps, etc.). Besides, another type of neural networks are the so-called Spiking Neural Networks (SNNs) in which learning takes place through the superposition of voltage spikes launched by the neurons. Their behavior is much closer to the brain functioning mechanisms they can be used with supervised and unsupervised learning rules. Since learning and inference is based on short voltage spikes, energy efficiency improves substantially. Up to this moment, all these ANNs (spiking and conventional) have been implemented as software tools running on conventional computing units based on the von Neumann architecture. However, this approach reaches important limits due to the required computing power, physical size and energy consumption. This is particularly true for applications at the edge of the internet. Thus, there is an increasing interest in developing AI tools directly implemented in hardware for this type of applications. The first hardware demonstrations have been based on Complementary Metal-Oxide-Semiconductor (CMOS) circuits and specific communication protocols. However, to further increase training speed andenergy efficiency while reducing the system size, the combination of CMOS neuron circuits with memristor synapses is now being explored. It has also been pointed out that the short time non-volatility of some memristors may even allow fabricating purely memristive ANNs. The memristor is a new device (first demonstrated in solid-state in 2008) which behaves as a resistor with memory and which has been shown to have potentiation and depression properties similar to those of biological synapses. In this Special Issue, we explore the state of the art of neuromorphic circuits implementing neural networks with memristors for AI applications.

Keywords: artificial intelligence; neural networks; resistive switching; memristive devices; deep learning networks; spiking neural networks; electronic synapses; crossbar array; pattern recognition

1. Introduction

The applications of Artificial Intelligence (AI) and their impact on global society are currently growing at an exponential pace. Image recognition, speech processing, business management and optimization, stock markets, medical diagnosis, global climate forecast, autonomous cars, and science discovery are only some of the present AI applications. The term AI was coined back in the late fifties, but it is only in the last decade that, due to the impressive improvements in computing power driven by the Moore's law, AI has been successfully applied in many areas, even overcoming humans in some tasks [1]. At this point, it is convenient to distinguish between conventional (narrow) AI applications, which are designed for one specific task, and Artificial General Intelligence (AGI) programs that aim at emulating human in the most general situations. All big players such as IBM, Google, Facebook, Microsoft, Baidu and practically everybody who's anybody in the AI field is committed to achieve AGI. The main idea behind AGI research programs is that once you solve intelligence, you can use it to solve everything else. AI is heralded as a revolutionary technology for the 21st century, it has many applications for the good but, in its AGI version, it has also been signaled as one of the significant risks for the future of humanity [2].

1.1. Artificial Intelligence and Its Implementation in Software

The internet has fueled AI applications providing huge amounts of data which can be fed into artificial neural networks (ANNs) to reveal relevant information about complex systems which could not otherwise be analyzed. ANNs are inspired in the low-level structure of the brain and are formed by artificial neurons interconnected by artificial synapses exhibiting plasticity effects. During the training of an ANN, large amounts of data are provided through the input neurons and the strength of the synaptic interconnections are progressively modified until the network learns how to classify not only the training data but also unforeseen data of a similar kind. The process of data recognition of the trained network is most often called inference. In the training phase, we can distinguish between supervised and unsupervised learning algorithms. Supervised learning requires the labelling of the raw data while unsupervised learning can directly deal with unstructured data. Supervised learning is implemented with the so-called Deep Neural Networks (DNNs) but also with other types of ANNs DNNs consist in an ordered arrangement of neuron layers interconnected with the adjacent layers by synapses. There is an input layer through which the data are supplied, an output layer which provides the processed information and, one or several hidden layers with different hierarchical levels of data representation. The actual architecture of interconnections gives rise to different types of networks optimized for different applications (fully connected networks, convolutional networks, recurrent networks, etc.). DNNs are trained using the backpropagation algorithm which consists in calculating an error function (the cost function) as the sum of the squared differences between the obtained and the expected outputs for mini batches (a subset of whole training database, which are called epochs. The cost function is progressively minimized using the stochastic gradient descent method and the back propagation of errors from output to input allows modifying the synaptic weights and train the system. In unsupervised learning networks, the expected response is not a priori known and hence, no cost function can be minimized and the backpropagation technique cannot be used. These networks learn to classify the data by themselves and the meaning of the classification results has to be finally interpreted. These systems are very promising to reveal previously unnoticed features in unstructured data and have the advantage of not requiring data labelling. For a nice recent review of DNNs characteristics and applications, see the work of Hinton [1].

Another type of networks are the so-called Spiking Neural Networks (SNN), in which the data moves back and forward through the network in the form of spikes generated by the neurons. These spikes progressively modify the synaptic weights in a way which is much more similar to the way synapses are potentiated or depressed in the human brain. In general, these systems are energetically much more efficient and use bioinspired learning rules. One example of these rules is the so-called Spike Time-Dependent Plasticity (STDP) in which a synapsis is potentiated or depressed when forward and backwards voltage spikes overlap at the terminals of the device. When the forward pulse arrives before than the backwards pulse (stimulus-response causal relation), the synapsis is potentiated, while if the backwards pulse arrives first, the synapsis is depressed. The STPD learning rules is very typically and easily applied for unsupervised learning in SNNs. However, there are also many works developing supervised learning algorithms to SNN like, for example, the spiking spatio-temporal back-propagation technique. The overwhelming success of DNNs has somehow slowed down the progress of SNNs applicationsHowever, these are certainly the most promising systems for the future, including applications which continue learning along their operation live. Nice reviews about SNNs can be found in the works of Brette et al. [3] and Tavanaei et al. [4].

Most AI algorithms have been implemented by software programs which run on conventional computing systems with a Von Neumann architecture such as central processing units (CPUs), graphical processing units (GPUs) and field programmable gate arrays (FPGAs). Recently, especially designed application specific integrated circuits such as the tensor processing unit (TPU) have been introduced to optimize the type of operations required for training and inference. In all these computing systems, the memory and processing units are physically separated so that significant amounts of data need to be shuttled back and forth during computation. This creates a performance bottleneck both in processing speed due to the memory latency and in power consumption due to the energy requirements for data retrieving, transportation and storage. It must be noticed that most of the involved energy is related to memory operations which can consume up to more than 1000X the energy consumed in arithmetic operations. [5] The problem is aggravated by the fact that deep learning systems are growing significantly in size (more and more hidden layers) in order to improve output accuracy and, as a consequence, training time, cost and energy consumption significantly increase. This growth of size has also the drawback that it is difficult to distribute large models through over-the-air update for applications at the edge of the internet, such as autonomous cars or mobile phone applications. As for the size increase and the associated reduction of training speed, we can consider the evolution of Microsoft ResNet system for image recognition. ResNet18 (18 layers of neurons) required 2.5 days of training to reach an error rate of about 10.8% while ResNet152 training takes 1.5 weeks to reach a prediction failure rate of 6.2%. Let us consider the case of AlphaGo as a last example. In 2016, AlphaGo, a complex AI tool developed by DeepMing (Google), defeated the top-ranking professional player, Lee Sedol, in the ancient game of Go which, according to the developers is 10^{100} times more complex than chess [6]. AlphaGo used deep neural networks trained by a combination of supervised learning from human expert games, and reinforcement learning, based on a reward for success, a way of learning inspired in phycology. The two neural networks of AlphaGo used Monte Carlo tree search programs to simulate thousands of random games of self-play [6]. It its largest distributed version, running on multiple machines, used 40 search threads, 1920 CPUs and 280 GPUs. On the other hand, while Lee Sedol consumed about 20 Watts of power to play, AlphaGo power consumption was of approximately 1 MW (200 W per CPU and 200 W per GPU), i.e. an electricity bill of USD 300 was genenerated for a single game. Given the required complexity of computing resources and huge amounts of energy consumption, alternative approaches to the implementation of AI tools are required. In this regard, the hardware implementation of AI and, in particular, neural networks built with memristors, might be the next step in the way towards reduced size, energy efficient AI systems with performace much closer to that of the human brain.

1.2. Artificial Intelligence and Its Hardware Implementation

Nowadays, there is a rising interest for the hardware implementation of ANNs using neuromorphic circuits. These are ordered networks of electron devices implementing artificial neurons and their synaptic interconnections. These hardware networks allow in-memory computing (computation performed directly on a non-volatile memory array), massive parallelism and huge improvements in power consumption. Moreover, they are highly suited for applications at the edge of the internet.

The first hardware implementations of neural networks are those based on CMOS technology. In these systems, neurons are based on CMOS circuits (both for computing and memory) and the required high density of interconnections is usually implemented by a virtual wiring system consisting in a digital bus and a special purpose communication protocol. Using this approach, large-scale SNN chips have been developed, reaching up to one million neurons per chip [7]. Interconnecting these chips on a board or a wafer and assembling them to form more complex systems have also been demonstrated. This approach is scalable to implement very complex neuromorphic systems. However, these systems require large amounts of circuitry and are costly in terms of area and energy consumption. Scaling these systems to the complexity of the brain (roughly 10^{11} neurons and 10^{15} synapses) would require a space of the size of a room. These drawbacks have motivated the exploration of other hardware alternatives such as those which combine CMOS for neuron implementation and memristors for synapses. This is the scope of this special issue namely, the application of memristors to build improved neuromorphic systems for AI.

The solid-state nanoelectronic implementation of the memristor was reported for the first time in 2008 by the HP group led by Stanley Williams [8]. In 1971, Leon Chua used symmetry arguments to predict a device which should relate electric charge and magnetic flux [9], just as inductors relate current and magnetic flux or capacitors relate charge and voltage. However, the memristor is better understood as a resistor with memory. A resistor whose value depends on an internal variable that changes with the applied voltages or currents and hence, it is able to store information in an analogue and non-volatile manner. On the other hand, these devices (with can be scaled down to 10 nm) can be fabricated in dense crossbar arrays (an array of perpendicular wires with a memristor at each crossing point) in the back-end of the CMOS process. Moreover, these layers can be stacked one on top of another to provide a highly dense 3D array of non-volatile memory (an implementation of the so-called storage-class memory) or, alternatively, an array of interconnections with synaptic properties for neuromorphic circuits. These memory arrays allow toperform computing tasks within the data themselves using for example their capability to perform operations such as matrix-vector multiplication (MVM) in an analogue, highly parallel and energy-efficient way. This type of one-step MVM calculations are based on physical laws such as the Ohm's law and the Kirchoff's law and they are the basis of in-memory computing. This is a very important change of paradigm which overcomes the limitations of the Von Neumann architecture for some tasks. On the other hand, these hybrid CMOS/memristor based neuromorphic systems will allow reducing the energy consumption by a factor of at least 10^3 with respect to pure CMOS implementations. Furthermore, there is a very relevant reduction of area so that a complex neural system with the density of the brain neurons and synapses could in principle be fabricated in a single board. The possibility of fabricating memristors with short-term non-volatility also points out to the possibility of implementing purely memristive DNNs and SNNs [10]. By purely memristive we refer to systems that implement both synapses and neurons with memristors.

In recent years, many different device concepts have been considered for implementing the memristor. These include the phase change memory (PCM), in which resistance is modified by partial crystallization/amorphization of a small volume of chalcogenide material; the Resistive Random Access Memory (RRAM) where conductance change is related to the electro-ionic modulation of a conducting filament across an oxide layer (mainly in binary oxides such as Ta_2O_5, Al_2O_3, HfO_2, TiO_2, ...) or to the homogenous modulation of an injection barrier (mainly in complex perovskite oxides); spintronic devices in which the memristor internal variable is the partial spin polarization, ferroelectric devices which use changes in the dielectric polarization to modify the device conductance, and others. Memristors have been implemented mainly in two-terminal devices (2T) but recently, three-terminal (3T) structures are also being explored to optimize some fundamental device properties for neuromorphic applications such as linearity in the conductance change and conduction symmetry.

Recently, there have been several hardware demonstrations of neural networks with synaptic interconnections implemented with memristors. The very first demonstration was that of Prezioso and coworkers [11] who implemented a single layer perceptron using a 12 × 12 passive crossbar array of RRAM. Using supervised training, they demonstrated classification of a small dataset of 3x3 images into three classes. Recently, the same research group presented another demonstrator of a perceptron classifier with one hidden layer implemented with two purely passive 20 × 20 crossbar arrays board-integrated with discrete conventional components [12]. With this system, they reached an error rate of only 3% with ex-situ supervised learning. Larger arrays have also been recently reported but all these incorporate an MOS transistor (selector) in series with the memristor (1T1R configuration) at each cross point. The transistor increases the required area and compromises the desired scalability. However, it is necessary to limit the current thus avoiding damaging the memristor during the forming/potentiation phases. On the other hand, the transistor allows to eliminate the crosstalk effects (sneak-path problem) which are increasingly significant for large synaptic arrays. With this 1T1R structure, a hardware accelerator based on 165,000 PCM synapses was implemented and used for image classification using the Modified National Institute of Standards and Technology (MNIST) database of handwritten digits [13]. The same set of MNIST data was also recently used for the in-situ supervised training of 1T1R RRAM synaptic crossbars of about 8000 memristors, showing high accuracy and tolerance to defective devices (stuck at low conductance) and reaching high recognition accuracy [14]. Also remarkable is the recent demonstration of the ex-situ training of a two-layer perceptron DNN implemented with a 4Kbit 1T1R RRAM array which not only achieved high accuracy but also very low power consumption [15].

Progress in the implementation of neural networks using memristors as synapses is remarkable. However, many issues still need to be resolved both at the material, device and system levels so as to simultaneously achieve high accuracy, low variability, high speed, energy efficiency, small area, low cost, and good reliability. This requires combined research efforts in these three interconnected areas: devices, circuits and systems. Towards this goal, high quality compact behavioral models are a very important ingredient to explore compare different devices at the circuit and system levels. In this regard, Stanley Williams recently made a call to the memristor research community requesting high quality compact models for the circuit designers and systems architects to use with confidence for their circuit and system simulations and validations [16].

2. Synopsis

In this special issue we are honored to have two invited review papers by recognized leaders in the field. Camuñas-Mesa, Linares-Barranco and Serrano-Gotarredona focus their review on the implementation of SNNs with hybrid memristor-CMOS hardware, and review the basics of neuromorphic computing and its CMOS implementation [17]. Milo, Malavena, Monzio Compagnoli and Ielmini, mainly focus on memristive devices implementing electronic synapses in neuromorphic circuits [18]. They consider different memory technologies for brain-inspired systems including mainstream flash memory technologies, and memristive technologies with 2T and 3T structures. Finally, they review recent results on the use of these devices in both SNN and DNN memristive/CMOS neuromorphic networks. Both reviews provide an updated complementary view of the state-of-the-art in the implementation of neuromorphic systems with memristive synapses. Besides these two featured papers, a total number of 11 contributed papers complete this special issue.

Truong proposes a method to correct the line resistances when writing the desired values of conductance in DNN for feedforward applications [19]. Circuit simulations of a 64 × 16 single layer perceptron for the recognition of 26 characters (8 × 8 grayscale pixels) support significant improvements of network recognition when line resistance increases above 1.5Ω.

Wang et al. report an optimized RRAM device with a forming-free Al_2O_3/TaO_X stacked oxide which shows non-filamentary switching, and an analog bipolar switching that permits to program the conductance in an ANN with a high precision (error rate < 10%) [20]. The device shows relevant synaptic properties such as long-term potentiation and depression, spike-time dependent plasticity and pulse-pair facilitation. Although the conductance change of such synapses as a function of the number of constant voltage amplitude pulses is highly nonlinear, optimization of the training method allows obtaining rather linear changes and this would allow good accuracy in ANNs.

Van Nguyen et al. contribute to this issue with two papers that deal with mimicking the brain's neocortical operation in hardware. In the first one, they propose a memristor-CMOS hybrid circuit for the temporal-pooling of sensory and hippocampal information [21]. This circuit is composed by an input layer which combines sensory and temporal/location information in a memristor crossbar. The output layer of neurons also contains a memristor crossbar and integrates the information to make predictions. Both input and output layers contain memristor crossbars and standard CMOS circuits such as current-voltage converters, comparators, AND gates, latches and other circuits. Instead of the backpropagation algorithm, they use the much simpler Hebbian learning, which can be suitable for online learning. Moreover, the authors verify their proposal by circuit simulation with a Verilog-A phenomenological model for the memristor. Application of the circuit to the Enhanced-MNIST database demonstrates very good accuracy in both word and sentence recognition. In their second paper, they deal with reducing the effects of defects in the memristor crossbars such a stuck-at faults and memristor variations [22]. First, they show that the boost-factor adjustment can make the system fault-tolerant by suppressing the activation of defective columns. Second, they propose a memristor-CMOS hybrid circuit with the boost-factor adjustment to realize a defect-tolerant Spatial Pooler in hardware. Using the MNIST database, they show that the recognition accuracy is reduced only by 0.6% by the presence of up to 10% crossbar defects, with a very low energy overhead related to boost factor adjustment.

Fernández-Rodríguez et al. deal with a new class of 3T memristive devices based on the Metal-Insulator-Transition (MIT) in $YBa_2Cu_3O_{7-\delta}$ (YBCO), a complex perovskite oxide with well-known high-T superconducting properties [23]. At 300K, YBCO doesn't show any sign of superconduction but, small changes in the oxygen concentration produce large changes in resistance due to the MIT so that reversible non-volatile memory effects are observed. The authors fabricate prototype 3T transistor-like devices (memistors) which allow demonstrating volume switching effects different from the widely studied filamentary or interfacial effects. The reported results allow the fabrication of highly functional trans-synaptic devices where the input signal modifies the conductance of the output channel.

Rodríguez et al. investigate the origin of novel laser-fabricated graphene oxide memristors [24]. They use numerical tools linked to Time Series Statistical Analysis to reveal that these memristors are based on a local change of the stoichiometry in a conducting filament (as it is the case in most of binary oxides memristor). For the filament conduction they use the widely known point-contact model.

Hajtó et al. deal with the problem of the high variability of memristor properties [25]. First, they thoroughly discuss the need of more reliable devices for ANNs and neuromorphic in-memory computation, which require multi-state digital memristors and analog memristors, respectively. To reduce variability, they propose to use several interconnected memristors (memristor emulator circuit) at each synaptic location. After having simulated these circuits in previous works, in this issue they present real measurements demonstrating the change of operation properties of the emulator circuits and the reduction of the variability index. The evident drawbacks of this approach are the increase of effective consumed chip area (either in 2D crossbars or 3D stacks of crossbars) and the reduction of energy efficiency.

Pedró et al. deal with the simulation of fully unsupervised learning in self-organized Kohonen networks [26]. After experimentally characterizing HfO_2 memristors and demonstrating STDP synaptic properties in these devices, they propose a set of waveforms to minimize conductance change non-linearity. Using a realistic compact behavioral model for these memristors, they simulated the neuromorphic system, thus testing the learning algorithm. They also discuss that the selected system design and learning scheme permits to concatenate multiple neuron layers for autonomous hierarchical computing.

The high complexity and limited knowledge about the physical processes taking place in RRAM memristors is nowadays hampering the development, optimization and application of these devices. Moreover, these devices are to be used in different applications, such as embedded non-volatile memories, SNNs and DNNs, and the device requirements change for each application. Thus, La Torraca et al. present a multi-scale simulation platform which includes all physical mechanisms such as charge transport, charge trapping, ion generation, diffusion, drift and recombination in an environment that considers the 3D distribution of temperature and electric field [27]. This multiscale approach allows simulating the performance of RRAM devices connecting their electrical properties to the underlying microscopic mechanisms, optimizing their analog switching performance as synapses, determining the role of electroforming and studying variability and reliability. Using this platform, the device performance can be optimized for different applications with different RRAM requirements.

Sun et al. discuss the application of 3D crossbar structures for the implementation of multi-layer neuromorphic networks (DNNs) [28]. They focus on RRAM memristors with a 3D structure and propose a new optimization method for machine learning weight changes that considers the properties of Vertical Resistive Random Access Memories (VRRAM). The operating principle of VRRAM allows to simplify the structure of the neuron circuit. The studied devices are promising for high-density neural network implementations.

Cisternas Ferri et al. use a phenomenological compact model for RRAM memristors, already experimentally validated in previous works, to construct a memristor emulator [29]. The main advantage of emulators over simulators is that they can be connected to external circuits to characterize their behavior in realistic environments. Moreover, the parameters of the emulated device can be arbitrarily changed so as to optimize the circuit performance and guide the ulterior fabrication of devices with optimum properties for a certain application. The memristor model is implemented using an Arduino microprocessor which solves the required differential equations. An analog-to-digital converter in the microcontroller measures the voltage on a digital potentiometer and the microprocessor changes its resistance accordingly. The emulator is validated comparing the obtained experimental results with model simulations (sinusoidal frequency memristive response, STDP, and response to voltage pulses). Finally, the emulator is introduced in a simple neuromorphic circuit that exhibits the main characteristics of Pavlovian conditioned learning.

Funding: This work was funded by the WAKeMeUP 783176 project, co-funded by grants from the Spanish Ministerio de Ciencia, Innovación y Universidades (PCI2018-093107 grant) and the ECSEL EU Joint Undertaking.

Conflicts of Interest: The authors declare no conflict of interest.

References

1. LeCun, Y.; Bengio, Y.; Hinton, G. Deep Learning. *Nature* **2015**, *521*, 436–444. [CrossRef] [PubMed]
2. Bostrom, N. *Superintelligence: Paths, Dangers, Strategies*; Oxford University Press: Oxford, UK, 2014.
3. Brette, R.; Rudolph, M.; Carnevale, T.; Hines, M.; Beeman, D.; Bower, J.M.; Diesmann, M.; Morrison, A.; Goodman, P.H.; Harris, F.C., Jr.; et al. Simulation of networks of spiking neurons: A review of tools and strategies. *J. Comput. Neurosci.* **2007**, *23*, 349. [CrossRef] [PubMed]
4. Tavanaei, A.; Ghodrati, M.; Reza Kheradpisheh, S.; Masquelier, T.; Maida, A. Deep learning in spiking neural networks. *Neural Networks* **2019**, *111*, 47. [CrossRef] [PubMed]
5. García-Martín, E.; Faviola Rodrigues, C.; Riley, G.; Grahna, H. Estimation of energy consumption in machine learning. *J. Parall Distr. Com.* **2019**, *134*, 75. [CrossRef]
6. Silver, D.; Huang, A.; Maddison, C.J.; Guez, A.; Sifre, L.; Van Den Driessche, G.; Schrittwieser, J.; Antonoglou, I.; Panneershelvam, V.; Lanctot, M.; et al. Mastering the game of Go with deep neural networks and tree search. *Nature* **2016**, *529*, 484. [CrossRef]
7. Merolla, P.A.; Arthur, J.V.; Alvarez-Icaza, R.; Cassidy, A.S.; Sawada, J.; Akopyan, F.; Jackson, B.L.; Imam, N.; Guo, C.; Nakamura, Y.; et al. A million spiking-neuron integrated circuit with a scalable communication network and interface. *Science* **2014**, *345*, 668–673. [CrossRef]

8. Strukov, D.B.; Snider, G.S.; Stewart, D.R.; Williams, R.S. The missing memristor found. *Nature* **2008**, *453*, 80–83. [CrossRef]
9. Chua, L.O. Memristor—The Missing Circuit Element. *IEEE Trans. Circuit Theory* **1971**, *18*, 507–519. [CrossRef]
10. Wang, Z.; Joshi, S.; Savel'ev, S.; Song, W.; Midya, R.; Li, Y.; Rao, M.; Yan, P.; Asapu, S.; Zhuo, Y.; et al. Fully memristive neural networks for pattern classification with unsupervised learning. *Nat. Electron.* **2019**, *1*, 137–145. [CrossRef]
11. Prezioso, M.; Merrikh-Bayat, F.; Hoskins, B.D.; Adam, G.C.; Likharev, K.K.; Strukov, D.B. Training and Operation of an Integrated Neuromorphic Network Based on Metal-Oxide Memristors. *Nature* **2015**, *521*, 61–64. [CrossRef]
12. Merrikh Bayat, F.; Prezioso, M.; Chakrabarti, B.; Nili, H.; Kataeva, I.; Strukov, D. Implementation of multilayer perceptron network with highly uniform passive memristive crossbar circuits. *Nature Comm.* **2018**, *9*, 2331. [CrossRef] [PubMed]
13. Burr, G.W.; Shelby, R.M.; Sidler, S.; Di Nolfo, C.; Jang, J.; Boybat, I.; Shenoy, R.S.; Narayanan, P.; Virwani, K.; Giacometti, E.U.; et al. Experimental demonstration and tolerancing of a large-scale neural network (165,000 synapses), using phase-change memory as the synaptic weight element. *IEEE Trans. Elect. Dev.* **2015**, *62*, 3498–3507. [CrossRef]
14. Li, C.; Belkin, D.; Li, Y.; Yan, P.; Hu, M.; Ge, N.; Jiang, H.; Montgomery, E.; Lin, P.; Wang, Z.; et al. Efficient and self-adaptive in-situ learning in multilayer memristor networks. *Nature Comm.* **2018**, *9*, 2385. [CrossRef] [PubMed]
15. Milo, V.; Zambelli, C.; Olivo, P.; Pérez, E.; Mahadevaiah, M.K.; Ossorio, O.G.; Wengr, C.; Ielmini, D. Multilevel HfO_2-based RRAM devices for low-power neuromorphic networks. *APL Mater.* **2019**, *7*, 081120. [CrossRef]
16. Williams, R.S. Summary of the Faraday Discussion on New memory paradigms: Memristive phenomena and neuromorphic applications. *Faraday Discuss.* **2019**, *213*, 579–587. [CrossRef] [PubMed]
17. Camuñas-Mesa, L.A.; Linares-Barranco, B.; Serrano-Gotarredona, T. Neuromorphic Spiking Neural Networks and Their Memristor-CMOS Hardware Implementations. *Materials* **2019**, *12*, 2745. [CrossRef]
18. Milo, V.; Malavena, G.; Monzio Compagnoni, C.; Ielmini, D. Memristive and CMOS Devices for Neuromorphic Computing. *Materials* **2020**, *13*, 166. [CrossRef]
19. Truong, S.N. A Parasitic Resistance-Adapted Programming Scheme for Memristor Crossbar-Based Neuromorphic Computing Systems. *Materials* **2019**, *12*, 4097. [CrossRef]
20. Wang, R.; Shi, T.; Zhang, X.; Wang, W.; Wei, J.; Lu, J.; Zhao, X.; Cao, R.; Long, S.; Liu, Q.; et al. Bipolar Analog Memristors as Artificial Synapses for Neuromorphic Computing. *Materials* **2018**, *11*, 2102. [CrossRef]
21. Van Nguyen, T.; Van Pham, K.; Min, K.-S. Memristor-CMOS Hybrid Circuit for Temporal-Pooling of Sensory and Hippocampal Responses of Cortical Neurons. *Materials* **2019**, *12*, 875. [CrossRef]
22. Van Nguyen, T.; Van Pham, K.; Min, K.-S. Hybrid Circuit of Memristor and Complementary Metal-Oxide Semiconductor for Defect-Tolerant Spatial Pooling with Boost-Factor Adjustment. *Materials* **2019**, *12*, 2122. [CrossRef] [PubMed]
23. Fernández-Rodríguez, A.; Alcalà, J.; Suñé, J.; Mestres, N.; Palau, A. Multi-Terminal Transistor-Like Devices Base don Strongly Correlated Metallic Oxides for Neuromorphic Applications. *Materials* **2020**, *13*, 281. [CrossRef] [PubMed]
24. Rodríguez, N.; Maldonado, D.; Romero, F.J.; Alonso, F.J.; Aguilera, A.M.; Godoy, A.; Jiménez-Molinos, F.; Ruiz, F.G.; Roldán, J.B. Resistive Switching and Charge Transport in Laser-Fabricated Graphene Oxide Memristors: A Time Series and Quantum Point Contact Approach. *Materials* **2019**, *12*, 3734. [CrossRef] [PubMed]
25. Hajtó, D.; Rák, A.; Cserey, G. Robust Memristor Networks for Neuromorphic Computation Applications. *Materials* **2019**, *12*, 3573. [CrossRef]
26. Pedró, M.; Martín-Martínez, J.; Maestro-Izquierdo, M.; Rodríguez, R.; Nafría, M. Self-Organizing Neural Networks Based on OxRAM Devices under a Fully Unsupervised Training Scheme. *Materials* **2019**, *12*, 3482. [CrossRef]
27. La Torraca, P.; Puglisi, F.M.; Padovani, A.; Larcher, L. Multiscale Modeling for Application-Oriented Optimization of Resistive Random-Access Memory. *Materials* **2019**, *12*, 3461. [CrossRef]

28. Sun, W.; Choi, S.; Kim, B.; Park, J. Three-Dimensional (3D) Vertical Resistive Random-Access Memory (VRRAM) Synapses for Neural Network Systems. *Materials* **2019**, *12*, 3451. [CrossRef]
29. Cisternas-Ferri, A.; Rapoport, A.; Fierens, P.I.; Patterson, G.A.; Miranda, E.; Suñé, J. On the application of a Diffusive Memristor Compact Model to Neuromorphic Circuits. *Materials* **2019**, *12*, 2260. [CrossRef]

materials

MDPI

Review

Neuromorphic Spiking Neural Networks and Their Memristor-CMOS Hardware Implementations

Luis A. Camuñas-Mesa *, Bernabé Linares-Barranco and Teresa Serrano-Gotarredona

Instituto de Microelectrónica de Sevilla (IMSE-CNM), CSIC and Universidad de Sevilla, 41092 Sevilla, Spain
* Correspondence: camunas@imse-cnm.csic.es

Received: 5 July 2019; Accepted: 10 August 2019; Published: 27 August 2019

Abstract: Inspired by biology, neuromorphic systems have been trying to emulate the human brain for decades, taking advantage of its massive parallelism and sparse information coding. Recently, several large-scale hardware projects have demonstrated the outstanding capabilities of this paradigm for applications related to sensory information processing. These systems allow for the implementation of massive neural networks with millions of neurons and billions of synapses. However, the realization of learning strategies in these systems consumes an important proportion of resources in terms of area and power. The recent development of nanoscale memristors that can be integrated with Complementary Metal–Oxide–Semiconductor (CMOS) technology opens a very promising solution to emulate the behavior of biological synapses. Therefore, hybrid memristor-CMOS approaches have been proposed to implement large-scale neural networks with learning capabilities, offering a scalable and lower-cost alternative to existing CMOS systems.

Keywords: neuromorphic systems; spiking neural networks; memristors; spike-timing-dependent plasticity

1. Introduction

The outstanding evolution of computers during the last 50 years has been based on the architecture proposed by Von Neumann in the 1940s [1]. In this model of stored-programme computer, data storage and processing are two independent tasks performed in separated areas with a high need of data communication between them. With the development of integrated circuits, Gordon Moore predicted in the 1960s that the number of transistors in an integrated circuit would double every 18 to 24 months [2]. This exponential evolution allowed for the development of more efficient computing systems, with increasing processing speed and decreasing power consumption. However, even the current technologies for semiconductor manufacturing are reaching the limits of Moore's law [3], so different solutions have been proposed to keep the future evolution of processing systems [4]. Two different strategies suggest the development of new processing paradigms and novel devices beyond conventional Complementary Metal–Oxide–Semiconductor (CMOS) technologies.

In parallel with the development of computing platforms, in the 1960s some researchers used the emerging electronic technologies as a mechanism for modeling neural systems, from individual neurons [5–10] to more complex networks [11]. The increasing understanding of the structure and fundamental principles of behavior of the human brain revealed a very different processing paradigm from the traditional computer architecture with a much better performance. Even when comparing with current supercomputers which excel at speed and precision, the human brain is still much more powerful when dealing with novelty, complexity and ambiguity for practical tasks like visual recognition and motion control, while presenting a negligible power consumption around 20W [12]. This comparison between conventional computers and the brain led to the emergence of neuromorphic computing. The term neuromorphic engineering was first coined by Carver Mead to refer to developing microelectronic information processing systems mimicking the operation of their biological counterparts [13,14]. During the 1980s, Carver Mead highlighted the analogy between the physics in biological neurons and the behavior of transistors in sub-threshold regime [13,14], developing neural networks based on analog circuits; leading to the implementation of the first silicon retinas [15] and proposing a new computing paradigm where data and processing tasks are performed by indivisible entities, taking inspiration from biological neural systems. Along the years, the neuromorphic engineering field has broaden its inspiration. Today's neuromorphic computing engineers not only try to mimic the highly parallel architecture of biological brains and the use of in-memory computing architectures as a way of improving the speed and energy performance, but also have deeply studied the signal information encoding, computational principles and learning paradigms that enable even simple biological brains with admiring performance in the interaction and adaptation to complex and unexpected environments with high reaction speeds and minimal power consumption despite relying on very simple and highly unreliable computation units [16].

Alternatively, many novel beyond-CMOS technologies have been proposed to overcome the limits of Moore's law. One of the most promising available devices is the nanoscale memristor. The memristor was first described theoretically by Chua in the 1970s as the fourth passive element establishing a relationship between electric charge and magnetic flux [17]. Much later in 2008, a team at HP Labs claimed to have found Chua's memristor experimentally based on a thin film of titanium oxide [18]. This 2-terminal device behaves as a variable resistor whose value can be modifed by applying certain voltages or currents. The most common structure for this device is a union metal-dielectric(s)-metal, where the dielectric layer can be as thin as a few nanometers. The application of electric fields and controlled currents across the dielectric produces an alteration of its resistance by growing a filament or other mechanisms like barrier modulation. Currently available memristors are mostly binary devices, as they can switch between two resistance values: HRS (High-Resistance State) and LRS (Low-Resistance State) [19]. Since the appearance of the memristors, many logic families based on memristors for digital computation have been proposed [20,21], their potential as digital long-term non-volatile memory technology has also been demonstrated [22–25], and their use as biosensing devices looks also promising [26]. In the field of neuromorphic engineering, the memristors have attracted a special interest due to its particular plasticity behaviour which ressembles the adaptation rules observed in biological synapses. Memristors can adapt and change its behaviour over time in response to different stimulation patterns as it happens in the human brain. In particular, it has been demonstrated that if stimulated with pulse-trains simulating the input from spiking neurons, memristors may exhibit a biologically inspired learning rule [27–30] resembling the spike-timing-dependent plasticity (STDP) observed in biological neurons [31–36]. Hence, memristors have been considered as artificial inorganic synapses.

In this paper, we analyze the current trend towards using memristors over CMOS platforms to implement neuromorphic systems, demonstrating a new paradigm which overcomes current limitations in conventional processing systems. In Section 2, we give a general overview of the basis of neuromorphic computing, while in Section 3 we review the main large-scale CMOS hardware implementations of neuromorphic systems. In Section 4, we describe proposed hybrid Memristor-CMOS approaches, while in Section 5 we emphasize the suitability of this strategy to implement learning algorithms in neural systems. Finally, in Section 6 we give our future perspective for this field.

2. Neuromorphic Computing

As already stated, neuromorphic computing systems take inspiration on the architecture, the technology and the computational principles of biological brains. Morphologically, the human brain is composed of approximately 10^{11} elementary processing units called neurons, massively interconnected by plastic adaptable interconnections called synapses. Each neuron connects approximately to 10^3–10^4 other neurons through synaptic connections. The neurons are known to be distributed in layers, and most of the synaptic interconnections are devoted to interconnect neurons belonging to successive layers.

The first computing systems inspired by this structure of biological brains were published in the 1940s–1950s and were called Artificial Neural Networks (ANNs) [37,38]. They appeared as powerful computational tools that proved to solve, by iteratively training algorithms that adapted the strength of the interconnection weights, complex pattern recognition, classification or function estimation problems not amenable to be solved by analytic tools. The first generations of neural networks did not involve any notion of time nor any temporal aspect in the computation.

Mc Culloch and Pitts, proposed in 1943, one of the first computational models of the biological neurons. Figure 1 illustrates the operation of each proposed neural computational unit. As illustrated in Figure 1, a neuron N_j receives inputs from n other previous neurons $x_1, x_2, ..., x_n$. The output of each neuron $x_1, x_2, ..., x_n$ in the previous layer is multiplied by the corresponding synaptic weight $w_{1j}, w_{2j}, ..., w_{nj}$, also know as synaptic efficacy. The combined weighted input is transformed mathematically using a certain non-linear transfer function or an activation function φ, generating an output o_j. In the original Mc Culloch and Pitts' neural model the activation function was a thresholding gate, giving as neural output a digital signal [37]. This digital output neuron was the core of the first generation of neural networks.

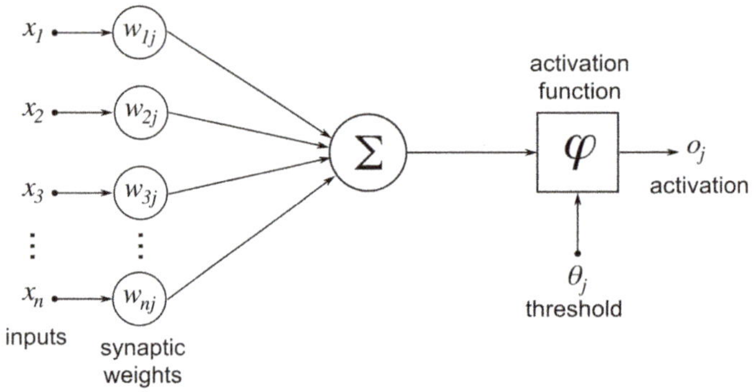

Figure 1. Diagram of an artificial neuron with n inputs with their corresponding synaptic weights. All weighted inputs are added and an activation function controls the generation of the output signal.

In 1958, Rosenblatt proposed the perceptron. The architecture of the perceptron is shown in Figure 2a. In Figure 2, the computational units or neurons are represented by circles, interconnected through trainable weights representing the synaptic connections. The original perceptron consisted of a single layer of input neurons fully interconnected in a feedforward way to a layer of output neurons. A learning hebbian rule [39] to adapt the weights was proposed [38]. This single layer perceptron was able to solve only linearly separable problems [40].

In the 1950–60s, a second generation of computational units arose were the thresholding activation function was replaced by a continuous analog valued output like a smooth sigmoid, radial basis function or a continuous piece-wise linear function [41,42]. Recently, the rectifying non-linear activation function, also known as ReLU has become very popular for its better training convergence and its hardware friendly implementation [43]. Furthermore, gradient descent based learning algorithms could be now applied to optimize the network weights. Alternative learning rules were proposed as the delta rule based on the Least Mean Squares (LSM) algorithm published by Widrow [44,45]. This second generation proved to be universal approximators for any analog continuous function, that is, any analog continuous function could be approximated by a network of this type with a single hidden unit [41].

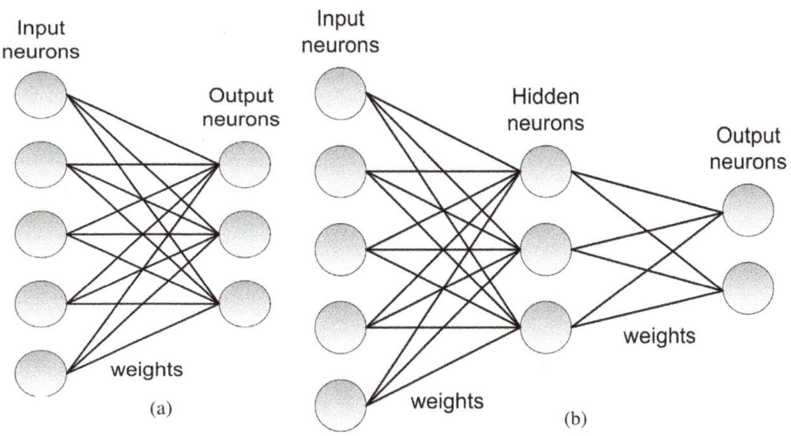

Figure 2. (**a**) Architecture of a single layer perceptron. The architecture consists of a layer on input neurons fully connected to a single layer of output neurons. (**b**) Extension to a multi-layer perceptron including more than one layer of trainable weights. In this example, the network includes 3 layers: input, hidden and output layer. Each connection between two neurons is given by a certain weight.

The backpropagation algorithm extended the application of the gradient descent techniques to networks with any number of hidden layers, popularly known as Deep Neural Networks (DNNs) [46–48]. Figure 2b illustrates a case with 3 layers: a first layer of input neurons, a second layer of hidden neurons, and a third layer of output neurons, although a general architecture can contain any given number of hidden layers.

The ANN architectures shown in Figure 2a,b are pure feedforward architectures as the signal propagates from input to output in an unidirectional way. Other architectures, known as recurrent neural networks, including feedback connections from upper layers in the architecture to lower layers, have been proposed. The Adaptive Resonance Theory (ART) architectures by Grossberg [49], the Kohonen self-organizing maps [50] or the Hopfield models [51] can be cited among the pioneering ones.

The presented ANNs have been typically developed in software, and trained offline. The training of DNNs requires a vast amount of annotated data to correctly generalize the problem without overfitting [52] and intensive computation resources. However, in recent years, the increase in the computation capabilities of modern computers and the availability of vast amounts of information have made DNN very popular allowing the development of many DNN-based applications [53,54] that use complex architectures like LeNet for handwritten digit recognition [55], Microsoft's speech recognition system [56] or AlexNet for image recognition [43]. As a consequence we have witnessed the explosion of DNNs and machine learning.

Despite the impressive advances that DNNs have demonstrated in recent years, their performance in terms of efficiency (speed and power consumption) compared with the human brain is still low as it is low their resemblance to the human brain in terms of information coding. In the biological brain, the information is processed in a continuous way in time, not just as a sequence of static frames as DNNs recognition systems do. Furthermore, in conventional DNNs, the output of the different neural layers are computed in a sequential way. Each layer has to wait until the output of the previous layer has been computed to perform its computation, thus introducing a significant recognition delay in the network. On the contrary, biological neurons transmit their information to the next neuronal layers in the form of spikes. Whenever a neuron emits a spike, the spike is transmitted to its afferent connected neurons and processed with just the delay of the synaptic connection. In 1996, Thorpe demonstrated that the human brain was able to recognize a visual familiar object in the time that just one spike propagates through all the layers of the visual cortex [57]. Similar visual processing speeds have been measured in the macaque monkeys by Rolls [58]. These experiments reveal an extremely efficient information coding in the biological brains. In this context, the 3rd generation of neural networks, spiking neural networks (SNNs), aims to bridge the gap between neuroscience and machine learning, using biologically-realistic models of neurons to carry out information coding and computation trying to fully exploit the efficiency in the spatio-temporal signal coding and processing and the corresponding power efficiency observed in the biological brains. SNNs operate using spikes in a similar way as biological neurons do. That way, in addition to the state of the neuron and the synaptic weight, SNNs also incorporate the concept of time into their model of operation. In these neurons, there is no propagation cycle, so each neuron fires an output spike only when its state reaches a certain threshold. Therefore, the information flows in these networks are spike trains which propagate between neurons asynchronously, and temporal correlation between spikes is crucial [41]. Spike trains offer the possibility of exploiting the richness of the temporal information contained in real-world sensory data. This allows SNNs to be applied to solve tasks which dynamically changing information like visual gesture recognition or speech recognition in a more natural way than current conventional (non spiking) artificial intelligent systems do. When dealing with dynamic information (as video sequences), conventional artificial systems perform computations using sequences of static images sampled at a constant periodic time (photogram time in the case of vision). Recognition of dynamic sequences may involve the use of recurrent neural network architectures or the resolution of continuous time differential equations. These computations are quite intensive using conventional framed ANN. However, the use of SNN where computation is driven in a continuous time way naturally and driven only by the occurrence of spikes detecting certain spatio-temporal correlations can be much more advantageous.

Many different coding methods for these spike trains have been proposed. Many authors have proposed to code the activity level of the neurons as the frequency of the firing rate. However, this type of coding does not benefit from the spike sparsity that should characterize SNN processing and thus, it does not enable the corresponding low power communication and computation due to the sparsity of the spike coding. Regarding the fast computation capability expected from SNN, this firing rate coding introduces a latency in the computation of the output firing rate. Furthermore, it is not biologically plausible as evidenced by the experiments of Thorpe [57] and Rolls [58] which demonstrated that the computation of a single cortical area is completed in 10–20 ms while the firing rate of the neurons involved in the computation is below 100 Hz, which does not make possible the computation based on the coding of analog variables in firing rates. However, as discussed by Thorpe et al. [59], there are many other biologically plausible and more efficient coding strategies. Other coding schemes that have been considered are in the timing between spikes [60], in the delay relative to a given synchronization time also known as time to first spike (TFS) [59] encoding, just coding the values in the order of spikes which is known as rank order coding [61], or synchronous detection coding [59].

Regarding the SNN neuron models, there are many neuron models that describe the behaviour of biological neurons with different levels of complexity [5–10]. The classic Hodgkin-Huxley model [5] is a 4-th order biophysical model that describes the behaviour of the currents flowing into the neuron ion channels in a biologically realistic way. However, due to its complexity, different 2nd order simplified models have been proposed like the one proposed by FitzHugh and Nagumo [6,7] and the Morris-Lecar model [8], among others. In the last years, the Izhikevich model [10] and the Adaptive Exponential Integrate and Fire (AdEx) model [9] have become very popular for their ability to reproduce a large variety of spiking regimes observed in the biological neurons just by varying a reduced number of model parameters. However, while detailed biophysical models can reproduce electrophisiological activity of biological neurons with great accuracy, they are difficult to analyze computationally and not friendly for hardware implementations. Because of these reasons, for computational purposes simple first-order phenomenological models like the Integrate and Fire model are frequently used.

The behavior of a single integrate-and-fire spiking neuron is illustrated in Figure 3. A spiking neuron receives input spikes from several dendrites and sends out spikes from its output axon, as shown in Figure 3a. Every time an input spike arrives, the state of the neuron is updated, and when it reaches the threshold, it generates an output spike and reset its state, as seen in Figure 3b. In this case, spikes are fully characterized by their firing time. In Figure 3, it can be observed that there is a constant slope decay of the membrane potential between two arriving spikes as it is the case of a leaky integrate and fire neuron. Mathematically, a leaky integrate-and-fire neuron can be described as:

$$i_{in}(t) = \frac{v_{mem}(t) - v_{rest}}{R} + C\frac{dv_{mem}(t)}{dt} \tag{1}$$

where $v_{mem}(t)$ represents the membrane potential, $i_{in}(t)$ the injected current, v_{rest} the resting value of the membrane potential, C the equivalent capacitance of the membrane, and R the leak resistance. A leaky integrate-and-fire neuron can be easily implemented in hardware following the resistance-capacitance (RC) "text book" concept scheme presented in Figure 4, where an input current i_{in} is integrated in capacitor C with leak resistance R. The integrated voltage v_{mem} is compared with a reference v_{th}, generating an output given by v_{out}. Additionally, integrate-and-fire neurons may consider a refractory period that forces a minimum time interval between two consecutive spikes of a neuron. A comprehensive overview of circuit realizations of spiking neurons with different levels of complexity can be found in [62].

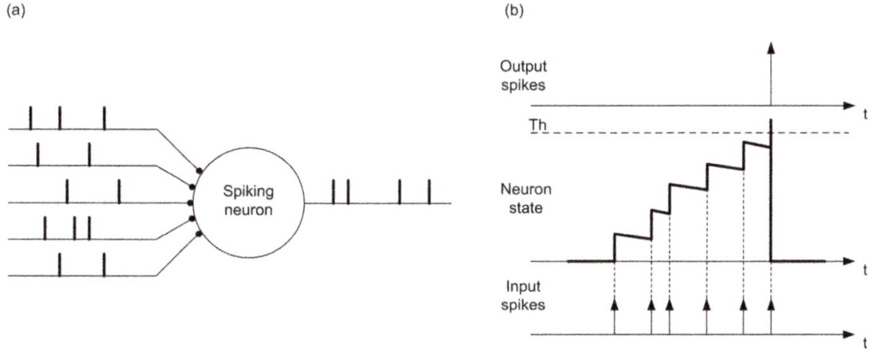

Figure 3. Illustration of the behavior of a leaky integrate-and-fire spiking neuron. (**a**) A spiking neuron receives spikes from several inputs, processes them, and generates output spikes from its output node. (**b**) Temporal evolution of the neuron state while it receives input spikes. When the threshold is reached, it generates an output spike.

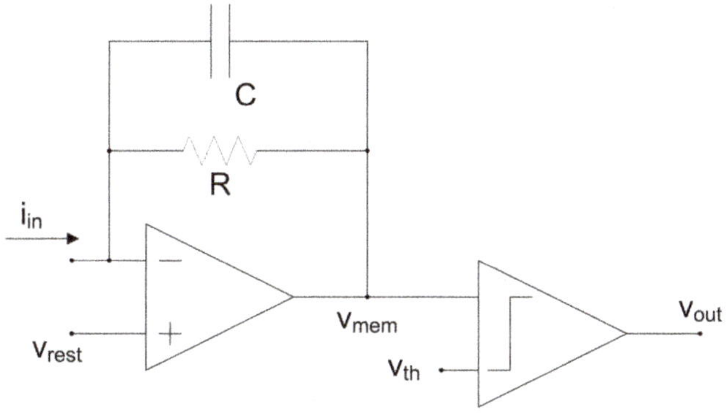

Figure 4. Example of a hardware implementation of an RC leaky integrate-and-fire neuron.

In terms of connectivity, the most general type of neural network is fully connected, meaning that each single neuron in layer i is connected to all neurons in layer $i+1$. This scheme applies no limitation to the learning capabilities of the network; however, it presents some difficulties for practical implementations. A very popular way of reducing the amount of interconnections is represented by Convolutional Neural Networks (ConvNets), where each neuron in layer i is connected to a subset of neurons in layer $i+1$ representing a projective field. This receptive field can be represented as a convolutional kernel, with shared weights for each layer [63]. This scheme is inspired by biology, as it has been observed in the visual cortex [64]. In a similar way to the biological visual cortex, this convolutional neural network architecture is commonly used for image processing applications in the earlier more massive parallel feature extraction layers, as it implies an important reduction of the number of connections.

Table 1 (adapted from [65]) contains a comparison of the main distinctive features between ANNs and SNNs. As previously stated, the latency in each computation stage in an ANN is high as the whole computation in each stage has to be completed on the input image to generate the corresponding output. On the contrary, in an SNN processor the computation is performed spike by spike so that, output spikes in a computational layer are generated as soon as enough spikes evidencing the existence of a certain feature has been collected. In that way, the output of a computation stage is a flow of spikes that is almost simultaneous with its input spike flow. This property of SNN systems has been called "pseudo-simultaneity" [65,66]. The latency between the input and output spike flows of a processing SNN convolution layer has been measured to be as low as 155 ns [67]. Regarding the recognition speed, whereas in an ANN the recognition speed is strongly dependent on the computation capabilities of the hardware and the number of total operations to be computed (which is dependent on the system complexity), in an SNN, each input spike is processed in almost real time by the processing hardware and the recognition is performed as soon as there are enough input events that allow the system to take a decision. This recognition speed strongly depends on the input statistics and signal coding schemes as previously discussed. In terms of power consumption, the ANNs power depends on the consumption of the processor and the memory reading and writing operations but for a giving input sampling frequency and size does not depend on the particular visual stimulus. However, in an SNN, the power consumption depends also strongly on the statistics of the stimulus and coding strategies. If efficient coding strategies are used, the system should benefit from the power efficiency of sparse spike representations.

On the negative side, as it has been already pointed out, the addition of the time variable makes SNN neuron models more complex than ANN ones. Also, as the computation of ANN is time-sampled, in each sampling time the algorithmic computation is performed using the available hardware resources that can be time multiplexed by fetching data and storing intermediate variables. However, in true SNN the spikes should be processed as they are generated in real time, requiring parallel hardware resources which cannot be multiplexed. The scaling up of the system can be done by modular expansion of the hardware resources.

However, where SNN should have major advantage is in applications requiring recurrent neural architectures, such as, in recognition of dynamic stimulus. The computation of recurrent connections in ANN requires computationally intensive iterations until convergence is reached, while the convergence of recurrent connections in SNN is almost instantaneous due to their pseudo-simultaneity property.

In terms of accuracy, as it will be discussed in Section 5, the learning methods that have been developed for ANN are not directly applicable to SNN. Although the learning theory of SNN still lacks behind its equivalent methods for ANN, some recent work reports for the same architecture an error increment of only 0.15% for the ImageNet dataset and 0.38% for the CIFAR10 dataset [68]. However, the temporal dependence introduces complexity so that once a SNN has been trained, its accuracy drops if the input temporal coding changes. But it also introduces the potential to recognize dynamic sequences in a more efficient way.

Table 1. Table comparing different features of ANNs and SNNs.

Feature	ANN	SNN
Data processing	Frame-based	Spike-based
Latency	High	Low Pseudo-simultaneity
Time resolution	Low	High Preservation of spatio-temporal correlation
Time processing	Sampled	Continuous
Neuron model complexity	Low	High
Recognition accuracy	Higher	Lower
Hardware multiplexing	Possible	Not possible
System scale-up	Ad hoc	Adding modules
Recognition speed	Low Independent on input stimulus	High Dependent on input statistics
Power consumption	Dependent on hardware resources Dependent on system complexity Determined by processor power and memory fetching Independent on input stimulus	Not dependent on system complexity Determined by power-per-event processing in modules Dependent on stimulus statistics
Recurrent topologies	Need to iterate until converge	Instantaneous

3. CMOS Neuromorphic Systems

Simulating SNNs on normal hardware is very computationally-intensive since it requires simulating coupled differential equations of large neuron populations running in parallel. Fully exploiting the coding and computation capabilities of biological brains requires the adequacy of the corresponding hardware platform to the peculiarities of the algorithm at different levels: from signal coding up to high level architectures. At the architectural level, the intrinsic parallelism of neural networks lends to the development of neuromorphic custom parallel hardware resembling the architecture of the biological brain to emulate its computing capabilities [62,69,70]. Furthermore, at the signal level, SNNs are better suited than ANNs for hardware implementation, as neurons are active only when they receive an input spike, reducing power consumption and simplifying computation.

One of the major issues when trying to implement in a parallel hardware large arrays of neural populations is the implementation of the synaptic interconnections. In a parallel 2D hardware, the physical wiring does allow to implement connections between just neighbouring neurons, while the biological neurons are distributed in 3D and massively interconnected among populations. Address-Event-Representation (AER) [71] is an asynchronous communication protocol that was conceived to massively interconnect neuron populations that can be located in the same or different chips as a 'virtual wiring' system. Figure 5 illustrates two neural populations communicated through an AER bus. In the particular case of this figure, neurons in the emitter population code their activity as a density of output pulses which is proportional to their activation level. However, the AER communication scheme can be applied to any type of pulse signal encoding [59]. Whenever a neuron in the emitter population generates a spike, it codes its physical coordinates (x, y) or address in a digital word in a fast digital bus and activates an asynchronous request (Rqst) signal. The coded address is sent through the fast digital bus to the receiver population. Upon reception of an active request, the receiver decodes the arriving neuron address and activates the acknowledge (Ack) signal. The received pulse can be sent to the corresponding neuron where the original activity of the sending neurons can be reproduced (as illustrated in Figure 5) or to a group of virtually connected neurons in the receiving population implementing a projection field [72]. The high-speed of the inter-population digital bus (in the order of nanoseconds) compared to the inter spike interval of biological neurons (in the order of milliseconds) allows to multiplex the connections of a million neurons in a shared time-multiplexed digital bus. Most of the developed large-scale CMOS neuromorphic computing platforms make use of this AER communication protocol. As neuromorphic systems have scaled up in size and architectural complexity, many variations of the original point-to-point AER communication scheme [71,73,74] have been proposed trying to improve the overall system communication bandwidth. The broadcast-mesh-AER [75–77] proposes a generic approach to interconnect a mesh of AER devices using a global mapper and interconnecting the devices in a chain architecture. The pre-structured hierarchical AER approach [78] uses the knowledge of the network topology to interconnect AER devices through different AER links. Mappers can be used in every link, however, once the AER devices have been physically interconnected the changes in the configuration are limited. The Hierarchical-Fractal AER [79] proposes different levels of interconnection by adding address bits at higher level based on the idea that the traffic of spikes is going to be more intense at a local level. The router-mesh AER [80] proposes to avoid an external mapper by placing a router with a mapping table inside every AER module taking ideas from traditional NoC topologies [81]. The multicasting-mesh AER approach [82] proposes a simplification of the router-mesh AER by employing routing tables that contain only information of the connectivity between modules instead of allowing full neuron to neuron connectivity programming. Another approach developed to allow programmable interconnections inside the same chip or at wafer scale has been to implement massive programmable cross-point interconnects to configure the network topology [83] and including off-wafer rerouting for longer range interconnects [84]. Recently, the Hierarchical Routing AER has been proposed that establishes different hierarchical levels of nested AER links where each link has a dynamically reconfigurable synaptic routing table which allows programmable connectivity of the neurons without restriction on the spatial range of connectivity [85]. Moradi et al. have proposed a mixed-mode hierarchical-mesh routing scheme that exploits a clustered connectivity structure to reduce memory requirements and get a balance among memory overhead and reconfigurability [86].

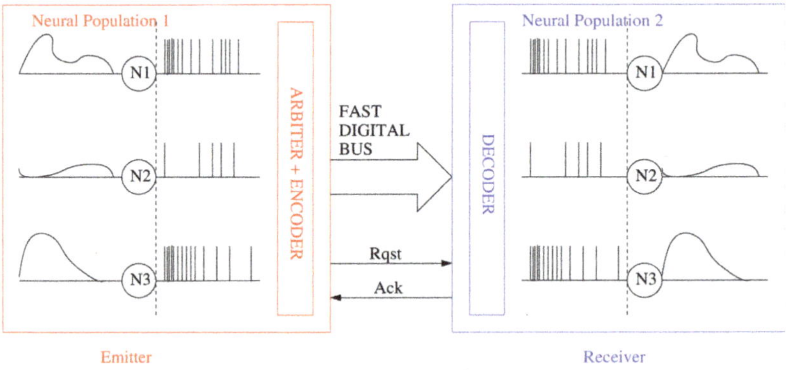

Figure 5. Illustration of two neural populations communicated through a point-to-point AER bus. Each neuron in the emitter population can be virtually connected to every neuron in the receiver population.

The above mentioned spike routing schemes have allowed the implementation of highly parallel massively interconnected spiking neural networks and the multichip integration of SNN hardware devoted to realize different specific parts of the cognitive function including integration of spike-based sensors and neural processors.

CMOS spike-based vision sensors have been developed since the very beginning of the neuromorphic engineering field [15]. Since then, a variety of AER visual sensors can be found in the literature that use different approaches to encode the luminance such as simple luminance to frequency transformation sensors [87], Time-to-First-Spike (TFS) coding sensors [88–91], foveated sensors [92,93], sensors encoding the spatial contrast [94,95], spatial and temporal filtering sensors that adapt to illumination and spatio-temporal contrast [96] and temporal transient detectors [97–104]. Among them, the temporal transient detectors also know as Dynamic Vision Sensors (DVSs) have recently become very popular. They produce as output a stream of asynchronous events where each pixel codes the temporal variation of the illumination inpinging on the pixel. Figure 6 illustrates the operation of a DVS sensor. One of the advantages of this sensor is that it codes the information in a compressive way sending only spikes when there is a relevant change in the illumination and thus removing the static background features of the scene from the moving object. Another advantage is that all the exact spatio-temporal information of the object is preserved with a reported precision in the spiking times of the order of 10 µs. This converts these sensors in ideal candidates for high-speed processing and recognition systems. Several companies are nowadays making an effort to develop commercial prototypes of high-resolution DVS cameras: iniVation, Insightness, Samsung [105], CelePixel [106], and Prophesee, aiming to develop high-speed autonomous intelligent vision systems. Other types of spiking sensors have been developed such as cochleas [107–109] and tactile sensors [110,111] following similar principles of encoding the sensed signal relative changes as a flow of neural spikes, thus, generating a compressed information.

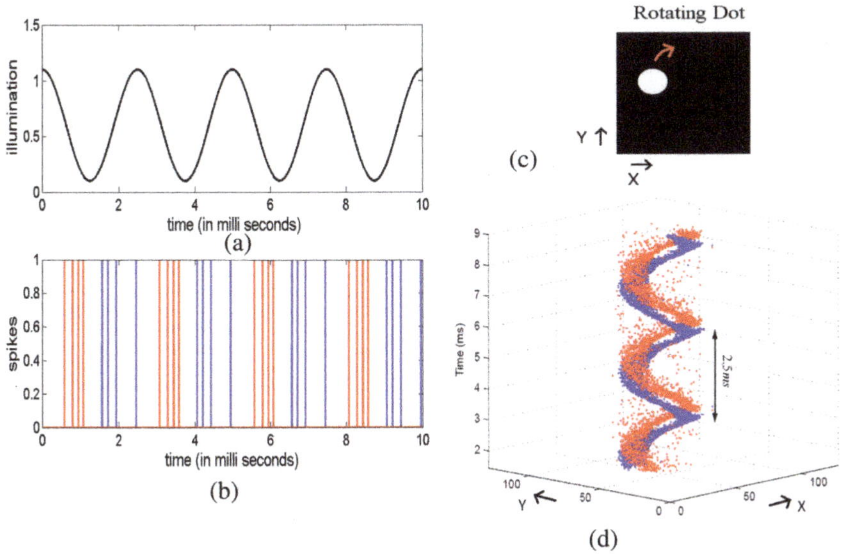

Figure 6. Illustration of the operation of a Dynamic Vision Sensor. (**a**,**b**) illustrate the operation a DVS pixel. (**a**) plots the illumination inpinging on a pixel that varies as a sinusoidal waveform along time with period 2.5 ms, and (**b**) illustrates the output spikes generated by the corresponding DVS pixel. The blue traces correspond to positive output spikes which are generated when the illumination increases, while the red traces illustrate the negative signed spikes generated by an illumination decreasing over time. (**d**) illustrates real measurements of the response of a DVS when observing a white rotating dot on a black background rotating with a 2.5 ms period, as shown in (**c**).

Regarding the neuromorphic hardware for processing, it should be distinguished between the hardware implementing specific functionalities of the cognitive function and general purpose SNN hardware platforms intended for emulating massive neural arrays. Among the specific functional neuromorphic circuits, researchers have developed SNN neuromorphic chips implementing computational primitives and operations performed in the brain such as:

- Winner-Take-All (WTA) is a brain inspired mechanism implemented by inhibitory interactions between neurons in a population that compete to inhibit each other. The result is that the neuron in the population receiving the highest input remains active while silencing the output of the rest of the neurons. Hardware modules of spiking Winner-take-all networks have been reported [112].

- Spiking Convolutional Networks (ConvNets): neural networks implementing in real time the behaviour of the feature extraction layers of the cortex region have been implemented in hardware [113–115].
- Hardware implementations of spiking neural networks for saliency maps detection have been proposed as emulators of brain attention mechanisms [116].
- Spiking Liquid State Machines have also been implemented for recognition of sequential patterns such as speech recognition tasks [117,118].

The specific SNN neuromorphic chips can be combined in a modular and scalable way [78] to achieve optimum performance in terms of complexity, speed, and power consumption depending on the specific application. However, the current evolution of hardware neuromorphic platforms tends to large-scale modular computing systems with increasing numbers of neurons and synapses [62,119] that are meant to be easily reconfigurable for different applications. Some of the most remarkable large-scale neuromorphic systems developed until the present are:

- The IBM TrueNorth chip is based upon distributed digital neural models aimed at real-time cognitive applications [120].
- The Stanford NeuroGrid uses real-time sub-threshold analogue neural circuits [121]. It has been recently reversioned with the Braindrop chip prototype [122] which is a single core planned to be part of the 1-million-neuron Brain Storm System [123].
- The Heidelberg BrainScaleS system uses wafer-scale above threshold analogue neural circuits running 10,000 times faster than biological real time aimed at understanding biological systems, and in particular, long-term learning [124].
- The Manchester SpiNNaker is a real-time digital many-core system that implements neural and synapse models in software running on small embedded processors, again primarily aimed at modelling biological nervous systems [125].
- The Intel Loihi chip consists of a mesh of 128 neuromorphic cores with an integrated learning engine on-chip [126].
- The Darwin Neural Processing Unit is a hardware co-processor with digital logic specifically designed for resource-constrained embedded applications [127].
- The ROLLS chip was developed at ETHZ-INI including 256 neurons and 128 k on-line learning synapses [128]. Recently, it has been updated to the Dynamic Neuromorphic Asynchronous Processor (DYNAPs) with 1 K neurons and 64 k on-line learning synapses [86].
- A digital realization of a neuromorphic chip (ODIN) containing 256 neurons and 64 K 4-bit synapses exhibiting a spike-driven synaptic plasticity in FDSOI 28 nm technology has recently been developed in the University of Leuven [129].

A comparison of the main features of these generic neuromorphic systems and the human brain is shown in Table 2. In general, these systems are based on a processing chip which is part of a multi-chip board (or wafer for BrainScaleS), and in some cases these boards can be assembled in multi-board racks, scaling up more and more the size of the implemented network. Some of the most recent approaches have not reported yet such multi-chip platforms.

Table 2. Comparison of the major features of the human brain and the large-scale neuromorphic systems described in this work.

Platform	Human Brain	Neurogrid	BrainScaleS	Truenorth	SpiNNaker	Loihi	Darwin	ROLLS	DYNAPs	ODIN
Technology	Biology	Analog, sub-threshold	Analog, over threshold	Digital, fixed	Digital, programmable	Digital, programmable	Digital, programmable	Mixed-signal, sub-threshold	Mixed-signal, subthreshold	Digital, programamble
Feature size	10 µm	180 nm	180 nm	28 nm	130 nm	14 nm	180 nm	180 nm	180 nm	28 nm
# transistors		23 M	15 M	5.4 B	100 M	2.07 B	≈M	12.2 M	-	-
Chip size		1.7 cm^2	0.5 cm^2	4.3 cm^2	1 cm^2	60 mm^2	25 mm^2	51.4 mm^2	43.79 mm^2	0.086 mm^2
# neurons (chip)		65 k	512	1 M	16 k	131 k	≈M	256	1 k	256
# synapses (chip)		100 M	100 k	256 M	16 M	126 M	Programmable	128 k	64 k	64 k
# chips per board		16	352	16	48	-	-	-	-	-
# neurons (board)	10^{11}	1 M	200 k	16 M	768 k	-	-	-	-	-
# synapses (board)	10^{15}	4 B	40 M	4 B	768 M	-	-	-	-	-
Energy per connection	10 fJ	100 pJ	100 pJ	25 pJ	10 nJ	81 pJ	10 nJ	>77 fJ	30 pJ	12.7 pJ
On-chip learning	Yes	No	Yes	No	Yes	Yes	Yes	Yes	No	Yes

4. Hybrid Memristor-CMOS Systems

As was mentioned in Section 1, progress in silicon technologies is reaching physical limitations which are causing the end of Moore's law, and traditional Von Neumann computing architectures are reaching scalability limits in terms of computing speed and power consumption. Novel brain inspired architectures have emerged as alternative computing platforms specially suitable for cognitive tasks that require the processing of massively parallel data. As already stated in Section 3, one of the main bottlenecks of the CMOS implementation of these neuromorphic parallel architectures is the physical implementation of the massive synaptic interconnections among neurons and the synaptic adaptability. The implementation of adaptable synaptic connections in CMOS technology requires the use of large amount of circuitry for analog memory or digital memory blocks that are costly in terms of area and energy requirements. Furthermore, learning rules to update these synaptic memory devices have to be implemented. The interest in developing a compact adaptable device obeying biological learning rules to implement the synaptic connections has motivated the investigation on alternative nanotechnologies to complement the CMOS technology in this regard. Memristive devices are novel two terminal devices able to change their conductance as a function of the voltage/current applied to their terminals that were predicted in 1971 by Chua based on circuit theory reasoning [17] and whose existence was experimentally demonstrated in nanomaterials devices much later in 2008 [18]. Different materials with different conductance switching mechanisms have been proposed [130] such as Phase-Change-Memory (PCM) [131], Conductive Bridge Memory (CBRAM) [132], Ferroelectric Memories (FeRAM) [133], Redox-based resistive switching Memories (ReRAM) [134], or organic memristive devices (OMD) [135–139]. Each of them presents different characteristics in terms of compactness, reliability, endurance, memory retention term, programmable states, and energy efficiency [69,140].

These devices present some properties specially valuable as electronic synaptic elements [141]:

- Memristors can be scaled down to feature sizes below 10 nm.
- They can retain memory states for years.
- They can switch with nanosecond timescales.
- They undergo spike-based learning in real time under biologically inspired learning rules as Spike-Time-Dependent Plasticity (STDP) [31,32,34–36].

The characteristic i/v equations of a memristive element can be approximated by:

$$\begin{aligned} i_{MR} &= G(w, v_{MR})v_{MR} \\ dw/dt &= f_{MR}(w, v_{MR}) \end{aligned} \quad (2)$$

where i_{MR}, v_{MR} are the current and the voltage drop at the terminal devices, respectively (as shown in Figure 7a, $G(w, v_{MR})$ is the conductance of the device that changes as function of the applied voltage (supposing a voltage or flux controlled device model [142]), and w is some physical parametric characteristic whose change is typically governed by a nonlinear function f_{MR} of the applied voltage including a threshold barrier. A typical f_{MR} observed in memristive devices [142] can be mathematically approximated by [28–30,143]

$$f_{MR} = \begin{cases} I_o * sign(v_{MR})(e^{|v_{MR}|/v_o} - e^{v_{TH}/v_o}) & if \quad |v_{MR}| > v_{Th} \\ 0 & otherwise \end{cases} \quad (3)$$

Figure 7b depicts the typical non-linear memristive adaptation curve f_{MR}.

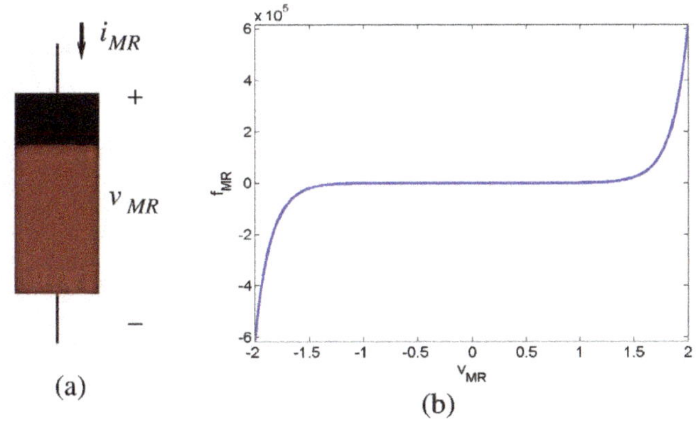

Figure 7. (**a**) Memristor symbol and (**b**) typical thresholded memristive adaptation curve

According to Equations (2) and (3), when a voltage higher than v_{TH} is applied between the terminals of a voltage-controlled memristor, its resistance changes. This property has been used to adapt supervisely the weights of simple perceptron networks [38] by applying voltage pulses controlled by some error function to memristive devices. The performance of correct categorization has been experimentally demonstrated [144–146]. Although these novel memristive devices open very promising alternatives for electronic technologies, they are still far from the maturity reached by CMOS sytems during the last decades. Instead, they are very promising technologies for being integrated in 3D with CMOS technology providing a high-density memory closely tight to computational units, thus overcoming the limitations of Von Neumann's architecture. Very dense architectures for 3D-integration of CMOS computing units with crossbar arrays of nanodevices like the semiconductor/nanowire/molecular integrated circuits (CMOL) [147] architecture have been proposed. A CMOL system combines the advantages of CMOS technology (flexibility and high fabrication yield) with the high density of crossbar arrays of nanoscale devices. This structure consists of a dense nanowire crossbar fabric on top of the CMOS substrate with memristor devices assembled in the crossings between nanowires as shown in Figure 8. Figure 8a shows a crossbar nanoarray where nanowires run in orthogonal directions. A memristive device is located at each cross point of a vertical and horizontal nanowire. Figure 8b shows the proposed CMOL structure. The nanowire crossbar is tilted with respect to the orientation of the 2D array of CMOS neurons. Each CMOS neuron has an output pin (red dots in Figure 8b) and an input pin (blue dots in Figure 8b). Each neuron output is connected to just one nanowire and each neuron input is connected to another nanowire in the perpendicular direction. The crosspoint memristive devices implement the synaptic connections between neurons. In the illustration of Figure 8b, the output of neuron 2 is connected to the input of neuron 1 through the synaptic memristive device located at the intersection point (marked as a black circle) of the two perpendicular nanowires (plotted as green lines) connected to neuron 2 output and neuron 1 input, respectively. Other alternative architectures for neuromorphic structures based on 3D integration of CMOS neurons and memristive synapses have been proposed as CrossNets [148]. A functional digital FPGA-like implementation of a small CMOL prototype where the memristors where used as digital switches to re-configure the digital hardware implemented in the CMOS cells has been demonstrated [149].

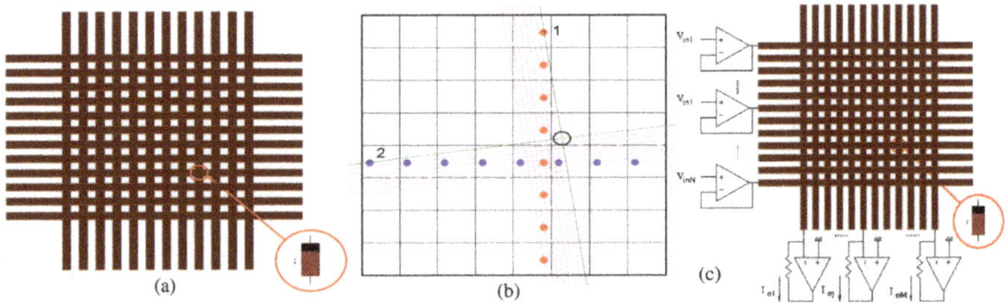

Figure 8. Illustration of the proposed hybrid CMOS/memristive CMOL architecture. (**a**) Memristive devices fabricated in the cross-points of a crossbar array and (**b**) proposed CMOL architecture. (**c**) Neuromorphic architecture composed of CMOS neurons connected to a crossbar array of memristors.

Neuromorphic architectures composed of CMOS neurons connected to a crossbar array of memristors as shown in Figure 8c have also been proposed as accelerators to perform the intensive matrix multiplications needed in deep machine learning architectures. In the memristive crossbar shown in Figure 8c, the input vector $[V_{in1}, V_{in2}, \ldots, V_{inN}]$ is applied as input voltages to the rows, each memristor in an (i,j) crossbar position is programmed with an analog value w_{ij} so that the currents flowing through the vertical columns are the result of the vector-matrix multiplication

$$I_j = \sum w_{ij} V_{ini}. \tag{4}$$

Many works have proposed including ReRAM memristive memory crossbars to implement Matrix-Vector-Multiplication Units in computer architectures to accelerate Neural Network applications [150–155] demonstrating great benefits in power consumption levels. PRIME [151] and RESPARC [150] report simulations of energy savings compared to fully CMOS Neural Processors Units in the order of 10^3 depending on the particular neural network architecture. Energy savings in the order of 10^3–10^5 respect to baseline CPU implementations have been reported [153,155]. However, in these works the memristor crossbars are included at a simulation level. A real hardware implementation of a hybrid CMOS system including an array of ReRAM crossbar as vector matrix multiplication elements for neural network computing acceleration at low energy consumption has been reported [22]. However, in this work the memristors are used in digital flip-flops as non-volatile digital devices. The real integration of CMOS neurons with a crossbar of CBRAM memristors is also demonstrated [156] for functional programming of a crossbar array of memristors in a digital way. More advanced fabrication techniques have been proposed to integrate up to 5 layers of 100 nm memristors in 3D crossbar arrays [157]. Some works have demonstrated the feasibility of integrating both carbon nanotube field-effect transistors (CNFETs) and RRAM on vertically stacked layers in a single chip on top of silicon logic circuitry, reporting 1952 CNFETs integrated with 224 RRAM cells for brain-inspired computing [158], or a prototype with more than 1 million RRAM cells with more than 2 million CNFETs in a single chip [25]. A recent work reported some circuit-level techniques for the design of a 65 nm 1 Mb pseudo-binary nonvolatile computing-in-memory RRAM macro which is capable of storing 512 k weights for Deep Neural Networks (DNN) [159].

However, so far experimental demonstrations of classification and training of memristive based analogue-memory learning systems have been on reduced systems and without achieving monolithic integration of the CMOS and memristive part [160], and suffered from classification inaccuracies due to device imperfections as control of the weight update, the programming of multilevel values, or variation in the device conductance range, limiting their application and severely degrading the performance of the network [161,162]. Another important shortcoming that limits the density of the implemented crossbars, as well as the practical hardware implementation of CMOL neuromorphic memristive systems, is the necessity of implementing a MOSFET in series with each memristive device (the so-called 1T1R devices) to limit the currents flowing through each memristor avoiding damage due to transient high-currents. When the transistor device is omitted, the current limitation is done in the peripheral CMOS circuitry, limiting the size of the array to reduce the risk of local high parasitic transient currents. In the 1T1R structures, the transistor also acts as a selection device to update individually each memristor avoiding alteration of the nearby devices. As a summary, although memristors are a very promising technology to implement high-density analog memories close to the computing system that could potentially implement high-speed low power learning cognitive system, there are still some technological limitations that are currently being investigated that have not allowed to implement such large scale systems.

5. Learning with Memristors (STDP)

Given that these SNNs are more powerful, in theory, than 2nd generation networks, it is natural to wonder why we do not see widespread use of them. One main issue that currently lies in practical use of SNNs is that of training. Learning mechanisms are crucial for the ability of neuromorphic systems to adapt to specific applications. In general, the goal of a learning algorithm is to modify the weights of the synaptic connections between neurons in order to improve the response of the network to a certain stimulus. Two main categories can be considered: supervised or unsupervised learning. In supervised learning, the dataset samples are labeled with the identification of the expected 'correct' network output. The measured deviation between the desired output and the real one is used to modify the synaptic weights. In unsupervised learning, there is no labeled information, so the own characteristics of the input data are analyzed by the network in order to self-organize.

As explained in Section 2, in the ANN field, the powerful computational capabilities of modern GPUs and CPUs and the availability of large amount of annotated data have made possible to train complex deep learning architectures using the supervised backpropagation learning algorithm [48] to solve complex cognitive problems in some cases with better accuracy than humans. However, there are no known effective supervised training methods for SNNs that offer higher performance than 2nd generation networks. The popular backpropagation learning strategies are not directly usable in SNN networks. On the one hand, if spikes are represented computationally as the occurrence of an output event at a particular time (as represented in Figure 3) they are not differentiable; on the other hand, differentiating the error back across the spatial layers (as it is done in the backpropagation algorithm) looses the precise temporal information contained in the spike timings. Therefore, in order to properly use SNNs for real-world tasks, we would need to develop an effective supervised learning method that takes space and time simultaneously into account [163]. Several approaches for SNN training have been adopted:

Training an ANN and conversion to SNN [66,164–167]. Some authors have proposed ANN to SNN direct conversion methods which are based on the training of ANN using static input images and directly mapping the network to an SNN converting the input stimulus to spikes using frequency rate encoding [164,165,167]. Bodo et al. implemented several optimizations achieving for a rate coded input similar performance than equivalent ANN implementations [165]. However, such encoding reduces the power efficiency of SNN. Other authors have proposed to train SNN with sensory data coming directly from a spike-based sensor (as a DVS recording). For that purpose, an equivalent ANN using static images generated from histograms of the input recordings of spiking stimulus is trained. Afterwards, a method to convert the weights of the ANN to the corresponding SNN is devised [66]. The additional timing parameters as leakage time or refractory period characteristics of SNN are optimized as hyper-parameters in the SNN resulting on different optimized parameter values for different input dynamics. Bodo et al. recently proposed an ANN to SNN conversion method based on time-to-first-spike input conversion code [166]. In all of these methods, training is done on static images and thus they do not fully exploit directly all the spatio-temporal information contained in the events.

Supervised training in the spiking domain. For the above mentioned reason, some methods for direct supervised learning in the spiking domain have been proposed [168–179]. Some of the earlier SNN training methods were based on an adaptation of the Delta Learning Rule [44] and were appropriate to train single layer architectures [169,171,172]. More recent SNN learning methods have been reported that try to apply the backpropagation learning rules to SNN with several learning layers. They include coding the spike times to have a differentiable relationship with a subset of previous spikes and hence compatible with the gradient descent back-propagation rule in the temporal domain [180], or approximating the spike shape response activity to be differentiable across neural layers [174,175,177]. Wu et al. introduced an SNN Spatio-Temporal BackPropagation algorithm [177]. Not only do they approximate the spike shape as a continuous differentiable function, but also they use a back-propagation-through-time (BTT) [163] which backpropagates the error in the space as well as the time dimension reporting the best recognition accuracy achieved by previously reported SNN on the MNIST and N-MNIST datasets and equivalent to the state-of-the-art of ANNs. Similarly, the SLAYER method [178] considers back-propagation in space and time and trains both weights and delays of the synaptic connections.

Unsupervised training in the spiking domain. The unsupervised SNN training methods are mostly based on the well known Spike-Timing-Dependent Plasticity (STDP) learning rule [31,32]. STDP is a Hebbian learning rule. The traditional Hebbian synaptic plasticity rule was formulated in 1940 suggesting that synapses increase their efficiency if they persistently take part in firing the post-synaptic neuron [39]. Much later in 1993, STDP learning algorithms were reported [31,32] as a refinement of this rule taking into account the precise relative timing of individual pre- and post-synaptic spikes, and not their average rates over time. In comparison with traditional Hebbian correlation-based plasticity, STDP proved to be better suited for explaining brain cortical phenomena [181,182], and demonstrated to be successful in learning hidden spiking patterns [183] or performing competitive spike pattern learning [184]. Interestingly, shortly after that, in 1997, STDP learning was experimentally observed in biological neurons [33–35]. Figure 9a,b illustrate the STDP learning rule as observed in biological synapses. Figure 9a plots a presynaptic neuron with a membrane potential V_{pre} which is connected through a synapse with synaptic strength w to a postsynaptic neuron with membrane potential V_{post}. The presynaptic neuron emits a spike at time t_{pre} which contributes to the generation of a postsynaptic spike at time t_{post}. The biological learning rule observed by Bi and Poo is illustrated in Figure 9b. When the two connected neurons generate spikes close in time, if $\Delta T = t_{post} - t_{pre}$ is positive, meaning that the presynaptic pulse contributed causally to generate the postsynaptic pulse, there is a positive variation in the efficacy of the synaptic connection $\xi(\Delta T) > 0$; on the contrary, if $\Delta T = t_{post} - t_{pre}$ is negative, the variation in the efficacy of the synaptic connection $\xi(\Delta T) < 0$ is negative. Being STDP a local learning rule, and memristors two-terminal devices exhibiting plasticity controlled by the local applied voltage/current to their terminals converts memristors as ideal candidates to implement high-density on-line STDP-based neuromorphic learning systems [27]. Linares et al. [28] showed that by combining the memristance model formulated in Equation (2) with the electrical wave signals of neural impulses (spikes) as shaped in Figure 9c applied to the pre- and post-synaptic terminals of the memristive synaptic-like device, the STDP behavior shown in Figure 9d emerges naturally. Considering the mathematical equation describing the spike shape shown in Figure 9c versus time

$$spk(t) = \begin{cases} A^{+}_{mp} \frac{e^{t/\tau^{+}} - e^{t^{+}_{tail}/\tau^{+}}}{1 - e^{t^{+}_{tail}/\tau^{+}}} & if \quad -t^{+}_{tail} < t < 0 \\ A^{-}_{mp} \frac{e^{-t/\tau^{-}} - e^{-t^{-}_{tail}/\tau^{-}}}{1 - e^{-t^{-}_{tail}/\tau^{-}}} & if \quad 0 < t < t^{-}_{tail} \\ 0 & otherwise \end{cases} \tag{5}$$

and a memristive synapse-like device where a presynaptic spike $spk(t)$ with attenuation α_{pre} arrives at time t to its negative terminal and a postsynaptic spike $spk(t + \Delta T)$ with attenuation α_{pos} arrives at time $t + \Delta T$ to its positive terminal, a voltage difference

$$v_{MR}(t+\Delta T) = \alpha_{pos}spk(t+\Delta T) - \alpha_{pre}spk(t) \quad (6)$$

is generated among the device terminals. The total change in the memristance parameter w can thus be computed as,

$$\Delta w(\Delta T) = \int f_{MR}(v_{MR}(t+\Delta T))dt = \xi(\Delta T) \quad (7)$$

Interestingly, for the memristor model considered in Equation (2) and the spike shape considered in Equation (5), the memristance learning rule shown in Figure 9d $\xi(\Delta T)$ is obtained which resembles the STDP rule observed by Gerstner in biological neurons. By playing with the spike shapes, many other STDP update rules can be tuned as demonstrated by Zamarreño et al. [29,30].

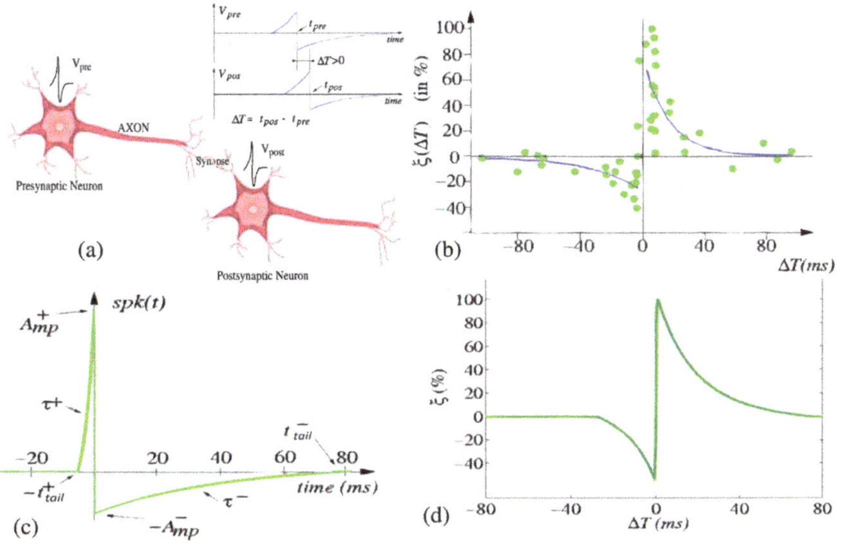

Figure 9. Illustration of STDP learning rule. (**a**) Pre-synaptic neuron generating a spike V_{pre} at time t_{pre} that arrives to a post-synaptic neuron that generates a spike V_{post} at time t_{post}, being $\Delta T = t_{post} - t_{pre}$, and (**b**) illustrates the variation of the synaptic efficacy $\xi(\Delta T)$ Vs ΔT, STDP learning rule, as the observed by Bi and Poo in biological synapses. (**c**) Illustrates the spike shape that applied to the memristive devices describes in Section 4 reproduces the STDP learning rule shown in (**d**).

In the last decade, many different works have demonstrated the emergence of STDP learning in memristive devices of different kinds of materials [137,180,185–189]. However, as already stated in Section 4, at a system level, the current limitations of the memristor technology in terms of control of the resolution of the weigh updating, have not made possible the implementation of working STDP memristive learning systems with analog synaptic elements. Precision in the weight update is difficult to control and most of the memristive devices operate changing between binary states. For that reason, stochastic STDP learning rules that operate with binary weights during inference and updating operation have been proposed. Seo et al. [190] applied this idea to simple classification problems, but they found that they could not learn to separate more than 5 patterns. Recently, Yousefzadeh et al. [191] were able to classify more elaborated databases (as MNIST) by introducing some other techniques that improved the performance.

Combining unsupervised feature extraction methods with supervised categorization training. While supervised learning methods like backpropagation are not energy efficient, are not appropriate for on-line chip learning, and do not look like biologically plausible, unsupervised learning rules are appropriate to extract repetitive structures in the training data but not appropriate to take decisions [192,193]. For example, Mozafari et al. propose to combine unsupervised STDP layer with supervised Reinforcement Learning STDP layers [193]. The resulting network is more robust to overfitting compared to backprogation training as it extracts common features and performs well with reduced number of training samples.

6. Future Perspective

It is well known that the human brain contains about 10^{11} neurons interconnected through 10^{15} synapses, and with a power consumption of around 20 W it is capable of performing complex sensing and cognitive processing, sophisticated motor control, learning and abstraction, and it can dynamically adapt to changing environments and unpredicted conditions. For this reason, neuromorphic engineers have been using the brain as a processing paradigm for several decades in order to fabricate artificial processing systems with similar capabilities. After the initial attempts of building the first spike-based processing systems demonstrated their feasibility and showed their promising potential [78], it became evident the need for scaling up these systems in terms of number of neurons and synapses [62]. Several works developed by both academic institutions [86,121–125,127–129] and industrial players like IBM [120] or Intel [126] fabricated neuromorphic chips with up to 1 M neurons and 256 M synapses, which could be ensembled in multi-chip boards and multi-board platforms, opening the way to implement large systems in the near future with numbers of neurons and synapses similar to the brain. However, these systems, based on different CMOS technologies, will be limited by the their large room-scale size. Besides, the complexity of current implementations of learning algorithms in CMOS limits their scalability.

The emergence of memristors and their synaptic-like behavior opened the possibility to overcome the limitations of CMOS technologies. Memristors can be a few nanometers size and can be packed densely in a two-dimensional layer with nanometer-range pitch, potentially offering higher neuron and synaptic density. With a fabrication process much cheaper than CMOS, memristor layers can be stacked in 3D. Assuming a reasonable 30-nm pitch, the superposition of 10 memristive layers could theoretically provide a memory density of 10^{11} non-volatile analog cells per cm^2. This approach could in principle reach the neuron and synaptic density of the human brain in a single board, including learning capabilities [194]. Furthermore, the close 3D dense packaging between the CMOS neural computation units and the memristive adaptive memory synaptic elements can significantly reduce the current consumption of the resulting systems.

Current available memristors are described as 1T1R devices, meaning that they are formed by the series connection of a MOS transistor and a memristive element. This transistor is used to limit the current flowing through the memristor during each operation (Forming, Writing, Erasing, Reading) to avoid damaging the device. However, this structure is limiting the density of memristors, as they are also consuming area in the CMOS substrate. An alternative to overcome this limitation is given by 1S1R devices (1-selector-1-resistor), where a volatile memristor (1S) is connected in series with a non-volatile memristor (1R), eluding any CMOS area consumption [195].

Hybrid systems with memristor layers fabricated on top of a CMOS substrate can provide highly parallel massive storage tightly coupled to CMOS computing circuitry. Therefore, computing and learning processes in the brain can be imitated by combining memristors with spiking processors and integrate-and-fire neurons in silicon. Using mesh techniques [82], grids of tens of chips can be assembled modularly on a Printed Circuit Board (PCB), allowing for scaling up the numbers of neurons and synapses in a neural system [65]. The combination of all these techniques together with the resolution of the multiple technical challenges currently associated to dense memristive layers (reliability, repeatability, reprogrammability) could provide an important step towards the hardware implementation of brain-scale low-power neuromorphic processing systems with online STDP learning.

Author Contributions: Writing—original draft preparation, L.A.C.-M. and T.S.-G.; writing—review and editing, L.A.C.-M., T.S.-G. and B.L.-B.; supervision, B.L.-B. and T.S.-G.; funding acquisition, T.S.-G. and L.A.C.-M.

Funding: This work was funded by EU H2020 grants 687299 "NEURAM3" and 824164 "HERMES", and by Spanish grant from the Ministry of Economy and Competitivity TEC2015-63884-C2-1-P (COGNET) (with support from the European Regional Development Fund). Luis A. Camuñas-Mesa was funded by the VI PPIT through the Universidad de Sevilla.

Conflicts of Interest: The authors declare no conflict of interest.

References

1. Von Neumann, J. First Draft of a Report on the EDVAC. *IEEE Ann. Hist. Comput.* **1945**, *15*, 27–75. [CrossRef]
2. Moore, G.E. Cramming more components onto integrated circuits. *Electronics* **1965**, *38*, 114–117. [CrossRef]
3. Waldrop, M.M. The chips are down for Moore's law. *Nature* **2016**, *530*, 144–147. [CrossRef] [PubMed]
4. Kaur, J. Life Beyond Moore: More Moore or More than Moore—A Review. *Int. J. Comput. Sci. Mob. Comput.* **2016**, *5*, 233–237.
5. Hodgkin, A.L.; Huxley, A.F. Currents carried by sodium and potassium ions through the membrane of the giant squid axon of loligo. *J. Physiol.* **1952**, *116*, 449–472. [CrossRef] [PubMed]
6. FitzHugh, R. Impulses and physiological states in models of nerve membrane. *Biophys. J.* **1961**, *1*, 445–466. [CrossRef]
7. Nagumo, J.S.; Arimoto, S.; Yoshizawa, S. An active pulse transmission line simulating nerve axon. *Proc. IRE* **1962**, *50*, 2061–2070. [CrossRef]
8. Morris, C.; Lecar, H. Voltage oscillations in the barnacle giant muscle fiber. *Biophys. J.* **1981**, *35*, 193–213. [CrossRef]
9. Brette, R.; Gerstner, W. Adaptive exponential integrate-and-fire model as an effective description of neuronal activity. *J. Neurophysiol.* **2005**, *94*, 3637–3642. [CrossRef]
10. Izhikevich, E.M. Simple Model of Spiking Neurons. *IEEE Trans. Neural Netw.* **2003**, *14*, 1569–1572. [CrossRef]
11. Runge, R.G.; Uemura, M.; Viglione, S.S. Electronic synthesis of the avian retina. *IEEE Trans. Biomed. Eng.* **1968**, *15*, 138–151. [CrossRef] [PubMed]
12. Furber, S. Large-scale neuromorphic computing systems. *J. Neural Eng.* **2016**, *13*, 051001. [CrossRef] [PubMed]
13. Mead, C. *Analog VLSI and Neural Systems*; Addison-Wesley: Boston, MA, USA, 1989.
14. Mead, C. Neuromorphic Electronic Systems. *Proc. IEEE* **1990**, *78*, 1629–1636. [CrossRef]
15. Mahowald, M.A.; Mead, C. The silicon retina. *Sci. Am.* **1991**, *264*, 76–82. [CrossRef] [PubMed]
16. Smith, L.S. Neuromorphic Systems: Past, Present and Future. *Br. Inspir. Cognit. Syst.* **2008**, 167–182.
17. Chua, L.O. Memristor—The Missing Circuit Element. *IEEE Trans. Circuit Theory* **1971**, *18*, 507–519. [CrossRef]
18. Strukov, D.B.; Snider, G.S.; Stewart, D.R.; Williams, R.S. The missing memristor found. *Nature* **2008**, *453*, 80–83. [CrossRef]
19. Hashem, N.; Das, S. Switching-time analysis of binary-oxide memristors via a non-linear model. *Appl. Phys. Lett.* **2012**, *100*, 262106. [CrossRef]
20. Kvatinsky, S.; Belousov, D.; Liman, S.; Satat, G.; Wald, N.; Friedman, E.G.; Kolodny, A.; Weiser, U.C. MAGIC—Memristor-Aided Logic. *IEEE Trans. Circuits Syst. II Express Br.* **2014**, *11*, 895–899. [CrossRef]
21. Kvatinsky, S.; Friedman, E.G.; Kolodny, A.; Weiser, U.C. Memristor-based material implication (IMPLY) logic: Design principles and methodologies. *IEEE Trans. Very Large Scale Integr. (VLSI)* **2013**, *10*, 2054–2066. [CrossRef]
22. Su, F.; Chen, W.H.; Xia, L.; Lo, C.P.; Tang, T.; Wang, Z.; Hsu, K.H.; Cheng, M.; Li, J.Y.; Xie, Y.; et al. A 462 GOPs/J RRAM-based nonvolatile intelligent processor for energy harvesting IoE system featuring nonvolatile logics and processing-in-memory. In Proceedings of the 2017 Symposium on VLSI Technology, Kyoto, Japan, 5–8 June 2017.
23. Liu, Y.; Wang, Z.; Lee, A.; Su, F.; Lo, C.; Yuan, Z.; Lin, C.; Wei, Q.; Wang, Y.; King, Y.; et al. A 65 nm ReRAM-Enabled Nonvolatile Processor with 6× Reduction in Restore Time and 4× Higher Clock Frequency Using Adaptive Data Retention and Self-Write-Termination Nonvolatile Logic. *Int. Conf. Solid-State Circuits* **2016**, *59*, 84–86.

24. Onuki, T.; Uesugi, W.; Tamura, H.; Isobe, A.; Ando, Y.; Okamoto, S.; Kato, K.; Yew, T.; Lin, C.; Wu, J.; et al. Embedded memory and ARM Cortex-M0 core using 60-nm C-axis aligned crystalline indium-gallium-zinc oxide FET integrated with 65-nm Si CMOS. *IEEE Symp. VLSI Circuits* **2017**, *52*, 925–932.
25. Shulaker, M.M.; Hills, G.; Park, R.; Howe, R.; Saraswat, K.; Wong, H.; Mitra, S. Three-dimensional integration of nanotechnologies for computing and data storage on a single chip. *Nature* **2017**, *547*, 74–78. [CrossRef]
26. Carrara, S.; Sacchetto, D.; Doucey, M.A.; Baj-Rossi, C.; De Micheli, G.; Leblebici, Y. Memristive-biosensors: A new detection method by using nanofabricated memristors. *Sens. Actuators B Chem.* **2012**, *171–172*, 449–457. [CrossRef]
27. Snider, G.S. Spike-time-dependent Plasticity in Memristive Nanotechnologies. In Proceedings of the IEEE/ACM International Symposium on Nanoscale Architectures, Washington, DC, USA, 12–13 June 2008.
28. Linares-Barranco, B.; Serrano-Gotarredona, T. Memristance can explain spike-time-dependent-plasticity in neural synapses. *Nat. Preced.* **2009**. [CrossRef]
29. Zamarreno-Ramos, C.; Camuñas-Mesa, L.A.; Pérez-Carrasco, J.A.; Masquelier, T.; Serrano-Gotarredona, T.; Linares-Barranco, B. On spike-timing-dependent-plasticity, memristive devices, and building a self-learning visual cortex. *Front. Neurosci.* **2011**, *5*, 26. [CrossRef]
30. Serrano-Gotarredona, T.; Masquelier, T.; Prodromakis, T.; Indiveri, G.; Linares-Barranco, B. STDP and STDP variations with memristors for spiking neuromorphic learning systems. *Front. Neurosci.* **2013**, *7*, 2. [CrossRef]
31. Gerstner, W.; Ritz, R.; Hemmen, J.L. Why spikes? Hebbian learning and retrieval of time-resolved excitation patterns. *Biol. Cybern.* **1993**, *69*, 503–515. [CrossRef]
32. Gerstner, W.; Kempter, R.; Leo van Hemmen, J.; Wagner, H. A neuronal learning rule for sub-millisecond temporal coding. *Lett. Nat.* **1996**, *383*, 76–78. [CrossRef]
33. Markram, H.; Lübke, J.; Frotscher, M.; Sakmann, B. Regulation of synaptic efficacy by coincidence of postsynaptic APS and EPSPS. *Science* **1997**, *275*, 213–215. [CrossRef]
34. Bi, G.; Poo, M. Synaptic modifications in cultured hippocampal neurons: Dependence on spike timing, synaptic strength, and postsynaptic cell type. *J. Neurosci.* **1998**, *18*, 10464–10472. [CrossRef]
35. Bi, G.; Poo, M. Synaptic modification by correlated activity: Hebb's postulate revisited. *Ann. Rev. Neurosci.* **2001**, *24*, 139–166. [CrossRef]
36. Jacob, V.; Brasier, D.J.; Erchova, I.; Feldman, D.; Shulz, D.E. Spike timing-dependent synaptic depression in the in vivo barrel cortex of the rat. *J. Neurosci.* **2007**, *27*, 1271–1284. [CrossRef]
37. McCulloch, W.S.; Pitts, W. A logical calculus of the ideas immanent in nervous activity. *Bull. Math. Biophys.* **1943**, *5*, 115–133. [CrossRef]
38. Rosenblatt, F. The Perceptron: A Probabilistic Model for Information Storage and Organization in the Brain. *Psychol. Rev.* **1958**, *65*, 386–408. [CrossRef]
39. Hebb, D. *The Organization of Behavior*; Wiley: New York, NY, USA, 1949.
40. Minsky, M.L.; Papert, S.A. *Perceptrons*; MIT Press: Cambridge, MA, USA, 1969.
41. Maass, W. Networks of spiking neurons: The third generation of neural network models. *Neural Netw.* **1997**, *10*, 1659–1671. [CrossRef]
42. Ghosh-Dastidar S.; Adeli H. Third Generation Neural Networks: Spiking Neural Networks. In *Advances in Computational Intelligence. Advances in Intelligent and Soft Computing*; Yu, W., Sanchez, E.N., Eds.; Springer: Berlin, Germany, 2009.
43. Krizhevsky, A.; Sutskever, I.; Hinton, G.E. Imagenet classification with deep convolutional neural networks. In Proceedings of the ImageNet Classification with Deep Convolutional Neural Networks NIPS, Lake Tahoe, CA, USA, 3–6 December 2012.
44. Widrow, B. *Adaptive "Adaline" Neuron Using Chemical "Memistors"*; Number Technical Report 1553-2; Stanford Electron. Labs.: Stanford, CA, USA, 1960.
45. Widrow, B.; Lehr, M.A. 30 years of Adaptive Neural Networks: Peceptron, Madaline, and Backpropagation. *Proc. IEEE* **1990**, *78*, 1415–1442. [CrossRef]
46. Werbos, P. Beyond Regression: New Tools for Prediction and Analysis in the Behavioral Sciences. Ph.D. Thesis, Harvard University, Cambridge, MA, USA, 1974.
47. Parker, D. *Learning-Logic*; Invention Report 581-64, File 1; Office of Technology Licensing, Stanford Univ.: Stanford, CA, USA, 1982.
48. Rumelhart, D.E.; Hinton, G.E.; Williams, R.J. Learning representations by back-propagating errors. *Nature* **1986**, 1476–4687. [CrossRef]

49. Carpenter, G.A.; Grossberg, S. A massively parallel architecture for a self-organizing neural pattern recognition machine. *Comput. Vis. Gr. Image Process.* **1983**, *37*, 54–115. [CrossRef]
50. Kohonen, T. Self-organized formation of topologically correct feature maps. *Biolog. Cybern.* **1982**, *43*, 59–69. [CrossRef]
51. Hopfield, J.J. Neural networks and physical systems with emergent collective computational abilities. *Proc. Natl. Acad. Sci. USA* **1982**, *79*, 2554–2558. [CrossRef]
52. Bishop, C.M. *Neural Networks for Pattern Recognition*; Clarendon Press: Oxford, UK, 1995.
53. Bengio, Y. Learning Deep Architectures for AI. *Found. Trends Mach. Learn.* **2009**, *2*, 1–127. [CrossRef]
54. Schmidhuber, J. Deep Learning in Neural Networks: An Overview. *Neural Netw.* **2015**, *61*, 85–117. [CrossRef]
55. LeCun, Y.; Jackel, L.D.; Boser, B.; Denker, J.S.; Graf, H.P.; Guyon, I.; Henderson, D.; Howard, R.E.; Hubbard, W. Handwritten digit recognition: Applications of neural network chips and automatic learning. *IEEE Commun. Mag.* **1989**, *27*, 41–46. [CrossRef]
56. Deng, L.; Li, J.; Huang, J.; Yao, K.; Yu, D.; Seide, F.; Seltzer, M.; Sweig, G.; He, X.; Williams, J.; et al. Recent advances in deep learning for speech research at Microsoft. In Proceedings of the 2013 IEEE International Conference on Acoustics, Speech and Signal Processing, Vancouver, BC, Canada, 26–31 May 2013 .
57. Thorpe, S.; Fize, D.; Marlot, C. Speed of processing in the human visual system. *Nature* **1996**, *381*, 520–522. [CrossRef]
58. Rolls, E.T.; Tovee, M.J. Processing speed in the cerebral cortex and the neurophysiology of visual masking. *Proc. R. Soc. London. Ser. B Biol. Sci.* **1994**, *257*, 9–15.
59. Thorpe, S.; Delorme, A.; Van Rullen, R. Spike-based strategies for rapid processing. *Neural Netw.* **2001**, *14*, 715–725. [CrossRef]
60. Huys, Q.; Zemel, R.; Natarajan, R.; Dayan, P. Fast population coding. *Neural Comput.* **2007**, *19*, 404–441. [CrossRef]
61. Rullen, R.V.; Thorpe, S.J. Rate coding versus temporal order coding: What the retinal ganglion cells tell the visual cortex. *Neural Comput.* **2001**, *13*, 1255–1283. [CrossRef]
62. Indiveri, G.; Linares-Barranco, B.; Hamilton, T.J.; Schaik, A.; Etienne-Cummings, R.; Delbrück, T.; Liu, S.; Dudek, P.; Häfliger, P.; Renaud, S.; et al. Neuromorphic silicon neuron circuits. *Front. Neurosci.* **2011**, *5*, 73. [CrossRef]
63. Fukushima, K. Neocognitron: A hierarchical neural network capable of visual pattern recognition. *Neural Netw.* **1988**, *1*, 119–130. [CrossRef]
64. Hubel, D.H.; Wiesel, T.N. Receptive fields and functional architecture of monkey striate cortex. *J. Physiol.* **1968**, *195*, 215–243. [CrossRef]
65. Farabet, C.; Paz, R.; Pérez-Carrasco, J.; Zamarreño-Ramos, C.; Linares-Barranco, A.; Lecun, Y.; Culurciello, E.; Serrano-Gotarredona, T.; Linares-Barranco, B. Comparison between frame-constrained fix-pixel-value and frame-free spiking-dynamic-pixel ConvNets for visual processing. *Front. Neurosci.* **2012**, *6*, 32. [CrossRef]
66. Perez-Carrasco, J.A.; Zhao, B.; Serrano, C.; Acha, B.; Serrano-Gotarredona, T.; Chen, S.; Linares-Barranco, B. Mapping from frame-driven to frame-free event-driven vision systems by low-rate rate coding and coincidence processing–application to feedforward ConvNets. *IEEE Trans. Pattern Anal. Mach. Intell.* **2013**, *35*, 2706–2719. [CrossRef]
67. Camunas-Mesa, L.; Acosta-Jiménez, A.; Zamarreño-Ramos, C.; Serrano-Gotarredona, T.; Linares-Barranco, B. A 32x32 Pixel Convolution Processor Chip for Address Event Vision Sensors With 155 ns Event Latency and 20 Meps Throughput. *IEEE Trans. Circuits Syst. I Regul. Pap.* **2011**, *58*, 777–790. [CrossRef]
68. Sengupta, A.; Ye, Y.; Wang, R.; Liu, C.; Roy, K. Going Deeper in Spiking Neural Networks: VGG and Residual Architectures. *Front. Neurosci.* **2019**. [CrossRef]
69. Bouvier, M.; Valentian, A.; Mesquida, T.; Rummens, F.; Reybox, M.; Vianello, E.; Biegne, E. Spiking Neural Networks Hardware Implementations and Challenges: A Survey. *ACM J. Emerg. Technlol. Comput. Syst.* **2019**, *15*, 1–35. [CrossRef]
70. Schmid, A. Neuromorphic microelectronics from devices to hardware systems and applications. *Nonlinear Theory Its Appl. IEICE* **2016**, *7*, 468–498. [CrossRef]
71. Sivilotti, M. Wiring Considerations in Analog VLSI Systems with Application to Field-Programmable Networks. Ph.D. Thesis, Computation and Neural Systems, California Inst. Technol., Pasadena, CA, USA, 1991.
72. Serrano-Gotarredona, T.; Andreou, A.G.; Linares-Barranco, B. AER image filtering architecture for vision-processing systems. *IEEE Trans. Circuits Syst. I* **1999**, *46*, 1064–1071. [CrossRef]

73. Boahen, K. Point-to-Point connectivity between neuromorphic chips using address events. *IEEE Trans. Circuits Syst. II* **2000**, *47*, 416–434. [CrossRef]
74. Boahen, K. A burst-mode word-serial address-event link-I,II,III. *IEEE Trans. Circuits Syst. I* **2004**, *51*, 1269–1280. [CrossRef]
75. Lin, J.; Merolla, P.; Arthur, J.; Boahen, K. Programmable connections in neuromorphic grids. In Proceedings of the 2006 49th IEEE International Midwest Symposium on Circuits and Systems, San Juan, Puerto Rico, 6–9 August 2006; pp. 80–84.
76. Merolla, P.; Arthur, J.; Shi, B.; Boahen, K. Expandable networks for neuromorphic chips. *IEEE Trans. Circuits Syst. I* **2007**, *54*, 301–311. [CrossRef]
77. Bamford, S.A.; Murray, A.F.; Willshaw, D.J. Large developing receptive fields using a distributed and locally reprogrammable address-event receiver. *IEEE Trans. Neural Netw.* **2010**, *21*, 286–304. [CrossRef]
78. Serrano-Gotarredona, R.; Oster, M.; Lichtsteiner, P.; Linares-Barranco, A.; Paz-Vicente, R.; Gomez-Rodriguez, F.; Camuñas-Mesa, L.; Berner, R.; Rivas-Perez, M.; Delbrück, T.; et al. CAVIAR: A 45k neuron, 5M synapse, 12G connects/s AER hardware sensory-processing-learning-actuating system for high-speed visual object recognition and tracking. *IEEE Trans. Neural Netw.* **2009**, *20*, 1417–1438. [CrossRef]
79. Joshi, S.; Deiss, S.; Arnold, M.; Park, J.; Yu, T.; Cauwenberghs, G. Scalable event routing in hierarchical neural array architecture with global synaptic connectivity. In Proceedings of the International Workshop Cellular Nanoscale Networks and Their Applications, Berkeley, CA, USA, 3–5 February 2010.
80. Khan, M.; Lester, D.; Plana, L.; Rast, A.; Jin, X.; Painkras, E.; Furber, S. SpiNNaker: Mapping neural networks onto a massively-parallel chip multiprocessor. In Proceedings of the 2008 IEEE International Joint Conference on Neural Networks, Hong Kong, China, 1–8 June 2008; pp. 2849–2856.
81. Benini, L.; Micheli, G.D. Networks on chips: A new SoC paradigm. *IEEE Comput.* **2002**, 70–78. [CrossRef]
82. Zamarreno-Ramos, C.; Linares-Barranco, A.; Serrano-Gotarredona, T.; Linares-Barranco, B. Multicasting mesh AER: A scalable assembly approach for reconfigurable neuromorphic structured AER systems. Application to ConvNets. *IEEE Trans. Biomed. Circuits Syst.* **2013**, *7*, 82–102. [CrossRef]
83. Fieres, J.; Schemmel, J.; Meier, K. Realizing biological spiking network models in a configurable wafer-scale hardware system. In Proceedings of the 2008 IEEE International Joint Conference on Neural Networks, Hong Kong, China, 1–8 June 2008; pp. 969–976.
84. Scholze, S.; Schiefer, S.; Partzsch, J.; Hartmann, S.; Mayr, C.; Höppner, S.; Eisenreich, H.; Henker, S.; Vogginger, B.; Schüffny, R. VLSI implementation of a 2.8 gevent/s packet based AER interface with routing and event sorting functionality. *Front. Neurosci.* **2011**, *5*, 117. [CrossRef]
85. Park, J.; Yu, T.; Joshi, S.; Maier, C.; Cauwenberghs, G. Hierarchical Address Event Routing for Reconfigurable Large-Scale Neuromorphic Systems. *IEEE Trans. Neural Netw. Learn. Syst.* **2017**, *28*, 2408–2422. [CrossRef]
86. Moradi, S.; Qiao, N.; Stefanini, F.; Indiveri, G. A Scalable Multicore Architecture with Heterogeneous Memory Structures for Dynamic Neuromorphic Asynchronous Processors (DYNAPs). *IEEE Trans. Biomed. Circuits Syst.* **2018**, *12*, 106–122. [CrossRef]
87. Culurciello, E.; Etienne-Cummings, R.; Boahen, K.A. A biomorphic digital image sensor. *IEEE J. Solid-State Circuits* **2003**, *38*, 281–294. [CrossRef]
88. Ruedi, P.F.; Heim, P.; Kaess, F.; Grenet, E.; Heitger, F.; Burgi, P.; Gyger, S.; Nussbaum, P. A 128 × 128 pixel 120-dB dynamic-range vision-sensor chip for image contrast and orientation extraction. *IEEE J. Solid-State Circuits* **2003**, *1*, 2325–2333. [CrossRef]
89. Barbaro, M.; Burgi, P.; Mortara, R.; Nussbaum, P.; Heitger, F. A 100 × 100 pixel silicon retina for gradient extraction with steering filter capabilities and temporal output coding. *IEEE J. Solid-State Circuits* **2002**, *37*, 160–172. [CrossRef]
90. Chen, S.; Bermak, A. Arbitrated time-to-first spike CMOS image sensor with on-chip histogram equalization. *IEEE Trans. Very Large Scale Integr. Syst.* **2007**, *15*, 346–357.
91. Qi, X.G.; Harris, J. A time-to-first-spike CMOS imager. In Proceedings of the 2004 IEEE International Symposium on Circuits and Systems (IEEE Cat. No.04CH37512), Vancouver, BC, Canada, 23–26 May 2004; pp. 824–827.
92. Azadmehr, M.; Abrahamsen, J.; Häfliger, P. A foveated AER imager chip. In Proceedings of the IEEE International Symposium on Circuits and Systems, Kobe, Japan, 23–26 May 2005; pp. 2751–2754.

93. Vogelstein, R.J.; Mallik, U.; Culurciello, E.; Etienne-Cummings, R.; Cauwenberghs, G. Spatial acuity modulation of an address-event imager. In Proceedings of the IEEE ICECS, Tel Aviv, Israel, Israel, 15 December 2004; pp. 207–210.
94. Costas-Santos, J.; Serrano-Gotarredona, T.; Serrano-Gotarredona, R.; Linares-Barranco, B. A Spatial Contrast Retina with On-chip Calibration for Neuromorphic Spike-Based AER Vision Systems. *IEEE Trans. Circuits Syst. I* **2007**, *54*, 1444–1458. [CrossRef]
95. Leñero-Bardallo, J.A.; Serrano-Gotarredona, T.; Linares-Barranco, B. A 5-Decade Dynamic Range Ambient-Light-Independent Calibrated Signed-Spatial-Contrast AER Retina with 0.1ms Latency and Optional Time-to-First-Spike Mode. *IEEE Trans. Circuits Syst I* **2010**, *57*, 2632–2643. [CrossRef]
96. Zaghloul, K.A.; Boahen, K. Optic nerve signals in a neuromorphic chip: Parts 1 and 2. *IEEE Trans. Biomed. Eng.* **2004**, *51*, 657–675. [CrossRef]
97. Leñero-Bardallo, J.A.; Serrano-Gotarredona, T.; Linares-Barranco, B. A 3.6us Asynchronous Frame-Free Event-Driven Dynamic-Vision-Sensor. *IEEE J. Solid-State Circuits* **2011**, *46*, 1443–1455. [CrossRef]
98. Kramer, J. An integrated optical transient sensor. *IEEE Trans. Circuits Syst. II Analog Digit. Signal Process* **2002**, *49*, 612–628. [CrossRef]
99. Lichtsteiner, P.; Posch, C.; Delbrück, T. A 128 × 128 120 dB 15 μs latency asynchronous temporal contrast vision sensor. *IEEE J. Solid-State Circuits* **2008**, *43*, 566–576. [CrossRef]
100. Serrano-Gotarredona, T.; Linares-Barranco, B. A 128x128 1.5% Contrast Sensitivity 0.9% FPN 3us Latency 4mW Asynchronous Frame-Free Dynamic Vision Sensor Using Transimpedance Amplifiers. *IEEE J. Solid-State Circuits* **2013**, 827–838. [CrossRef]
101. Brandli, C.; Berner, R.; Yang, M.; Liu, S.; Delbrück, T. A 240 × 180 130 dB 3 μs Latency Global Shutter Spatiotemporal Vision Sensor. *IEEE J. Solid-State Circuits* **2014**, 2333–2341. [CrossRef]
102. Moeys, D.P.; Corradi, F.; Li, C.; Bamford, S.; Longinotti, L.; Voigt, F.; Berry, S.; Taverni, G.; Helmchen, F.; Delbrück, T. A Sensitive Dynamic and Active Pixel Vision Sensor for Color or Neural Imaging Applications. *IEEE Trans. Biomed. Circuits Syst.* **2018**, *12*, 123–136. [CrossRef]
103. Posch, C.; Matolin, D.; Wohlgenannt, R. A QVGA 143 dB dynamic range frame-free PWM image sensor with lossless pixel-level video compression and time-domain CDS. *IEEE J. Solid-State Circuits* **2011**, *46*, 259–275. [CrossRef]
104. Posch, C.; Serrano-Gotarredona, T.; Linares-Barranco, B.; Delbrück, T. Retinomorphic Event-Based Vision Sensors: Bioinspired Cameras with Spiking Output. *Proc. IEEE* **2014**, *102*, 1470–1484. [CrossRef]
105. Son, B.; Suh, Y.; Kim, S.; Jung, H.; Kim, J.; Shin, C.; Park, K.; Lee, K.; Park, J.; Woo, J.; et al. A 640 × 480 dynamic vision sensor with a 9um pixel and 300Meps address-event representation. *IEEE Intl. Solid-State Circuits Conf.* **2017**. [CrossRef]
106. Guo, M.; Huang, J.; Chen, S. Live demonstration: A 768 × 640 pixels 200 Meps dynamic vision sensor. In Proceedings of the 2017 IEEE International Symposium on Circuits and Systems (ISCAS), Baltimore, MD, USA , 28–31 May 2017 .
107. Lyon, R.F.; Mead, C. An analog electronic cochlea. *IEEE Trans. Acoust. Speech Signal Process.* **1988**, *36*, 1119–1134. [CrossRef]
108. Chan, V.; Liu, S.; van Schaik, A. AER EAR: A Matched Silicon Cochlea Pair with Address Event Representation Interface. *IEEE Trans. Circuits Syst. I Regul. Pap.* **2007**, *54*, 48–59. [CrossRef]
109. Wen, B.; Boahen, K. A Silicon Cochlea With Active Coupling. *IEEE Trans. Biomed. Circuits Syst.* **2009**, *3*, 444–455. [CrossRef]
110. Caviglia, S.; Pinna, L.; Valle, M.; Bartolozzi, C. Spike-Based Readout of POSFET Tactile Sensors. *IEEE Trans. Circuits Syst. I* **2017**, *64*, 1421–1431. [CrossRef]
111. Ros, P.M.; Crepaldi, M.; Demarchi, D. A hybrid quasi-digital/neuromorphic architecture for tactile sensing in humanoid robots. In Proceedings of the International Workshop on Advances in Sensors and Interfaces, Gallipoli, Italy, 18–19 June 2015; pp. 126–130.
112. Oster, M.; Douglas, R.; Liu, S.C. Computation with Spikes in a Winner-Take-All Network. *Neural Comput.* **2009**, *21*, 2437–2465. [CrossRef]
113. Camuñas-Mesa, L.; Zamarreño-Ramos, C.; Linares-Barranco, A.; Acosta-Jiménez, A.; Serrano-Gotarredona, T.; Linares-Barranco, B. An event-driven multi-kernel convolution processor module for event-driven vision sensors. *IEEE J. Solid-State Circuits* **2012**, *47*, 504–517. [CrossRef]

114. Camuñas-Mesa, L.A.; Domínguez-Cordero, Y.L.; Linares-Barranco, A.; Serrano-Gotarredona, T.; Linares-Barranco, B. A Configurable Event-Driven Convolutional Node with Rate Saturation Mechanism for Modular ConvNet Systems Implementation. *Front. Neurosci.* **2018**, *12*, 63. [CrossRef]
115. Camuñas-Mesa, L.A.; Serrano-Gotarredona, T.; Linares-Barranco, B. Event-driven sensing and processing for high-speed robotic vision. In Proceedings of the IEEE Biomedical Circuits and Systems Conference (BioCAS) Proceedings, Lausanne, Switzerland, 22–24 October 2014; pp. 516–519.
116. Indiveri, G. Modeling Selective Attention Using a Neuromorphic Analog VLSI Device. *Neural Comput.* **2000**, *12*, 2857–2880. [CrossRef]
117. Schrauwen, B.; D'Haene, M.; Verstraeten, D.; Campenhout, J. Compact hardware liquid state machines on FPGA for real-time speech recognition. *Neural Netw.* **2008**, *21*, 511–523. [CrossRef]
118. Alomar, M.L.; Canals, V.; Morro, A.; Oliver, A.; Rossello, J.L. Stochastic hardware implementation of Liquid State Machines. In Proceedings of the International Joint Conference on Neural Networks, Vancouver, BC, Canada, 24–29 July 2016; pp. 1128–1133.
119. Liu, S.C.; Delbruck, T.; Indiveri, G.; Whatley, A.; Douglas, R. *Event-Based Neuromorphic Systems*; Wiley: Hoboken, NJ, USA, 2015.
120. Merolla, P.A.; Arthur, J.V.; Alvarez-Icaza, R.; Cassidy, A.S.; Sawada, J.; Akopyan, F.; Jackson, B.L.; Imam, N.; Guo, C.; Nakamura, Y.; et al. A million spiking-neuron integrated circuit with a scalable communication network and interface. *Science* **2014**, *345*, 668–673. [CrossRef]
121. Benjamin, B.V.; Gao, P.; McQuinn, E.; Choudhary, S.; Chandrasekaran, A.R.; Bussat, J.M.; Alvarez-Icaza, R.; Arthur, J.V.; Merolla, P.A.; Boahen, K. Neurogrid: A mixed-analog-digital multichip system for large-scale neural simuations. *Proc. IEEE* **2014**, *102*, 699–716. [CrossRef]
122. Neckar, A.S. Braindrop: A Mixed Signal Neuromorphic Architecture with a Dynamical Systems-Based Programming Model. Ph.D. Thesis, Stanford University, Stanford, CA, USA, 2018.
123. Neckar, A.; Fok, S.; Benjamin, B.; Stewart, T.; Oza, N.; Voelker, A.; Eliasmith, C.; Manohar, R.; Boahen, K. Braindrop: A Mixed-Signal Neuromorphic Architecture With a Dynamical Systems-Based Programming Model. *Proc. IEEE* **2019**, *107*, 144–164. [CrossRef]
124. Schemmel, J.; Briiderle, D.; Griibl, A.; Hock, M.; Meier, K.; Millner, S. A wafer-scale neuromorphic hardware system for large-scale neural modeling. In Proceedings of the 2010 IEEE International Symposium on Circuits and Systems, Paris, France, 30 May–2 June 2010; pp. 1947–1950.
125. Furber, S.B.; Galluppi, F.; Temple, S.; Plana, L.A. The SpiNNaker project. *Proc. IEEE* **2014**, *102*, 652–65. [CrossRef]
126. Davies, L.; Srinivasa, N.; Lin, T.; Chinya, G.; Cao, Y.; Choday, S.; Dimou, G.; Joshi, P.; Imam, N.; Jain, S.; et al. Loihi: A Neuromorphic Manycore Processor with On-Chip Learning. *IEEE Micro* **2018**, *38*, 82–99. [CrossRef]
127. Ma, D.; Shen, J.C.; Gu, Z.H.; Zhang, M.; Zhu, X.; Xu, X.; Xu, Q.; Shen, Y.; Pan, G. Darwin: A neuromorphic hardware co-processor based on Spiking Neural Networks. *Sci. China Inf. Sci.* **2016**, *59*, 023401. [CrossRef]
128. Qiao, N.; Mostafa, H.; Corradi, F.; Osswald, M.; Stefanini, F.; Sumislawska, D.; Indiveri, G. A re-configurable on-line learning spiking neuromorphic processor comprising 256 neurons and 128K synapses. *Front. Neurosci.* **2015**, *9*, 141. [CrossRef]
129. Frenkel, C.; Lefebvre, M.; Legat, J.; Bol, D. A 0.086-mm^2 12.7-pJ/SOP 64k-Synapse 256-Neuron Online-Learning Digital Spiking Neuromorphic Processor in 28-nm CMOS. *IEEE Trans. Biomed. Circuits Syst.* **2019**, *13*, 145–158.
130. Eryilmaz, S.B.; Joshi, S.; Neftci, E.; Wan, W.; Cauwenberghs, G.; Wong, H.P. Neuromorphic architectures with electronic synapses. In Proceedings of the 17th International Symposium on Quality Electronic Design (ISQED), Santa Clara, CA, USA, 15–16 March 2016; pp. 118–123.
131. Suri, M.; Bichler, O.; Querlioz, D.; Cueto, O.; Perniola, L.; Sousa, V.; Vuillaume, D.; Gamrat, C.; DeSalvo, B. Phase change memory as synapse for ultra-dense neuromorphic systems: Application to complex visual pattern extraction. In Proceedings of the IEEE International Electron Devices Meeting (IEDM), Washington, DC, USA, 5–7 December 2011.
132. Valov, I.; Waser, R.; Jameson, J.; Kozicki, M. Electrochemical metallization memories-fundamentals, applications, prospects. *Nanotechnology* **2011**, *22*, 254003. [CrossRef]
133. Chanthbouala, A.; Garcia, V.; Cherifi, R.; Bouzehouane, K.; Fusil, S.; Moya, X.; Xavier, S.; Yamada, H.; Deranlot, C.; Mathur, N.; et al. A ferroelectric memristor. *Nat. Mater.* **2012**, *11*, 860–864. [CrossRef]

134. Wei, Z.; Kanzawa, Y.; Arita, K.; Katoh, Y.; Kawai, K.; Muraoka, S.; Mitani, S.; Fujii, S.; Katayama, K.; Iijima, M.; et al. Highly reliable TaOx ReRAM and direct evidence of redox reaction mechanism. In Proceedings of the IEEE International Electron Devices Meeting, San Francisco, CA, USA, 15–17 December 2008; pp. 1–4.
135. Kaneto, K.; Asano, T.; Takashima, W. Memory device using a conducting polymer and solid polymer electrolyte. *Jpn J. Appl. Phys.* **1991**, *30*, L215. [CrossRef]
136. Battistoni, S.; Erokhin, V.; Iannotta, S. Frequency driven organic memristive devices for neuromorphic short term and long term plasticity. *Org. Electron.* **2019**, *65*, 434–438. [CrossRef]
137. Liu, G.; Wang, C.; Zhang, W.; Liang, P.; Zhang, C.; Yang, X.; Fan, F.; Chen, Y.; Li, R. Organic biomimicking memristor for information storage and processing applications. *Adv. Electron. Mater.* **2016**, *2*, 1500298. [CrossRef]
138. Alibart, F.; Pleutin, S.; Bichler, O.; Gamrat, C.; Serrano-Gotarredona, T.; Linares-Barranco, B.; Vuillaume, D. A memristive nanoparticle/organic hybrid synapstor for neuroinspired computing. *Adv. Funct. Mater.* **2012**, *22*, 609–616. [CrossRef]
139. Song, S.; Cho, B.; Kim, T.W.; Ji, Y.; Jo, M.; Wang, G.; Choe, M.; Kahng, Y.H.; Hwang, H.; Lee, T. Three-dimensional integration of organic resistive memory devices. *Adv. Mater.* **2010**, *22*, 5048–5052. [CrossRef]
140. Kuzum, D. Synaptic electronics: Materials, devices and applications. *Nanotechnology* **2013**, *24*, 382001. [CrossRef]
141. Zidan, M.A.; Strachan, J.P.; Lu, W.D. The future of electronics based on memristive systems. *Nat. Electron.* **2018**, *1*, 22–29. [CrossRef]
142. Jo, S.H.; Chang, T.; Ebong, I.; Bhadviya, B.B.; Mazumder, P.; Lu, W. Nanoscale Memristor Device as Synapse in Neuromorphic Systems. *Nano Lett.* **2010**, *10*, 1297–1301. [CrossRef] [PubMed]
143. Serrano-Gotarredona, T.; Prodromakis, T.; Linares-Barranco, B. A Proposal for Hybrid Memristor-CMOS Spiking Neuromorphic Learning Systems. *IEEE Circuits Syst. Mag.* **2013**, *13*, 74–88. [CrossRef]
144. Demin, V.A.; Erokhin, V.V.; Emelyanov, A.V.; Battistoni, S.; Baldi, G.; Iannotta, S.; Kashkarov, P.K.; Kovalchuk, M.V. Hardware elementary perceptron based on polyaniline memristive devices. *Org. Electron.* **2015**, *25*, 16–20. [CrossRef]
145. Lin, Y.P.; Bennett, C.H.; Cabaret, T.; Vodenicarevic, D.; Chabi, D.; Querlioz, D.; Jousselme, B.; Derycke, V.; Klein, J.O. Physical realization of a supervised learning system built with organic memristive synapses. *Sci. Rep.* **2016**, *6*, 31932 [CrossRef] [PubMed]
146. Emelyanov, A.V.; Lapkin, D.A.; Demin, V.A.; Erokhin, V.V.; Battistoni, S.; Baldi, G.; Dimonte, A.; Korovin, A.N.; Iannotta, S.; Kashkarov, P.K.; et al. First steps towards the realization of a double layer perceptron based on organic memristive devices. *Aip Adv.* **2016**, *6*, 111301. [CrossRef]
147. Likharev, K.; Strukov, D. CMOL: Devices, Circuits, and Architectures. In *Introducing Molecular Electronics*; Cuniberti, G., Fagas, G., Richter, K., Eds.; Springer: Berlin/Heidelberg, Germany, 2005; pp. 447–477.
148. Likharev, K. CrossNets: Neuromorphic Hybrid CMOS/Nanoelectronic Networks. *Sci. Adv. Mater.* **2011**, *3*, 322–331. [CrossRef]
149. Xia, Q.; Robinett, W.; Cumbie, M.W.; Banerjee, N.; Cardinali, T.J.; Yang, J.J.; Wu, W.; Li, X.; Tong, W.M.; Strukov, D.B.; et al. Memristor-CMOS Hybrid Integrated Circuits for Reconfigurable Logic. *Nano Lett.* **2009**, *9*, 3640–3645. [CrossRef]
150. Ankit, A.; Sengupta, A.; Panda, P.; Roy, K. RESPARC: A Reconfigurable and Energy-Efficient Archi-tecture with Memristive Crossbars for Deep Spiking Neural Networks. In Proceedings of the Design Automation Conference 2017, Austin, TX, USA, 18–22 June 2017.
151. Chi, P.; Li, S.; Xu, C.; Zhang, T.; Zhao, J.; Liu, Y.; Wang, Y.; Xie, Y. PRIME: A novel processing-in-memory architecture for neural network computation in ReRAM-based main memory. *Int. Symp. Comp. Arch.* **2016**, *44*, 27–39. [CrossRef]
152. Cheng, M.; Xia, L.; Zhu, Z.; Cai, Y.; Xie, Y.; Wang, Y.; Yang, H. TIME: A Training-in-memory Architecturefor Memristor-based Deep Neural Networks. In Proceedings of the Annual Design Automation Conference, Austin, TX, USA, 18–22 June 2017.
153. Ankit, A.; El Hajj, I.; Chalamalasetti, S.R.; Ndu, G.; Foltin, M.; Williams, R.S.; Faraboschi, P.; Hwu, W.M.; Strachan, J.P.; Roy, K.; et al. PUMA: A Programmable Ultra-efficient Memristor-based Accelerator for Machine Learning Inference. In Proceedings of the International Conference on Architectural Support for Programming Languages and Operating Systems, Providence, RI, USA, 13–17 April 2019.

154. Huang, H.; Ni, L.; Wang, K.; Wang, Y.; Yu, H. A highly parallel and energy efficient three-dimensional multilayer CMOS-RRAM accelerator for tensorized neural network. *IEEE Trans. Nanotechnol.* **2017**, *17*, 645–656. [CrossRef]
155. Ni, L.; Wang, Y.; Yu, H.; Yang, W.; Weng, C.; Zhao, J. An energy-efficient matrix multiplication accelerator by distributed in-memory computing on binary RRAM crossbar. In Proceedings of the Asia and South Pacific Design Automation Conference, Macau, China, 25–28 January 2016.
156. Kim, K.H.; Gaba, S.; Wheeler, D.; Cruz-Albrecht, J.M.; Hussain, T.; Srinivasa, N.; Lu, W. A functional hybrid memristor crossbar-array/CMOS system for data storage and neuromorphic. *Appl. Nano Lett.* **2011**, 389–395. [CrossRef]
157. Li, C.; Han, L.; Jiang, H.; Jang, M.H.; Lin, P.; Wu, Q.; Barnell, M.; Yang, J.J.; Xin, H.L.; Xia, Q. Three-dimensional crossbar arrays of self-rectifying Si/SiO2/Si memristors. *Nat. Commun.* **2017**, *8*, 15666. [CrossRef]
158. Wu, T.F.; Li, H.; Huang, P.C.; Rahimi, A.; Rabaey, J.M.; Wong, H.S.P.; Shulaker, M.M.; Mitra, S. Brain-inspired computing exploiting Carbon Nanotube FETs and Resistive RAM. Hyperdimensional computing case study. In Proceedings of the International Solid-State Circuits Conference (ISSCC), San Francisco, CA, USA, 11–15 February 2018; pp. 492–493.
159. Chen, W.H.; Li, K.X.; Lin, W.Y.; Hsu, K.H.; Li, P.Y.; Yang, C.H.; Xue, C.X.; Yang, E.Y.; Chen, Y.K.; Chang, Y.S.; et al. A 65 nm 1 Mb nonvolatile computing-in-memory ReRAM macro with sub-16ns multiply-and-accumulate for binary DNN AI edge processors. In Proceedings of the International Solid-State Circuits Conference, San Francisco, CA, USA, 11–15 February 2018; pp. 494–495.
160. Bayat, F.M.; Prezioso, M.; Chakrabarti, B.; Nili, H.; Kataeva, I.; Strukov, S. Implementation of multilayer perceptron network with highly uniform passive memristive crossbar circuits. *Nat. Commun.* **2018**, *9*, 2331. [CrossRef]
161. Kim, S.; Lim, M.; Kim, Y.; Kim, H.D.; Choi, S.J. Impact of Synaptic Device Variations on Pattern Recognition Accuracy in a Hardware Neural Network. *Sci. Rep.* **2018**, *8*, 2638. [CrossRef]
162. Ambrogio, S.; Narayanan, P.; Tsai, H.; Shelby, R.M.; Boybat, I.; di Nolfo, C.; Sidler, S.; Giordano, M.; Bodini, M.; Farinha, N.C.; et al. Equivalent-accuracy accelerated neural-network training using analogue memory. *Nature* **2018**, *558*, 60–67. [CrossRef]
163. Werbos, P.J. Backpropagation through time: What it does and how to do it. *Proc. IEEE* **1990**, *78*, 1550–1560. [CrossRef]
164. Diehl, P.U. Fast-classifying, high-accuracy spiking deep networks through weight and threshold balancing. In Proceedings of the International Joint Conference on Neural Networks, Killarney, Ireland, 12–17 July 2015; pp. 1–8.
165. Rueckauer, B.; Lungu, I.A.; Hu, Y.; Pfeiffer, M.; Liu, S.C. Conversion of continuous-valued deep networks to efficient event-driven networks for image classification. *Front. Neurosci.* **2017**, 682. [CrossRef]
166. Rueckauer, B.; Liu, S.C. Conversion of analog to spiking neural networks using sparse temporal coding. In Proceedings of the IEEE International Symposium on Circuits and Systems, Florence, Italy, 27–30 May 2018; pp. 1–5.
167. Cao, Y.; Chen, Y.; Khosla, D. Spiking deep convolutional neural networks for energy-efficient object recognition. *Int. J. Comput. Vis.* **2015**, *113*, 54–66. [CrossRef]
168. Bohte, S.M.; Kok, J.N.; Poutrã, H.L. Error-backpropagation in temporally encoded networks of spiking neurons. *Neurocomputing* **2002**, *48*, 17–37. [CrossRef]
169. Ponulak, F. *ReSuMe—New Supervised Learning Method for Spiking Neural Networks*; Technical Report; Institute of Control and Information Engineering, Poznan University of Technology: Poznań, Poland, 2005.
170. Gutig, R.; Sompolinsky, H. The tempotron: A neuron that learns spike timing-based decisions. *Nat Neurosci* **2006**, *9*, 420–428. [CrossRef]
171. Mohemmed, A.; Schliebs, S.; Matsuda, S.; Kasabov, N. SPAN: Spike pattern association neuron for learning spatio-temporal spike patterns. *Int. J. Neural Syst.* **2012**, *9*, 1250012. [CrossRef]
172. Florian, R.V. The chronotron: A neuron that learns to fire temporally precise spike patterns. *PLoS ONE* **2012**, *7*, e40233. [CrossRef]
173. Florian, R.V. Reinforcement learning through modulation of spike-timing-dependent synaptic plasticity. *Neural Comput.* **2007**, *19*, 1468–1502. [CrossRef]

174. Yu, Q.; Tang, H.; Tan, K.C.; Li, H. Precise-spike-driven synaptic plasticity: Learning hetero-association of spatiotemporal spike patterns. *PLoS ONE* **2013**, *8*, e78318 [CrossRef]
175. Lee, J.H.; Delbruck, T.; Pfeiffer, M. Training Deep Spiking Neural Networks Using Backpropagation. *Front. Neurosci.* **2016**, *10*, 508. [CrossRef]
176. Mostafa, H. Supervised Learning Based on Temporal Coding in Spiking Neural Networks. *IEEE Trans. Neural Netw. Learn. Syst.* **2018**, *29*, 3227–3235. [CrossRef]
177. Wu, Y.; Deng, L.; Li, G.; Zhu, J.; Shi, L. Spatio-Temporal Backpropagation for Training High-Performance Spiking Neural Networks. *Front. Neurosci.* **2018**, *12*, 331. [CrossRef]
178. Shrestha, S.B.; Orchard, G. SLAYER: Spike Layer Error Reassignment in Time. *Adv. Neural Inf. Process. Syst.* **2018**, *31*, 1412–1421.
179. Zheng, N.; Mazumder, P. Online Supervised Learning for Hardware-Based Multilayer Spiking Neural Networks Through the Modulation of Weight-Dependent Spike-Timing-Dependent Plasticity. *IEEE Trans. Neural Netw. Learn. Syst.* **2018**, *29*, 4287–4302. [CrossRef]
180. Mostafa, H.; Khiat, A.; Serb, A.; Mayr, C.G.; Indiveri, G.; Prodromakis, T. Implementation of a spike-based perceptron learning rule using TiO_{2-x} memristors. *Front. Neurosci.* **2015**, *9*, 357. [CrossRef]
181. Young, J.M. Cortical reorganization consistent with spike timing-but not correlation-dependent plasticity. *Nat. Neurosci.* **2007**, *10*, 887–895. [CrossRef]
182. Finelli, L.A.; Haney, S.; Bazhenov, M.; Stopfer, M.; Sejnowski, T.J. Synaptic learning rules and sparse coding in a model sensory system. *PLoS Comput. Biol.* **2008**, *4*, e1000062. [CrossRef]
183. Masquelier, T.; Guyonneau, R.; Thorpe, S.J. Spike timing dependent plasticity finds the start of repeating patterns in continuous spike trains. *PLoS ONE* **2008**, *3*, e1377. [CrossRef]
184. Masquelier, T.; Guyonneau, R.; Thorpe, S.J. Competitive STDP-based spike pattern learning. *Neural Comput.* **2009**, *21*, 1259–1276. [CrossRef]
185. Tan, Z.H.; Yang, R.; Terabe, K.; Yin, X.B.; Zhang, X.D.; Guo, X. Synaptic metaplasticity realized in oxide memristive devices. *Adv. Mater.* **2016**, *28*, 377–384. [CrossRef]
186. Prezioso, M.; Bayat, F.M.; Hoskins, B.D.; Adam, G.C.; Likharev, K.K.; Strukov, D.B. Training and operation of an integrated neuromorphic network based on metal-oxide memristors. *Nature* **2015**, *521*, 61–64. [CrossRef]
187. Matveyev, Y.; Kirtaev, R.; Fetisova, A.; Zakharchenko, S.; Negrov, D.; Zenkevich, A. Crossbar nanoscale HfO2-based electronic synapses. *Nanoscale Res. Lett.* **2016**, *11*, 147. [CrossRef]
188. Du, N.; Kiani, M.; Mayr, C.G.; You, T.; Bürger, D.; Skorupa, I.; Schmidt, O.G.; Schmidt, H. Single pairing spike-timing dependent plasticity in $BiFeO_3$ memristors with a time window of 25 ms to 125 µs. *Front. Neurosci.* **2015**, *9*, 227. [CrossRef]
189. Xiao, Z.; Huang, J. Energy-efficient hybrid perovskite memristors and synaptic devices. *Adv. Electron. Mater.* **2016**, *2*, 1600100. [CrossRef]
190. Seo, J.; Seok, M. Digital CMOS neuromorphic processor design featuring unsupervised online learning. In Proceedings of the IFIP/IEEE International Conference on Very Large Scale Integration, Daejeon, Korea, 5–7 October 2015; pp. 49–51.
191. Yousefzadeh, A.; Stromatias, E.; Soto, M.; Serrano-Gotarredona, T.; Linares-Barranco, B. On Practical Issues for Stochastic STDP Hardware With 1-bit Synaptic Weights. *Front. Neurosci.* **2018**. [CrossRef]
192. Mozafari, M.; Kheradpisheh, S.R.; Masquelier, T.; Nowzari-Dalini, A.; Ganjtabesh, M. First-spike-based visual categorization using reward-modulated STDP. *IEEE Trans. Neural Netw. Learn. Syst.* **2018**, *29*, 6178–6190. [CrossRef]
193. Mozafari, M.; Ganjtabesh, M.; Nowzari-Dalini, A.; Thorpe, S.J.; Masquelier, T. Bio-inspired digit recognition using reward-modulated spike-timing-dependent plasticity in deep convolutional networks. *Pattern Recognit.* **2019**, *94*, 87–95. [CrossRef]
194. Linares-Barranco, B. Memristors fire away. *Nat. Electron.* **2018**, *1*, 100. [CrossRef]
195. Chen, P.Y.; Yu, S. Compact Modeling of RRAM Devices and Its Applications in 1T1R and 1S1R Array Design. *IEEE Trans. Electron Devices* **2015**, *62*, 4022–4028. [CrossRef]

materials

MDPI

Review

Memristive and CMOS Devices for Neuromorphic Computing

Valerio Milo, Gerardo Malavena, Christian Monzio Compagnoni and Daniele Ielmini *

Dipartimento di Elettronica, Informazione e Bioingegneria, Politecnico di Milano and Italian Universities Nanoelectronics Team (IU.NET), Piazza L. da Vinci 32, 20133 Milano, Italy; valerio.milo@polimi.it (V.M.); gerardo.malavena@polimi.it (G.M.); christian.monzio@polimi.it (C.M.C.)

* Correspondence: daniele.ielmini@polimi.it

Received: 28 November 2019; Accepted: 18 December 2019; Published: 1 January 2020

Abstract: Neuromorphic computing has emerged as one of the most promising paradigms to overcome the limitations of von Neumann architecture of conventional digital processors. The aim of neuromorphic computing is to faithfully reproduce the computing processes in the human brain, thus paralleling its outstanding energy efficiency and compactness. Toward this goal, however, some major challenges have to be faced. Since the brain processes information by high-density neural networks with ultra-low power consumption, novel device concepts combining high scalability, low-power operation, and advanced computing functionality must be developed. This work provides an overview of the most promising device concepts in neuromorphic computing including complementary metal-oxide semiconductor (CMOS) and memristive technologies. First, the physics and operation of CMOS-based floating-gate memory devices in artificial neural networks will be addressed. Then, several memristive concepts will be reviewed and discussed for applications in deep neural network and spiking neural network architectures. Finally, the main technology challenges and perspectives of neuromorphic computing will be discussed.

Keywords: neuromorphic computing; Flash memories; memristive devices; resistive switching; synaptic plasticity; artificial neural network; spiking neural network; pattern recognition

1. Introduction

The complementary metal-oxide semiconductor (CMOS) technology has sustained tremendous progress in communication and information processing since the 1960s. Thanks to the continuous miniaturization of the metal-oxide semiconductor (MOS) transistor according to the Moore's law [1] and Dennard scaling rules [2], the clock frequency and integration density on the chip have seen an exponential increase. In the last 15 years, however, the Moore's scaling law has been slowed down by two fundamental issues, namely the excessive subthreshold leakage currents and the increasing heat generated within the chip [3,4]. To overcome these barriers, new advances have been introduced, including the adoption of high-k materials as the gate dielectric [5], the redesign of the transistor with multigate structures [6,7], and 3D integration [8]. Besides the difficult scaling, another crucial issue of today's digital computers is the physical distinction between the central processing unit (CPU) and the memory unit at the origin of extensive data movement during computation, especially for data-intensive tasks [9]. Solving the memory bottleneck requires a paradigm shift in architecture, where computation is executed in situ within the data by exploiting, e.g., the ability of memory arrays to implement matrix-vector multiplication (MVM) [10,11]. This novel architectural approach is referred to as in-memory computing, which provides the basis for several outstanding applications, such as pattern classification [12,13], analogue image processing [14], and the solution of linear systems [15,16] and of linear regression problems [17].

In this context, neuromorphic computing has been receiving increasing interest for its ability to mimic the human brain. A neuromorphic circuit consists of a network of artificial neurons and synapses capable of processing sensory information with massive parallelism and ultra-low power dissipation [18]. The realization of scalable, high density, and high-performance neuromorphic circuits generally requires the extensive adoption of memory devices serving the role of synaptic links and/or neuron elements. The device structure and operation of these memory devices may require specific optimization for neuromorphic circuits.

This work reviews the current status of neuromorphic devices, with a focus on both CMOS and memristive devices for implementation of artificial synapses and neurons in both deep neural networks (DNNs) and spiking neural networks (SNNs). The paper is organized as follows: Section 2 provides an overview of the major neuromorphic computing concepts from a historical perspective. Section 3 is an overview of the operating principles of mainstream NAND and NOR Flash technologies, and their adoption in neuromorphic networks. Section 4 describes the most important memristive concepts being considered for neuromorphic computing applications. Section 5 addresses the adoption of memristive devices in DNNs and SNNs for hardware demonstration of cognitive functions, such as pattern recognition and image/face classification. Finally, Section 6 discusses issues and future perspectives for large-scale hardware implementation of neuromorphic systems with CMOS/memristive devices.

2. Neuromorphic Computing Concepts

The origin of neuromorphic computing can be traced back to 1949, when McCulloch and Pitts proposed a mathematical model of the biological neuron. This is depicted in Figure 1a, where the neuron is conceived as a processing unit, operating (i) a summation of input signals ($x_1, x_2, x_3, \ldots$), each multiplied by a suitable synaptic weight ($w_1, w_2, w_3, \ldots$) and (ii) a non-linear transformation according to an activation function, e.g., a sigmoidal function [19]. A second landmark came in 1957, when Rosenblatt developed the model of a fundamental neural network called multiple-layer perceptron (MLP) [20], which is schematically illustrated in Figure 1b. The MLP consists of an input layer, one or more intermediate layers called hidden layers, and an output layer, through which the input signal is forward propagated toward the output. The MLP model constitutes the backbone for the emerging concept of DNNs. DNNs have recently shown excellent performance in tasks, such as pattern classification and speech recognition, via extensive supervised training techniques, such as the backpropagation rule [21–23]. DNNs are usually implemented in hardware with von Neumann platforms, such as the graphics processing unit (GPU) [24] and the tensor processing unit (TPU) [25], used to execute both training and inference. These hardware implementations, however, reveal all the typical limitations of the von Neumann architecture, chiefly the large energy consumption in contrast with the human brain model.

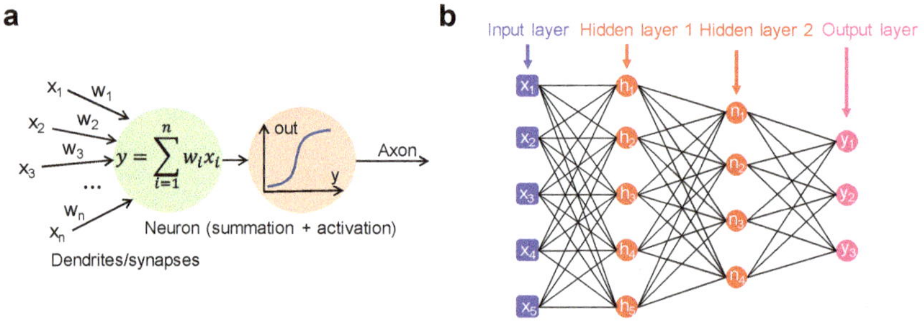

Figure 1. (**a**) Conceptual illustration of McCulloch and Pitts artificial neuron architecture, where the weighted sum of the input signals is subject to the application of a non-linear activation function yielding the output signal. (**b**) Schematic representation of a multilayer perceptron consisting of two hidden layers between the input and the output layer.

To significantly improve the energy efficiency of DNNs, MVM in crossbar memory arrays has emerged as a promising approach [26,27]. Memory devices also enable the implementation of learning schemes able to replicate the biological synaptic plasticity at the device level. CMOS memories, such as the static random access memory (SRAM) [28,29] and the Flash memory [30], were initially adopted to capture synaptic behaviors in hardware. In the last 10 years, novel material-based memory devices, generically referred to as memristors [31], have evidenced attractive features for the implementation of neuromorphic hardware, including non-volatile storage, low power operation, nanoscale size, and analog resistance tunability. In particular, memristive technologies, which include resistive switching random access memory (RRAM), phase change memory (PCM), and other emergent memory concepts based on ferroelectric and ferromagnetic effects, have been shown to achieve synapse and neuron functions, enabling the demonstration of fundamental cognitive primitives as pattern recognition in neuromorphic networks [32–35].

The field of neuromorphic networks includes both the DNN [36], and SNN, the latter more directly inspired by the human brain [37]. Contrary to DNNs, the learning ability in SNNs emerges via unsupervised training processes, where synapses are potentiated or depressed by bio-realistic learning rules inspired by the brain. Among these local learning rules, spike-timing-dependent plasticity (STDP) and spike-rate-dependent plasticity (SRDP) have received intense investigation for hardware implementation of brain-inspired SNNs. In STDP, which was experimentally demonstrated in hippocampal cultures by Bi and Poo in 1998 [38], the synaptic weight update depends on the relative timing between the presynaptic spike and the post-synaptic spike (Figure 2a). In particular, if the pre-synaptic neuron (PRE) spike precedes the post-synaptic neuron (POST) spike, namely the relative delay of spikes, $\Delta t = t_{post} - t_{pre}$, is positive, then the interaction between the two spikes causes the synapse to increase its weight, which goes under the name of synaptic potentiation. On the other hand, if the PRE spike follows the POST spike, i.e., Δt is negative, then the synapse undergoes a weight decrease or synaptic depression (Figure 2b). In SRDP, instead, the rate of spikes emitted by externally stimulated neurons dictates the potentiation or depression of the synapse, with high and low frequency stimulation leading to synaptic potentiation and depression, respectively [39]. Unlike STDP relying on pairs of spikes, SRDP has been attributed to the complex combination of three spikes (triplet) or more [40–43]. In addition to the ability to learn in an unsupervised way and emulate biological processes, SNNs also offer a significant improvement in energy efficiency thanks to the ability to process data by transmission of short spikes, hence consuming power only when and where the spike occurs [18]. Therefore, CMOS and memristive concepts can offer great advantages in the implementation of both DNNs and SNNs, providing a wide portfolio of functionalities, such as non-volatile weight storage, high scalability, energy efficient in-memory computing via MVM, and online weight adaptation in response to external stimuli.

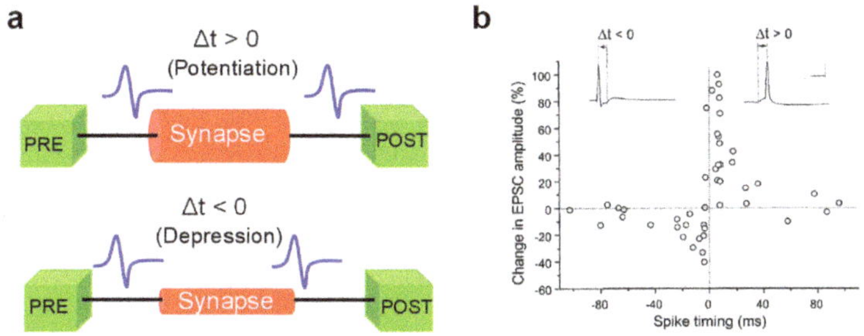

Figure 2. (**a**) Sketch of the spike-timing-dependent plasticity (STDP) learning rule. If the PRE spike arrives just before the POST spike at the synaptic terminal (Δt > 0), the synapse undergoes a potentiation process, resulting in a weight (conductance) increase (**top**). Otherwise, if the PRE spike arrives just after the POST spike (Δt < 0), the synapse undergoes a depression process, resulting in a weight (conductance) decrease (**bottom**). (**b**) Relative change of synaptic weight as a function of the relative time delay between PRE and POST spikes measured in hippocampal synapses by Bi and Poo. Reprinted with permission from [38]. Copyright 1998 Society for Neuroscience.

3. Mainstream Memory Technologies for Neuromorphic and Brain-Inspired Systems

3.1. Memory Transistors and Mainstream Flash Technologies

The memory transistor represents the elementary building unit at the basis of modern mainstream non-volatile storage technologies. It consists of a mainstream MOS transistor whose structure is modified to accommodate a charge-storage layer in its gate stack, allowing carriers to be confined in a well-defined region due to the resulting potential barriers. As shown in Figure 3, the most adopted solutions for such a layer are based either on highly doped polycrystalline silicon (polysilicon) or a dielectric material able to capture and release electrons and holes thanks to its peculiar high density of defects. The charge storage layer is usually referred to as floating gate in the former case, and charge-trap layer in the latter one. However, in both cases, storing a net charge in the memory transistor floating gate or charge-trap layer results in a shift of the drain current vs. gate voltage ($I_{DS} - V_{GS}$) curve due to the corresponding variation of the device threshold voltage (V_T). In particular, such variation is mainly ruled by the capacitance between the transistor gate and the charge-storage layer, C_{sg}, according to $\Delta V_T = -Q_s/C_{sg}$, meaning that a net positive or negative stored charge (Q_s) is reflected in a negative or positive V_T shift (ΔV_T), respectively. As a consequence, a proper discretization of the stored charge in each memory transistor allows one or multiple bits of information to be stored that can be accessed through a V_T read operation.

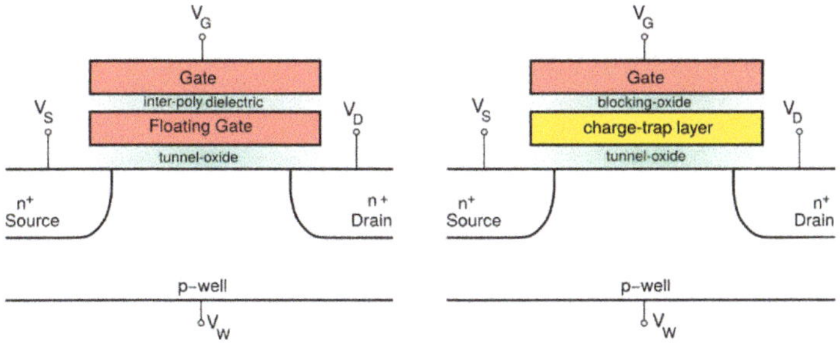

Figure 3. Schematic of a memory cell exploiting (**left**) a highly doped polysilicon layer and (**right**) a dielectric layer with a high density of microscopic defects for charge storage.

In order to reliably accomplish the tuning of the stored charge and, consequently, the modification of the information content through the program (making the stored charge more negative) and erase (making the stored charge more positive) operations, suitable physical mechanisms must be selected. As schematically depicted in Figure 4, the most widely adopted physical mechanisms are the Fowler–Nordheim (FN) tunneling, for both program and erase operations, and the channel hot electron injection (CHEI), for program operation only. In the former case, the bias voltages applied to the memory transistor contacts are chosen to generate large vertical electric fields that activate carrier exchange between the substrate and the storage layer by the quantum mechanical current through the energy barrier separating them. In the latter case, instead, CHEI is achieved by accelerating the transistor on-state current electrons by applying a positive drain-to-source voltage drop (V_{DS}). If V_{DS} is large enough, the energy acquired by the channel electrons is sufficient for them to overcome the tunnel-oxide energy barrier and to be redirected to the charge-storage layer due to the positive V_{GS}. Moreover, it is worth mentioning that, for a target ΔV_T to be achieved over comparable time scales, CHEI requires much lower voltages to be applied with respect to FN tunneling. On the contrary, its injection efficiency is of the order of 10^{-5} only, much smaller than that of FN tunneling (very close to one). A final but important remark is that for both CHEI and FN tunneling, the maximum number of program/erase cycles that can be performed on the devices is usually smaller than 10^5; in fact, for larger cycling doses, the number of defects generated in the tunnel oxide by the program/erase operations severely undermines the transistor reliability.

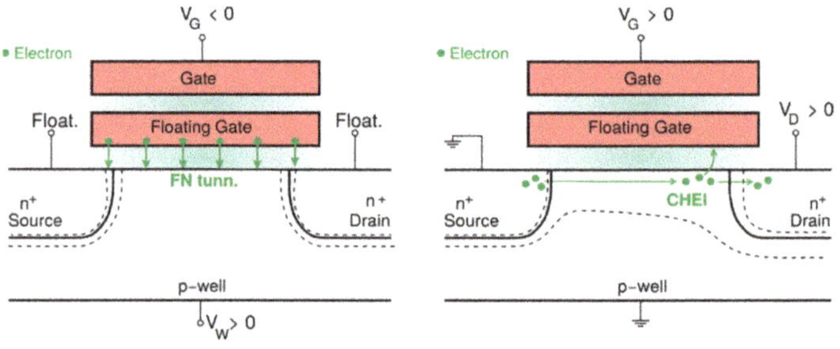

Figure 4. Physical mechanisms and corresponding voltage schemes exploited to change the amount of charge in the cell storage layer, consisting of (**left**) Fowler–Nordheim (FN) and (**right**) channel hot-electron injection (CHEI).

Starting from the schematic structure shown in Figure 3, the arrangement of memory transistors to build memory arrays and their working conditions are strictly related to the specific targeted application. In particular, two solutions that have ruled the non-volatile memory market since their very first introduction are the NAND Flash [44] and NOR Flash [45] architectures (Figure 5). Although they share the important peculiarity that the erase operation, exploiting FN tunneling to reduce the amount of the stored negative charge, involves a large number of cells at the same time (a block of cell), some relevant differences can be mentioned.

NAND Flash technology is the main solution for the storage of large amounts of data, therefore achieving large bit storage density, i.e., the ratio between the chip capacity and its area is a mandatory requirement. For this purpose, NAND Flash memory transistors are deeply scaled (up to a feature size as small as 15 nm) and arranged in series connection, making the memory cells belonging to each string accessible only through the contacts at their top and bottom ends (Figure 5a). In such a way, the area occupancy of each cell is minimized; on the other hand, the attempt to minimize the array fragmentation and to reduce the area occupancy of the control circuitry makes the random access time to the cells quite long (tens of µs), due to the consequent delays of the signals propagating over the long WLs and BLs. For this reason, programming schemes taking advantage of the low current and high injection efficiency of FN tunneling were developed to program many memory transistors at the same time, allowing extremely high throughputs (tens or even hundreds of Mbytes/s) to be achieved.

The NOR Flash technology, on the other hand, is mainly intended for code storage, making the storage and retrieval of small packets of data (a few bytes) as fast as possible a mandatory requirement. As a consequence, in order to make each memory cell directly accessible through dedicated contacts, the memory transistors are connected in parallel, as shown in Figure 5b. Thanks to this architecture, a fast and single-cell selective program operation can be easily achieved exploiting CHEI. From the cell design standpoint, this results in a limited channel scalability, due to the need for the cell to withstand relatively high V_{DS} during its operation. Even though these features determine a larger cell footprint and, in turn, a higher cost of NOR Flash with respect to NAND Flash technologies, they allow NOR Flash arrays to guarantee a superior array reliability, being an important requirement for code storage applications.

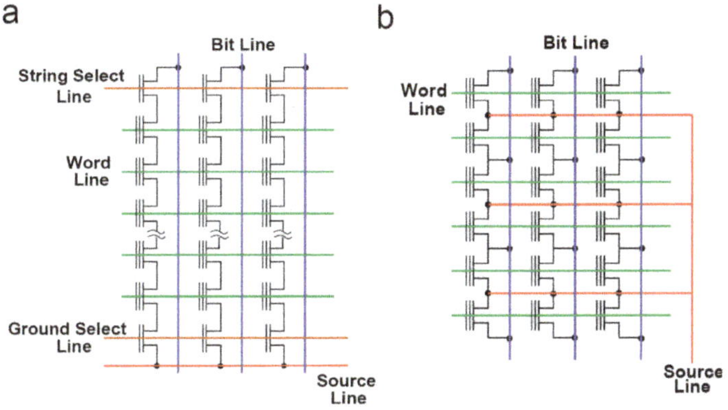

Figure 5. Schematic of memory arrays based on (**a**) NAND Flash and (**b**) NOR Flash architecture.

3.2. Memory Transistors as Synaptic Devices in Artificial Neural Networks

The first proposal of exploiting memory transistors as artificial synapses in artificial neural networks (ANNs) and brain-inspired neural networks dates back to the 1990s directly from the pioneering work presented in ref. [46]. The basic idea proposed there is to take advantage of the subthreshold characteristic $I_{DS} - V_{GS}$ of an n-channel floating-gate memory transistor to reproduce the biologically observed synaptic behavior and to exploit it to build large-scale neuromorphic systems. In fact, when operated in a subthreshold regime, a memory transistor exhibits an $I_{DS} - V_{GS}$ relation that can be expressed as:

$$I_{DS} = I_0 \cdot exp\left[\frac{q\alpha_G\left(V_{GS} - V_T^{ref}\right)}{mkT}\right] \cdot exp\left[\frac{-q\alpha_G \Delta V_T}{mkT}\right], \tag{1}$$

where I_0 is the current pre-factor, q is the elementary charge, m is the subthreshold slope ideality factor, kT is the thermal energy, α_G is the gate-to-floating-gate capacitive coupling ratio, and ΔV_T is the floating-gate transistor V_T shift from an arbitrary chosen V_T^{ref}.

With reference to the previous equation, I_{DS} can be decomposed in the product of two contributions. The first factor, $I_0 \cdot exp\left[\frac{q\alpha_G\left(V_{GS}-V_T^{ref}\right)}{mkT}\right]$, is a function of V_{GS} only, and represents the input presynaptic signal; the remaining scaling factor, $W = exp\left[\frac{-q\alpha_G \Delta V_T}{mkT}\right]$, instead, depending on ΔV_T but not on V_{GS}, can be thought of as the synaptic weight.

When compared with other modern approaches based on emerging memory technologies, this solution presents the clear advantages of (i) limited power consumption, thanks to the reduced currents peculiar of transistors operated below the threshold; (ii) fine weight granularity, coming to the virtually analog and bidirectional V_T tuning; and (iii) a mature and well-established CMOS fabrication technology. In particular, the relevance of the last point can be easily understood by considering the possibility of arranging a large number of floating-gate transistors in very dense and reliable memory arrays, normally employed for storage purposes. However, when exploited as synaptic arrays in neuromorphic applications, such memory arrays must meet the mandatory condition of single-cell selectivity during both program and erase operations, meaning that both the positive and negative tuning of the V_T (weight) of each memory cell (synapse) must be guaranteed. Even if this consideration makes a NOR-type array inherently more suitable to be used in these fields because of its architecture that allows direct access to each cell by dedicated contacts, its standard block-erase scheme must still be overcome. For this reason, since its very first proposal, the synaptic transistor introduced in refs. [46–48], and tested on LTD and LTP based on the STDP learning rule in refs. [30,48], includes an additional contact with respect to standard n-channel floating-gate transistors (Figure 6) to be connected to signal lines running orthogonal to the WLs [46]. While keeping CHEI for the program, the erase operation takes place by removing stored electrons by FN tunneling when a sufficiently high electric field is developed between the tunneling contact and the transistor floating gate that, as shown in Figure 3, is properly extended in close proximity of such a contact. Note that this erase scheme is indeed single-cell selective because the substrate contact, common to all the array cells, is kept to the ground.

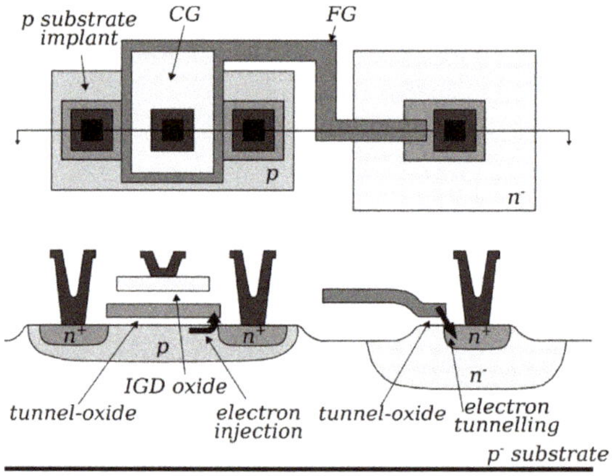

Figure 6. Top view (**up**) and side view (**down**) of the synaptic transistor. Physical mechanisms exploited for program (electron injection) and erase (electron tunneling) are highlighted too. Adapted with permission from [48]. Copyright 1997, IEEE.

Although, recently, some more effort was devoted to build new custom synaptic devices and test them in SNNs [49–51], a more convincing proof of the feasibility of the floating-gate transistor to build large-scale neuromorphic systems comes from a different approach. The basic idea consists in slightly modifying the routing of commercially available NOR Flash memory arrays to enable a single-cell selective erase operation while keeping the cell structure unchanged. For this purpose, NOR memory arrays developed with a 180 nm technology by Silicon Storage Technology, Inc. (SST) [52] are chosen in refs. [53–56]. The basic memory cell, as depicted in Figure 7a, features a highly asymmetric structure presenting a floating gate only near the source side, with the gate stack at the drain side made only of the tunneling oxide. In spite of this structure, the program operation can still be performed by CHEI at the source side; as for the erase operation, instead, a positive voltage is applied between the gate and source, resulting in the emission of stored electrons toward the gate by FN tunneling.

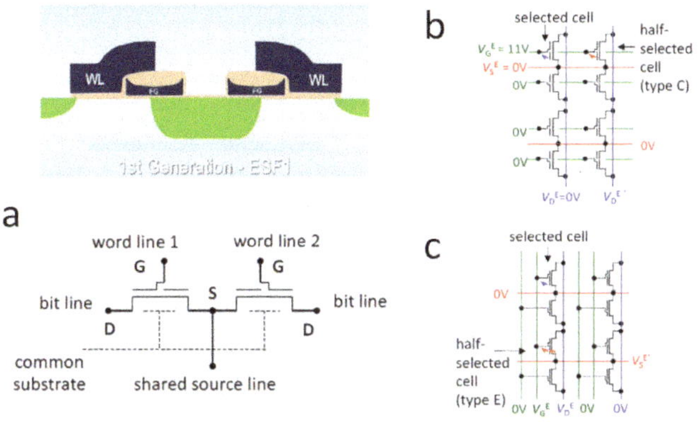

Figure 7. (**a**) Schematic cross-section of the Silicon Storage Technology (SST) cell structure (**top**) and its equivalent circuit (**bottom**) and NOR array with (**b**) classic and (**c**) modified routing together with the respective erase protocol. Reprinted with permission from [53]. Copyright 2015, IEEE.

The arrangement of such SST cells to make a NOR array is shown in Figure 7b, where the erase voltages are highlighted too. Since both WLs and SLs run parallel to each other and orthogonal to the BLs, the erase protocol involves all the cells in a row at the same time. For this reason, in refs. [54], a modification to the array routing as reported in Figure 7c is proposed, with the WLs now running parallel to the BLs. In this way, single-cell selectivity is achieved during both the program (involving WL, BL, and SL) and erase (involving WL and SL only).

In refs. [54,55], two SST NOR arrays, re-routed as explained before, are employed to build and test a fully integrated three-layer (784 × 64 × 10) ANN, trained offline on the Modified National Institute of Standards and Technology (MNIST) database for handwritten digit recognition via the backpropagation algorithm [21–23]. In particular, in order to enable the implementation of negative weights, and also to reduce random drifts and temperature sensitivity, a differential solution is adopted. As shown in Figure 8a, following this approach, each couple of adjacent memory cells implements a synaptic weight, with the resulting BL currents summed and read by CMOS artificial neurons built exploiting a differential current operational amplifier. The whole one-chip integrated network, whose schematic structure, including two synaptic arrays together with two neuron layers and some additional circuitry, is reported in Figure 8b, has shown a 94.7% classification fidelity with one-pattern classification time and energy equal to 1 μs and less than 20 nJ, respectively. Moreover, a reduction of the total chip active area, amounting to 1 mm^2 in the discussed work, is expected together with an increase of its performance when moving to the next 55 nm SST technology. In this regard, some preliminary results about MVM were already presented in ref. [56].

Although this solution based on re-routing commercially available NOR arrays appears promising, it comes together with its main drawback consisting in the increased area occupancy (the single-cell area in the modified array is 2.3 times larger than the original one). A different approach aiming at avoiding this disadvantage is proposed in [57–59]. Here, the authors suggest a modified working scheme for a mainstream double-polysilicon common-ground NOR Flash arrays developed in a 40 nm embedded technology by STMicroelectronics (Figure 9a) without any change needed in the cell or array design. While keeping CHEI as the physical mechanism for the program, single-cell selectivity during the erase is achieved by employing hot-hole injection (HHI) in the cell floating gate. In particular, by keeping the source and substrate contacts to the ground while applying a positive and negative voltage to the drain and to the gate, respectively, the developed electric field triggers the generation of holes by band-to-band tunneling at the drain side and accelerates them (Figure 9b); if the applied voltages are high enough, the energy acquired by the holes allows them to overcome the energetic barrier of the tunnel oxide and to be redirected toward the floating gate thanks to the negative gate voltage.

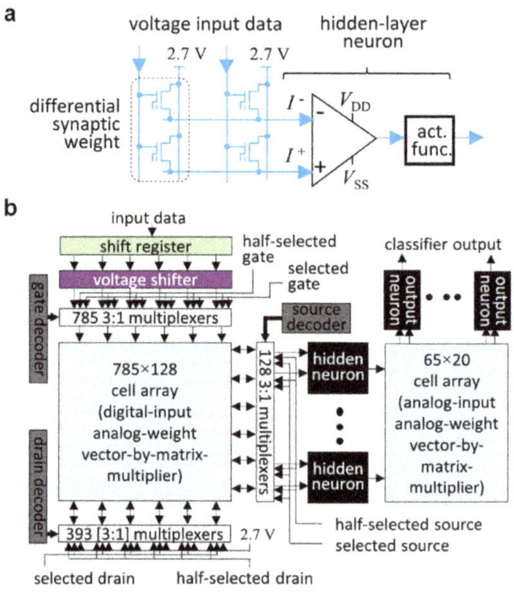

Figure 8. (**a**) Differential implementation of a synaptic connection followed by a hidden-layer neuron, consisting of a differential summing operational amplifier and an activation-function block. (**b**) High-level architecture of the artificial neural network and needed additional circuitry. Reprinted with permission from [55]. Copyright 2018, IEEE.

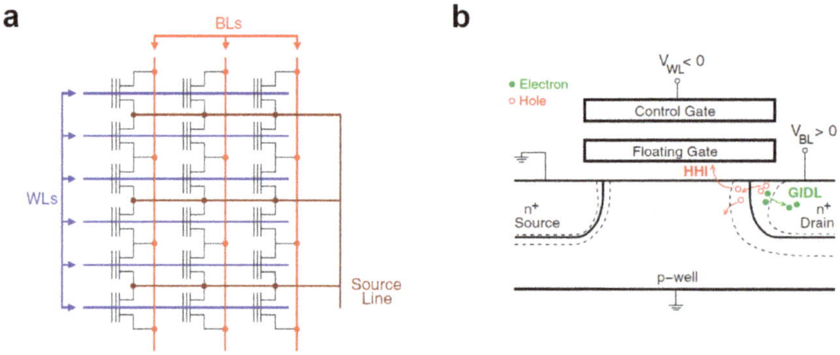

Figure 9. (**a**) Schematic for a mainstream common-ground NOR Flash array and (**b**) proposed physical mechanism exploited for the erase operations. Reprinted with permission from [57]. Copyright 2018, IEEE.

To validate this program/erase scheme in a brain-inspired neural network, the authors demonstrated long-term potentiation/depression through the design of the presynaptic and postsynaptic waveforms as shown in Figure 10a. The short rectangular pulse applied to the BL as a consequence of a postsynaptic fire event overlaps with a positive or negative WL voltage according to the time distance between the presynaptic and postsynaptic spike, Δt. In particular, $\Delta t > 0$ leads to long-term potentiation by HHI and Δt < 0 leads to long-term depression by CHEI. To further confirm the validity of this protocol, a prototype two layers 8 × 1 SNN was tested on pattern recognition, producing encouraging results as shown in Figure 10b; in fact, as expected, while the synapses corresponding to the input pattern are quickly potentiated, the remaining ones are gradually depressed.

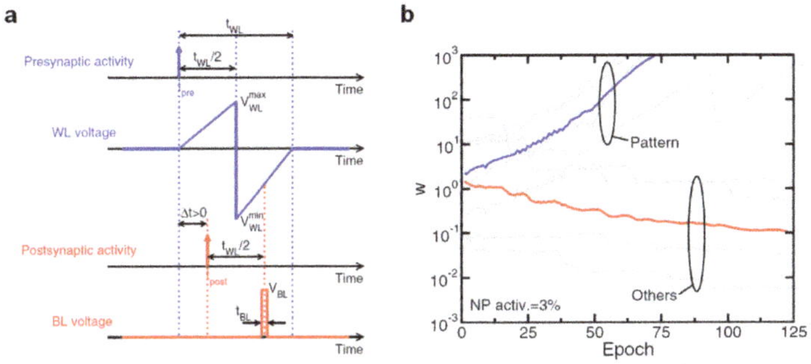

Figure 10. (**a**) Pulse scheme proposed to implement the spike-timing-dependent plasticity (STDP) waveform exploiting the erase mechanism shown in Figure 9b and (**b**) evolution of the weights of the implemented NOR Flash-based spiking neural network during the learning phase. Reprinted with permission from [57]. Copyright 2018, IEEE.

A final remark, being of great relevance especially in DNN inference, is the finite tuning precision of the cells array, V_T, and its stability after the offline training phase. In the case of ANN based on NOR Flash memory arrays, two of the most relevant physical mechanisms causing reliability issues of this kind are program noise (PN), determining an inherent uncertainty during the program phase due to the statistical nature of electron injection in the floating gate, and random telegraph noise (RTN), inducing V_T instabilities arising from the capture and release of charge carriers in tunnel-oxide defects. In ref. [60], the authors assess the impact of both PN and RTN on a neuromorphic digit classifier through parametric Monte-Carlo simulations. The main result, relevant in terms of projection of the previously discussed results on future technological nodes, is that such non-idealities play a non-negligible role, setting a stringent requirement both on the maximum scalability of the array cell and on the adopted program/erase schemes.

4. Memristive Technologies

To replicate neural networks in hardware, memristive devices have been recently investigated for the realization of compact circuits capable of emulating neuron and synapse functionalities. Increasing interest toward these novel device concepts first results from their ability to store information at the nanoscale in an analogue and non-volatile way. Also, they allow the memory to be combined with the computing function, enabling in-situ data processing, also referred to as in-memory computing [11], which is currently the major approach toward the achievement of energy-efficient computing paradigms beyond the von Neumann bottleneck. In detail, the landscape of memristive technologies can be divided into the classes of memristors with two or three terminals, which are explained in the following subsections.

4.1. Memristive Devices with 2-Terminal Structure

As shown in Figure 11, the class of memristive devices with a two-terminal structure covers various physical concepts, such as resistive switching random access memory (RRAM), phase change memory (PCM), spin-transfer torque magnetic random access memory (STT-MRAM), and ferroelectric random access memory (FeRAM), which share a very simple structure consisting of a metal-insulator-metal (MIM) stack, where an insulating layer is sandwiched between two metallic electrodes called the top electrode (TE) and bottom electrode (BE), respectively. As a voltage pulse is applied, these devices undergo a change of physical properties of the material used as the switching layer, which results in a change of the resistance for RRAM and PCM, magnetic polarization for STT-MRAM, and electrical polarization for FeRAM. Importantly, all these memristive elements offer the opportunity to read, write, and erase the information in memory states by electrical operations on the device, thus making them potentially more attractive in terms of scalability than other memory concepts, such as the Flash memories based on charge storage.

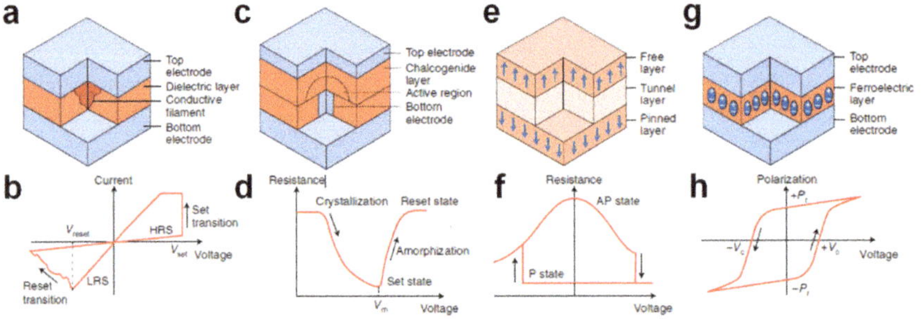

Figure 11. Sketch of the most promising two-terminal memristive devices used in neuromorphic computing applications. (**a**) Structure of resistive switching random access memory (RRAM) device where the insulating switching layer is sandwiched between two metal electrodes. (**b**) Current-voltage characteristics of RRAM displaying that the application of a positive voltage causes an abrupt resistance transition, called set, leading the device from the high resistance state (HRS) to the low resistance state (LRS) while the application of a negative voltage causes a more gradual resistance transition, called reset, leading the device from LRS to HRS. (**c**) Structure of phase change memory (PCM) device where a chalcogenide active layer is sandwiched between two metal electrodes. (**d**) Resistance-voltage characteristics of PCM displaying that the crystallization process in the active layer gradually leading the PCM from HRS to LRS is achieved at voltages below the melting voltage, V_m, while the amorphization process gradually leading the PCM from LRS to HRS is achieved at voltages above V_m. (**e**) Structure of spin-transfer torque magnetic random access memory (STT-MRAM) device, where a tunnel layer is sandwiched between two ferromagnetic metal electrodes. (**f**) Resistance-voltage characteristics of STT-MRAM displaying two binary resistance transitions leading the device from the anti-parallel (AP) to the parallel (P) state (set) at positive voltage and from P to AP (reset) at negative voltage. (**g**) Structure of ferroelectric random access memory (FeRAM) device, where a ferroelectric layer is sandwiched between two metal electrodes. (**h**) Polarization-voltage characteristics displaying binary operation between two states with a positive residual polarization, $+P_r$, and a negative residual polarization, $-P_r$, achieved by application of a positive and negative voltage, respectively. Reprinted with permission from [11]. Copyright 2018, Springer Nature.

Figure 11a shows the MIM stack of the RRAM device, where an insulating oxide material serves as the switching layer [61–63]. To initiate the device, a preliminary electrical operation called forming is performed by application of a positive voltage at TE by causing a soft breakdown process, leading to the creation of a high conductivity path containing oxygen vacancies and/or metallic impurities, also known as a conductive filament (CF), within the oxide layer. This results in the change of the resistance of the device from the initial high resistance state (HRS) to the low resistance state (LRS). After forming, in the case of bipolar RRAM devices, the application of negative/positive voltage pulses at TE leads the device to experience reset and set transitions, respectively. The application of a negative pulse causes the rupture of CF (reset process), leading to the opening of a depleted gap via drift/diffusion migration of ion defects from BE to TE, hence to the HRS. On the other hand, the application of a positive pulse allows the gap to be filled via field-driven migration of ion defects from TE to BE, thus leading the device back to LRS (set process) [64,65]. Two resistance transitions can be noted by the current-voltage characteristics shown in Figure 11b, which evidence both the abrupt nature of the set process due to the positive feedback loop involving the two driving forces for ion migration, namely the electric field and temperature, and the more gradual dynamics of the reset process due to the negative feedback occurring within the device as a negative pulse is applied [66]. Similar to the bipolar RRAM described in Figure 11b, which typically relies on switching layers, including HfO_x [67], TaO_x [68], TiO_x [69], SiO_x [70], and WO_x [71], the conductive-bridge random access memory (CBRAM), where metallic CFs are created/disrupted between active Cu/Ag electrodes, has also received strong interest in recent years [72]. In addition to bipolar RRAM concepts, another type of filamentary RRAM called unipolar RRAM, typically based on NiO [73–75], has been widely investigated, evidencing that pulses with the same polarity can induce both set and reset processes as a result of the key role played by Joule heating for the creation/disruption of CF [73,75]. Moreover, the RRAM concept also includes non-filamentary devices referred to as uniform RRAM, exhibiting an interface resistive switching due to the uniform change of a Schottky or tunneling barrier on the whole cell area [76]. One of the fundamental features making RRAM suitable for in-memory computing is the opportunity to modulate its resistance in an analog way, thus enabling multilevel operation via the storage of at least 3 bit [77–81]. In addition to multilevel operation, it also combines high scalability up to 10 nm in size [82] and the opportunity to achieve 3D integration [83].

Figure 11c shows the schematic structure of a PCM device, which relies on a chalcogenide material, such as $Ge_2Sb_2Te_5$ (GST) [84], as the switching layer. Here, resistance variation arises from an atomic configuration change within the active layer from the crystalline to the amorphous phase and vice-versa via application of unipolar voltage pulses at TE [85–87]. As a voltage higher than the voltage, V_m, needed to induce the melting process within the active layer is applied across the cell, local melting takes place within the chalcogenide material, leading the device to HRS as a result of the pinning of the Fermi level at the midgap. Otherwise, if the applied voltage is below V_m, a gradual crystallization process is triggered via local Joule heating, leading PCM to LRS [88]. These physical processes can be better visualized by the resistance-voltage characteristics in Figure 11d, where the set transition displays a gradual behavior due to the gradual crystallization process induced by Joule heating while the reset transition displays faster dynamics than the set transition. Compared to RRAM, where the HRS/LRS ratio is about 10, PCM offers a higher resistance window, ranging from 100 to 1000, which makes PCM very attractive for multilevel operation as reported in [89], where a 3 bits/cell PCM device was demonstrated. Moreover, in addition to classic GST, other materials, such as GeSb [90], doped In-Ge-Te [91], and Ge-rich GST [92], have been investigated, receiving strong interest since they offer higher crystallization temperatures for enhanced retention performances.

Figure 11e shows the schematic structure of an STT-MRAM device based on an MIM stack called magnetic tunnel junction (MTJ), including an ultrathin tunneling layer (TL), typically in MgO, interposed between two ferromagnetic (FM) metal electrodes, typically in CoFeB, called the pinned layer (PL) and free layer (FL), respectively [93–95]. Unlike RRAM and PCM enabling multilevel operation, STT-MRAM allows only two states to be stored, with a very small resistance window of the order of a factor 2 [94] because of the tunnel magneto-resistance (TMR) effect [96]. The two states are encoded in the relative orientation between PL magnetic polarization, which is fixed, and FL magnetic polarization, which is instead free to change via the spin-transfer torque physical mechanism discovered by Slonczewski [97] and Berger [98] in 1996. As a positive voltage is applied at TE, a current of electrons with the same spin-polarization of the fixed layer is transmitted through the tunneling layer, causing the transition of the polarization orientation from anti-parallel (AP) to parallel (P), which leads the device to LRS. In contrast, as a negative bias is applied, the reflection back of electrons entering from the free layer with the opposite magnetization takes place, thus causing the transition from the P to AP state, hence from LRS to HRS. Figure 11f shows the resistance response of the STT-MRAM device as a function of the applied voltage, evidencing that the application of positive/negative voltage pulse induces set/reset transition with very abrupt dynamics, which further supports the incompatibility of

STT-MRAM with multilevel applications. However, STT-MRAM has shown high potential in scalability, as reported in ref. [99], fast switching speed [100], and almost unlimited cycling endurance [101,102].

Figure 11g shows the MIM stack of FeRAM, where an insulating layer based on a ferroelectric (FE) material, typically in doped HfO_2 [103] or perovskite materials [104,105], is sandwiched between two metal electrodes. Its operation principle relies on the polarization switching within the FE layer due to the rotation of electrical dipoles under an external bias [106]. As shown by the polarization-voltage characteristics in Figure 11h, a positive voltage above the coercive voltage, $+V_c$, at TE induces the set transition, leading the device to exhibit a positive residual polarization, $+P_r$, whereas a voltage more negative than $-V_c$ leads the device to exhibit a negative residual polarization, $-P_r$. Importantly, note that the FE switching process does not impact on the device resistance, which makes FeRAM unusable as resistive memory.

4.2. Memristive Devices with Three-Terminal Structure

In addition to the two-terminal devices, memristive concepts also include the class of three-terminal devices whose main examples are those depicted in Figure 12, namely (a) the ferroelectric field-effect transistor (FeFET) [107], (b) the electro-chemical random access memory (ECRAM) [108], and (c) the spin-orbit torque magnetic random access memory (SOT-MRAM) [109]. Other interesting three-terminal concepts that have been recently investigated for neuromorphic computing applications are the 2D semiconductor-based mem-transistors [110,111] and the domain-wall-based magnetic memories [112,113].

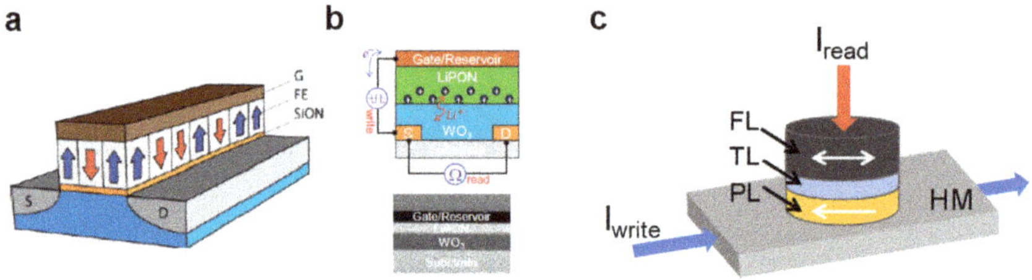

Figure 12. Sketch of three fundamental examples of three-terminal memristive devices. (**a**) Schematic structure of ferroelectric field-effect transistor (FeFET) device, where the ferroelectric switching phenomenon allows the transistor threshold voltage to be modulated, thus gradually changing the channel conductivity. (**b**) Schematic structure of electro-chemical random access memory (ECRAM) device, where the channel conductivity is controlled by the migration of ion species, e.g., Li^+ ions, into an electrolyte material being induced by the voltage applied at the gate terminal. (**c**) Schematic structure of spin-orbit torque magnetic random access memory (SOT-MRAM), where the current flow in a heavy metal (HM) line causes a polarization switching in the MTJ-free layer, resulting in a device conductance change. Reprinted with permission from [107,108]. Copyright 2017, IEEE. Copyright 2018, IEEE.

Figure 12a shows the structure of the FeFET consisting of an MOS transistor with an FE material, such as doped-HfO_2 [103], and perovskites [106], serving as the gate dielectric. Here, the application of external pulses at the gate terminal induces a non-volatile polarization switching within the FE dielectric, leading to a change of the transistor threshold, hence of the channel conductivity, which can be probed simply by reading the current at the drain terminal. As a result, the FeFET concept allows significant issues due to transient read currents and destructive read operation limiting FeRAM operation to be overcome. This three-terminal device has recently been operated into memory arrays with 28 nm CMOS technology [114] and exhibits a strong potential for the development of 3D structures [115]. Also, it has been operated to replicate synapse [116] and neuron [117,118] functions, which, combined with 3D integration opportunity, makes it a strong candidate for neuromorphic computing applications.

Figure 12b illustrates the device structure of the ECRAM consisting of an MOS transistor where a solid-state electrolyte based on inorganic materials, such as lithium phosphorous oxynitride (LiPON) [108,119], or organic materials, such as poly (3, 4-ethylenedioxythiophene):polystyrene sulfonate (PEDOT:PSS) [120], is used as the gate dielectric. Its operation relies on the intercalation/de-intercalation of ions in a channel layer to tune the device conductance. As reported in [108], the intercalation of Li^+ ions into the WO_3 layer by application of a positive voltage at the gate terminal leads the device to experience a conductance increase whereas the de-intercalation of Li^+ ions under negative bias leads the device to experience a conductance decrease. The linear conductance change is achievable in ECRAM thanks to the decoupling of read/write paths, which makes this device concept very attractive for synaptic applications, mainly for hardware implementation of synaptic weights in ANNs, where analog and symmetric weight updates play a crucial role. Also, the device investigated in [108] provides fast operation at the nanosecond timescale, thus opening the way toward a significant acceleration of the training process in hardware ANNs.

Figure 12c shows the device structure of the SOT-MRAM, where a heavy metal (HM) line, typically in Pt [121] or Ta [122], is located under an MTJ. This three-terminal device is programmed by the flow of a horizontal current through the HM line, which induces a spin accumulation as a result of the spin Hall or the Rashba effects [123,124], leading to the switching of magnetic polarization in the MTJ FL. Unlike the program operation, the read operation can be performed by measuring the vertical current flowing in MTJ as a result of the TMR effect, which means that the three-terminal structure of SOT-MRAM offers the opportunity to decouple read/write current paths and consequently improve the endurance performance compared with STT-MRAM. Regarding device applications, SOT-MRAM was used to implement neuromorphic computing in ANNs, by exhibiting the synapse function [125], the neuron function [126], and the associative memory operation [127].

5. Memristive Neuromorphic Networks

Thanks to their rich physics and nanoscale size, memristive concepts are believed to be promising candidates to achieve the huge density and behavior of real synapses and neurons, thus enabling brain-like cognitive capabilities in hardware neural networks. Based on this appealing approach, many hardware or mixed hardware/simulation implementations of the neural networks currently dominating the neuromorphic computing scenario, namely the DNNs and the SNNs, have been proposed.

5.1. DNNs with Memristive Synapses

DNNs encompass various ANN architectures, such as feedforward MLP and convolutional neural network (CNN) [36], that have attracted wide interest in the neuromorphic computing scenario thanks to the excellent performance achieved in machine learning tasks, such as image classification [128], face verification [129], and speech recognition [130]. Because of the very high complexity of the CNN architecture, which consists of a deep hierarchy of convolutional layers followed by some fully connected layers, and processing strategy, which is based on the extraction of the most significant features of submitted images via the application of large sets of filters, hardware implementation of DNN tasks with memory devices has mostly been focused on feedforward MLP networks. In this type of ANN, the training phase is based on a supervised learning algorithm called backpropagation [21–23] and consists of three sub-procedures called forward propagation, backward propagation, and weight update [36]. Note that although the backpropagation algorithm is chiefly considered lacking in biological plausibility [131], recent works have questioned this aspect [132]. During training, upon any input presentation from a training database containing images of objects, digits, or faces, the input signal propagates in the forward direction from the input to output layer, passing through the multiplication by synaptic weights of each layer and the summation at the input of each hidden/output neuron. Forward propagation yields an output signal, which is compared with the target response of the network, namely the label of the submitted image, thus leading to the calculation of the corresponding error signal. At this point, the calculated error signal is propagated in the backward direction from the output to the input layer and is used to update all the synaptic weights, hence the name backpropagation. Repeating this scheme for every image of the training database for a certain number of presentation cycles or epochs, the optimization of synaptic weights is achieved, leading the network to specialize on the training database. After, the training phase is followed by the test phase, namely the phase where the classification ability of DNN is evaluated by submitting another database, called the test dataset, only once, via forward propagation of the signal encoded in all the test examples [36].

The downside of the outstanding results achieved running DNNs in software on high-performance digital computers, such as GPU and TPU, or very large servers is given by the excessive power consumption and latency due to the von Neumann architecture. To overcome this issue, memristive devices, in particular RRAM and PCM, have been intensively investigated to accelerate artificial intelligence (AI) applications in hardware thanks to their ability to execute in-memory computing with extremely high energy efficiency and speed by exploiting basic physical laws, such as the Ohm's law and Kirchhoff's law [11]. However, hardware implementation of a real in-situ weight update for DNN training has been challenged by critical non-idealities affecting the conductance response of the majority of memristive devices, mainly RRAM and PCM, during set (potentiation) and reset (depression) processes, such as the non-linearity, the asymmetry, and the stochasticity [34,133,134]. Motivated by these significant limitations, a wide range of alternative materials and technologies have been intensively investigated, leading to the recent emergence of novel concepts, such as ECRAM [108] and the ionic floating gate [135], thanks to their highly linear, symmetric, and analog conductance behavior.

In the last 10 years, great advances in crossbar-based demonstrations of DNNs for pattern classification have been achieved using RRAM and PCM devices [12,13,136–138]. In ref. [12], a medium-scale crossbar array containing 165,000 PCM devices with a one-transistor-one-resistor (1T1R) structure was used to demonstrate an image classification task by hardware implementation of the three-layer DNN schematically shown in Figure 13a. This network is based on an input layer with 528 input neurons, a first hidden layer with 250 neurons, a second hidden layer with 125 neurons, and an output layer with 10 neurons, and was operated on a cropped version (22 × 24 pixels) of handwritten digit images from the MNIST database for training and test operations. To implement positive and negative synaptic weights of the network, Burr et al. proposed a differential configuration based on pairs of 1T1R PCM cells with conductance, G^+ and G^-, respectively, as shown in Figure 13b. According to this structure, each weight can be potentiated or depressed by increasing G^+ with fixed G- or increasing G- with fixed G^+, respectively. Also, the network was implemented with software neurons, providing the conversion of the sum of input currents into an output voltage by application of the tanh non-linear function. After the training process, which was carried out on 5000 MNIST images by using a complex pulse overlap scheme, the network's classification ability was evaluated, leading to a best performance of only 83% due to the asymmetry and non-linearity of the PCM G-response (Figure 13c). To tackle this limitation, a novel artificial synapse combining the 1T1R differential pair with a three-transistor/one-capacitor (3T1C) analog device was presented in ref. [138]. This led the PCM-based DNNs with improved hardware synapses to match the software performance on both the MNIST and CIFAR databases [139]. Later, other DNN implementations in small-scale 1T1R RRAM crossbar arrays were demonstrated, enabling MNIST classification with 92% test performance [137] and gray-scale face classification on the Yale face database with 91.5% performance [136], thanks to the RRAM conductance responses displaying high linearity and symmetry in both update directions. Moreover, an alternative approach aiming at combining high performance with high energy efficiency was proposed in ref. [140]. Here, after an off-line training resulting in the optimization of synaptic weights in the software, the floating-point accuracy of synaptic weights was reduced only to five levels, which were stored in a hardware 4 kbit HfO_2 RRAM array using a novel multilevel programming scheme. The following execution of the inference phase with the experimental conductances stored into the 4 kbit RRAM array led to a maximum classification accuracy of 83%. A simulation-based study showed that the implementation of synaptic weights using more conductance levels can move performance beyond 90% with larger arrays.

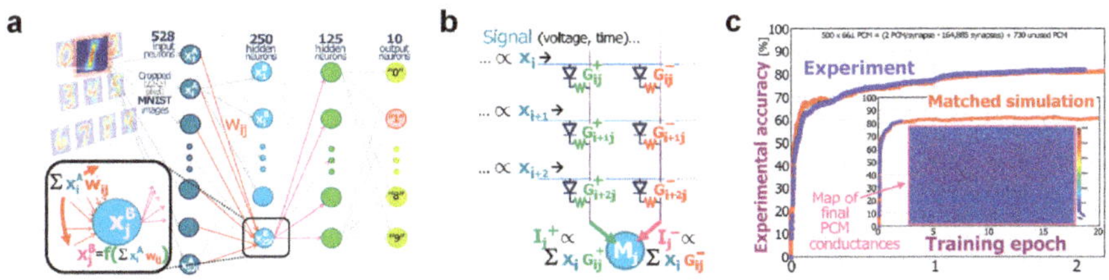

Figure 13. (**a**) Schematic representation of a three-layer DNN operated on the MNIST database for an image classification task. (**b**) Weight implementation in DNN by differential pairs of 1T1R PCM cells with conductances G_{ij}^{+} and G_{ij}^{-}, which provide a positive current and a negative current, respectively. (**c**) Experimental classification accuracy achieved by three-layer DNN during the inference phase. Reprinted with permission from [12]. Copyright 2014, IEEE. Deep neural networks, DNNs; Modified National Institute of Standards and Technology, MNIST; one-transistor-one-resistor, 1T1R.

5.2. *SNNs with Memristive Synapses*

Although DNNs have shown to be capable of excellent performance in fundamental cognitive functions, exceeding the human ability in some cases [128,141], the interest in SNNs is rapidly increasing thanks to their attempt to replicate structure and operation principles of the most efficient computing machine found in nature, which is the biological brain. The brain can efficiently learn, recognize, and infer in an unsupervised way thanks to the plasticity of biological synapses controlled by local rules, such as STDP, which has recently inspired many hardware implementations of synaptic plasticity at the device and network level exploiting the attractive physical properties of memristive devices.

One of the earliest STDP demonstrations at the memristive device level was performed by Jo and coauthors in ref. [142] by using an Ag/Si-based CBRAM device as the synapse and a time-division multiplexing approach based on synchronous time frames which was designed to achieve STDP characteristics thanks to the conversion of the time delay into the amplitude of the pulse to be applied across the synaptic device. After this precursor implementation, another scheme based on voltage overlap at the terminals of memristive synapses was experimentally demonstrated in both RRAM [143] and PCM [144]. Both works demonstrate potentiation and depression characteristics very close to biological STDP, exploiting the analog modulation of device conductance achieved via the superposition of voltage spikes with suitably tailored waveforms. Specifically, Kuzum et al. proposed the voltage waveforms shown in Figure 14a as PRE and POST spikes for achieving potentiation in PCM devices [144]. As the relative delay is positive, in this case $\Delta t = 20$ ms, the overlap of the PRE spike, which consists of a sequence of high positive pulses with increasing amplitudes followed by another sequence of small positive pulse with decreasing amplitudes, with the POST spike, which consists of a single 8 ms long negative pulse, leads the total voltage across the PCM cell, $V_{pre} - V_{post}$, to only cross the minimum threshold for potentiation, v_P, thus leading the synapse to undergo potentiation via a set process within PCM. Changing the sign of Δt, depression was also demonstrated, thus allowing the STDP characteristics shown in Figure 14b to be achieved, which exhibit a very nice agreement with the Bi and Poo measurements [38]. Moreover, note that this scheme offers the opportunity to finely tune the shape of STDP characteristics, by suitably designing the PRE spike waveform [144]. Taking inspiration from this approach based on overlapping spikes across the memristive device, more recently, other significant STDP demonstrations were achieved in individual two-terminal memristive devices, thus enabling unsupervised learning in small-scale memristive SNNs [145–149]. However, the synapse implementation using individual two-terminal memristive devices might suffer from serious issues, such as (i) the requirement to control the current during set transition in RRAM devices to avoid an uncontrollable CF growth [64], which would reduce the synapse reliability during potentiation; (ii) the sneak paths challenging the operation of crossbar arrays; and (iii) the high energy consumption.

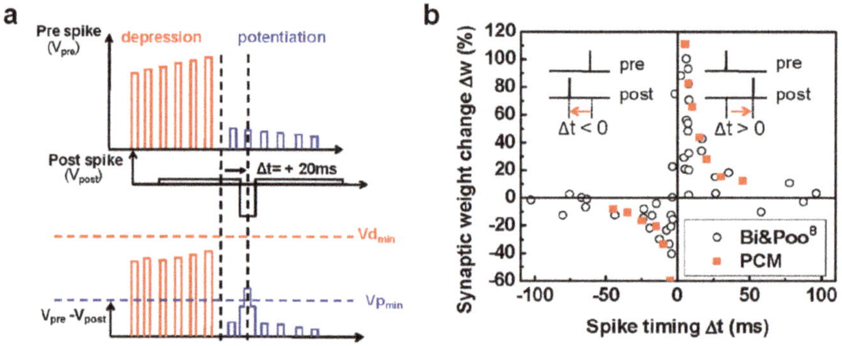

Figure 14. (**a**) PRE and POST spike waveforms applied at terminals of a PCM-based synaptic device to change its weight via an overlap-based STDP scheme. The application of a positive time delay of 20 ms leads to a conductance increase (potentiation) in the PCM synapse since the spike overlap leads the effective voltage across the PCM to cross the potentiation threshold whereas the higher depression threshold is not hit. (**b**) Measured weight change as a function of the spike timing achieved using a PCM synapse against experimental data collected by Bi and Poo in biological synapses. Reprinted with permission from [144]. Copyright 2012, American Chemical Society.

To overcome these drawbacks, a novel hybrid CMOS/memristive STDP synapse using the 1T1R structure was proposed in refs. [150,151]. Figure 15a shows the schematic structure of the 1T1R device presented in ref. [151], where a Ti/HfO_x/TiN RRAM is serially connected to the drain of an MOS transistor acting as selector and current limiter. As schematically shown in Figure 15b, the ability of the 1T1R cell to operate as a synapse capable of STDP was validated in the hardware [152]. The 1T1R synapse operation can be explained as follows. The application of a pulse designed as a PRE spike at the gate terminal of the transistor combined with the low voltage bias applied at the TE of the RRAM device activates a current flowing toward the BE. At this point, the current enters in an integrate-and-fire circuit implementing POST where it is integrated, causing an increase of the POST internal potential, V_{int}. As a sequence of PRE spikes leads the POST to cross its internal threshold, the POST emits both a forward spike toward the next neuron layer and a suitably designed spike, including a positive pulse followed by a negative pulse, being delivered at TE, thus creating the conditions for synaptic weight update according to STDP [151]. As shown in Figure 15c, if the PRE spike anticipates the POST spikes ($\Delta t > 0$), only the positive pulse of the POST spike with amplitude V_{TE+} ($V_{TE+} > V_{set}$) overlaps with the PRE spike, thus inducing a set transition within the RRAM device, leading RRAM to LRS, and, therefore, the synapse to be potentiated. Otherwise, if the PRE spike follows the POST spike ($\Delta t < 0$), only the negative pulse with amplitude V_{TE-} ($|V_{TE-}| > |V_{reset}|$) overlaps with the PRE spike, thus inducing a reset transition within the RRAM device, leading RRAM to HRS, and, therefore, the synapse to be depressed (not shown). Thanks to this operation principle, the 1T1R synapse was shown to capture STDP functionality implementing the 3D characteristics shown in Figure 15d, where the relative change in conductance, $\eta = \log_{10}(R_0/R)$, is plotted as a function of the initial resistance state, R_0, and relative delay, Δt. They support potentiation/depression at positive/negative Δt, evidencing that maximum potentiation is obtained for R_0 = HRS, whereas maximum depression is obtained for R_0 = LRS. If the 1T1R synapse is initially in LRS/HRS, no potentiation/depression occurs because it cannot overcome the boundary conductance values set by LRS and HRS [151–153]. Importantly, note that the weight change in the 1T1R synapse can be induced only via spike overlap, hence only for delays in the range -10 ms $< \Delta t <$ 10 ms in this experiment [152].

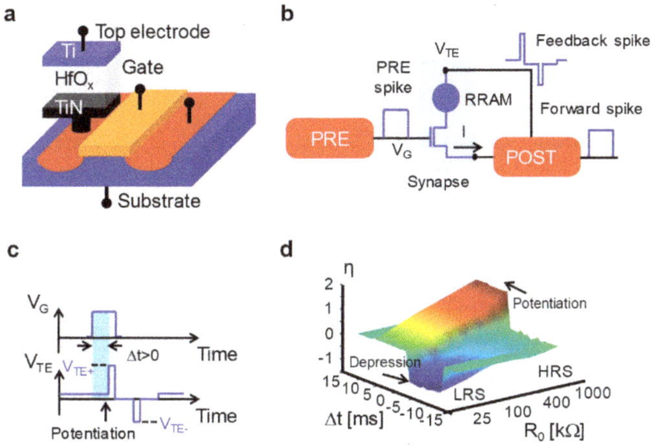

Figure 15. (**a**) Schematic structure of the 1T1R RRAM structure. (**b**) Schematic representation of the 1T1R structure as a synapse to achieve STDP in hardware via overlapping PRE and POST voltage spikes applied at the gate terminal and RRAM top electrode, respectively. (**c**) Schematic sketch of PRE and POST overlapping spikes leading to synapse potentiation via the activation of a set process in the RRAM cell. (**d**) STDP characteristics experimentally demonstrated in the 1T1R RRAM synapse. Adapted with permission from [151,152]. Copyright 2016, IEEE.

Although the STDP characteristics achieved in the 1T1R RRAM synapse [151,152] display a squared shape due to binary operation of the RRAM cell instead of the exponentially decaying behavior observed in biological experiments, the plasticity of the 1T1R synapse was exploited in many SNN implementations enabling neuromorphic tasks, such as unsupervised learning of space/spatiotemporal patterns [151,152,154,155], the extraction of auditory/visual patterns [156,157], pattern classification [158–160], and associative memory [161–163], in both simulation and hardware.

Figure 16a shows the schematic representation of the RRAM-based SNN used in ref. [152] to demonstrate unsupervised learning of visual patterns in hardware. This perceptron SNN consists of 16 PREs connected to a single POST via individual synapses with the 1T1R RRAM structure of Figure 15a. Pattern learning experiment is based on three sequential phases where only one 4×4 visual pattern among Pattern #1, Pattern #2, and Pattern #3 shown in Figure 16b is submitted to the input layer, and was conducted using a stochastic approach according to which the probability to submit the pattern image or a random noise image similar to the last 4×4 pattern in Figure 16b at every epoch is 50%. Using this training approach, Figure 16c shows that the submission of three patterns alternated with noise resulted in the on-line adaptation of SNN synapses to the presented pattern in all three phases, evidencing a selective potentiation of synapses within the submitted pattern due to the correlated spiking activity of corresponding PREs and the depression of synapses outside the pattern, typically called background synapses, due to the uncorrelated nature of noise inducing POST spike-PRE spike depression sequences for the background with a high probability [151,152]. Note that the frequency and amount of submitted noise has to be carefully designed to prevent learning dynamics from becoming unstable [164]. To further support the unsupervised pattern learning ability of SNN with 1T1R RRAM synapses, Figure 16d shows the raster plot of spikes generated by PREs during the whole experiment, leading to the time evolution of synaptic conductance evidenced in Figure 16e, where the pattern/background synaptic conductance converges to LRS/HRS at the end of each training phase. Note that the stochastic approach used in this experiment also allowed for the implementation of multiple pattern learning by a winner-take-all scheme [165] based on the use of software inhibitory synapses between 2 POSTs, and unsupervised learning of gray-scale images [152].

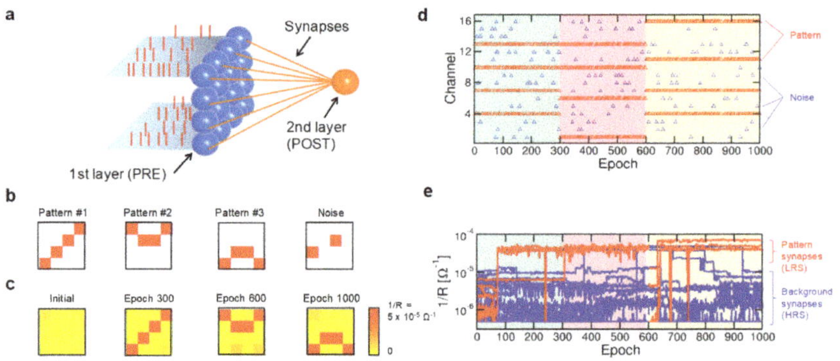

Figure 16. (**a**) Schematic sketch of a single-layer perceptron network where a 4 x 4 input layer is fully connected to a single POST. (**b**) Sequence of three visual patterns (Pattern #1, Pattern #2, and Pattern #3) submitted to the neural network during training process and an example of a random noise image, which is alternatively applied to patterns according to a stochastic approach. (**c**) Conductance/weight color plots measured at epochs 0, 300, 600, and 1000 evidencing the ability of the synaptic weights to adapt to submitted patterns thanks to selective potentiation of pattern synapses and noise-induced depression of background synapses. (**d**) Raster plot of PRE spikes applied to pattern and background input channels during the learning experiment. (**e**) Time evolution of the measured synaptic conductance during three phases of the unsupervised learning experiment showing convergence of pattern/background synapses to LRS/HRS. Reprinted from [152].

The main drawbacks generally limiting the implementation of synaptic plasticity in overlap-based synaptic concepts, such as the 1T1R synapse, are the pulse duration and energy efficiency. Overlap-based implementations first require a pulse width of the order of time delays to allow for conductance change within the device, which results in pulses with a long duration causing a high power consumption. In addition to this, the need for long pulses to program overlap-based memristive devices also causes too slow signal processing in large neuromorphic networks, which leads to low throughput performance [166].

An alternative approach to achieve synaptic plasticity overcoming the limitations affecting overlap-based memristive devices consists of the adoption of non-overlap memristive devices, such as the second-order memristor [167,168]. Unlike first-order memristors, such as RRAM and PCM, where device conductance can change only if overlapping voltage pulses are applied at device terminals, resistive switching in second-order memristors can take place by sequential application of two spikes with a certain Δt at device terminals as a result of short-term memory effects encoded in the time evolution of second-order variables, e.g., the internal temperature. As shown in Figure 17a, if Δt is long, two sequential spikes applied at terminals of a second-order memristor induce small independent changes in temperature, which results in no conductance change. On the contrary, if Δt is short, the superposition of the effects of applied spikes results in a large change in temperature thanks to a limited thermal constant of about 500 ns, thus leading to a long-term conductance variation in the device as a result of short-term memory effects. Importantly, short memory effects observed in second-order memristors have recently attracted great interest because they can allow for the emulation in hardware of a fundamental biological process playing a key role in the real synapse response as the Ca^{2+} ion dynamics [169,170] and to finely replicate biological STDP and SRDP [168,171]. An interesting STDP demonstration by a second-order memristor is reported in ref. [168]. Here, a $Pt/Ta_2O_{5-x}/TaO_y/Pd$ RRAM device was operated as a non-overlap synapse to achieve STDP via sequential application of PRE and POST voltages. As shown in Figure 17b, the PRE spike consists of a positive pulse with amplitude of 1.6 V and duration of 20 ns followed after 1 μs by a longer positive pulse with amplitude of 0.7 V and duration of 1 μs whereas the POST spike includes a positive pulse with amplitude of 1.1 V and duration of 20 ns followed after 1 μs by a longer positive pulse with amplitude of 0.7 V and 1 μs width. Note that both the first pulse, called the programming element, and the second pulse, called the heating element, within PRE and POST spikes cannot cause independently a conductance change in the RRAM device. The application of the PRE/POST spike at TE/BE of the RRAM device results in an effective voltage drop across the device, evidencing a PRE–POST spike sequence for positive Δt and POST–PRE spike sequence for negative Δt, as shown in Figure 17c. In the case of the PRE–POST spike sequence (Δt > 0), the heating effect of the PRE spike affects the POST spike, making the positive change in conductance due to the negative programming pulse in the POST higher than the negative change in conductance due to the positive programming pulse in the PRE, hence causing the non-overlap RRAM synapse to undergo potentiation. On the other hand, in the case of the POST–PRE sequence (Δt < 0), the opposite occurrence order of spikes results in an effective negative conductance change in the $Pt/Ta_2O_{5-x}/TaO_y/Pd$ RRAM device, resulting in the depression of the non-overlap synapse. Figure 17d shows the STDP characteristics experimentally measured in the $Pt/Ta_2O_{5-x}/TaO_y/Pd$ RRAM device for variable Δt in the range –6 μs – 6 μs, which exhibit strong similarity with biological data and a good agreement with simulation results achieved by a numerical model of the second-order memristor.

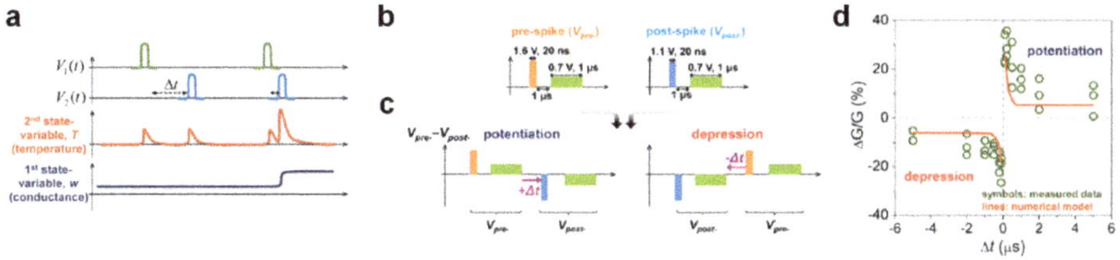

Figure 17. (**a**) Schematic representation of a non-overlap scheme enabling STDP in second-order memristors. Short-term memory effects observed in second-order physical variables, e.g., internal temperature, allow for the implementation of potentiation/depression for short/long delays. (**b**) PRE and POST spike waveforms applied at top electrode (TE) and bottom electrode (BE) to implement non-overlap STDP. (**c**) Effective voltage across a second-order memristor to induce potentiation (**left**) and depression (**right**). (**d**) STDP characteristics measured in a second-order memristor against calculated curves achieved by numerical modeling. Reprinted with permission from [168]. Copyright 2015, American Chemical Society.

Similar to the second-order memristor device, other memristive concepts also allowed bio-realistic synaptic plasticity to be demonstrated using non-overlap schemes. In ref. [172], an atomic switch RRAM, whose stack includes a silver BE, an Ag_2S-based solid electrolyte, and a metal TE separated from the Ag_2S layer by a nanogap, was proposed as an artificial synapse thanks to the short-term memory effects controlling its physical processes. In fact, the application of voltage pulses at TE induces the gradual creation of an Ag atomic bridge within the nanogap leading to a short-term potentiation process after a few pulses, resulting in an incomplete atomic bridge, which is followed by a long-term potentiation process achieved after many pulses resulting in the formation of a complete atomic bridge. In addition to short-term plasticity due to the spontaneous relaxation process of the atomic bridge, this non-overlap device also offers the opportunity to capture SRDP potentiation and depression depending on whether the frequency of the applied pulses is high or low. Thanks to this functionality, the sequential learning of visual patterns was demonstrated in a 7 × 7 array of Ag_2S inorganic synaptic devices.

Another memristive concept to implement non-overlap synapses in hardware was recently presented in ref. [171]. Here, a hybrid device based on the serial configuration of a volatile RRAM with a SiO_xN_y:Ag stack serving as the select device and a non-volatile RRAM serving as the resistive device, also known as a one-selector-one-resistor (1S1R) structure, was designed to demonstrate non-overlap synaptic plasticity for neuromorphic computing. Exploiting spontaneous relaxation of CF similar to the one taking place in atomic switches, the introduction of a volatile RRAM or diffusive memristor in series to a non-volatile RRAM, where conductance change can only be induced by the electric field, enabled 1S1R synapses capable of both SRDP and STDP depending on the rate or occurrence timing of PRE and POST spikes applied in sequence at TE. Note that the strong potential of 1S1R synapses for neuromorphic computing applications was also investigated in simulation in [173,174]. Moreover, diffusive memristors developed in ref. [171] were used as neurons to build in hardware a fully memristive neural network, which was shown to achieve outstanding performance in a pattern classification task by the implementation of unsupervised learning [175].

6. Discussion

While neuromorphic networks have recently demonstrated an excellent ability in fundamental cognitive computing applications, such as image classification and speech recognition, their large-scale hardware implementation is still a major challenge. Achieving such a goal primarily requires nanoscale, energy-efficient, and fast devices capable of emulating faithfully high-density, ultra-low power operation and low latency of biological synapses and neurons. Moreover, depending on the architecture (DNN or SNN) and the application of neuromorphic networks, such devices should also fulfill other significant requirements, such as high retention, high linearity in conductance response, and long endurance [35]. In Table 1, the CMOS-based and memristive emerging memory devices investigated for neuromorphic computing we discussed in Sections 3 and 4 are compared in terms of performance, reliability, and suitability for DNN, with the distinction between training and inference phases, and SNN applications; however, it is evidenced that no emerging memory device can currently optimize all the metrics for any network architecture and application.

Table 1. Comparison of key features exhibited by CMOS mainstream memory devices and memristive emerging memory devices under investigation to implement neuromorphic computing in hardware. Adapted from [35].

Technology	CMOS Mainstream Memories		Memristive Emerging Memories						
	NOR Flash	NAND Flash	RRAM	PCM	STT-MRAM	FeRAM	FeFET	SOT-MRAM	Li-ion
ON/OFF Ratio	10^4	10^4	10–10^2	10^2–10^4	1.5-2	10^2–10^3	5–50	1.5–2	40–10^3
Multilevel operation	2 bit	4 bit	2 bit	2 bit	1 bit	1 bit	5 bit	1 bit	10 bit
Write voltage	<10 V	>10 V	<3V	<3V	<1.5 V	<3 V	<5 V	<1.5 V	<1 V
Write time	1–10 µs	0.1–1 ms	<10 ns	~50 ns	<10 ns	~30 ns	~10 ns	<10 ns	<10 ns
Read time	~50 ns	~10 µs	<10 ns	<10 ns	<10 ns	<10 ns	~10 ns	<10 ns	<10 ns
Stand-by power	Low	Low	Low	Low	Low	Low	Low	Low	Low
Write energy (J/bit)	~100 pJ	~10 fJ	0.1–1 pJ	10 pJ	~100 fJ	~100 fJ	<1 fJ	<100 fJ	~100 fJ
Linearity	Low	Low	Low	Low	None	None	Low	None	High
Drift	No	No	Weak	Yes	No	No	No	No	No
Integration density	High	Very High	High	High	High	Low	High	High	Low
Retention	Long	Long	Medium	Long	Medium	Long	Long	Medium	-
Endurance	10^5	10^4	10^5–10^8	10^6–10^9	10^{15}	10^{10}	$>10^5$	$>10^{15}$	$>10^5$
Suitability for DNN training	No	No	No	No	No	No	Moderate	No	Yes
Suitability for DNN inference	Yes	Yes	Moderate	Yes	No	No	Yes	No	Yes
Suitability for SNN applications	Yes	No	Yes	Yes	Moderate	Yes	Yes	Moderate	Moderate

To efficiently execute DNN online training in hardware, high speed and low energy consumption are two essential features of synaptic devices to maximize the network throughput, namely the rate of trained patterns, and enable DNNs in embedded systems, respectively. In addition to these features, high accuracy in weight update operation imposes the use of devices exhibiting a conductance response with a high degree of linearity. This functionality makes almost all the emerging devices unsuitable as synaptic devices for online training. The only exception is represented by novel Li-ion devices, which appear to be very promising, with a simulated performance of around 98% [119], even though the necessary technology maturity and high-density integration have not been reached yet. Alternatively, more complex structures, including multiple pair of memristive devices, such as PCM and RRAM, could mitigate the need for high linearity, but at the expense of a lower integration density [176].

Differently from DNN online training consisting of forward propagation, backpropagation, and weight update operations, DNN inference only relies on forward propagation, which means that the high linearity needed to accurately update the weights is not an essential feature of synaptic devices for this task. Specifically, hardware suitable for optimizing the inference process should primarily exhibit low latency to accelerate the classification of each test pattern and low-power consumption to enable DNN inference at the edge. In addition to these features, high retention of analogue states is also essential to prevent charge fluctuations in CMOS devices [177], stochastic noise in RRAM [178], and resistance drift in PCM [179] from degrading the weights programmed in one shot after the off-line training procedure. These requirements can be fulfilled not only by Li-ion devices, as in the case of DNN training, but also by CMOS floating gate memory [55], RRAM [137], and PCM [148] devices thanks to their ability to finely tune the conductance with analog precision to encode the stored weights.

On the other hand, hardware implementation of brain-inspired SNNs for sensors or embedded systems primarily requires high energy efficiency to enable sensory information processing for long times even in limited-energy environments. The high endurance of synaptic and neuron devices is also strongly required in that SNN operation relies on a learning approach based on continuous synaptic updates and continuous reset operations of integrate-and-fire neurons upon fire events. In addition to these features, a high resistance window could be useful for accurate continual learning although multilevel weight storage could be not strictly needed, as shown by significant applications using binary stochastic memory devices, such as STT-MRAM. Therefore, both NOR Flash memory [57], despite higher operating voltages, and all the memristive emerging devices show a strong potential for hardware implementation of SNNs emulating the efficiency and 3D architecture of the biological brain.

Although some limitations currently hinder the large-scale industrialization of memory-centric neuromorphic technology, the rich physics of memory devices can also offer additional biologically inspired functionalities and more. For instance, besides synaptic implementation, integrate-and-fire neuron functionality has been recently demonstrated in various types of memristive devices, including RRAM [180], volatile RRAM [175], Mott memristor [181], PCM [182], STT-MRAM [183,184], SOT-MRAM [126], and paramagnetic MTJs [185], thus opening the way for hardware implementation of high-density fully memristive neural networks with a high area and energy efficiency. Also, thanks to the short-term memory effects observed in some materials, a more realistic implementation of biological synaptic behavior taking into account the impact of spatiotemporal patterns has been achieved [171–173]. Moving from the standpoint of the device to that of the system, in-memory computing with memristive devices is opening the way to the exploration of new learning algorithms exhibiting strong similarity with human experience, such as reinforcement learning [186], which has already been shown to enable complex tasks [187].

Finally, memristive devices are receiving increasing interest for the development of other computing concepts by neuromorphic networks with high computational power, such as the Hopfield recurrent neural network [188]. Although high acceleration performance has been achieved for the solution of hard constraint-satisfaction problems (CSPs), such as the Sudoku puzzle, via CMOS-based circuits [189], FPGA [190], and quantum computing circuits [191], the use of memristive devices in crossbar-based neural networks can further speed up computation by the introduction of a key resource as the noise [192] without the requirement of additional sources [193]. Moreover, very recent studies have also evidenced the strong potential of memristive devices for the execution of complex algebraic tasks, including the solution of linear systems and differential equations, such as the Schrödinger and Fourier equations, in crossbar arrays in only one computational step [16], thus overcoming the latency of iterative approaches [15]. Therefore, these achievements suggest CMOS/memristive devices as enablers of novel high-efficiency computing paradigms capable of revolutionizing many fields of our society.

7. Conclusions

This work provides an overview of the most promising devices for neuromorphic computing covering both CMOS and memristive device concepts. Physical MVM in memristive/CMOS crossbar arrays implementing DNNs and SNNs has enabled both fundamental cognitive applications, such as image and speech recognition, and the solution of algebraic and constraint-satisfaction problems in hardware. These milestones can thus pave the way to highly powerful and energy-efficient neuromorphic hardware based on CMOS/memristive technologies, making AI increasingly pervasive in future society.

Author Contributions: Writing—original draft preparation, V.M. and G.M.; writing—review and editing, V.M., G.M., D.I. and C.M.C.; visualization, V.M. and G.M.; supervision, D.I. and C.M.C.; funding acquisition, D.I. All authors have read and agreed to the published version of the manuscript.

Funding: This work has received funding from the European Research Council (ERC) under the European Union's Horizon 2020 research and innovation programme (grant agreement no. 648635).

Conflicts of Interest: The authors declare no conflict of interest.

References

1. Moore, G.E. Cramming more components onto integrated circuits. *Electronics* **1965**, *38*, 114–117. [CrossRef]
2. Dennard, R.H.; Gaensslen, F.H.; Yu, H.-N.; Rideout, V.L.; Bassous, E.; LeBlanc, A.R. Design of ion-implanted MOSFET's with very small physical dimensions. *IEEE J. Solid State Circuits* **1974**, *9*, 256–268. [CrossRef]
3. Horowitz, M. Computing's energy problem (and what we can do about it). In Proceedings of the 2014 IEEE International Solid-State Circuits Conference (ISSCC), San Francisco, CA, USA, 9–13 February 2014; pp. 10–14. [CrossRef]
4. Waldrop, M.M. The chips are down for Moore's law. *Nature* **2016**, *530*, 144–147. [CrossRef] [PubMed]
5. Robertson, J. High dielectric constant oxides. *Eur. Phys. J. Appl. Phys.* **2004**, *28*, 265–291. [CrossRef]
6. Ferain, I.; Colinge, C.A.; Colinge, J.-P. Multigate transistor as the future of classical metal-oxide-semiconductor field-effect transistors. *Nature* **2011**, *479*, 310–316. [CrossRef]
7. Kuhn, K. Considerations for ultimate CMOS scaling. *IEEE Trans. Electron Devices* **2012**, *59*, 1813–1828. [CrossRef]
8. Shulaker, M.M.; Hills, G.; Park, R.S.; Howe, R.T.; Saraswat, K.; Wong, H.-S.P.; Mitra, S. Three-dimensional integration of nanotechnologies for computing and data storage on a single chip. *Nature* **2017**, *547*, 74–78. [CrossRef]
9. Wong, H.-S.P.; Salahuddin, S. Memory leads the way to better computing. *Nat. Nanotechnol.* **2015**, *10*, 191–194. [CrossRef]
10. Truong, S.N.; Min, K.-S. New memristor-based crossbar array architecture with 50–% area reduction and 48–% power saving for matrix-vector multiplication of analog neuromorphic computing. *J. Semicond. Technol. Sci.* **2014**, *14*, 356–363. [CrossRef]
11. Ielmini, D.; Wong, H.-S.P. In-memory computing with resistive switching devices. *Nat. Electron.* **2018**, *1*, 333–343. [CrossRef]
12. Burr, G.W.; Shelby, R.M.; di Nolfo, C.; Jang, J.W.; Shenoy, R.S.; Narayanan, P.; Virwani, K.; Giacometti, E.U.; Kurdi, B.; Hwang, H. Experimental demonstration and tolerancing of a large-scale neural network (165,000 synapses) using phase-change memory as the synaptic weight element. In Proceedings of the 2014 IEEE International Electron Devices Meeting (IEDM), San Francisco, CA, USA, 15–17 December 2014; pp. 697–700. [CrossRef]
13. Prezioso, M.; Merrikh-Bayat, F.; Hoskins, B.D.; Adam, G.C.; Likharev, K.K.; Strukov, D.B. Training and operation of an integrated neuromorphic network based on metal-oxide memristors. *Nature* **2015**, *521*, 61–64. [CrossRef] [PubMed]

14. Li, C.; Hu, M.; Li, Y.; Jiang, H.; Ge, N.; Montgomery, E.; Zhang, J.; Song, W.; Dávila, N.; Graves, C.E.; et al. Analogue signal and image processing with large memristor crossbars. *Nat. Electron.* **2018**, *1*, 52–59. [CrossRef]
15. Le Gallo, M.; Sebastian, A.; Mathis, R.; Manica, M.; Giefers, H.; Tuma, T.; Bekas, C.; Curioni, A.; Eleftheriou, E. Mixed-precision in-memory computing. *Nat. Electron.* **2018**, *1*, 246–253. [CrossRef]
16. Sun, Z.; Pedretti, G.; Ambrosi, E.; Bricalli, A.; Wang, W.; Ielmini, D. Solving matrix equations in one step with crosspoint resistive arrays. *Proc. Natl. Acad. Sci. USA* **2019**, *116*, 4123–4128. [CrossRef]
17. Sun, Z.; Pedretti, G.; Bricalli, A.; Ielmini, D. One-step regression and classification with crosspoint resistive memory arrays. *Sci. Adv.* **2019**, in press.
18. Indiveri, G.; Liu, S.-C. Memory and information processing in neuromorphic systems. *Proc. IEEE* **2015**, *103*, 1379–1397. [CrossRef]
19. McCulloch, W.S.; Pitts, W.A. A logical calculus of the ideas immanent in nervous activity. *Bull. Math. Biophys.* **1943**, *5*, 115–133. [CrossRef]
20. Rosenblatt, F. *The Perceptron: A Perceiving and Recognizing Automaton Project Para*; Report 85-460-1; Cornell Aeronautical Laboratory: Buffalo, NY, USA, 1957.
21. Rumelhart, D.E.; Hinton, G.E.; Williams, R.J. Learning representation by backpropagating errors. *Nature* **1986**, *323*, 533–536. [CrossRef]
22. LeCun, Y.; Bottou, L.; Bengio, Y.; Haffner, P. Gradient-based learning applied to document recognition. *Proc. IEEE* **1998**, *86*, 2278–2324. [CrossRef]
23. LeCun, Y.; Bengio, Y.; Hinton, G. Deep learning. *Nature* **2015**, *521*, 436–444. [CrossRef]
24. Coates, A.; Huval, B.; Wang, T.; Wu, D.; Ng, A.Y.; Catanzaro, B.C. Deep learning with COTS HPC systems. In Proceedings of the 30th International Conference on Machine Learning (ICML), Atlanta, GA, USA, 16–21 June 2013; Volume 28, pp. 1337–1345.
25. Jouppi, N.P.; Young, C.; Patil, N.; Patterson, D.; Agrawal, G.; Bajwa, R.; Bates, S.; Bathia, S.; Boden, N.; Borchers, A.; et al. In-Datacenter performance analysis of a Tensor Processing Unit^{TM}. In Proceedings of the 44th International Symposium on Computer Architecture (ISCA), Toronto, ON, Canada, 24–28 June 2017; pp. 1–12. [CrossRef]
26. Hu, M.; Graves, C.E.; Li, C.; Li, Y.; Ge, N.; Montgomery, E.; Davila, N.; Jiang, H.; Williams, R.S.; Yang, J.J.; et al. Memristor-based analog computation and neural network classification with a dot product engine. *Adv. Mater.* **2018**, *30*, 1705914. [CrossRef] [PubMed]
27. Xia, Q.; Yang, J.J. Memristive crossbar arrays for brain-inspired computing. *Nat. Mater.* **2019**, *18*, 309–323. [CrossRef] [PubMed]
28. Merolla, P.A.; Arthur, J.V.; Alvarez-Icaza, R.; Cassidy, A.S.; Sawada, J.; Akopyan, F.; Jackson, B.L.; Imam, N.; Guo, C.; Nakamura, Y.; et al. A million spiking-neuron integrated circuit with a scalable communication network and interface. *Science* **2014**, *345*, 668–673. [CrossRef] [PubMed]
29. Moradi, S.; Qiao, N.; Stefanini, F.; Indiveri, G. A scalable multicore architecture with heterogeneous memory structures for dynamic neuromorphic asynchronous processors (DYNAPs). *IEEE Trans. Biomed. Circuits Syst.* **2017**, *12*, 106–122. [CrossRef] [PubMed]
30. Ramakrishnan, S.; Hasler, P.; Gordon, C. Floating gate synapses with spike-time-dependent plasticity. *IEEE Trans. Biomed. Circuits Syst.* **2011**, *5*, 244–252. [CrossRef] [PubMed]
31. Strukov, D.B.; Snider, G.S.; Stewart, D.R.; Williams, R.S. The missing memristor found. *Nature* **2008**, *453*, 80–83. [CrossRef]
32. Kuzum, D.; Yu, S.; Wong, H.-S.P. Synaptic electronics: Materials, devices and applications. *Nanotechnology* **2013**, *24*, 382001. [CrossRef]
33. Burr, G.W.; Shelby, R.M.; Sebastian, A.; Kim, S.; Kim, S.; Sidler, S.; Virwani, K.; Ishii, M.; Narayanan, P.; Fumarola, A.; et al. Neuromorphic computing using non-volatile memory. *Adv. Phys. X* **2017**, *2*, 89–124. [CrossRef]
34. Yu, S. Neuro-inspired computing with emerging nonvolatile memory. *Proc. IEEE* **2018**, *106*, 260–285. [CrossRef]
35. Ielmini, D.; Ambrogio, S. Emerging neuromorphic devices. *Nanotechnology* **2020**, *31*, 092001. [CrossRef]
36. Sze, V.; Chen, Y.H.; Yang, T.-J.; Emer, J.S. Efficient processing of Deep Neural Networks: A tutorial and survey. *Proc. IEEE* **2017**, *105*, 2295–2329. [CrossRef]

37. Maass, W. Networks of spiking neurons: The third generation of neural network models. *Neural Netw.* **1997**, *10*, 1659–1671. [CrossRef]
38. Bi, G.-Q.; Poo, M.-M. Synaptic modifications in cultured hippocampal neurons: Dependence on spike timing, synaptic strength, and postsynaptic cell type. *J. Neurosci.* **1998**, *18*, 10464–10472. [CrossRef] [PubMed]
39. Sjostrom, P.J.; Turrigiano, G.G.; Nelson, S.B. Rate, timing, and cooperativity jointly determine cortical synaptic plasticity. *Neuron* **2001**, *32*, 1149–1164. [CrossRef]
40. Gjorgjieva, J.; Clopath, C.; Audet, J.; Pfister, J.P. A triplet spike timing dependent plasticity model generalizes the Bienenstock-Cooper-Munro rule to higher-order spatiotemporal correlations. *Proc. Natl. Acad. Sci. USA* **2011**, *108*, 19383–19388. [CrossRef] [PubMed]
41. Pfister, J.-P.; Gerstner, W. Triplets of spikes in a model of spike timing-dependent plasticity. *J. Neurosci.* **2006**, *26*, 9673–9682. [CrossRef]
42. Rachmuth, G.; Shouval, H.-Z.; Bear, M.F.; Poon, C.-S. A biophysically-based neuromorphic model of spike rate- and timing-dependent plasticity. *Proc. Natl. Acad. Sci. USA* **2011**, *108*, E1266–E1274. [CrossRef]
43. Milo, V.; Pedretti, G.; Carboni, R.; Calderoni, A.; Ramaswamy, N.; Ambrogio, S.; Ielmini, D. A 4-Transistors/1-Resistor hybrid synapse based on resistive switching memory (RRAM) capable of spike-rate-dependent plasticity (SRDP). *IEEE Trans. Very Large Scale Integrat. (VLSI) Syst.* **2018**, *26*, 2806–2815. [CrossRef]
44. Monzio Compagnoni, C.; Goda, A.; Spinelli, A.S.; Feeley, P.; Lacaita, A.L.; Visconti, A. Reviewing the evolution of the NAND Flash technology. *Proc. IEEE* **2017**, *105*, 1609–1633. [CrossRef]
45. Bez, R.; Camerlenghi, E.; Modelli, A.; Visconti, A. Introduction to Flash memory. *Proc. IEEE* **2003**, *91*, 489–502. [CrossRef]
46. Hasler, P.; Diorio, C.; Minch, B.A.; Mead, C. Single transistor learning synapses. In Proceedings of the 7th International Conference on Neural Information Processing Systems (NIPS), Denver, CO, USA, 28 November–1 December 1994; pp. 817–824.
47. Diorio, C.; Hasler, P.; Minch, B.A.; Mead, C.A. A single-transistor silicon synapse. *IEEE Trans. Electron Devices* **1996**, *43*, 1972–1980. [CrossRef]
48. Diorio, C.; Hasler, P.; Minch, B.A.; Mead, C.A. A floating-gate MOS learning array with locally computed weight updates. *IEEE Trans. Electron Devices* **1997**, *44*, 2281–2289. [CrossRef]
49. Kim, H.; Park, J.; Kwon, M.-W.; Lee, J.-H.; Park, B.-G. Silicon-based floating-body synaptic transistor with frequency-dependent short- and long-term memories. *IEEE Electron Device Lett.* **2016**, *37*, 249–252. [CrossRef]
50. Kim, H.; Hwang, S.; Park, J.; Yun, S.; Lee, J.-H.; Park, B.-G. Spiking neural network using synaptic transistors and neuron circuits for pattern recognition with noisy images. *IEEE Electron Device Lett.* **2018**, *39*, 630–633. [CrossRef]
51. Kim, C.-H.; Lee, S.; Woo, S.Y.; Kang, W.-M.; Lim, S.; Bae, J.-H.; Kim, J.; Lee, J.-H. Demonstration of unsupervised learning with spike-timing-dependent plasticity using a TFT-type NOR Flash memory array. *IEEE Trans. Electron Devices* **2018**, *65*, 1774–1780. [CrossRef]
52. Technology is driving the latest automotive designs. Available online: http://www.sst.com (accessed on 20 December 2019).
53. Merrikh Bayat, F.; Guo, X.; Om'mani, H.A.; Do, N.; Likharev, K.K.; Strukov, D.B. Redesigning commercial floating-gate memory for analog computing applications. In Proceedings of the IEEE International Symposium on Circuits and Systems (ISCAS), Lisbon, Portugal, 24–27 May 2015; pp. 1921–1924. [CrossRef]
54. Guo, X.; Merrikh Bayat, F.; Bavandpour, M.; Klachko, M.; Mahmoodi, M.R.; Prezioso, M.; Likharev, K.K.; Strukov, D.B. Fast, energy-efficient, robust, and reproducible mixed-signal neuromorphic classifier based on embedded NOR flash memory technology. In Proceedings of the 2017 IEEE International Electron Devices Meeting (IEDM), San Francisco, CA, USA, 2–6 December 2017; pp. 151–154. [CrossRef]
55. Merrikh Bayat, F.; Guo, X.; Klachko, M.; Prezioso, M.; Likharev, K.K.; Strukov, D.B. High-performance mixed-signal neurocomputing with nanoscale floating-gate memory cell arrays. *IEEE Trans. Neural Netw. Learning Syst.* **2018**, *29*, 4782–4790. [CrossRef] [PubMed]
56. Guo, X.; Merrikh Bayat, F.; Prezioso, M.; Chen, Y.; Nguyen, B.; Do, N.; Strukov, D.B. Temperature-insensitive analog vector-by-matrix multiplier based on 55 nm NOR flash memory cells. In Proceedings of the IEEE Custom Integrated Circuits Conference (CICC), Austin, TX, USA, 30 April–3 May 2017; pp. 1–4. [CrossRef]

57. Malavena, G.; Spinelli, A.S.; Monzio Compagnoni, C. Implementing spike-timing-dependent plasticity and unsupervised learning in a mainstream NOR Flash memory array. In Proceedings of the 2018 IEEE International Electron Devices Meeting (IEDM), San Francisco, CA, USA, 1–5 December 2018; pp. 35–38. [CrossRef]
58. Malavena, G.; Filippi, M.; Spinelli, A.S.; Monzio Compagnoni, C. Unsupervised learning by spike-timing-dependent plasticity in a mainstream NOR Flash memory array: Part I—Cell operation. *IEEE Trans. Electron Devices* **2019**, *66*, 4727–4732. [CrossRef]
59. Malavena, G.; Filippi, M.; Spinelli, A.S.; Monzio Compagnoni, C. Unsupervised learning by spike-timing-dependent plasticity in a mainstream NOR Flash memory array: Part II—Array learning. *IEEE Trans. Electron Devices* **2019**, *66*, 4733–4738. [CrossRef]
60. Malavena, G.; Petrò, S.; Spinelli, A.S.; Monzio Compagnoni, C. Impact of program accuracy and random telegraph noise on the performance of NOR Flash-based neuromorphic classifier. In Proceedings of the 49th European Solid-State Device Research Conference (ESSDERC), Cracow, Poland, 23–26 September 2019; pp. 122–125. [CrossRef]
61. Waser, R.; Aono, M. Nanoionics-based resistive switching memories. *Nat. Mater.* **2007**, *6*, 833–840. [CrossRef] [PubMed]
62. Wong, H.-S.P.; Lee, H.-Y.; Yu, S.; Chen, Y.-S.; Wu, Y.; Chen, P.-S.; Lee, B.; Chen, F.T.; Tsai, M.-J. Metal oxide RRAM. *Proc. IEEE* **2012**, *100*, 1951–1970. [CrossRef]
63. Ielmini, D. Resistive switching memories based on metal oxides: Mechanisms, reliability and scaling. *Semicond. Sci. Technol.* **2016**, *31*, 063002. [CrossRef]
64. Ielmini, D. Modeling the universal set/reset characteristics of bipolar RRAM by field- and temperature-driven filament growth. *IEEE Trans. Electron Devices* **2011**, *58*, 4309–4317. [CrossRef]
65. Larentis, S.; Nardi, F.; Balatti, S.; Gilmer, D.C.; Ielmini, D. Resistive switching by voltage-driven ion migration in bipolar RRAM—Part II: Modeling. *IEEE Trans. Electron Devices* **2012**, *59*, 2468–2475. [CrossRef]
66. Ambrogio, S.; Balatti, S.; Gilmer, D.C.; Ielmini, D. Analytical modeling of oxide-based bipolar resistive memories and complementary resistive switches. *IEEE Trans. Electron Devices* **2014**, *61*, 2378–2386. [CrossRef]
67. Lee, H.Y.; Chen, P.S.; Wu, T.Y.; Chen, Y.S.; Wang, C.C.; Tzeng, P.J.; Lin, C.H.; Chen, F.; Lien, C.H.; Tsai, M.-J. Low power and high speed bipolar switching with a thin reactive Ti buffer layer in robust HfO_2 based RRAM. In Proceedings of the 2008 IEEE International Electron Devices Meeting (IEDM), San Francisco, CA, USA, 15–17 December 2008; pp. 1–4. [CrossRef]
68. Lee, M.-J.; Lee, C.B.; Lee, D.; Lee, S.R.; Chang, M.; Hur, J.H.; Kim, Y.-B.; Kim, C.-J.; Seo, D.H.; Seo, S.; et al. A fast, high-endurance and scalable non-volatile memory device made from asymmetric Ta_2O_{5-x}/TaO_{2-x} bilayer structures. *Nat. Mater.* **2011**, *10*, 625–630. [CrossRef] [PubMed]
69. Park, S.-G.; Magyari-Köpe, B.; Nishi, Y. Impact of oxygen vacancy ordering on the formation of a conductive filament in TiO_2 for resistive switching memory. *IEEE Electron Device Lett.* **2011**, *32*, 197–199. [CrossRef]
70. Bricalli, A.; Ambrosi, E.; Laudato, M.; Maestro, M.; Rodriguez, R.; Ielmini, D. Resistive switching device technology based on silicon oxide for improved on-off ratio—Part I: Memory devices. *IEEE Trans. Electron Devices* **2018**, *65*, 115–121. [CrossRef]
71. Chien, W.C.; Chen, Y.C.; Lai, E.K.; Lee, F.M.; Lin, Y.Y.; Chuang, A.T.H.; Chang, K.P.; Yao, Y.D.; Chou, T.H.; Lin, H.M.; et al. A study of switching mechanism and electrode material of fully CMOS compatible tungsten oxide ReRAM. *Appl. Phys. A* **2011**, *102*, 901–907. [CrossRef]
72. Kozicki, M.N.; Barnaby, H.J. Conductive bridge random access memory—materials, devices and applications. *Semicond. Sci. Technol.* **2016**, *31*, 113001. [CrossRef]
73. Russo, U.; Ielmini, D.; Cagli, C.; Lacaita, A.L. Filament conduction and reset mechanism in NiO-based resistive-switching memory (RRAM) devices. *IEEE Trans. Electron Devices* **2009**, *56*, 186–192. [CrossRef]
74. Lee, H.D.; Magyari-Köpe, B.; Nishi, Y. Model of metallic filament formation and rupture in NiO for unipolar switching. *Phys. Rev. B* **2010**, *81*, 193202. [CrossRef]
75. Ielmini, D.; Bruchhaus, R.; Waser, R. Thermochemical resistive switching: Materials, mechanisms and scaling projections. *Phase Transit.* **2011**, *84*, 570–602. [CrossRef]
76. Sawa, A. Resistive switching in transition metal oxides. *Mater. Today* **2008**, *11*, 28–36. [CrossRef]
77. Russo, U.; Kamalanathan, D.; Ielmini, D.; Lacaita, A.L.; Kozicki, M.N. Study of multilevel programming in Programmable Metallization Cell (PMC) memory. *IEEE Trans. Electron Devices* **2009**, *56*, 1040–1047. [CrossRef]

78. Balatti, S.; Larentis, S.; Gilmer, D.C.; Ielmini, D. Multiple memory states in resistive switching devices through controlled size and orientation of the conductive filament. *Adv. Mater.* **2013**, *25*, 1474–1478. [CrossRef] [PubMed]
79. Yu, S.; Gao, B.; Fang, Z.; Yu, H.; Kang, J.; Wong, H.-S.P. A low energy oxide-based electronic synaptic device for neuromorphic visual systems with tolerance to device variation. *Adv. Mater.* **2013**, *25*, 1774–1779. [CrossRef]
80. Zhao, L.; Chen, H.-Y.; Wu, S.-C.; Jiang, Z.; Yu, S.; Hou, T.-H.; Wong, H.-S.P.; Nishi, Y. Multi-level control of conductive nano-filament evolution in HfO_2 ReRAM by pulse-train operations. *Nanoscale* **2014**, *6*, 5698–5702. [CrossRef]
81. Prakash, A.; Park, J.; Song, J.; Woo, J.; Cha, E.-J.; Hwang, H. Demonstration of low power 3-bit multilevel cell characteristics in a TaO_x-based RRAM by stack engineering. *IEEE Electron Device Lett.* **2015**, *36*, 32–34. [CrossRef]
82. Govoreanu, B.; Kar, G.S.; Chen, Y.-Y.; Paraschiv, V.; Kubicek, S.; Fantini, A.; Radu, I.P.; Goux, L.; Clima, S.; Degraeve, R.; et al. 10×10 nm^2 Hf/HfO_x crossbar resistive RAM with excellent performance, reliability and low-energy operation. In Proceedings of the 2011 IEEE International Electron Devices Meeting (IEDM), Washington, DC, USA, 5–7 December 2011; pp. 729–732. [CrossRef]
83. Baek, I.G.; Park, C.J.; Ju, H.; Seong, D.J.; Ahn, H.S.; Kim, J.H.; Yang, M.K.; Song, S.H.; Kim, E.M.; Park, S.O.; et al. Realization of vertical resistive memory (VRRAM) using cost effective 3D process. In Proceedings of the 2011 IEEE International Electron Devices Meeting (IEDM), Washington, DC, USA, 5–7 December 2011; pp. 737–740. [CrossRef]
84. Yamada, N.; Ohno, E.; Nishiuchi, K.; Akahira, N.; Takao, M. Rapid-phase transitions of GeTe-Sb_2Te_3 pseudobinary amorphous thin films for an optical disk memory. *J. Appl. Phys.* **1991**, *69*, 2849–2856. [CrossRef]
85. Raoux, S.; Welnic, W.; Ielmini, D. Phase change materials and their application to non-volatile memories. *Chem. Rev.* **2010**, *110*, 240–267. [CrossRef]
86. Burr, G.W.; BrightSky, M.J.; Sebastian, A.; Cheng, H.Y.; Wu, J.Y.; Kim, S.; Sosa, N.E.; Papandreou, N.; Lung, H.-L.; Pozidis, H.; et al. Recent progress in Phase-Change Memory technology. *IEEE J. Emerg. Sel. Top. Circuits Syst. JETCAS* **2016**, *6*, 146–162. [CrossRef]
87. Fong, S.W.; Neumann, C.M.; Wong, H.-S.P. Phase-Change Memory—Towards a storage-class memory. *IEEE Trans. Electron Devices* **2017**, *64*, 4374–4385. [CrossRef]
88. Ielmini, D.; Lacaita, A.L.; Pirovano, A.; Pellizzer, F.; Bez, R. Analysis of phase distribution in phase-change nonvolatile memories. *IEEE Electron Device Lett.* **2004**, *25*, 507–509. [CrossRef]
89. Athmanathan, A.; Stanisavljevic, M.; Papandreou, N.; Pozidis, H.; Eleftheriou, E. Multilevel-cell Phase-Change Memory: A viable technology. *IEEE J. Emerg. Sel. Top. Circuits Syst. JETCAS* **2016**, *6*, 87–100. [CrossRef]
90. Chen, Y.C.; Rettner, C.T.; Raoux, S.; Burr, G.W.; Chen, S.H.; Shelby, R.M.; Salinga, M.; Risk, W.P.; Happ, T.D.; McClelland, G.M.; et al. Ultra-thin phase-change bridge memory device using GeSb. In Proceedings of the 2006 IEEE International Electron Devices Meeting (IEDM), San Francisco, CA, USA, 11–13 December 2006; pp. 1–4. [CrossRef]
91. Morikawa, T.; Kurotsuchi, K.; Kinoshita, M.; Matsuzaki, N.; Matsui, Y.; Fujisaki, Y.; Hanzawa, S.; Kotabe, A.; Terao, M.; Moriya, H.; et al. Doped In-Ge-Te Phase Change Memory featuring stable operation and good data retention. In Proceedings of the 2007 IEEE International Electron Devices Meeting (IEDM), Washington, DC, USA, 10–12 December 2007; pp. 307–310. [CrossRef]
92. Zuliani, P.; Varesi, E.; Palumbo, E.; Borghi, M.; Tortorelli, I.; Erbetta, D.; Dalla Libera, G.; Pessina, N.; Gandolfo, A.; Prelini, C.; et al. Overcoming temperature limitations in phase change memories with optimized $Ge_xSb_yTe_z$. *IEEE Trans. Electron Devices* **2013**, *60*, 4020–4026. [CrossRef]
93. Chappert, C.; Fert, A.; Van Dau, F.N. The emergence of spin electronics in data storage. *Nat. Mater.* **2007**, *6*, 813–823. [CrossRef]
94. Kent, A.D.; Worledge, D.C. A new spin on magnetic memories. *Nat. Nanotech.* **2015**, *10*, 187–191. [CrossRef]
95. Locatelli, N.; Cros, V.; Grollier, J. Spin-torque building blocks. *Nat. Mater.* **2014**, *13*, 11–20. [CrossRef]
96. Julliere, M. Tunneling between ferromagnetic films. *Phys. Lett. A* **1975**, *54*, 225–226. [CrossRef]
97. Slonczewski, J.C. Current-driven excitation of magnetic multilayers. *J. Magn. Magn. Mater.* **1996**, *159*, L1–L7. [CrossRef]

98. Berger, L. Emission of spin waves by a magnetic multilayer traversed by a current. *Phys. Rev. B* **1996**, *54*, 9353–9358. [CrossRef] [PubMed]
99. Novak, J.J. Dependence of voltage and size on write error rates in spin-transfer torque magnetic random-access memory. *IEEE Magn. Lett.* **2016**, *7*, 1–4. [CrossRef]
100. Saida, D.; Kashiwada, S.; Yakabe, M.; Daibou, T.; Hase, N.; Fukumoto, M.; Miwa, S.; Suzuki, Y.; Nuguchi, H.; Fujita, S.; et al. Sub-3 ns pulse with sub-100 µA switching of 1x-2x nm perpendicular MTJ for high-performance embedded STT-MRAM towards sub-20 nm CMOS. In Proceedings of the 2016 IEEE Symposium on VLSI Technology, Honolulu, HI, USA, 14–16 June 2016; pp. 1–2. [CrossRef]
101. Carboni, R.; Ambrogio, S.; Chen, W.; Siddik, M.; Harms, J.; Lyle, A.; Kula, W.; Sandhu, G.; Ielmini, D. Understanding cycling endurance in perpendicular spin-transfer torque (p-STT) magnetic memory. In Proceedings of the 2016 IEEE International Electron Devices Meeting (IEDM), San Francisco, CA, USA, 3–7 December 2016; pp. 572–575. [CrossRef]
102. Kan, J.J.; Park, C.; Ching, C.; Ahn, J.; Xie, Y.; Pakala, M.; Kang, S.H. A study on practically unlimited endurance of STT-MRAM. *IEEE Trans. Electron Devices* **2017**, *64*, 3639–3646. [CrossRef]
103. Böscke, T.S.; Mueller, J.; Brauhaus, D.; Schroeder, U.; Boettger, U. Ferroelectricity in hafnium oxide thin films. *Appl. Phys. Lett.* **2011**, *99*, 102903. [CrossRef]
104. Takashima, D.; Takeuchi, Y.; Miyakawa, T.; Itoh, Y.; Ogiwara, R.; Kamoshida, M.; Hoya, K.; Doumae, S.M.; Ozaki, T.; Kanaya, H.; et al. A 76-mm^2 8-Mb chain ferroelectric memory. *IEEE J. Solid State Circuits* **2001**, *36*, 1713–1720. [CrossRef]
105. Sakai, S.; Takahashi, M.; Takeuchi, K.; Li, Q.H.; Horiuchi, T.; Wang, S.; Yun, K.Y.; Takamiya, M.; Sakurai, T. Highly scalable Fe(Ferroelectric)-NAND Cell with MFIS(Metal-Ferroelectric-Insulator-Semiconductor) structure for sub-10nm Tera-bit capacity NAND Flash memories. In Proceedings of the Joint Non-Volatile Semiconductor Memory Workshop and International Conference on Memory Technology and Design, Opio, France, 18–22 May 2008; pp. 103–105. [CrossRef]
106. Mikolajick, T.; Dehm, C.; Hartner, W.; Kasko, I.; Kastner, M.J.; Nagel, N.; Moert, M.; Mazure, C. FeRAM technology for high density applications. *Microelectron. Reliab.* **2001**, *41*, 947–950. [CrossRef]
107. Mulaosmanovic, H.; Ocker, J.; Müller, S.; Noack, M.; Müller, J.; Polakowski, P.; Mikolajick, T.; Slesazeck, S. Novel ferroelectric FET based synapse for neuromorphic systems. In Proceedings of the 2017 IEEE Symposium on VLSI Technology, Kyoto, Japan, 5–8 June 2017; pp. T176–T177. [CrossRef]
108. Tang, J.; Bishop, D.; Kim, S.; Copel, M.; Gokmen, T.; Todorov, T.; Shin, S.H.; Lee, K.-T.; Solomon, P.; Chan, K.; et al. ECRAM as scalable synaptic cell for high-speed, low-power neuromorphic computing. In Proceedings of the 2018 IEEE International Electron Devices Meeting (IEDM), San Francisco, CA, USA, 1–5 December 2018; pp. 292–295. [CrossRef]
109. Cubukcu, M.; Boulle, O.; Drouard, M.; Garello, K.; Avci, C.O.; Miron, I.M.; Langer, J.; Ocker, B.; Gambardella, P.; Gaudin, G. Spin-orbit torque magnetization switching of a three-terminal perpendicular magnetic tunnel junction. *Appl. Phys. Lett.* **2014**, *104*, 042406. [CrossRef]
110. Sangwan, V.K.; Lee, H.-S.; Bergeron, H.; Balla, I.; Beck, M.E.; Chen, K.-S.; Hersam, M.C. Multi-terminal memtransistors from polycrystalline monolayer molybdenum disulfide. *Nature* **2018**, *544*, 500–504. [CrossRef]
111. Zhu, X.; Li, D.; Liang, X.; Lu, W.D. Ionic modulation and ionic coupling effects in MoS_2 devices for neuromorphic computing. *Nat. Mater.* **2019**, *18*, 141–148. [CrossRef]
112. Bhowmik, D.; Saxena, U.; Dankar, A.; Verma, A.; Kaushik, D.; Chatterjee, S.; Singh, U. On-chip learning for domain wall synapse based fully connected neural network. *J. Magn. Magn. Mater.* **2019**, *489*, 165434. [CrossRef]
113. Sharad, M.; Augustine, C.; Panagopoulos, G.; Roy, K. Spin-based neuron model with domain wall magnets as synapse. *IEEE Trans. Nanotech.* **2012**, *11*, 843–853. [CrossRef]
114. Trentzsch, M.; Flachowsky, S.; Richter, R.; Paul, J.; Reimer, B.; Utess, D.; Jansen, S.; Mulaosmanovic, H.; Müller, S.; Slesazeck, S.; et al. A 28nm HKMG super low power embedded NVM technology based on ferroelectric FETs. In Proceedings of the 2016 IEEE International Electron Devices Meeting (IEDM), San Francisco, CA, USA, 3–7 December 2016; pp. 294–297. [CrossRef]
115. Florent, K.; Pesic, M.; Subirats, A.; Banerjee, K.; Lavizzari, S.; Arreghini, A.; Di Piazza, L.; Potoms, G.; Sebaai, F.; McMitchell, S.R.C.; et al. Vertical ferroelectric HfO_2 FET based on 3-D NAND architecture: Towards dense low-power memory. In Proceedings of the 2018 IEEE International Electron Devices Meeting (IEDM), San Francisco, CA, USA, 1–5 December 2018; pp. 43–46. [CrossRef]

116. Jerry, M.; Chen, P.-Y.; Zhang, J.; Sharma, P.; Ni, K.; Yu, S.; Datta, S. Ferroelectric FET analog synapse for acceleration of deep neural network training. In Proceedings of the 2017 IEEE International Electron Devices Meeting (IEDM), San Francisco, CA, USA, 2–6 December 2017; pp. 139–142. [CrossRef]
117. Mulaosmanovic, H.; Chicca, E.; Bertele, M.; Mikolajick, T.; Slesazeck, S. Mimicking biological neurons with a nanoscale ferroelectric transistor. *Nanoscale* **2018**, *10*, 21755–21763. [CrossRef] [PubMed]
118. Fang, Y.; Gomez, J.; Wang, Z.; Datta, S.; Khan, A.I.; Raychowdhury, A. Neuro-mimetic dynamics of a ferroelectric FET-based spiking neuron. *IEEE Electron Device Lett.* **2019**, *40*, 1213–1216. [CrossRef]
119. Fuller, E.J.; El Gabaly, F.; Leonard, F.; Agarwal, S.; Plimpton, S.J.; Jacobs-Gedrim, R.B.; James, C.D.; Marinella, M.J.; Talin, A.A. Li-ion synaptic transistor for low power analog computing. *Adv. Mater.* **2017**, *29*, 1604310. [CrossRef] [PubMed]
120. Van de Burgt, Y.; Lubberman, E.; Fuller, E.J.; Keene, S.T.; Faria, G.C.; Agarwal, S.; Marinella, M.J.; Talin, A.A.; Salleo, A. A non-volatile organic electrochemical device as a low-voltage artificial synapse for neuromorphic computing. *Nat. Mater.* **2017**, *16*, 414–418. [CrossRef] [PubMed]
121. Garello, K.; Avci, C.O.; Miron, I.M.; Baumgartner, M.; Ghosh, A.; Auffret, S.; Boulle, O.; Gaudin, G.; Gambardella, P. Ultrafast magnetization switching by spin-orbit torques. *Appl. Phys. Lett.* **2014**, *105*, 212402. [CrossRef]
122. Lo Conte, R.; Hrabec, A.; Mihai, A.P.; Schulz, T.; Noh, S.-J.; Marrows, C.H.; Moore, T.A.; Kläui, M. Spin-orbit torque-driven magnetization switching and thermal effects studied in Ta\CoFeB\MgO nanowires. *Appl. Phys. Lett.* **2014**, *105*, 122404. [CrossRef]
123. Garello, K.; Miron, I.M.; Avci, C.O.; Freimuth, F.; Mokrousov, Y.; Blügel, S.; Auffret, S.; Boulle, O.; Gaudin, G.; Gambardella, P. Symmetry and magnitude of spin-orbit torques in ferromagnetic heterostructures. *Nat. Nanotechnol.* **2013**, *8*, 587–593. [CrossRef]
124. Miron, I.M.; Garello, K.; Gaudin, G.; Zermatten, P.-J.; Costache, M.V.; Auffret, S.; Bandiera, S.; Rodmacq, B.; Schuhl, A.; Gambardella, P. Perpendicular switching of a single ferromagnetic layer induced by in-plane current injection. *Nature* **2011**, *476*, 189–193. [CrossRef]
125. Borders, W.A.; Fukami, S.; Ohno, H. Characterization of spin-orbit torque-controlled synapse device for artificial neural network applications. *Jpn. J. Appl. Phys.* **2018**, *57*, 1002B2. [CrossRef]
126. Sengupta, A.; Choday, S.H.; Kim, Y.; Roy, K. Spin orbit torque based electronic neuron. *Appl. Phys. Lett.* **2015**, *106*, 143701. [CrossRef]
127. Borders, W.A.; Akima, H.; Fukami, S.; Moriya, S.; Kurihara, S.; Horio, Y.; Sato, S.; Ohno, H. Analogue spin-orbit torque device for artificial-neural-network-based associative memory operation. *Appl. Phys. Express* **2017**, *10*, 013007. [CrossRef]
128. He, K.; Zhang, X.; Ren, S.; Sun, J. Delving deep into rectifiers: Surpassing human-level performance on ImageNet classification. In Proceedings of the IEEE International Conference on Computer Vision (ICCV), Santiago, Chile, 7–13 December 2015; pp. 1026–1034. [CrossRef]
129. Taigman, Y.; Yang, M.; Ranzato, M.; Wolf, L. DeepFace: Closing the gap to human-level performance in face verification. In Proceedings of the IEEE Conference on Computer Vision and Pattern Recognition (CVPR), Columbus, OH, USA, 23–28 June 2014; pp. 1701–1708. [CrossRef]
130. Xiong, W.; Droppo, J.; Huang, X.; Seide, F.; Seltzer, M.L.; Stolcke, A.; Yu, D.; Zweig, G. Toward human parity in conversational speech recognition. *IEEE/ACM Trans. Audio Speech Lang. Process.* **2017**, *25*, 2410–2423. [CrossRef]
131. Grossberg, S. Competitive learning: From interactive activation to adaptive resonance. *Cogn. Sci.* **1987**, *11*, 23–63. [CrossRef]
132. Whittington, J.C.R.; Bogacz, R. Theories of error back-propagation in the brain. *Trends Cogn. Sci.* **2019**, *23*, 235–250. [CrossRef] [PubMed]
133. Burr, G.W.; Shelby, R.M.; Sidler, S.; di Nolfo, C.; Jang, J.; Boybat, I.; Shenoy, R.S.; Narayanan, P.; Virwani, K.; Giacometti, E.U.; et al. Experimental demonstration and tolerancing of a large-scale neural network (165,000 synapses) using phase-change memory as the synaptic weight element. *IEEE Trans. Electron Devices* **2015**, *62*, 3498–3507. [CrossRef]
134. Woo, J.; Yu, S. Resistive memory-based analog synapse: The pursuit for linear and symmetric weight update. *IEEE Nanotechnol. Mag.* **2018**, *12*, 36–44. [CrossRef]

135. Fuller, E.J.; Keene, S.T.; Melianas, A.; Wang, Z.; Agarwal, S.; Li, Y.; Tuchman, Y.; James, C.D.; Marinella, M.J.; Yang, J.J.; et al. Parallel programming of an ionic floating-gate memory array for scalable neuromorphic computing. *Science* **2019**, *364*, 570–574. [CrossRef]
136. Yao, P.; Wu, H.; Gao, B.; Eryilmaz, S.B.; Huang, X.; Zhang, W.; Zhang, Q.; Deng, N.; Shi, L.; Wong, H.-S.P.; et al. Face classification using electronic synapses. *Nat. Commun.* **2017**, *8*, 15199. [CrossRef]
137. Li, C.; Belkin, D.; Li, Y.; Yan, P.; Hu, M.; Ge, N.; Jiang, H.; Montgomery, E.; Lin, P.; Wang, Z.; et al. Efficient and self-adaptive in-situ learning in multilayer memristor neural networks. *Nat. Commun.* **2018**, *9*, 2385. [CrossRef]
138. Ambrogio, S.; Narayanan, P.; Tsai, H.; Shelby, R.M.; Boybat, I.; di Nolfo, C.; Sidler, S.; Giordano, M.; Bodini, M.; Farinha, N.C.P.; et al. Equivalent-accuracy accelerated neural-network training using analogue memory. *Nature* **2018**, *558*, 60–67. [CrossRef] [PubMed]
139. Krizhevsky, A. Learning Multiple Layers of Features from Tiny Images. 2009. Ch. 3. Available online: https://www.cs.toronto.edu/~{}kriz/cifar.html (accessed on 20 December 2019).
140. Milo, V.; Zambelli, C.; Olivo, P.; Pérez, E.; Mahadevaiah, M.K.; Ossorio, O.G.; Wenger, C.; Ielmini, D. Multilevel HfO_2-based RRAM devices for low-power neuromorphic networks. *APL Mater.* **2019**, *7*, 081120. [CrossRef]
141. Silver, D.; Huang, A.; Maddison, C.J.; Guez, A.; Sifre, L.; van den Driessche, G.; Schrittwieser, J.; Antonoglou, I.; Panneershelvam, V.; Lanctot, M.; et al. Mastering the game of Go with deep neural networks and tree search. *Nature* **2016**, *529*, 484–489. [CrossRef] [PubMed]
142. Jo, S.H.; Chang, T.; Ebong, I.; Bhadviya, B.B.; Mazumder, P.; Lu, W. Nanoscale memristor device as synapse in neuromorphic systems. *Nano Lett.* **2010**, *10*, 1297–1301. [CrossRef]
143. Yu, S.; Wu, Y.; Jeyasingh, R.; Kuzum, D.; Wong, H.-S.P. An electronic synapse device based on metal oxide resistive switching memory for neuromorphic computation. *IEEE Trans. Electron Devices* **2011**, *58*, 2729–2737. [CrossRef]
144. Kuzum, D.; Jeyasingh, R.G.D.; Lee, B.; Wong, H.-S.P. Nanoelectronic programmable synapses based on phase change materials for brain-inspired computing. *Nano Lett.* **2012**, *12*, 2179–2186. [CrossRef]
145. Serb, A.; Bill, J.; Khiat, A.; Berdan, R.; Legenstein, R.; Prodromakis, T. Unsupervised learning in probabilistic neural networks with multi-state metal-oxide memristive synapses. *Nat. Commun.* **2016**, *7*, 12611. [CrossRef]
146. Prezioso, M.; Mahmoodi, M.R.; Merrikh-Bayat, F.; Nili, H.; Kim, H.; Vincent, A.; Strukov, D.B. Spike-timing-dependent plasticity learning of coincidence detection with passively integrated memristive circuits. *Nat. Commun.* **2018**, *9*, 5311. [CrossRef]
147. Hansen, M.; Zahari, F.; Kohlstedt, H.; Ziegler, M. Unsupervised Hebbian learning experimentally realized with analogue memristive crossbar arrays. *Sci. Rep.* **2018**, *8*, 8914. [CrossRef]
148. Boybat, I.; Le Gallo, M.; Nandakumar, S.R.; Moraitis, T.; Parnell, T.; Tuma, T.; Rajendran, B.; Leblebici, Y.; Sebastian, A.; Eleftheriou, E. Neuromorphic computing with multi-memristive synapses. *Nat. Commun.* **2018**, *9*, 2514. [CrossRef]
149. Vincent, A.F.; Larroque, J.; Locatelli, N.; Romdhane, N.B.; Bichler, O.; Gamrat, C.; Zhao, W.S.; Klein, J.-O.; Galdin-Retailleau, S.; Querlioz, D. Spin-transfer-torque magnetic memory as a stochastic memristive synapse for neuromorphic systems. *IEEE Trans. Biomed. Circ. Syst.* **2015**, *9*, 166–174. [CrossRef] [PubMed]
150. Ambrogio, S.; Ciocchini, N.; Laudato, M.; Milo, V.; Pirovano, A.; Fantini, P.; Ielmini, D. Unsupervised learning by spike timing dependent plasticity in phase change memory (PCM) synapses. *Front. Neurosci.* **2016**, *10*, 56. [CrossRef] [PubMed]
151. Ambrogio, S.; Balatti, S.; Milo, V.; Carboni, R.; Wang, Z.; Calderoni, A.; Ramaswamy, N.; Ielmini, D. Neuromorphic learning and recognition with one-transistor-one-resistor synapses and bistable metal oxide RRAM. *IEEE Trans. Electron Devices* **2016**, *63*, 1508–1515. [CrossRef]
152. Pedretti, G.; Milo, V.; Ambrogio, S.; Carboni, R.; Bianchi, S.; Calderoni, A.; Ramaswamy, N.; Spinelli, A.S.; Ielmini, D. Memristive neural network for on-line learning and tracking with brain-inspired spike timing dependent plasticity. *Sci. Rep.* **2017**, *7*, 5288. [CrossRef] [PubMed]
153. Prezioso, M.; Merrikh-Bayat, F.; Hoskins, B.; Likharev, K.; Strukov, D. Self-adaptive spike-timing-dependent plasticity of metal-oxide memristors. *Sci. Rep.* **2016**, *6*, 21331. [CrossRef] [PubMed]

154. Milo, V.; Pedretti, G.; Carboni, R.; Calderoni, A.; Ramaswamy, N.; Ambrogio, S.; Ielmini, D. Demonstration of hybrid CMOS/RRAM neural networks with spike time/rate-dependent plasticity. In Proceedings of the 2016 IEEE International Electron Devices Meeting (IEDM), San Francisco, CA, USA, 3–7 December 2016; pp. 440–443. [CrossRef]
155. Wang, W.; Pedretti, G.; Milo, V.; Carboni, R.; Calderoni, A.; Ramaswamy, N.; Spinelli, A.S.; Ielmini, D. Learning of spatiotemporal patterns in a spiking neural network with resistive switching synapses. *Sci. Adv.* **2018**, *4*, eaat4752. [CrossRef]
156. Suri, M.; Bichler, O.; Querlioz, D.; Palma, G.; Vianello, E.; Vuillaume, D.; Gamrat, C.; DeSalvo, B. CBRAM devices as binary synapses for low-power stochastic neuromorphic systems: Auditory (cochlea) and visual (retina) cognitive processing applications. In Proceedings of the 2012 IEEE International Electron Devices Meeting (IEDM), San Francisco, CA, USA, 10–13 December 2012; pp. 235–238. [CrossRef]
157. Suri, M.; Bichler, O.; Querlioz, D.; Cueto, O.; Perniola, L.; Sousa, V.; Vuillaume, D.; Gamrat, C.; DeSalvo, B. Phase change memory as synapse for ultra-dense neuromorphic systems: Application to complex visual pattern extraction. In Proceedings of the 2011 IEEE International Electron Devices Meeting (IEDM), Washington, DC, USA, 5–7 December 2011; pp. 79–82. [CrossRef]
158. Ambrogio, S.; Balatti, S.; Milo, V.; Carboni, R.; Wang, Z.; Calderoni, A.; Ramaswamy, N.; Ielmini, D. Novel RRAM-enabled 1T1R synapse capable of low-power STDP via burst-mode communication and real-time unsupervised machine learning. In Proceedings of the IEEE Symposium on VLSI Technology, Honolulu, HI, USA, 14–16 June 2016; pp. 1–2. [CrossRef]
159. Garbin, D.; Vianello, E.; Bichler, O.; Rafhay, Q.; Gamrat, C.; Ghibaudo, G.; De Salvo, B.; Perniola, L. HfO_2-based OxRAM devices as synapses for convolutional neural networks. *IEEE Trans. Electron Devices* **2015**, *62*, 2494–2501. [CrossRef]
160. Muñoz-Martín, I.; Bianchi, S.; Pedretti, G.; Melnic, O.; Ambrogio, S.; Ielmini, D. Unsupervised learning to overcome catastrophic forgetting in neural networks. *IEEE J. Exp. Solid State Comput. Devices Circuits* **2019**, *5*, 58–66. [CrossRef]
161. Eryilmaz, S.B.; Kuzum, D.; Jeyasingh, R.; Kim, S.B.; BrightSky, M.; Lam, C.; Wong, H.-S.P. Brain-like associative learning using a nanoscale non-volatile phase change synaptic device array. *Front. Neurosci.* **2014**, *8*, 205. [CrossRef]
162. Milo, V.; Ielmini, D.; Chicca, E. Attractor networks and associative memories with STDP learning in RRAM synapses. In Proceedings of the 2017 IEEE International Electron Devices Meeting (IEDM), San Francisco, CA, USA, 2–6 December 2017; pp. 263–266. [CrossRef]
163. Milo, V.; Chicca, E.; Ielmini, D. Brain-inspired recurrent neural network with plastic RRAM synapses. In Proceedings of the IEEE International Symposium on Circuits and Systems (ISCAS), Florence, Italy, 27–30 May 2018; pp. 1–5. [CrossRef]
164. Pedretti, G.; Milo, V.; Ambrogio, S.; Carboni, R.; Bianchi, S.; Calderoni, A.; Ramaswamy, N.; Spinelli, A.S.; Ielmini, D. Stochastic learning in neuromorphic hardware via spike timing dependent plasticity with RRAM synapses. *IEEE J. Emerg. Sel. Top. Circuits Syst. JETCAS* **2018**, *8*, 77–85. [CrossRef]
165. Masquelier, T.; Guyonneau, R.; Thorpe, S.J. Competitive STDP-based spike pattern learning. *Neural Comput.* **2009**, *21*, 1259–1276. [CrossRef] [PubMed]
166. Nair, M.V.; Muller, L.K.; Indiveri, G. A differential memristive synapse circuit for on-line learning in neuromorphic computing systems. *Nano Futures* **2017**, *1*, 035003. [CrossRef]
167. Pershin, Y.V.; Di Ventra, M. Neuromorphic, digital, and quantum computation with memory circuit elements. *Proc. IEEE* **2012**, *100*, 2071–2080. [CrossRef]
168. Kim, S.; Du, C.; Sheridan, P.; Ma, W.; Choi, S.H.; Lu, W.D. Experimental demonstration of a second-order memristor and its ability to biorealistically implement synaptic plasticity. *Nano Lett.* **2015**, *15*, 2203–2211. [CrossRef]
169. Zucker, R.S.; Regehr, W.G. Short-term synaptic plasticity. *Ann. Rev. Physiol.* **2002**, *64*, 355–405. [CrossRef]
170. Markram, H.; Wang, Y.; Tsodyks, M. Differential signaling via the same axon of neocortical pyramidal neurons. *Proc. Natl. Acad. Sci. USA* **1998**, *95*, 5323–5328. [CrossRef]
171. Wang, Z.; Joshi, S.; Savel'ev, S.E.; Jiang, H.; Midya, R.; Lin, P.; Hu, M.; Ge, N.; Strachan, J.P.; Li, Z.; et al. Memristors with diffusive dynamics as synaptic emulators for neuromorphic computing. *Nat. Mater.* **2017**, *16*, 101–108. [CrossRef]

172. Ohno, T.; Hasegawa, T.; Tsuruoka, T.; Terabe, K.; Gimzewski, J.K.; Aono, M. Short-term plasticity and long-term potentiation mimicked in single inorganic synapses. *Nat. Mater.* **2011**, *10*, 591–595. [CrossRef]
173. Wang, W.; Bricalli, A.; Laudato, M.; Ambrosi, E.; Covi, E.; Ielmini, D. Physics-based modeling of volatile resistive switching memory (RRAM) for crosspoint selector and neuromorphic computing. In Proceedings of the 2018 IEEE International Electron Devices Meeting (IEDM), San Francisco, CA, USA, 1–5 December 2018; pp. 932–935. [CrossRef]
174. Wang, W.; Laudato, M.; Ambrosi, E.; Bricalli, A.; Covi, E.; Lin, Y.-H.; Ielmini, D. Volatile resistive switching memory based on Ag ion drift/diffusion—Part II: Compact modeling. *IEEE Trans. Electron Devices* **2019**, *66*, 3802–3808. [CrossRef]
175. Wang, Z.; Joshi, S.; Savel'ev, S.; Song, W.; Midya, R.; Li, Y.; Rao, M.; Yan, P.; Asapu, S.; Zhuo, Y.; et al. Fully memristive neural networks for pattern classification with unsupervised learning. *Nat. Electron.* **2018**, *1*, 137–145. [CrossRef]
176. Cristiano, G.; Giordano, M.; Ambrogio, S.; Romero, L.P.; Cheng, C.; Narayanan, P.; Tsai, H.; Shelby, R.M.; Burr, G.W. Perspective on training fully connected networks with resistive memories: Device requirements for multiple conductances of varying significance. *J. Appl. Phys.* **2018**, *124*, 151901. [CrossRef]
177. Nicosia, G.; Paolucci, G.M.; Monzio Compagnoni, C.; Resnati, D.; Miccoli, C.; Spinelli, A.S.; Lacaita, A.L.; Visconti, A.; Goda, A. A single-electron analysis of NAND Flash memory programming. In Proceedings of the 2015 IEEE International Electron Devices Meeting (IEDM), Washington, DC, USA, 7–9 December 2015; pp. 378–381. [CrossRef]
178. Ambrogio, S.; Balatti, S.; Cubeta, A.; Calderoni, A.; Ramaswamy, N.; Ielmini, D. Statistical fluctuations in HfO_x resistive-switching memory (RRAM): Part I—Set/Reset variability. *IEEE Trans. Electron Devices* **2014**, *61*, 2912–2919. [CrossRef]
179. Ielmini, D.; Lacaita, A.L.; Mantegazza, D. Recovery and drift dynamics of resistance and threshold voltages in phase change memories. *IEEE Trans. Electron Devices* **2007**, *54*, 308–315. [CrossRef]
180. Lashkare, S.; Chouhan, S.; Chavan, T.; Bhat, A.; Kumbhare, P.; Ganguly, U. PCMO RRAM for integrate-and-fire neuron in spiking neural networks. *IEEE Electron Device Lett.* **2018**, *39*, 484–487. [CrossRef]
181. Pickett, M.D.; Medeiros-Ribeiro, G.; Williams, R.S. A scalable neuristor built with Mott memristors. *Nat. Mater.* **2013**, *12*, 114–117. [CrossRef]
182. Tuma, T.; Pantazi, A.; Le Gallo, M.; Sebastian, A.; Eleftheriou, E. Stochastic phase-change neurons. *Nat. Nanotechnol.* **2016**, *11*, 693–699. [CrossRef]
183. Torrejon, J.; Riou, M.; Araujo, F.A.; Tsunegi, S.; Khalsa, G.; Querlioz, D.; Bortolotti, P.; Cros, V.; Yakushiji, K.; Fukushima, A.; et al. Neuromorphic computing with nanoscale spintronic oscillators. *Nature* **2017**, *547*, 428–431. [CrossRef]
184. Wu, M.-H.; Hong, M.-C.; Chang, C.-C.; Sahu, P.; Wei, J.-H.; Lee, H.-Y.; Sheu, S.-S.; Hou, T.-H. Extremely compact integrate-and-fire STT-MRAM neuron: A pathway toward all-spin artificial deep neural network. In Proceedings of the IEEE Symposium on VLSI Technology, Kyoto, Japan, 9–14 June 2019; pp. T34–T35. [CrossRef]
185. Mizrahi, A.; Hirtzlin, T.; Fukushima, A.; Kubota, H.; Yuasa, S.; Grollier, J.; Querlioz, D. Neural-like computing with populations of superparamagnetic basis functions. *Nat. Commun.* **2018**, *9*, 1533. [CrossRef]
186. Wittenberg, G.M.; Sullivan, M.R.; Tsien, J.Z. Synaptic reentry reinforcement based network model for long-term memory consolidation. *Hippocampus* **2002**, *12*, 637–647. [CrossRef]
187. Wang, Z.; Li, C.; Song, W.; Rao, M.; Belkin, D.; Li, Y.; Yan, P.; Jiang, H.; Lin, P.; Hu, M.; et al. Reinforcement learning with analogue memristor arrays. *Nat. Electron.* **2019**, *2*, 115–124. [CrossRef]
188. Hopfield, J.J. Searching for memories, Sudoku, implicit check bits, and the iterative use of not-always-correct rapid neural computation. *Neural Comput.* **2008**, *20*, 1119–1164. [CrossRef] [PubMed]
189. Mostafa, H.; Müller, L.K.; Indiveri, G. An event-based architecture for solving constraint satisfaction problems. *Nat. Commun.* **2015**, *6*, 8941. [CrossRef] [PubMed]
190. Traversa, F.L.; Ramella, C.; Bonani, F.; Di Ventra, M. Memcomputing *NP*-complete problems in polynomial time using polynomial resources and collective states. *Sci. Adv.* **2015**, *1*, e1500031. [CrossRef] [PubMed]
191. Denchev, V.S.; Boixo, S.; Isakov, S.V.; Ding, N.; Babbush, R.; Smelyanskiy, V.; Martinis, J.; Neven, H. What is the computational value of finite-range tunneling? *Phys. Rev. X* **2016**, *6*, 031015. [CrossRef]

192. Maass, W. Noise as a resource for computation and learning in networks of spiking neurons. *Proc. IEEE* **2014**, *102*, 860–880. [CrossRef]
193. Cai, F.; Kumar, S.; Van Vaerenbergh, T.; Liu, R.; Li, C.; Yu, S.; Xia, Q.; Yang, J.J.; Beausoleil, R.; Lu, W.; et al. Harnessing intrinsic noise in memristor Hopfield neural networks for combinatorial optimization. *arXiv* **2019**, arXiv:1903.11194.

materials

MDPI

Article

Multi-Terminal Transistor-Like Devices Based on Strongly Correlated Metallic Oxides for Neuromorphic Applications

Alejandro Fernández-Rodríguez [1], Jordi Alcalà [1], Jordi Suñe [2,*], Narcis Mestres [1] and Anna Palau [1,*]

[1] Institut de Ciència de Materials de Barcelona, ICMAB-CSIC, Campus UAB, 08193 Bellaterra, Barcelona, Spain; afernandez3@icmab.es (A.F.-R.); jalcala@icmab.es (J.A.); narcis@icmab.es (N.M.)

[2] Departament d'Enginyeria Electrònica, Universitat Autònoma de Barcelona, 08193 Bellaterra, Barcelona, Spain

* Correspondence: jordi.sune@uab.cat (J.S.); palau@icmab.es (A.P.)

Received: 14 November 2019; Accepted: 3 January 2020; Published: 8 January 2020

Abstract: Memristive devices are attracting a great attention for memory, logic, neural networks, and sensing applications due to their simple structure, high density integration, low-power consumption, and fast operation. In particular, multi-terminal structures controlled by active gates, able to process and manipulate information in parallel, would certainly provide novel concepts for neuromorphic systems. In this way, transistor-based synaptic devices may be designed, where the synaptic weight in the postsynaptic membrane is encoded in a source-drain channel and modified by presynaptic terminals (gates). In this work, we show the potential of reversible field-induced metal-insulator transition (MIT) in strongly correlated metallic oxides for the design of robust and flexible multi-terminal memristive transistor-like devices. We have studied different structures patterned on $YBa_2Cu_3O_{7-\delta}$ films, which are able to display gate modulable non-volatile volume MIT, driven by field-induced oxygen diffusion within the system. The key advantage of these materials is the possibility to homogeneously tune the oxygen diffusion not only in a confined filament or interface, as observed in widely explored binary and complex oxides, but also in the whole material volume. Another important advantage of correlated oxides with respect to devices based on conducting filaments is the significant reduction of cycle-to-cycle and device-to-device variations. In this work, we show several device configurations in which the lateral conduction between a drain-source channel (synaptic weight) is effectively controlled by active gate-tunable volume resistance changes, thus providing the basis for the design of robust and flexible transistor-based artificial synapses.

Keywords: strongly correlated oxides; resistive switching; neuromorphic computing; transistor-like devices

1. Introduction

Digital computers can process a large amount of data with high precision and speed. However, compared to the brain, the computer still cannot approach a comparable performance considering cognitive functions such as perception, recognition, and memory. Neuromorphic computing, operating with a parallel architecture connecting low-power computing elements (neurons) with multiple adaptive memory elements (synapses), appears as a very attractive alternative to von-Neuman based algorithms in future cognitive computers [1,2]. The advantages of using analogue with very large-scale integration include: Inherent parallelism, as well as reducing the chip area and power consumption in comparison with digital implementations [3]. Design of computational systems mimicking the way that brain works, with intrinsically massive parallel information processing, is completely unfeasible by using the existing hardware which is based on conventional digital logic. Although stable learning has been achieved with digital logic for low-precision applications using binary weights [4,5], the development of novel functional materials, and individual device components able to resemble the properties of neurons and synapses, are mandatory to bring a revolutionary technological leap toward the implementation of a fully neuromorphic computer.

Resistive-switching devices, modeled as memristors, have become a leading candidate to mimic basic functionalities of biological components in a neural network, while providing clear advantages in energy and scalability [3,6]. The resistive switching effect consists of a non-volatile reversible switch between different resistance states, induced by an electric field [7]. Strongly correlated metal oxides showing metal–Mott insulating transitions (MIT) appear as particularly interesting materials for future neuromorphic device architectures, because they show large resistance variations, induced by small carrier concentration modulations, driven by an electric field, allotted to obtain multilevel analogue states [8–10]. The ability to continuously tune the electrical resistance, as well as to induce both volatile and non-volatile transitions, put them in a unique position to mimic neurons and synapses on a device level [11,12].

In particular, to achieve useful synaptic plasticity, a multistate behavior should be changed in an analog continuous fashion with long retention time so that the device resistance continuously depends on the electrical history. Spike time dependent plasticity (STDP) has been successfully demonstrated in different memristive devices based on two-terminal (2T) metal-insulator-metal passive circuit elements [13,14]. However, in biological systems, signal transmission and synapse learning are both generally regarded to occur concurrently in synapse-connected neuron pairs. Current 2T artificial synaptic devices operate by separating the signal transmission and self-learning processes in time. In this context, three-terminal (3T) synaptic devices, being able to realize both functions simultaneously, offer a promising solution for efficient synapse simulation [11,15,16]. Another reason why research on multiterminal devices is relevant is the possibility of having several gates which can obtain signals from different sources simultaneously, and they can therefore experience spatiotemporal effects, which 2T devices cannot [15]. Lately, new multiterminal devices that are able to mimic important aspects of biological sensing functions have been developed. In this sense, through the utilization of a simple organic electrochemical transistor based device with multiple gates, a sensing system has been demonstrated that is analogous to the orientation selectivity from the thalamus (the center part of the brain) to the visual cortex, which governs the vision process in the brain [17]. In a second example, a series of split-gate molybdenum sulfide transistors were implemented to mimic the coincidence nerve network in the owl's brain [18]. Given the huge number of neurons and synaptic connections in the human brain, multi-terminal memristors are also needed to perform complex functions as heterosynaptic plasticity [19–22].

We have recently demonstrated stable volume field-induced resistive switching in structures based on strongly correlated metallic perovskite oxides ($La_{1-x}Sr_xMnO_3$ (LSMO) and $YBa_2Cu_3O_{7-\delta}$ (YBCO)), modulated through oxygen diffusion [23,24]. Optimally doped LSMO and YBCO materials are metallic in its initial state and they evolve into the insulating state by decreasing the oxygen content [25,26]. Multiple resistance states, needed for synaptic applications, can be achieved by tuning the oxygen doping with the applied voltage. In order to elucidate this behavior, Figure 1 displays different curves obtained by measuring the $R(T)$ evolution of a switched contact in a YBCO film, after applying different voltage pulses. A clear MIT transition from the optimally doped metallic state to an underdoped insulating state is observed.

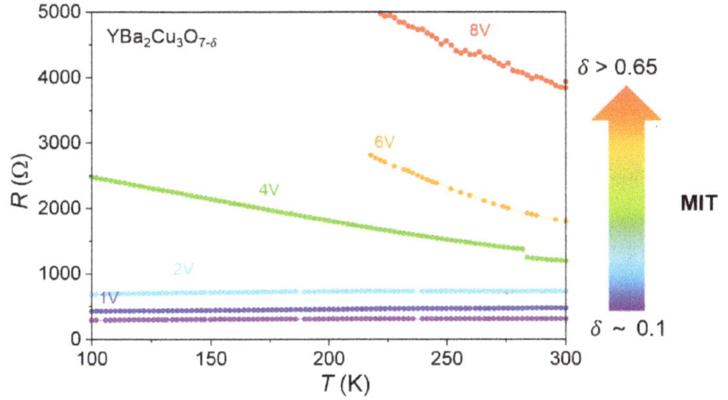

Figure 1. Resistance versus temperature obtained for a YBCO film after applying a series of voltage pulses to a silver contact of 100 μm.

The key advantage of these systems is that the resistive switching is based on the MIT, which being an intrinsic property of the material, causes a homogeneous change of resistance in a gate modulable volume, allowing the design of flexible transistor-like devices (memristors) [23]. It is worth noting that the volume resistance modulation, observed in metallic perovskites, offers enhanced robustness, in terms of cycle-to-cycle and device-to-device variations, when compared with that induced in strongly correlated oxides that are insulating in the pristine state, where the switching phenomena is strongly localized at the contact interface or in confined filaments [7,27].

Here, we report on the study of the oxygen diffusion in YBCO based multi-terminal memristor devices in which the oxygen redistribution, and thus the conductance of a drain-source channel, may be tuned by using various gates. A sketch of the oxygen diffusion mechanism occurring below the gate, emulating a synaptic process, is shown in Figure 2.

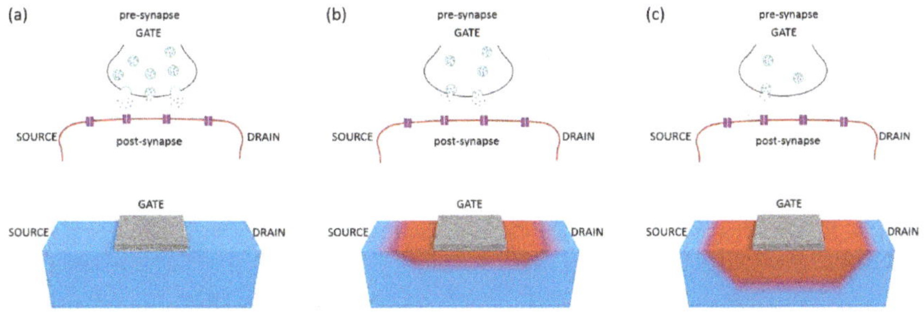

Figure 2. Schematic representation of a transistor-like device emulating a biological synapse. Blue and red in the bottom pictures depict optimally doped and under-doped YBCO, respectively. According to the oxygen doping, the schemes represent (**a**) high, (**b**) intermediate, and (**c**) low source-drain conductance.

The conductance between a source-drain channel (post-synaptic membrane) is controlled through modulatory gate terminals (pre-synaptic inputs). By the application of a gate voltage, oxygen vacancies are redistributed within the YBCO channel, locally changing its doping level, thereby their resistance (conductance). Synaptic plasticity characteristics may be obtained with intermediate synaptic weight states achieved by tuning the amount of oxygen vacancies created. Multiple pre-synaptic input terminals have been emulated by using multiple intermediate gates between the drain-source channel.

2. Materials and Methods

The geometry of YBCO transistor-like devices consist of a drain-source channel with different gate terminals to modulate the channel conductance. Optimally doped, epitaxial $YBa_2Cu_3O_{7-\delta}$ (YBCO) thin films, with thickness of 100 nm, were grown by pulsed laser deposition (PLD) on (001)-$LaAlO_3$ single crystal substrates. The parameters used in this process were previously optimized for our purposes. The substrate was heated up to T = 800–810 °C, with an O_2 partial pressure of 0.3 mbar during the deposition and a fixed target-substrate distance of 52.5 mm. A high fluence laser (~2 J/cm^2) working at a frequency of 5 Hz was used. During the cooling ramp, we increase the P(O_2) in the chamber in order to obtain well oxygenated samples. The thickness of the film is mainly determined by the number of pulses. For these samples, 2600 pulses were applied obtaining a thickness of 100 nm. Topography shows a high-quality flat surface in all cases, the root-mean-square (rms) value of surface roughness is found to be below 1 nm. The structural features of YBCO films have been studied by theta-2theta X-ray diffraction (Siemens Diffractometer D5000, Siemens AG, Munich, Germany). The epitaxial nature of the films was evidenced by the detection of only (001) peaks along with the corresponding (001) peaks originating from the (001)-LAO substrates in the theta-2theta X-ray diffraction spectra. Photolithography and wet etching were used to pattern channels with different widths, w = 5–100 µm. After the patterning, multiple 50 nm thick, 100 × 100 µm^2 silver contacts, spaced different distances apart, d = 100–300 µm, were deposited by sputtering and lift-off.

Electrical measurements were performed at room temperature with a Keithley 2450 source-meter at ambient pressure and temperature. Voltage pulses of 4 s, were applied between two top gates (top–top configuration), located at different positions of the channel, while measuring the current–voltage (I–V), and associated resistance–voltage (R–V) characteristics, in a two-point configuration. The variation of the drain-source conductance through the channel, obtained after applying the gate pulses, was evaluated by measuring the resistance at intermediate segments of the channel, N, (R_N, N = 1, 2, 3, 4, 5) in a standard four-point method, using two external electrodes to inject the current and intermediate contacts to measure the voltage. In this way, we avoid the contribution of the contact resistance and thus we obtain the bulk resistance change. Figure 3a shows a schematic representation of the proposed device and Figure 3b an optical microscopy image of several devices with different channel widths (w = 100, 50, 20, 10, and 5 µm).

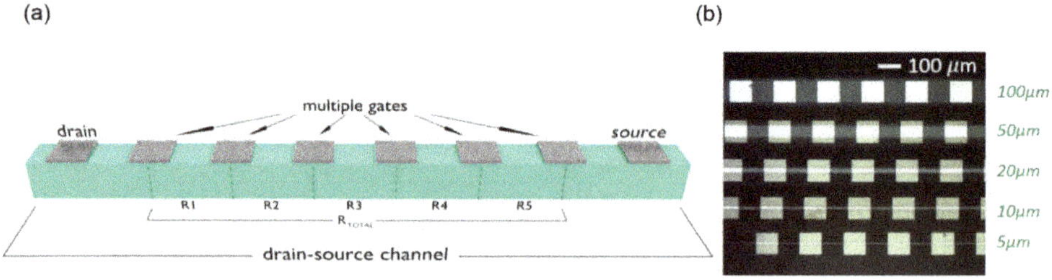

Figure 3. (**a**) Schematic representation of a transistor-like device with a source-drain channel and multiple tunable gates. The channel conductance is evaluated by measuring intermediate resistances (R_N); (**b**) optical microscope image of several devices patterned with different channel widths from 5 to 100 µm.

3. Results and Discussion

3.1. Switching Characteristics between Two Gates

Figure 4 shows repeated I–V scans (Figure 4a), and the associated R–V curves (Figure 4b), obtained for a device with a channel of w = 50 µm, by applying positive and negative voltage pulses within two gate electrodes placed d = 200 µm apart. A complementary switching behavior was reproduced, since the two gates, see opposite voltage polarities in opposite directions [28,29]. Thus, for a given polarity, one electrode undergoes a set process (incorporating oxygen and thus switching from a high resistance state (HRS) to a low resistance state (LRS)) while in the other one a reset transition is produced (losing oxygen and switching from an LRS to an HRS). The set (V_{set}) and reset (V_{reset}) voltages, associated to each gate electrode, are depicted in Figure 4b. In general, for both polarities, V_{set} occurs at lower voltage values than V_{reset}, due to a fast motion of oxygen in the low conductivity regions [23]. In a device with symmetrical gates, the resistance values obtained at the HRS and LRS for a given voltage pulse are the same thus providing a symmetrical loop, as the one shown in Figure 4b.

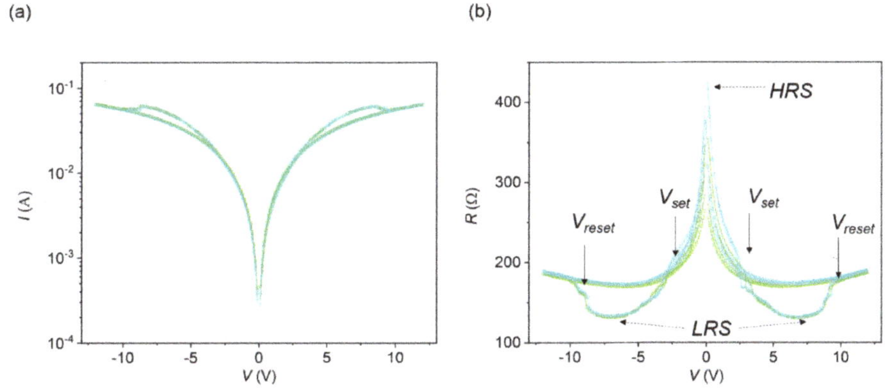

Figure 4. Typical (**a**) *I*–*V* and (**b**) *R*–*V*, obtained by using a two-point measurement, for a YBCO transistor-like device with a channel width of w = 50 μm, obtained by applying several voltage pulses through two identical gates separated at a distance of d = 200 μm, in a top–top electrode configuration.

The evolution of V_{set} and V_{reset} have been investigated by evaluating different *I*–*V* curves obtained for devices with different channel widths applying the minimum voltage pulse able to reversibly switch the gates at different distances (see Figure 5a). The values of V_{set} and V_{reset} increase linearly with the electrode distance, according to a constant dependence with the set and reset electric field (E_{set} and E_{reset}, respectively) which are of the order of, $E_{set} \sim (1\text{–}1.5) \times 10^4$ V/m, $E_{reset} \sim (1.5\text{–}2) \times 10^4$ V/m. Bias voltages of $V \sim 2$ V are needed to switch gates placed 10 μm apart and lower values, favorable for practical applications, are expected by reducing the device dimensions. Figure 5b shows the HRS and LRS resistances obtained for devices of different widths. The HRS have been read at $V \sim 0$ V, whereas for the LRS we considered the minimum value of the loop resistance. Both values are indicated in Figure 4b by dashed arrows.

It is clearly observed that the resistance values for the HRS and LRS increase with decreasing the channel width, with a behavior that is essentially linear, which is completely consistent with a volume resistive switching process [23]. Deviations of the linear dependence at low channel widths may be attributed to fabrication factors or border effects. In this way, by changing the gate area or unbalancing the applied positive/negative voltage pulse, one can modulate the weight of resistance variation in each gate. Figure 6a shows a typical example of a device with different gate areas in which the HRS and LRS of each gate exhibit different resistance changes, thus producing an asymmetrical *R*–*V* curve. Figure 6b shows an example of an asymmetrical *R*–*V* curve obtained in a device with equal gates but applying asymmetrical voltage pulses. In this case, the maximum applied negative voltage is lower than V_{reset} and thus the contact that should switch at the HRS at this polarity does not change. Both situations will be better described in the following.

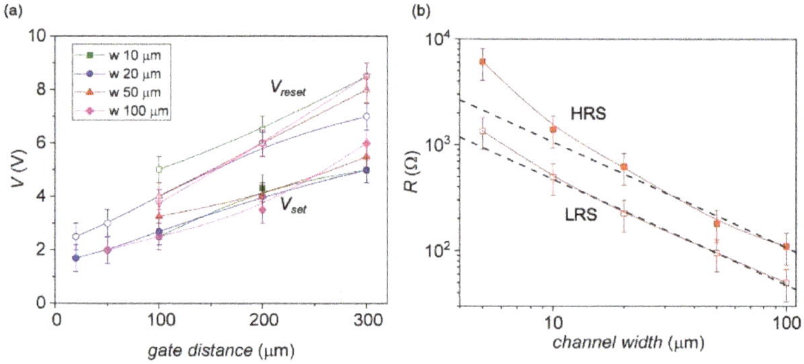

Figure 5. (**a**) Set (closed symbols) and reset (open symbols) voltages as a function of the gate distance obtained for devices of different widths; (**b**) evolution of the HRS and LRS resistance values with the device width. Dashed lines correspond to a linear dependence of R with the channel width, solid lines are guides to the eye. All values have been obtained by using a two-point configuration.

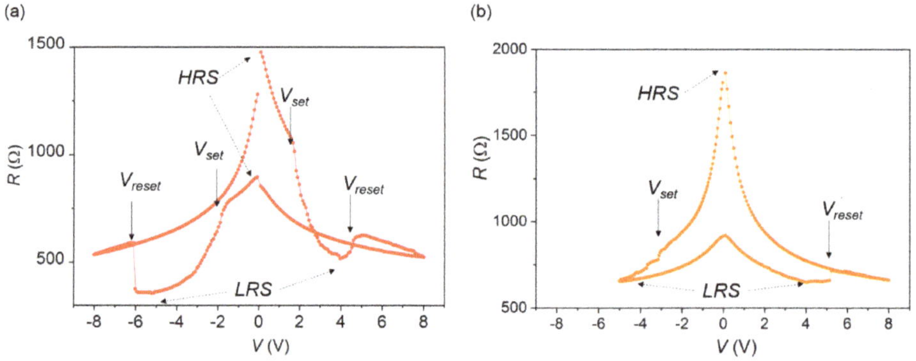

Figure 6. Typical *I*–*V* characteristics, obtained by using a two-point measurement, for YBCO transistor-like devices by applying (**a**) symmetrical voltage pulses using two gates with different switching performance; (**b**) asymmetrical voltages pulses to switch just one gate.

Next, we will demonstrate that the reversible gate resistance modulation, which occurs through a field-induced MIT driven by oxygen diffusion, is not just occurring below the gates, but also effectively modifies the volume resistance of the drain-source channel.

3.2. Conductance Modulation in a Drain-Source Channel

The conductance modulation of the device channels has been evaluated by measuring the relative variation of volume resistance at different segments of it (in a four-point configuration), after applying several positive and negative voltage pulses between two intermediate gates, in a two-point configuration. Figure 7a shows a schematic representation of the active gates (in yellow) and voltage probe positions considered for a device with a track of w = 10 μm and gate distance d = 100 μm. Figure 7b shows the *R*–*V* curves measured through the yellow gates by applying a maximum voltage of 12 V. A complementary switch of the two contact gates is clearly evidenced with a rather symmetrical *R*–*V* hysteresis curve. We plot in Figure 7c the percentage resistance change, measured at different segments of the channel, ΔR_N, calculated by using Equation (1).

$$\Delta R_N = 100 \times [R_N(t) - R_N(i)]/R_N(i) \quad (1)$$

were $R_N(i)$ and $R_N(t)$ are the resistance values measured at the N segment at the initial state and after several voltage pulses, respectively, using a four-point configuration. A clear correlation between ΔR_N and the applied pulses is observed in Figure 7c. Large resistance variations (ΔR_N ~ 15–35%) are obtained at the segments close to the gates (N = 2, 3, 4), whereas the resistance does not change on those segments located further away from the gates (N =1, 5). It is worth pointing out that the variation of resistance at different regions of the channel compensate each other, providing a nearly constant resistance when measured through the whole channel (R_{TOTAL}). This is in agreement with a redistribution of oxygen vacancies within the channel, with no external oxygen exchange, as modeled in [23].

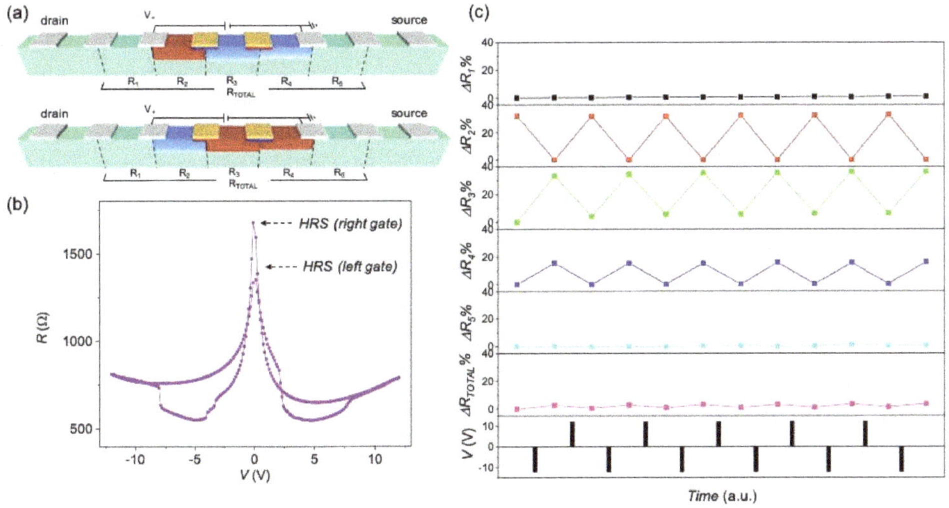

Figure 7. (**a**) Schematic representation of the oxygen redistribution in a YBCO device with a channel of w = 10 µm, by applying positive (top) and negative (bottom) voltage pulses between the two yellow gates separated at d = 100 µm. Red and blue colors represent HRS and LRS, respectively; (**b**) R–V characteristics, obtained by applying voltage pulses between the gates in two-point configuration; (**c**) percentage resistance change, measured at different segments of the device, using a four-point configuration, after a series of gate voltage pulses. The initial resistance of all segments was R_N ~ 1500–2000 µm.

The major effect of field induced oxygen diffusion is a drift of oxygen vacancies going from the negatively charged gate to the positive one. Thus, an accumulation of oxygen vacancies confined below the right gate occurs for positive voltage pulses (top Figure 7a), that is detected with a switching of this gate to the HRS in the two-point configuration measurement (Figure 7b). The complementary effect is obtained for negative voltage pulses with an accumulation of oxygen vacancies below the left gate (bottom Figure 7a) thus inducing a switching of this gate to the HRS. We have depicted this localized gate effect (from now on referred as gate switching) by coloring blue and red regions (not at scale) below the gates for LRS and HRS, respectively. The gate switching cycles produce a non-trivial reversible oxygen redistribution within the channel, that have been evaluated by measuring the resistance at different segments in a four-point configuration. The measured resistance at a given segment of the channel is directly correlated with its local oxygen concentration, being higher by increasing the amount of oxygen vacancies [25,30]. Thus, assuming a homogenous switch and considering that the resistivity of the HRS is much higher than that of the LRS, the amount of switched channel volume can be directly correlated from the resistance variation as schematically represented in Figure 7a. When one of the gate electrodes is switched to the LRS, there is a region nearby the gate that loses oxygen, i.e., segment $N = 2$ for the left gate (top Figure 7a) and segments $N = 3$ and $N = 4$ for the right (bottom Figure 7a). Although the device presents a rather symmetrical R–V curve (Figure 7b), the slightly different gate performance produces an asymmetry in the oxygen redistribution. That is, the right gate (with a higher HRS value) is able to inject oxygen vacancies in a wider lateral distance than the left one. It is worth noting that the oxygen vacancy accumulation/decrease produces a large effect in the oxygen redistribution within the channel that induces resistance changes not only in the segments localized between the gates but also in the concomitant ones, envisaging the large oxygen mobility occurring in these devices.

Conductivity modulation along the track can be tuned by further unbalancing the weight of the resistance switch in each gate. Figure 8 shows conductance measurements performed in a device with $w = 100$ μm and a gate distance $d = 500$ μm, considering the configuration schematically shown in Figure 8a. In this case the R–V hysteresis curves measured are clearly asymmetric, with very different high-resistance states achieved in the two gates (Figure 8b). The resistance variation at different segments of the channel for this device is shown in Figure 8c. In this case, the oxygen distribution is highly inhomogeneous, with a larger resistance change (~200%) concentrated close to the right gate (segment $N = 4$), and a complementary smoother resistance variation, that occupies a large region of the channel, nearby the left gate (segments N = 1, 2, and 3). As in the previous case, the gate that undergoes a transition to a more insulating state (left gate in this case) is the one that is able to inject oxygen vacancies to further lateral distances.

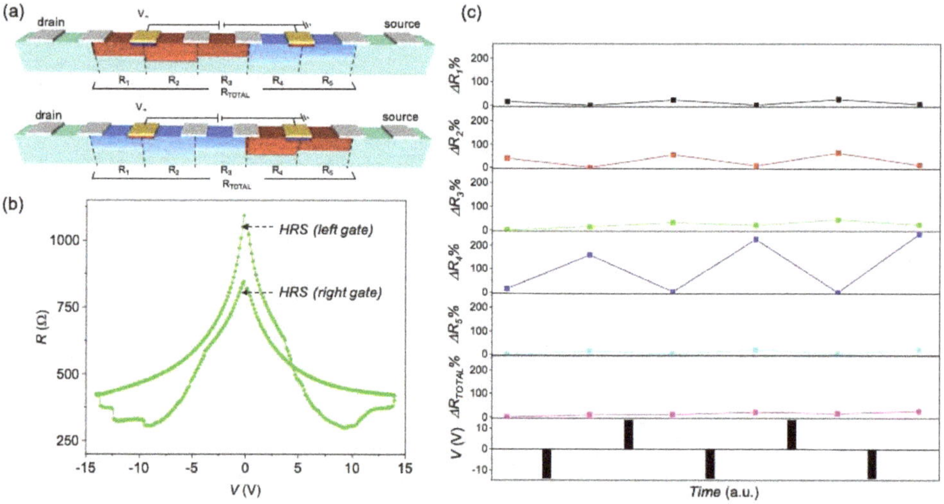

Figure 8. (**a**) Schematic representation of the oxygen redistribution in a YBCO device with a channel of $w = 100$ μm, by applying positive (top) and negative (bottom) voltage pulses between the two yellow gates separated at $d = 500$ μm. Red and blue colors represent HRS and LRS, respectively; (**b**) R–V characteristics, obtained by applying voltage pulses between the gates in two-point configuration; (**c**) percentage resistance change, measured at different segments of the device, using a four-point configuration, after a series of gate voltage pulses. The initial resistance of all segments was R_N ~ 150–200 μm.

The maximum applied voltage in the I–V curves may also be used as a tuning knob to control the oxygen redistribution (and thus the conductance) through the channel. We show in Figure 9 an extreme case, for a device with $w = 30$ μm and $d = 500$ μm, in which we just switch one of the two gates, maintaining the other at the LRS. To do so, we apply a negative voltage pulse higher than V_{reset} to switch the left contact to the HRS (Figure 9b). This contact is then switched back by to the LRS by applying a positive voltage higher than V_{set} but lower than that needed to switch the right contact to the HRS (V_{reset}).

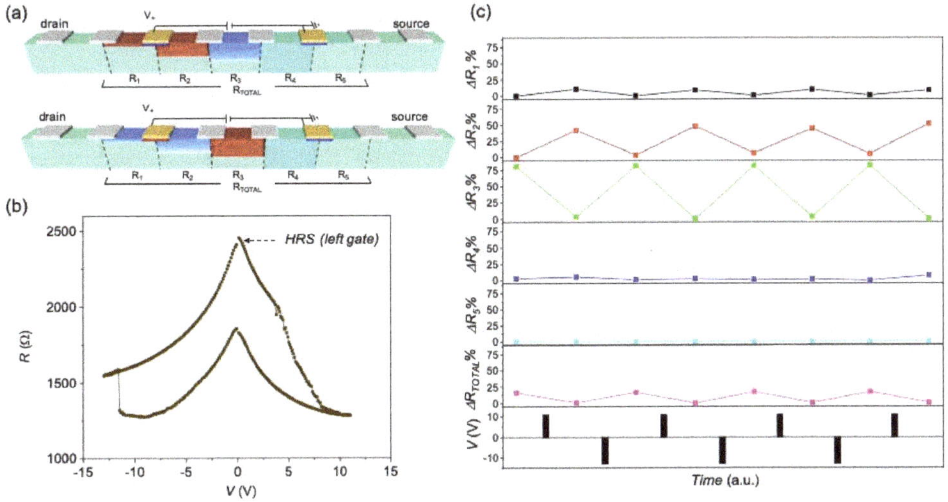

Figure 9. (**a**) Schematic representation of the oxygen redistribution in a YBCO device with a channel of w = 30 µm, by applying positive (top) and negative (bottom) voltage pulses between the two yellow gates separated at d = 500 µm. Red and blue colors represent HRS and LRS, respectively; (**b**) R–V characteristics, obtained by applying voltage pulses between the gates in two-point configuration. Maximum applied positive voltage pulse has been kept below V_{reset} in order to maintain the right contact at the LRS; (**c**) percentage resistance change, measured at different segments of the device, using a four-point configuration, after a series of gate voltage pulses. The initial resistance of all segments was R_N ~ 400–500 µm.

The resistance variation through the channel is shown in Figure 9c and the associated oxygen redistribution is schematically depicted in Figure 9a. In this case, we observe that by switching the left gate to the LRS, oxygen vacancies are injected in the segments nearby (N = 1, 2). Subsequent voltage cycles produce a reversible motion of oxygen vacancies form $N = 1, 2$ to $N = 3$. Note that the conductance is not affected in the sections near the right gate, N = 4, 5, which is kept at the LRS.

Resistance experiments directly confirm that the conductance between a drain-source channel can be effectively modulated by using different active gates and that the oxygen redistribution in it strongly depends on the switching performance of each gate, and the applied voltage pulse. These results provide a proof-of-concept of resistance modulation in multi-gate memristor structures based on the strongly correlated materials showing the MIT. However, the top–top application of voltage strongly limits not only the device performance but also the complete characterization of synaptic functions. For practical applications, top–bottom configurations should be used to increase the on-off ratio, to allow reliable programming intermediate states and to design the required devices characteristics (linear conductance change, symmetric set and reset, retention, etc.). The proposed devices provide a wide design space based on material engineering (oxide doping, oxygen scavenging layers, etc.) and geometrical engineering (oxide thickness, separation between gates, number of gates, etc.) which may help to achieve the desired device characteristics for synapses and neurons.

4. Conclusions

Our work shows the potential of multi-terminal memristive structures, based on strongly correlated YBCO metallic oxide, as a promising approach for the design of neuromorphic devices, exploiting the tuneability of field-induced oxygen doping. Results demonstrate that multiple gates can be used to change the conductance (local oxygen doping) between a source-drain channel, thus emulating the synaptic weight. The movement and redistribution of oxygen vacancies within the channel, and thus its conductance, may be controlled by the device geometry, gate dimensions and position, and bias voltage. A large design flexibility can be obtained by changing the switching performance of different gates, thus offering the possibility to locally adjust the conductance response as required to implement neuromorphic functionalities.

Author Contributions: A.P., N.M., and A.F.-R. conceived and designed the experiments. A.F.-R., J.A., and A.P. performed sample fabrication and the experiments. A.F.-R analyzed the results. J.S., A.P., and N.M. wrote the manuscript. All authors contributed to results interpretation and reviewed the manuscript. All authors have read and agreed to the published version of the manuscript.

Funding: This research was founded by the Spanish Ministry of Economy and Competitiveness through the "Severo Ochoa" Programme for Centres of Excellence in R&D (SEV-2015-0496), SUPERSWITCH project (FUNMAT-FIP-2017), COACHSUPENERGY (MAT2014-51778-C2-1-R), and SuMaTe (RTI2018-095853-B-C21) projects, co-financed by the European Regional Development Fund, MCIU/AEI/FEDER, UE. We also thank support from the European Union for NanoSC Cost Action NANOCOHYBRI (CA 16218) and from the Catalan Government with 2017-SGR-1519. A.F.-R thanks the Spanish Ministry of Economy for the FPI Spanish grant (BES-2016-077310). J.S. was supported by the Spanish Ministerio de Ciencia, Innovación y Universidades and the ECSEL EU Joint Undertaking through the WAKeMeUP 783176 Project.

Conflicts of Interest: The authors declare no conflict of interest.

References

1. Solomon, P.M. Analog neuromorphic computing using programmable resistor arrays. *Solid-State Electron.* **2019**, *155*, 82–92. [CrossRef]
2. Gokmen, T.; Vlasov, Y. Acceleration of deep neural network training with resistive cross-point devices: Design considerations. *Front. Neurosci.* **2016**, *10*, 333. [CrossRef]
3. Burr, G.W.; Shelby, R.M.; Sebastian, A.; Kim, S.; Sidler, S.; Virwani, K.; Ishii, M.; Narayanan, P.; Fumarola, A.; Sanches, L.L.; et al. Neuromorphic computing using non-volatile memory. *Adv. Phys. X* **2017**, *2*, 89–124. [CrossRef]
4. Suri, M.; Querlioz, D.; Bichler, O.; Palma, G.; Vianello, E.; Vuillaume, D.; Gamrat, C.; De Salvo, B.; Suri, M.; Querlioz, D.; et al. Bio-inspired stochastic computing using binary CBRAM synapses. *IEEE Trans. Electron Devices* **2013**, *60*, 2402–2409. [CrossRef]
5. Yu, S.; Gao, B.; Fang, Z.; Yu, H.; Kang, J.; Wong, H.-S.P. Stochastic learning in oxide binary synaptic device for neuromorphic computing. *Front. Neurosci.* **2013**, *7*, 186. [CrossRef]
6. Zidan, M.A.; Strachan, J.P.; Lu, W.D. The future of electronics based on memristive systems. *Nat. Electron.* **2018**, *1*, 22–29. [CrossRef]
7. Sawa, A. Resistive switching in transition metal oxides. *Mater. Today* **2008**, *11*, 28–36. [CrossRef]
8. Janod, E.; Tranchant, J.; Corraze, B.; Querré, M.; Stoliar, P.; Rozenberg, M.; Cren, T.; Roditchev, D.; Phuoc, V.T.; Besland, M.P.; et al. Resistive switching in Mott insulators and correlated systems. *Adv. Funct. Mater.* **2015**, *25*, 6287–6305. [CrossRef]
9. Bagdzevicius, S.; Maas, K.; Boudard, M.; Burriel, M. Interface-type resistive switching in perovskite materials. *J. Electroceramics* **2017**, *39*, 157–184. [CrossRef]
10. Bi, C.; Meng, X.; Almasi, H.; Rosales, M.; Wang, W. Metal based nonovolatile field-effect transistors. *Adv. Funct. Mater.* **2016**, *26*, 3490–3495. [CrossRef]
11. Zhou, B.Y.; Ramanathan, S. Mott memory and neuromorphic devices. *Proc. IEEE* **2015**, *103*, 1289–1310. [CrossRef]
12. Stoliar, P.; Tranchant, J.; Corraze, B.; Janod, E.; Besland, M.P.; Tesler, F.; Rozenberg, M.; Cario, L. A leaky-integrate-and-fire neuron analog realized with a Mott insulator. *Adv. Funct. Mater.* **2017**, *27*, 1604740. [CrossRef]
13. Kuzum, D.; Yu, S.; Wong, H.S. Synaptic electronics: Materials, devices and applications. *Nanotechnology* **2013**, *24*, 382001. [CrossRef] [PubMed]
14. Jo, S.H.; Chang, T.; Ebong, I.; Bhadviya, B.B.; Mazumder, P.; Lu, W. Nanoscale memristor device as synapse in neuromorphic systems. *Nano Lett.* **2010**, *10*, 1297–1301. [CrossRef]

15. Han, H.; Yu, H.; Wei, H.; Gong, J.; Xu, W. Recent progress in three-terminal artificial synapses: From device to system. *Small* **2019**, *15*, 1900695. [CrossRef]
16. Yang, C.S.; Shang, D.S.; Liu, N.; Fuller, E.J.; Agrawal, S.; Talin, A.A.; Li, Y.Q.; Shen, B.G.; Sun, Y. All-solid-state synaptic transistor with ultralow conductance for neuromorphic computing. *Adv. Funct. Mater.* **2018**, *28*, 1804170. [CrossRef]
17. Gkoupidenis, P.; Koutsouras, D.A.; Lonjaret, T.; Fairfield, J.A.; Malliaras, G.G. Orientation selectivity in a multi-gated organic electrochemical transistor. *Sci. Rep.* **2016**, *6*, 27007. [CrossRef]
18. Das, S.; Dodda, A.; Das, S. A biomimetic 2D transistor for audiomorphic computing. *Nat. Commun.* **2019**, *10*, 1–10. [CrossRef]
19. Sangwan, V.K.; Lee, H.-S.; Bergeron, H.; Balla, I.; Beck, M.E.; Chen, K.-S.; Hersam, M.C. Multi-terminal memtransistors from polycrystalline monolayer molybdenum disulfide. *Nature* **2018**, *554*, 500–504. [CrossRef]
20. Stoddart, A. Electronic devices: Making multi-terminal memtransistors. *Nat. Rev. Mater.* **2018**, *3*, 18014. [CrossRef]
21. Gou, G.; Sun, J.; Qian, C.; He, Y.; Kong, L.A.; Fu, Y.; Dai, G.; Yang, J.; Gao, Y. Artificial synapses based on biopolymer electrolyte-coupled SnO_2 nanowire transistors. *J. Mater. Chem. C* **2016**, *4*, 11110–11117. [CrossRef]
22. Zhu, L.Q.; Wan, C.J.; Guo, L.Q.; Shi, Y.; Wan, Q. Artificial synapse network on inorganic proton conductor for neuromorphic systems. *Nat. Commun.* **2014**, *5*, 3158. [CrossRef] [PubMed]
23. Palau, A.; Fernandez-rodriguez, A.; Gonzalez-rosillo, J.C.; Granados, X.; Coll, M.; Bozzo, B.; Ortega-hernandez, R.; Sun, J.; Obradors, X.; Puig, T. Electrochemical tuning of metal insulator transition and nonvolatile resistive switching in superconducting films. *ACS Appl. Mater. Interfaces* **2018**, *10*, 30522–30531. [CrossRef] [PubMed]
24. Gonzalez-Rosillo, J.C.; Ortega-Hernandez, R.; Arndt, B.; Coll, M.; Dittmann, R.; Obradors, X.; Palau, A.; Suñe, J.; Puig, T. Engineering oxygen migration for homogeneous volume resistive switching in 3-terminal devices. *Adv. Electron. Mater.* **2019**, *5*, 1800629. [CrossRef]
25. Wuyts, B.; Moshchalkov, V.V.; Bruynseraede, Y. Resistivity and Hall effect of metallic oxygen-deficient $YBa_2Cu_3O_x$ films in the normal state. *Phys. Rev. B* **1996**, *53*, 9418. [CrossRef]
26. Sakai, J.; Ito, N.; Imai, S. Oxygen content of $La_{1-x}Sr_xMnO_{3-y}$ thin films and its relation to electric-magnetic properties. *J. Appl. Phys.* **2006**, *99*, 08Q318. [CrossRef]
27. Waser, R.; Dittmann, R.; Staikov, C.; Szot, K. Redox-based resistive switching memories nanoionic mechanisms, prospects, and challenges. *Adv. Mater.* **2009**, *21*, 2632–2663. [CrossRef]
28. Linn, E.; Rosezin, R.; Kügeler, C.; Waser, R. Complementary resistive switches for passive nanocrossbar memories. *Nat. Mater.* **2010**, *9*, 403–406. [CrossRef]
29. Nardi, F.; Balatti, S.; Larentis, S.; Gilmer, D.C.; Ielmini, D. Complementary switching in oxide-based bipolar resistive-switching random memory. *IEEE Trans. Electron Devices* **2012**, *60*, 70–77. [CrossRef]
30. Lee, Y.S.; Segawa, K.; Li, Z.Q.; Padilla, W.J.; Dumm, M.; Dordevic, S.V.; Homes, C.C.; Ando, Y.; Basov, D.N. Electrodynamics of the nodal metal state in weakly doped high-T_c cuprates. *Phys. Rev. B-Condens. Matter Mater. Phys.* **2005**, *72*, 054529. [CrossRef]

materials

MDPI

Article

Bipolar Analog Memristors as Artificial Synapses for Neuromorphic Computing

Rui Wang [1,2], Tuo Shi [1,2,*], Xumeng Zhang [1,2], Wei Wang [1], Jinsong Wei [1,3], Jian Lu [1,3], Xiaolong Zhao [1], Zuheng Wu [1,2], Rongrong Cao [1,2], Shibing Long [3], Qi Liu [1,2,*] and Ming Liu [1,2]

1 Institute of Microelectronics of Chinese Academy of Sciences, Beijing 100029, China; wangrui@ime.ac.cn (R.W.); zhangxumeng@ime.ac.cn (Xr.Z.); wangwei_esss@nudt.edu.cn (W.W.); weijinsong@ime.ac.cn (J.W.); lujian@ime.ac.cn (J.L.); zhaoxiaolong@ime.ac.cn (X.Z.); wuzuheng@ime.ac.cn (Z.W.), caorongrong@ime.ac.cn (R.C.); liuming@ime.ac.cn (M.L.)

2 University of Chinese Academy of Sciences, Beijing 100049, China

3 University of Science and Technology of China, Hefei 230026, China; longshibing@ime.ac.cn

* Correspondence: shituo@ime.ac.cn (T.S.); liuqi@ime.ac.cn (Q.L.); Tel.: +86-10-8299-5582 (T.S.); +86-01-8299-5798 (Q.L.)

Received: 10 September 2018; Accepted: 23 October 2018; Published: 26 October 2018

Abstract: Synaptic devices with bipolar analog resistive switching behavior are the building blocks for memristor-based neuromorphic computing. In this work, a fully complementary metal-oxide semiconductor (CMOS)-compatible, forming-free, and non-filamentary memristive device ($Pd/Al_2O_3/TaO_x/Ta$) with bipolar analog switching behavior is reported as an artificial synapse for neuromorphic computing. Synaptic functions, including long-term potentiation/depression, paired-pulse facilitation (PPF), and spike-timing-dependent plasticity (STDP), are implemented based on this device; the switching energy is around 50 pJ per spike. Furthermore, for applications in artificial neural networks (ANN), determined target conductance states with little deviation (<1%) can be obtained with random initial states. However, the device shows non-linear conductance change characteristics, and a nearly linear conductance change behavior is obtained by optimizing the training scheme. Based on these results, the device is a promising emulator for biology synapses, which could be of great benefit to memristor-based neuromorphic computing.

Keywords: memristor; artificial synapse; neuromorphic computing

1. Introduction

Over the last decades, rapid advances in digital computing system based on complementary metal-oxide semiconductor (CMOS) integrated circuit technology have substantially changed society. However, due to the limitations of classical von-Neumann computers (the von-Neumann bottleneck) in speed, power efficiency, and parallel processing, there are urgent demands for novel computing structures and systems [1]. The human brain is likely to be the most efficient computing system, because the operating frequency of our brain is in the range of 1–10 Hz, and it consumes only around 1–10 W of power, which means the energy consumption per synaptic event is only approximately 1–100 fJ [2]. Therefore, the novel computing system—neuromorphic computing, inspired by the brain—has attracted scientists' attention in recent years for its advantages, such as being massively parallel and fault-tolerant. The weight modulation ability of synapses is known as synaptic plasticity, which is believed to be the primary reason for learning and memory in the brain. In order to implement neuromorphic computing, such as artificial neural networks (ANN), an electronic synaptic device is necessary.

Recently, the implementation of artificial synapses with memristors has been proposed. Memristors are two compact terminal devices that change their resistances when subjected to electrical stimulation [3–6]. Several memristors, ranging from resistive random access memory (RRAM) [7–11], to phase change memory (PCM) [12], to ferroelectric RAM [13–15], have been proposed for neuromorphic computing applications as artificial synapses. Several memristors based on new materials [16,17] have been proposed for neuromorphic computing. However, when memristors are employed in neuromorphic computing systems (e.g., artificial neuron networks), binary memristors with only two resistance states (i.e., high resistance state (HRS) and low resistance state (LRS)) have been proven to be effective only in some specific applications [18,19]. In some neuromorphic computing systems designed for complex applications, such as image recognition, the use of only two states as synaptic weights presents disadvantages in performances [20,21]—for example, low accuracy or area-efficiency. On the other hand, in biology neuromorphic systems, synaptic weights are continuously tunable in depression and potentiation; thus, memristors with gradually changing conductance in bipolarity could be more like the biology synapse, and can therefore emulate brain functions better than binary memristors. As artificial synapses, memristors with tunable conductance have attracted growing attention for being promising candidates for weight storage in neuromorphic computing systems, owing to the advantages in accuracy and area-efficiency. Several methods have been discussed to implement analog-resistive switching behavior, including using multiple memristors to construct one synapse [22], utilizing a unipolar analog behavior in some metal oxide-based filamentary memristors [11,23,24], optimizing programming schemes [25,26], adding heat enhancement layers [27], or using non-filamentary memristors [28–30]. Compared with the filamentary memristors, non-filamentary memristors can implement multilevel states more easily, but usually have poorer retention [31–33] However, realizing bipolar analog conductance change in both SET (transition from HRS to LRS) and RESET (transition from LRS to HRS) processes with satisfying retention time remains an open challenge.

In this paper, a fully CMOS-compatible, forming-free, and non-filamentary memristor device based on $Ta/TaO_x/Al_2O_3/Pd$, with analog SET and RESET processes, is proposed for neuromorphic computing as an artificial synapse. The direct current (DC) sweeping results demonstrate that the device has bipolar analog resistance switching behavior, and the multilevel conductance states can be obtained with satisfying retention time. Synaptic plasticity, including long-term potentiation/depression (LTP/LTD), paired-pulse facilitation (PPF), and spiking-time-dependent plasticity (STDP), can be mimicked by our devices. For the applications in ANN, determined target conductance states and the linearity of conductance change are carefully examined.

2. Materials and Methods

The metal–insulator (double functional layer)–metal structure and the cross-sectional transmission electron microscopy (TEM) image of the $Ta/TaO_x/Al_2O_3/Pd$ device are shown in Figure 1a,b, respectively. The fabrication process of the device is shown in Figure 1c. First, the Si substrate was cleaned with acetone, ethanol, and de-ionized water. 30 nm-thick Pd and 15 nm-thick Ta as the bottom electrode were deposited on the Si substrate by magnetron sputtering. A TaO_x layer was formed by rapid thermal annealing (RTA) carried out for 300 s in plasma O_2 by plasma-enhanced chemical vapor deposition (PECVD) at 275 °C. Direct oxygen plasma with a power of 100 W was applied on the Ta film. After RTA, 7 nm-thick Al_2O_3 was deposited by atom layer deposition (ALD). Finally, 40 nm Pd as the top electrode was deposited by magnetron sputtering after the lithography process. For our device, the highest temperature of the process is only 275 °C (below 400 °C), and all the materials (Pd, Ta, Al) were CMOS compatible. As a result, our device was fully CMOS compatible.

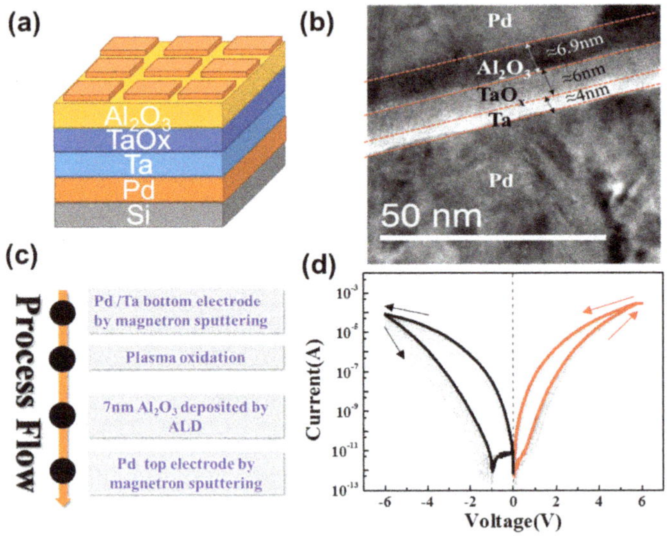

Figure 1. (**a**) The schematic, (**b**) a cross sectional transmission electron microscopy (TEM) image of the Ta/TaO_x/Al_2O_3/Pd device, (**c**) the fabrication processes of the Ta/TaO_x/Al_2O_3/Pd device, and (**d**) typical *I–V* curves of the Ta/TaO_x/Al_2O_3/Pd showing bipolar analog switching (SET voltage = 6 V, RESET voltage = −6 V).

The DC electrical characteristics of the device were measured by an Agilent B1500A semiconductor parameter analyzer (Santa Rosa, CA, US). During the electrical measurement, the voltage was applied to the top Pd electrode, while the Ta/Pd bottom electrode was tied to ground.

3. Results and Discussions

The resistive switching characteristics of the device were evaluated under DC programming conditions. The typical current–voltage (*I–V*) characteristic of the Ta/TaO_x/Al_2O_3/Pd device under DC sweep mode from −6 V to 6 V is shown in Figure 1d. The device is forming-free, and no abrupt change of current in both SET and RESET switching processes is observed, indicating a bipolar analog resistive switching feature. Within 6 V and −6 V stop voltages on SET and RESET processes, a ~10^3 ratio between HRS and LRS can be obtained (read voltage is 1 V), which is larger than our recent work of similar TaO_x/Al_2O_3 stack device (~10^2 ratio, Ti/AlO_x/TaO_x/Pt) [34].

To further demonstrate the analog characteristics, the DC sweep with different working voltages and without compliance currents (SET voltage: 2.5 V, 3 V to 5.5 V; and RESET voltage: −2 V, −2.5 to −6 V) and the DC sweep with different compliance currents during SET process are shown in Figure 2. The initial resistance of the device is ~10^{11} Ω (read at 1 V). When the positive sweeping voltage is applied to the device, the resistance of the device is retained until the voltage reaches 2.5 V, then the resistance gradually decreases. During the consecutive SET process, as shown in an inset of Figure 2b, the responding currents (read at 1 V) can gradually increase with the increment of the stop voltages, indicating that different conductance states can be obtained in the SET process. Various conductance states can also be obtained by setting different compliance currents during the SET process. With compliance currents from 500 nA to 2.2 mA, the corresponding *I–V* curves and the 60 different resulting conductance states are shown in Figure 2c and the inset, respectively. The RESET process can be implemented by applying a negative DC sweeping voltage to the device. As shown in Figure 2a, eight consecutive negative DC sweeps with various stop voltages are applied to the device. As the voltages decrease from −2 to −6 V with a −0.5 V step, the device is switched to a higher resistance state after each step. Moreover, the multilevel resistance states can be preserved within satisfying retention time, as shown in Figure 2d. The multilevel resistance states are obtained by consecutive positive voltage sweepings (2 to 6 V with a 0.25 V step). After each sweeping, the device resistance states are monitored by a series of 1 V reading pulses at 0.5 s intervals. As it is shown in Figure 2d, though with slightly decay, nine different states can be clearly distinguished after 1000 s.

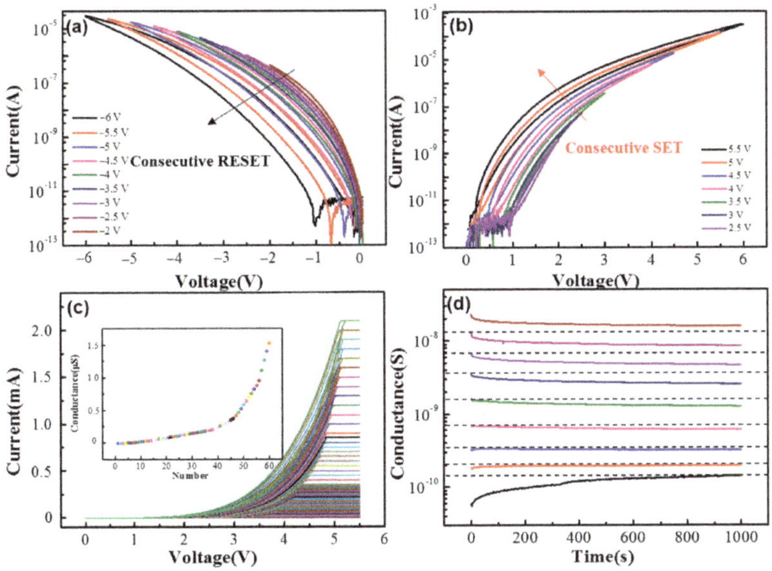

Figure 2. Bipolar analog-resistive switching characteristics of the $Ta/TaO_x/Al_2O_3/Pd$ device under the DC sweeping mode: (**a**) consecutive DC sweeping with different stop voltages from −2 to −6 V in the RESET process; (**b**) consecutive DC sweeping with different stop voltages from 2.5 to 5.5 V in the SET process; (**c**) consecutive DC sweeping with different compliance currents from 500 nA to 2.2 mA in the SET process (inset: 60 different conductance states obtained by modulating different compliance currents); and (**d**) retention characteristics of nine different resistance states of the $Ta/TaO_x/Al_2O_3/Pd$ device.

The characteristics of the bipolar analog-resistive switching in pulse mode are investigated via positive (0 to 4.5 V) and negative (0 to −5 V) triangle pulses, as shown in Figure 3a,b, respectively. The curves of current and voltage versus time for the SET and RESET processes are shown in the insets of Figure 3a,b, respectively. These results further confirm the analog resistive switching characteristics under both positive and negative pulses. The results reveal that in both the SET and RESET processes, gradual tuning of the multilevel conductance states can be obtained. Bipolar analog resistive switching characteristics are fully analogous to the biology synapse; thus, the devices have the potential to mimic synaptic functions in neuromorphic computing system.

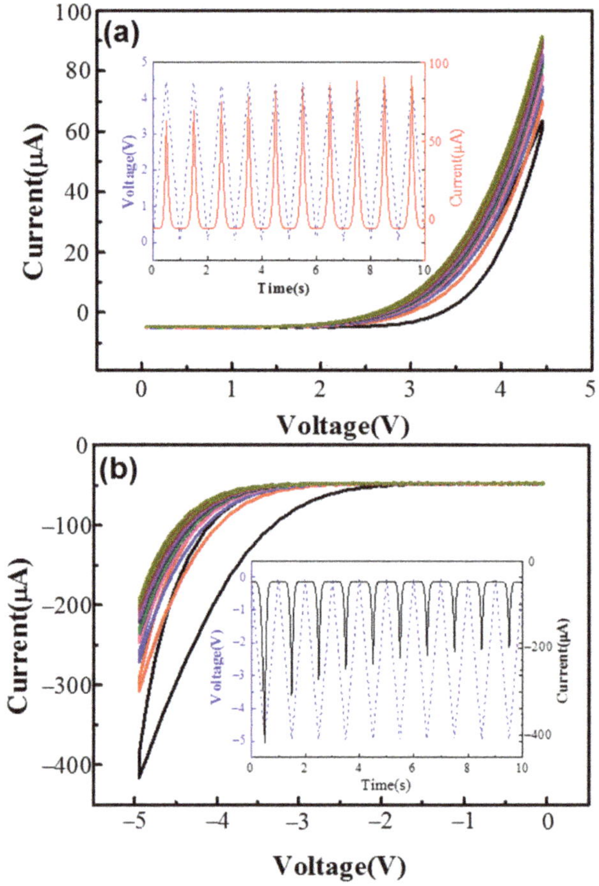

Figure 3. (**a**) Gradual SET under positive triangle pulses (from 0 to 4.5 V) (inset: the *I*-*t* and *V*-*t* curves of (**a**), representing the gradual increasing of current with time); (**b**) gradual RESET under negative triangle pulses (from 0 to −5 V) (inset: the *I*-*t* and *V*-*t* curves of (**b**), representing the gradual decreasing of current with time).

Long-term potentiation/depression (LTP/LTD) is when the synaptic weight can be changed gradually under spiking signals and the changed weight can be maintained from several minutes to years [35]. To evaluate the long-term potentiation/depression of a device, 50 consecutive pulses with different pulse amplitudes and widths are applied to the device, as shown in Figure 4. All the conductance of the device is monitored by 1 V reading voltage. The change of conductance can be modulated by different amplitudes and widths. As shown in Figure 4a,b, the amplitude here was fixed at 5.5 V during potentiation and −5.5 V during depression, with different widths (1 μs, 10 μs, and 100 μs). In addition, Figure 4c,d show the potentiation and depression with a fixed 100 μs width and different amplitudes (potentiation: from 4.5 to 5.5 V; depression: from −4.5 to −5.5 V). With a higher amplitude or larger width, the change of the conductance is increased in both potentiation and depression. For our device, when the pulse amplitude (write voltage) is ~±4.5 V and the pulse width is 1 μs, the write current is around ~10^{-5} A; thus, the switching energy is 50 pJ per spike. To conclude, the device conductance is continuously increased by positive pulses, which can mimic long-term potentiation. In addition, the device conductance is continuously decreased by negative pulses, which can mimic long-term depression.

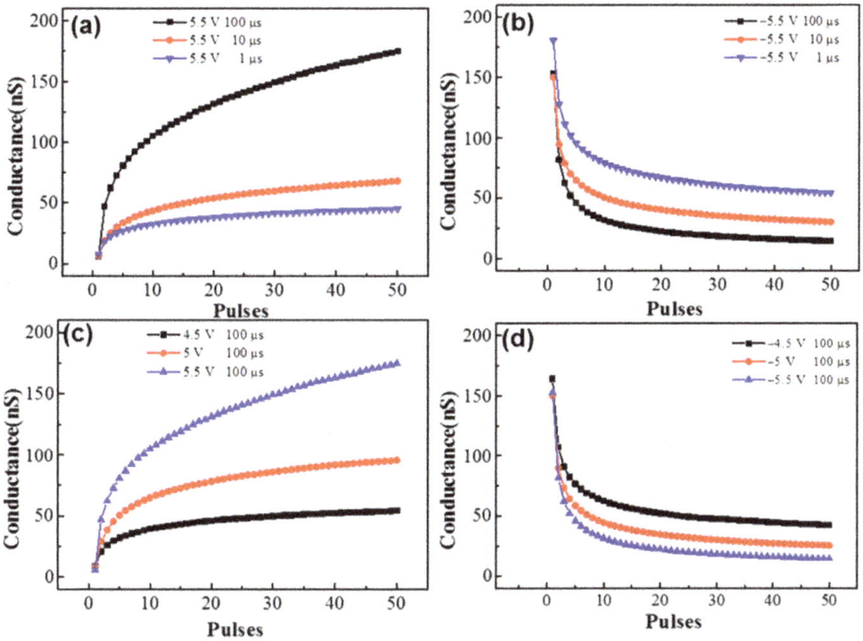

Figure 4. The measured long-term potentiation and long-term depression synaptic function with identical pulses. A total of 50 pulses with 5.5 V pulse amplitude and different pulse widths for (**a**) potentiation (1 µs, 10 µs, and 100 µs); (**b**) depression (1 µs, 10 µs, and 100 µs); 50 pulses with 100 µs pulse width and a different pulse amplitude (**c**) for potentiation (4.5 V, 5 V, and 5.5 V) and (**d**) for depression (−4.5 V, −5 V, and −5.5 V).

Moreover, the device can emulate other synaptic features, such as paired-pulse facilitation (PPF) and spiking-time-dependent plasticity (STDP), as shown in Figure 5. Most research on artificial synapses focuses on the long-term plasticity, because long-term changes provide a physiological substrate for learning and memory. However, short-term plasticity is also significant, since it supports a variety of computations, such as synaptic filtering, adaptation, and enhancement of transients, decorrelation, burst detection, and sound localization [36]. PPF is an important kind of short-term plasticity. In biological synapses, PPF functions can be described as follows: the second post-synaptic response current becomes larger than the first under two successive spike stimuli, with the interval time of spikes less than recovery time [8]. The experimental demonstration of PPF functions in our device is shown in Figure 5a. When a pair of pulses is applied to the device, the conductance gradually increases during the positive pulses, and the maximum responding current of the second pulse is clearly larger than the first, and a decay phenomenon can be observed during the pulse interval, which is similar to the PPF in the biological system.

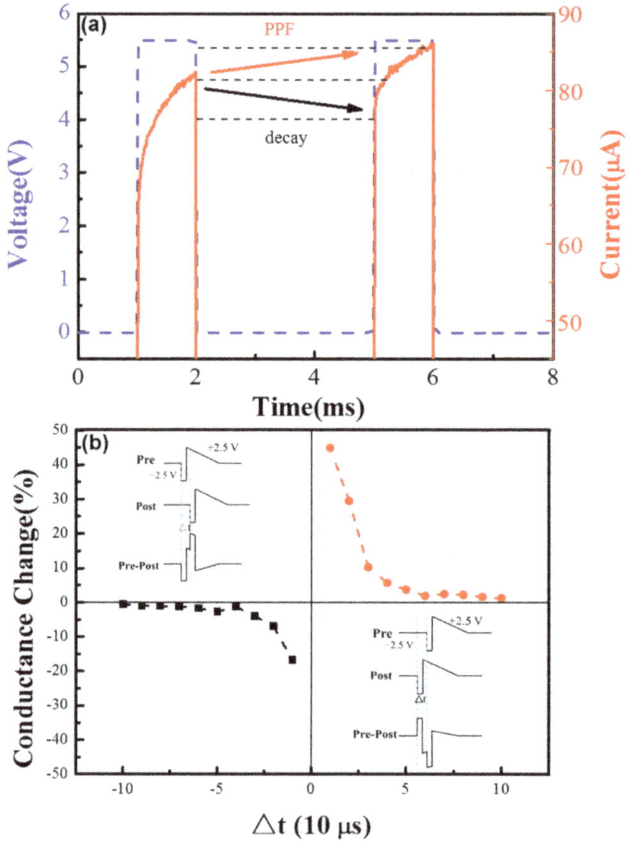

Figure 5. (**a**) The short-term plasticity: paired-pulse facilitation (PPF) synaptic function of the $Ta/TaO_x/Al_2O_3/Pd$ device; (**b**) illustration of spike signals and spiking-time-dependent plasticity (STDP) function of the device. The individual pre-synaptic or post-synaptic spike signal is designed as a pair of pulses (−2.5 V, 10 μs pulse and 2.5 V triangle pulse) applied to the top and bottom electrode, respectively.

In biological systems, synaptic weight can be modulated by the temporal relationship of the activity between the pre- and post-synaptic neurons, which is called spiking-time-dependent plasticity (STDP). According to STDP, the change of synaptic weight (ΔW) is a function of the time difference between pre- and post-synaptic activity (Δt). To emulate the STDP function in the device, a pair of pulses acting as the spiking signals with different time intervals is applied to the device. Individual pre-synaptic or post-synaptic spiking signals are designed as a pair of pulses (−2.5 V, 10 μs pulse and a 2.5 V triangle pulse) applied to the top and bottom electrode, respectively, as shown in Figure 5b. It should be noted that an individual positive signal or an individual negative signal is not strong enough to modulate the resistance of the device. As shown in Figure 5b, the effective signal to the device is the pre-synaptic signal minus the post-synaptic signal. When the pre-spike appears before the post-spike ($\Delta t > 0$), the conductance (synaptic weight) of the device is enhanced (potentiation), and the change in weight decreases with the increase of Δt. On the contrary, when the pre-spike appears after the post-spike, the conductance of the device depresses and the change of the weight decreases with the increase of Δt. The measurement result shows that the $Ta/TaO_x/Al_2O_3/Pd$ device can emulate the STDP learning rules successfully, which has potential to be used in the spiking neuron network (SNN).

To fully explore bipolar conductance tuning characteristics and demonstrate the potential application of the device in some specific neuromorphic computing systems like ANN, determined target conductance states with different initial states have been tested. As shown in Figure 6a, the initial state is 2.41 nS, after two tuning processes: 5.7 V positive pulses with 10 µs width for rough-tuning, and −5 V negative pulses with 10 µs width for fine-tuning. The target conductance state of 5.5 nS can be obtained with little deviation (<1%). The same target conductance state can also be obtained when the initial conductance state is 13.5 nS, by −5.7 V negative pulses with 10 µs width for rough-tuning and 5 V positive pulses with 10 µs width for fine-tuning, as shown in Figure 6b. As shown in Figure 6c,d, another target conductance state (10 nS), can be obtained with little deviation. It is worth noting that the target conductance states are determined randomly. Based on this result, it can be proven that precision is achieved across a wide dynamic range. Writing error is a standard plot when characterizing resistive switching write noise. The write error of the device has been tested, as shown in Figure 7. A DC sweeping with 100 µA compliance current is used to get nearly the same initial states. Only one programming pulse (4.5 V/10 µs for potentiation and −4.5 V/10 µs for depression) is applied after each DC sweeping. The conductance states (total 10 cycles) are obtained by 1 V reading voltage. As shown in Figure 7b,d the standard deviation is 0.079 nS after one potentiation pulse, and 0.11 nS after one depression pulse, respectively. The dynamic range is around 20 nS under 4.5 V/10 µs training pulses. As a result, the write error is only around 0.6% of the total dynamic range.

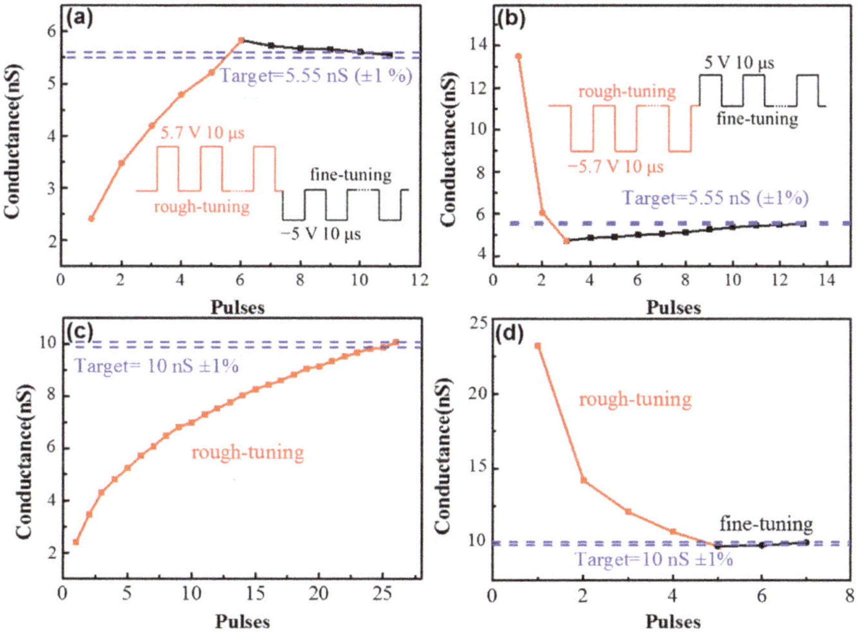

Figure 6. The bipolar conductance tuning to randomly determined target states (5.5 nS ± 1% and 10 nS ± 1%) under pulses with different initial states: (**a**) the initial state is 2.41 nS, and the target conductance state is obtained by 5.7 V positive pulses for rough-tuning and −5 V negative pulses for fine-tuning; (**b**) the initial state is 13.5 nS, and the target conductance state is obtained by −5.7 V negative pulses for rough-tuning and 5 V positive pulses for fine-tuning; (**c**) the initial state is 2.2 nS, and the target state is obtained only by rough-tuning; and (**d**) the initial state is 23 nS, and the target state is obtained by rough-tuning and fine-tuning methods.

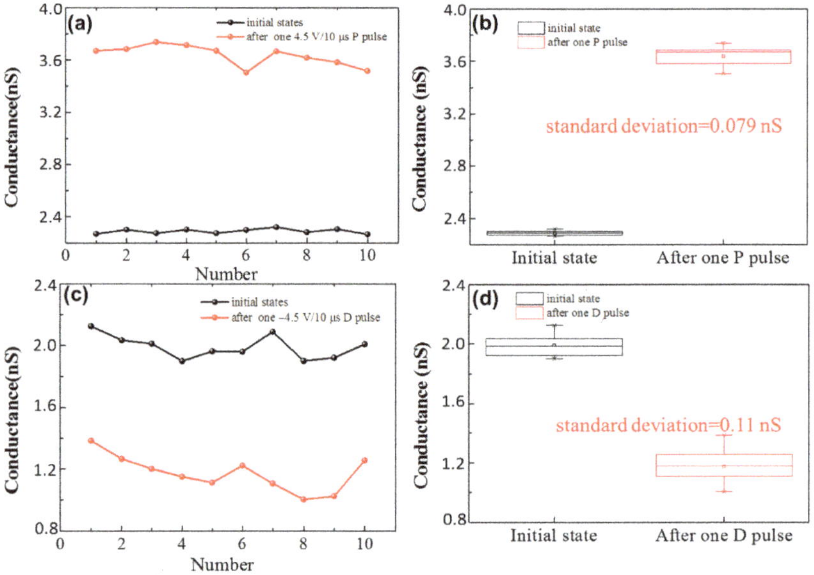

Figure 7. (**a**) The conductance states after one 5 V/10 μs P pulse from nearly the same initial states. (**b**) Conductance distribution from (a), where the standard deviation is 0.079 nS. (**c**) The conductance states after one −5 V/10 μs P pulse from nearly the same initial states. (**d**) Conductance distribution from (c), where the standard deviation is 0.11 nS.

The recognition accuracy of the ANN highly depended on the linearity of the synaptic weight change—i.e., the recognition accuracy is low under high non-linearity [37,38]. However, as shown in Figure 4, the device is highly non-linear. To improve the linearity of the conductance change of the device, a non-identical pulse scheme is adopted, as shown in Figure 8. The training pulses are fixed at width but with increasing amplitudes. The amplitude range of the potentiation process is from 2 to 6 V with 0.1 V steps, and the range of the depression process is from −2 to −6 V with −0.1 V steps. The weight updates are recorded in four training cycles, as shown in Figure 8. The non-linearity factor (NL) has been calculated by NL = average $(\frac{G-G_{linear}}{G_{linear}})$ [39], so the non-linearity factors of the normal training method are 1.09, 1.427, and 1.332 respectively, based on the data in Figure 4a. In addition, the non-linearity factors of the incremental training method are −0.62 for long-term potentiation and 0.13 for long-term depression, based on the data in Figure 8a.

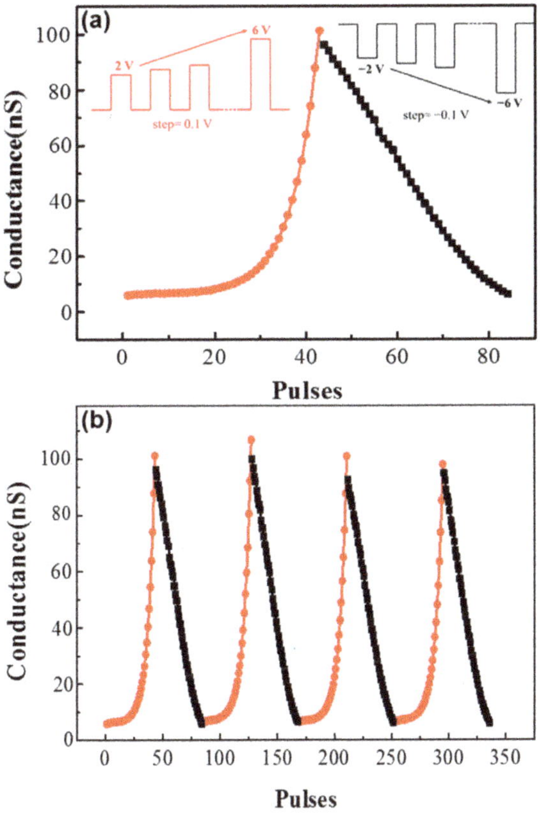

Figure 8. The measured long-term potentiation/depression synaptic function with non-identical training pulses: (**a**) the training pulses with increasing amplitudes (potentiation: from 2 to 6 V, 100 μs; depression: from −2 to −6 V, 100 μs); and (**b**) the weight updates, recorded in four training cycles.

The investigation of the switching mechanism of the device is shown in Figure 9. The conductance of the filamentary memristors mostly depends on the size and morphology of the conductive filament with several nanometers diameter in the device. Thus, the conductance of filamentary memristor does not significantly change with the change of the electrode areas. The *I*–*V* curves of the 1st SET process and conductance distribution of 25 different devices at LRS with various electrode areas (from 10 to 100 μm^2) are shown in Figure 9a,b, respectively. In Figure 9a, the current level after SET shows a positively proportional relationship with the electrode area. In statistical analysis of 25 devices at LRS in Figure 9b, such a trend can be more clearly seen in the plotting of the conductance with the electrode area. As shown in inset of Figure 9b, the linear fit result confirms that the device conductance scales linearly with the device area. As a result, the switching occurs across the entire electrode area, but not just within a local filament, suggesting a non-filamentary switching mechanism of Ta/TaO_x/Al_2O_3/Pd device. The temperature dependencies of the device conductance at LRS and HRS are studied in Figure 9c,d, respectively. With the increase of temperature, the conductance at both LRS and HRS increases as well, indicating the semiconductor conduction behavior of the device. To explain the switching mechanism of the device, we proposed a simple model [40], shown in Figure 9e. The device can be divided into three parts: a barrier layer (Al_2O_3), a switching area (interface of Al_2O_3 and TaO_x), and a conductive oxidation layer (TaO_x). The switching area is located at the interface of Al_2O_3 and TaO_x. During SET operation, a positive voltage is applied on the top electrode, the oxygen ions in the barrier layer are pulled away from the interface layer, and the materials in the interface are reduced. During RESET operation, a negative voltage is applied on the top electrode, the oxygen ions in the barrier layer are pushed into the interface layer, and the materials in the interface are oxidized. The push-and-pull of the oxygen ions in the surface can change the resistance of the device.

To implement neuromorphic computing, the device should be integrated into an array. To operate an array, a half-bias scheme is a common method. However, our device has a low ON/OFF ratio (<100) between the selected voltage and the half-selected voltage, which may cause a sneak path issue during write operation. As a result, it is hard for our device to implement a dense crossbar array without the help of a transistor or selector device. A one transistor one resistor (1T1R) or one selector one resistor (1S1R) structure should be adopted to overcome the sneak path issue during writing operation. The device structure can still be optimized to improve the linearity of the conductance changes and decrease the working voltage. In addition, the detailed non-filamentary switching mechanism in this device needs to be further explored.

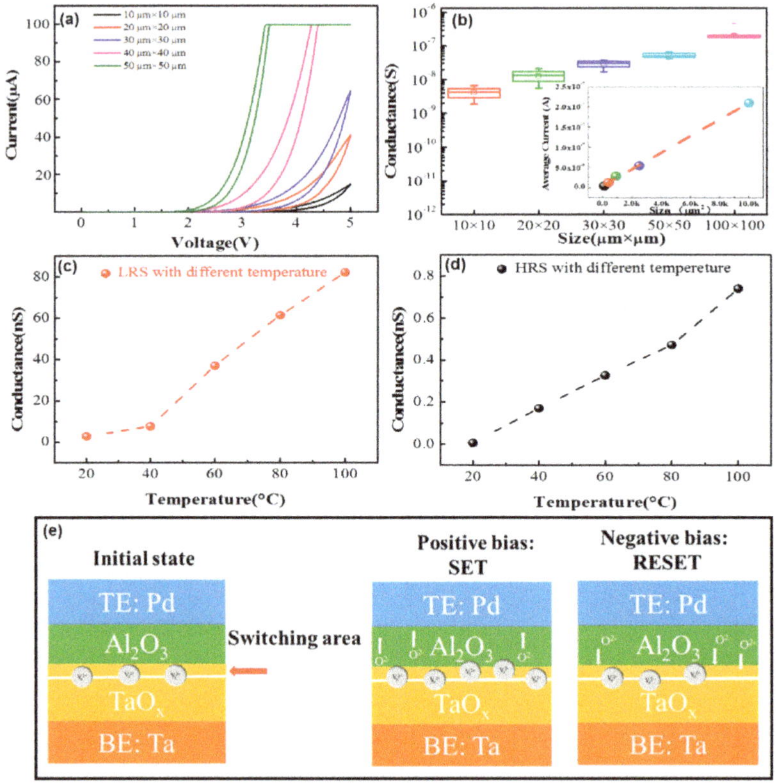

Figure 9. (**a**) The *I–V* curves of the first SET process with different electrode area sizes (from 10 μm × 10 μm to 100 μm × 100 μm). (**b**) Conductance distribution at LRS with different sized areas (the conductance states are obtained by 1 V reading voltage in 25 different devices) (inset: the linear fit result confirms that the device conductance scales linearly with device areas). (**c**) Conductance of LRS with different temperatures from 20 to 100 °C; (**d**) Conductance of HRS with different temperatures from 20 to 100 °C. (**e**) The schematic of the switching mechanism of the device; the switching area is the interface of TaO_x-Al_2O_3, and the push-and-pull of the oxygen ions in the surface can change the resistance of the interface layer.

4. Conclusions

In this paper, a $Ta/TaO_x/Al_2O_3/Pd$ memristor is fabricated, to be used as artificial synapse. The device shows bipolar analog-resistive switching behavior. Moreover, multilevel conductance states with a satisfying retention time (>1000 s) can be obtained by modulating voltages or compliance currents under DC sweeping mode. Based on the bipolar analog switching, synaptic functions, including long-term potentiation/depression, paired-pulse facilitation, and spiking time dependent plasticity are successfully mimicked. For ANN applications, the determined target conductance, the linearity, and the writing errors are carefully examined. The results suggest that as an artificial synapse, the $Ta/TaO_x/Al_2O_3/Pd$ memristor is a promising candidate for neuromorphic computing.

Author Contributions: Conceptualization: R.W.; data curation: R.W.; formal analysis: X.Z. (Xumeng Zhang); funding acquisition: Q.L.; investigation: R.W. and X.Z. (Xumeng Zhang); project administration: T.S. and Q.L.; resources: X.Z. (Xiaolong Zhao), Z.W. and R.C.; software: W.W. and J.L.; supervision, T.S., S.L., Q.L. and M.L.; visualization: J.W.; writing (original draft): R.W.

Funding: This work is supported by the National High Technology Research Development Program under Grant No. 2017YFB0405603; and the National Natural Science Foundation of China under Grant Nos. 61521064, 61732020, 61751401, and 61522408.

Conflicts of Interest: The authors declare no conflict of interest.

References

1. Fusi, S.; Annunziato, M.; Badoni, D.; Salamon, A.; Amit, D.J. Spike-driven synaptic plasticity: Theory, simulation, VLSI implementation. *Neural Comput.* **2000**, *12*, 2227–2258. [CrossRef] [PubMed]
2. Laughlin, S.B.; van Steveninck, R.R.D.; Anderson, J.C. The metabolic cost of neural information. *Nat. Neurosci.* **1998**, *1*, 36–41. [CrossRef] [PubMed]
3. Saremi, M. Modeling and Simulation of the Programmable Metallization Cells (PMCs) and Diamond-Based Power Devices. Ph.D. Thesis, Arizona State University, Tempe, AZ, USA, 2017.
4. Strukov, D.B.; Snider, G.S.; Stewart, D.R.; Williams, R.S. The missing memristor found. *Nature* **2008**, *453*, 80–83. [CrossRef] [PubMed]
5. Saremi, M. A physical-based simulation for the dynamic behavior of photodoping mechanism in chalcogenide materials used in the lateral programmable metallization cells. *Solid State Ion.* **2016**, *290*, 1–5. [CrossRef]
6. Saremi, M. Carrier mobility extraction method in ChGs in the UV light exposure. *Micro Nano Lett.* **2016**, *11*, 762–764. [CrossRef]
7. Jo, S.H.; Chang, T.; Ebong, I.; Bhadviya, B.B.; Mazumder, P.; Lu, W. Nanoscale Memristor Device as Synapse in Neuromorphic Systems. *Nano Lett.* **2010**, *10*, 1297–1301. [CrossRef] [PubMed]
8. Zhang, X.M.; Liu, S.; Zhao, X.L.; Wu, F.C.; Wu, Q.T.; Wang, W.; Cao, R.R.; Fang, Y.L.; Lv, H.B.; Long, S.B. Emulating short-term and long-term plasticity of bio-synapse based on cu/a-Si/Pt memristor. *IEEE Electron Device Lett.* **2017**, *38*, 1208–1211. [CrossRef]
9. Yu, S.M.; Wu, Y.; Jeyasingh, R.; Kuzum, D.G.; Wong, H.S.P. An electronic synapse device based on metal oxide resistive switching memory for neuromorphic computation. *IEEE Trans. Electron Devices* **2011**, *58*, 2729–2737. [CrossRef]
10. Yu, S.M.; Gao, B.; Fang, Z.; Yu, H.Y.; Kang, J.F.; Wong, H.S.P. A low energy oxide-based electronic synaptic device for neuromorphic visual systems with tolerance to device variation. *Adv. Mater.* **2013**, *25*, 1774–1779. [CrossRef] [PubMed]
11. Saremi, M.; Rajabi, S.; Barnaby, H.J.; Kozicki, M.N. The effects of process variation on the parametric model of the static impedance behavior of programmable metallization cell (PMC). *MRS Proc.* **2014**, *1692*. [CrossRef]
12. Suri, M.; Bichler, O.; Querlioz, D.; Cueto, O.; Perniola, L.; Sousa, V.; Vuillaume, D.; Gamrat, C.; DeSalvo, B. Phase change memory as synapse for ultra-dense neuromorphic systems: Application to complex visual pattern extraction. In Proceedings of the 2011 IEEE International Electron Devices Meeting (IEDM), Washington, DC, USA, 5–7 December 2011.
13. Kaneko, Y.; Nishitani, Y.; Ueda, M. Ferroelectric artificial synapses for recognition of a multishaded image. *IEEE Trans. Electron Devices* **2014**, *61*, 2827–2833. [CrossRef]

14. Jerry, M.; Chen, P.Y.; Zhang, J.C.; Sharma, P.; Ni, K.; Yu, S.M.; Datta, S. Ferroelectric FET analog synapse for acceleration of deep neural network training. In Proceedings of the 2017 IEEE International Electron Devices Meeting (IEDM), San Francisco, CA, USA, 2–6 December 2017.
15. Oh, S.; Kim, T.; Kwak, M.; Song, J.; Woo, J.; Jeon, S.; Yoo, I.K.; Hwang, H. $HfZrO_x$-based ferroelectric synapse device with 32 levels of conductance states for neuromorphic applications. *IEEE Electron Device Lett.* **2017**, *38*, 732–735. [CrossRef]
16. Suri, M.; Querlioz, D.; Bichler, O.; Palma, G.; Vianello, E.; Vuillaume, D.; Gamrat, C.; DeSalvo, B. Bio-inspired stochastic computing using binary CBRAM synapses. *IEEE Trans. Electron Devices* **2013**, *60*, 2402–2409. [CrossRef]
17. Yan, X.; Zhang, L.; Chen, H.; Li, X.; Wang, J.; Liu, Q.; Lu, C.; Chen, J.; Wu, H.; Zhou, P. Graphene oxide quantum dots based memristors with progressive conduction tuning for artificial synaptic learning. *Adv. Funct. Mater.* **2018**, *28*, 1803728. [CrossRef]
18. Shi, Y.; Liang, X.; Yuan, B.; Chen, V.; Li, H.; Hui, F.; Yu, Z.; Yuan, F.; Pop, E.; Wong, H.S.P.; et al. Electronic synapses made of layered two-dimensional materials. *Nat. Electron.* **2018**, *1*, 458. [CrossRef]
19. Yu, S.M.; Gao, B.; Fang, Z.; Yu, H.Y.; Kang, J.F.; Wong, H.S.P. Stochastic learning in oxide binary synaptic device for neuromorphic computing. *Front. Neurosci.* **2013**, *7*. [CrossRef] [PubMed]
20. Garbin, D.; Vianello, E.; Bichler, O.; Rafhay, Q.; Gamrat, C.; Ghibaudo, G.; DeSalvo, B.; Perniola, L. HfO2-based OxRAM devices as synapses for convolutional neural networks. *IEEE Trans. Electron Devices* **2015**, *62*, 2494–2501. [CrossRef]
21. Bill, J.; Legenstein, R. A compound memristive synapse model for statistical learning through STDP in spiking neural networks. *Front. Neurosci.* **2014**, *8*, 412. [CrossRef] [PubMed]
22. Piccolboni, G.; Molas, G.; Portal, J.M.; Coquand, R.; Bocquet, M.; Garbin, D.; Vianello, E.; Carabasse, C.; Delaye, V.; Pellissier, C.; et al. Investigation of the potentialities of Vertical Resistive RAM (VRRAM) for neuromorphic applications. In Proceedings of the 2015 IEEE International Electron Devices Meeting (IEDM), Washington, DC, USA, 7–9 December 2015.
23. Yu, S.M.; Gao, B.; Fang, Z.; Yu, H.Y.; Kang, J.F.; Wong, H.S.P. A neuromorphic visual system using RRAM synaptic devices with sub-pJ energy and tolerance to variability: Experimental characterization and large-scale modeling. In Proceedings of the 2012 IEEE International Electron Devices Meeting (IEDM), San Francisco, CA, USA, 10–13 December 2012.
24. Yan, X.; Zhao, J.; Liu, S.; Zhou, Z.; Liu, Q.; Chen, J.; Liu, X.Y. Memristor with Ag-cluster-doped TiO_2 films as artificial synapse for neuroinspired computing. *Adv. Funct. Mater.* **2018**, *28*. [CrossRef]
25. Wang, I.T.; Chang, C.C.; Chiu, L.W.; Chou, T.Y.; Hou, T.H. 3D $Ta/TaO_x/TiO_2/Ti$ synaptic array and linearity tuning of weight update for hardware neural network applications. *Nanotechnology* **2016**, *27*. [CrossRef] [PubMed]
26. Jeong, Y.; Kim, S.; Lu, W.D. Utilizing multiple state variables to improve the dynamic range of analog switching in a memristor. *Appl. Phys. Lett.* **2015**, *107*. [CrossRef]
27. Wu, W.; Wu, H.Q.; Gao, B.; Deng, N.; Yu, S.M.; Qian, H. Improving analog switching in HfO_x-based resistive memory with a thermal enhanced layer. *IEEE Electron Device Lett.* **2017**, *38*, 1019–1022. [CrossRef]
28. Shi, T.; Wu, J.F.; Liu, Y.; Yang, R.; Guo, X. Behavioral plasticity emulated with lithium lanthanum titanate-based memristive devices: Habituation. *Adv. Electron. Mater.* **2017**, *3*, 10–1002. [CrossRef]
29. Geoffrey, W.; Burr, R.M.S.; Abu, S.; Sangbum, K.; Seyoung, K.; Severin, S.; Kumar, V.; Masatoshi, I.; Pritish, N.; Alessandro, F.; et al. Neuromorphic computing using non-volatile memory. *Adv. Phys. X* **2017**, *2*, 89–124. [CrossRef]
30. Yang, R.; Terabe, K.; Yao, Y.; Tsuruoka, T.; Hasegawa, T.; Gimzewski, J.K.; Aono, M. Synaptic plasticity and memory functions achieved in a WO_{3-x}-based nanoionics device by using the principle of atomic switch operation. *Nanotechnology* **2013**, *24*, 384003. [CrossRef] [PubMed]
31. Pan, R.B.; Li, J.; Zhuge, F.; Zhu, L.Q.; Liang, L.Y.; Zhang, H.L.; Gao, J.H.; Cao, H.T.; Fu, B.; Li, K. Synaptic devices based on purely electronic memristors. *Appl. Phys. Lett.* **2016**, *108*. [CrossRef]
32. Wang, Y.F.; Lin, Y.C.; Wang, I.T.; Lin, T.P.; Hou, T.H. Characterization and modeling of nonfilamentary $Ta/TaO_x/TiO_2/Ti$ analog synaptic device. *Sci. Rep.* **2015**, *5*. [CrossRef] [PubMed]
33. Shi, T.; Yang, R.; Guo, X. Coexistence of analog and digital resistive switching in BiFeO3-based memristive devices. *Solid State Ion.* **2016**, *296*, 114–119. [CrossRef]

34. Sun, Y.; Xu, H.; Wang, C.; Song, B.; Liu, H.; Liu, Q.; Liu, S.; Li, Q. A Ti/AlO_x/TaO_x/Pt analog synapse for memristive neural network. *IEEE Electron Device Lett.* **2018**, *39*, 1298–1301. [CrossRef]
35. Lynch, M.A. Long-term potentiation and memory. *Physiol. Rev.* **2004**, *84*, 87–136. [CrossRef] [PubMed]
36. Abbott, L.F.; Regehr, W.G. Synaptic computation. *Nature* **2004**, *431*, 796–803. [CrossRef] [PubMed]
37. Jang, J.W.; Park, S.; Burr, G.W.; Hwang, H.; Jeong, Y.H. Optimization of conductance change in $Pr_{1-x}Ca_xMnO_3$-Based synaptic devices for neuromorphic systems. *IEEE Electron Device Lett.* **2015**, *36*, 457–459. [CrossRef]
38. Woo, J.; Yu, S. Resistive memory-based analog synapse: The pursuit for linear and symmetric weight update. *IEEE Nanotechnol. Mag.* **2018**, *12*, 36–44. [CrossRef]
39. Bae, J.-H.; Lim, S.; Park, B.-G.; Lee, J.-H. High-density and near-linear synaptic device based on a reconfigurable gated Schottky diode. *IEEE Electron Device Lett.* **2017**, *38*, 1153–1156. [CrossRef]
40. Luo, Q.; Zhang, X.; Hu, Y.; Gong, T.; Xu, X.; Yuan, P.; Ma, H.; Dong, D.; Lv, H.; Long, S. Self-rectifying and forming-free resistive-switching device for embedded memory application. *IEEE Electron Device Lett.* **2018**, *39*, 664–667. [CrossRef]

materials

MDPI

Article

Three-Dimensional (3D) Vertical Resistive Random-Access Memory (VRRAM) Synapses for Neural Network Systems

Wookyung Sun [1,*], Sujin Choi [1], Bokyung Kim [1] and Junhee Park [2,*]

[1] Department of Electronic and Electrical Engineering, Ewha Womans University, Seoul 03760, Korea; sujinchoi26@gmail.com (S.C.); bkkim0505@hanmail.net (B.K.)
[2] Medical Research Institute, Ewha Womans University, Seoul 03760, Korea
* Correspondence: wkyungsun@ewha.ac.kr (W.S.); junhee.park@ewha.ac.kr (J.P.)

Received: 11 September 2019; Accepted: 18 October 2019; Published: 22 October 2019

Abstract: Memristor devices are generally suitable for incorporation in neuromorphic systems as synapses because they can be integrated into crossbar array circuits with high area efficiency. In the case of a two-dimensional (2D) crossbar array, however, the size of the array is proportional to the neural network's depth and the number of its input and output nodes. This means that a 2D crossbar array is not suitable for a deep neural network. On the other hand, synapses that use a memristor with a 3D structure are suitable for implementing a neuromorphic chip for a multi-layered neural network. In this study, we propose a new optimization method for machine learning weight changes that considers the structural characteristics of a 3D vertical resistive random-access memory (VRRAM) structure for the first time. The newly proposed synapse operating principle of the 3D VRRAM structure can simplify the complexity of a neuron circuit. This study investigates the operating principle of 3D VRRAM synapses with comb-shaped word lines and demonstrates that the proposed 3D VRRAM structure will be a promising solution for a high-density neural network hardware system.

Keywords: RRAM; vertical RRAM; neuromorphics; neural network hardware; reinforcement learning

1. Introduction

In recent years, neuromorphic computing has emerged as a complementary system to the von Neumann architecture. Much of the research on neural network hardware implementation discusses how to connect large numbers of neurons and synapses. As a consequence, various memory devices such as static random-access memory, resistive random-access memory (RRAM), floating-gate (FG) memory, and phase change memory have been implemented as the synapse model in neural network hardware systems [1–4].

The most popular device-level component chosen to implement the synapses is the "memory resistor", or memristor, because the resistance value of a memristor is a function of its historical activity. Moreover, energy efficiency is a key challenge of neuromorphic computing and RRAM is attractive for large-scale system demonstration due to its relatively lower energy consumption as compared with other synaptic devices [5]. The most common use of the memristor two-dimensional (2D)-crossbar is as a multiple memristor synapse since a single memristor cannot represent the positive and negative weights of synapses. However, 2D crossbar array synapses are not suitable for the implementation of deep neural networks (DNN) because the chip area depends on both the depth of the neural network and the number of input and output nodes.

The three-dimensional (3D) vertical resistance random-access memory (VRRAM) promises to minimize the area of a resistive memory. It can be categorized into two types based on its word line structures [6]: 3D VRRAM with a word line (WL) planar structure uses metal planes as WL electrodes, while a 3D VRRAM with a WL even/odd structure has comb-shaped WLs separated by etching. This structure is more promising than a WL plane structure for the VRRAM architecture because it has the same performance as a double cell bit [7,8]. Therefore, if a 3D VRRAM is used for synapses instead of a 2D crossbar array, as shown in Figure 1, the chip area of a DNN system can be effectively reduced. Recently, several works have evaluated the synaptic RRAM using 3D VRRAM. A high-density 3D synaptic architecture based on Ta/TaOx/TiO_2/Ti RRAM is proposed as a neuromorphic computation hardware and the analog synaptic plasticity is simulated using the physical and compact models [9]. The potentiality of the VRRAM concept for various neuromorphic applications is investigated with one synapse being emulated by one VRRAM pillar [10]. Yet many of these studies have focused on experimental demonstration at a single RRAM cell level, and the idea that neuromorphic applications are possible is only presented as a concept. There are some previous studies related to 3D VRRAM with a WL planar structure. For example, the four-layer 3D RRAM integrated with FinFET (Fin Field-Effect Transistor) was developed for brain-inspired computing and in-memory computing [11], and 3D vertical array of RRAM was proposed for storing and computing large-scale weight matrices in the neural network [12]. However, a 3D VRRAM with comb-shaped WLs is more promising for a more efficient synaptic RRAM architecture because it has a double cell bit. Although research on 3D VRRAM with comb-shaped WLs has been published, it has focused on RRAM device variation, and explored the concept of many devices connected to one pillar operating as one synapse to overcome the variation [13]. Implementing a single synapse with multiple devices reduces the benefits of using 3D VRRAM. Moreover, reported previously related studies did not evaluate the circuit level properties of 3D VRRAM with comb-shaped WLs. Theoretical investigations are insufficient for exploring the relationship between synapse weight change and memory device resistance in 3D VRRAM.

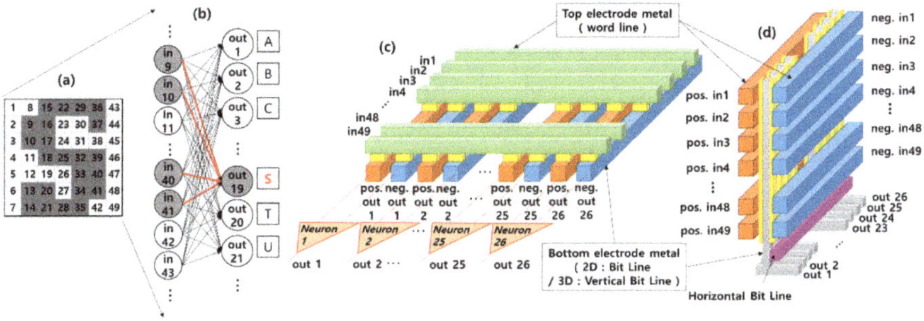

Figure 1. (**a**) The input pattern for letter 'S'. (**b**) A neural network consisting of 49 input neurons and 26 output neurons (red lines = increased weights in the learning process) (**c**) Two-dimensional (2D) crossbar array synapses for implementing the neural network as shown in (b). (**d**) 3D vertical resistive random-access memory (VRRAM) synapses with the same performance as the synapses in (c).

In this study, we propose a new optimization method for machine learning weight changes that considers the structural characteristics of 3D VRRAM. This study investigates the operating principle of 3D VRRAM synapses with comb-shaped WLs and demonstrates that this structure is a promising synaptic model for neural network systems. The remainder of this paper is organized as follows: Section 2 describes a new 3D VRRAM crossbar array synapse incorporating a synaptic memristor model and learning operations for a guide training algorithm [14,15]. In Section 3, the accuracy of a neural network with 3D VRRAM synapses is measured by classifying 7 × 7 alphabet letter images using HSPICE circuit simulation. The conclusions are presented in Section 4.

2. Materials and Methods

2.1. A Neural Network Learning Method Using a 3D VRRAM Synapse

A neural network system design with 3D VRRAM synapses is shown in Figure 1. We evaluated the accuracy of the proposed 3D VRRAM synapses circuit by classifying 7 × 7 images representing alphabet letters as shown in Figure 2. Figure 1b shows a neural network consisting of 49 input neurons and 26 output neurons designed to classify input letter images into 26 classes as shown in Figure 1a. For the letter 'S', the nodes or neurons that generate the output spike are represented in gray, and increased weights in the learning process are indicated by red lines. The most common memristor application in neuromorphic systems is as the synapses in a 2D crossbar array as shown in Figure 1c. The weight of one synapse is represented by the conductance difference between two memristors because a single memristor cannot have both positive and negative weight values for a synapse [2]. For example, neuron 1 compares the total current of "positive out 1" in the red line with that of the "negative out 1" as shown in Figure 1c. If the "positive out 1" current is greater than the "negative out 1" current, neuron 1 spikes, which means the output of neuron 1 is a '1'. In contrast, when the "negative out 1" current is greater than the "positive out 1" current, the output of neuron 1 is '0'. The learning architecture for this implementation is constructed as a 49 × 52 2D memristor crossbar array.

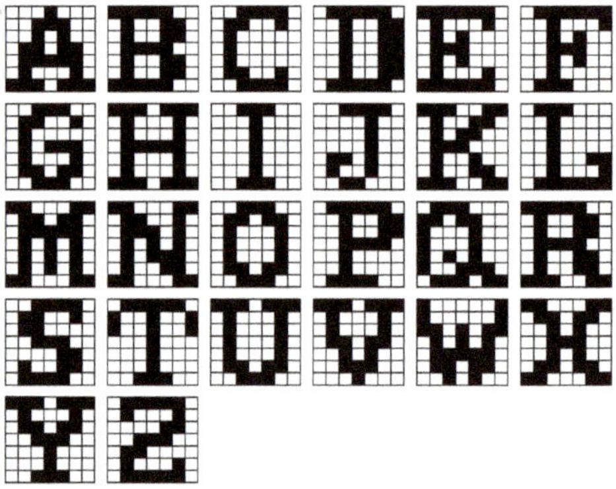

Figure 2. 7 × 7 original alphabet images.

If a 3D VRRAM is used for synapses, however, the chip area efficiency can be increased. Figure 1d shows a 3D VRRAM synapses structure with the same performance as Figure 1c. The 'red' and 'blue' word lines in Figure 1d represent "positive" and "negative" outputs, respectively. Therefore, only the area for 26 vertical pillars is needed to implement 26 classes in contrast to the need for 52 column lines in the 2D crossbar array. Moreover, the pillar structure of 3D VRRAM makes it simpler to build neuron circuits because there is no need for a circuit to a compare positive and negative current.

A "guide training" algorithm is used to verify the accuracy and the performance of the 3D VRRAM synapses in HSPICE simulation [14,15]. This is a modified reinforcement learning algorithm and it is optimized for hardware implementation because it does not include a backpropagation algorithm. The algorithm was applied to image classification using the 2D crossbar memristor synaptic circuit, and its performance has been verified by showing a high learning success rate. The initial synaptic weights were randomized before the new training event was started. The single data set of 26 images (Figure 2), one for each alphabet letter, was defined as one epoch. After training, testing was performed to classify 20 test image sets consisting of the original or inverted pixel images, as shown in Figure 3. For example, the noise 0% test set consisted of 520 original images, and the noise 4% test set consisted of 520 images with two randomly selected pixels inverted.

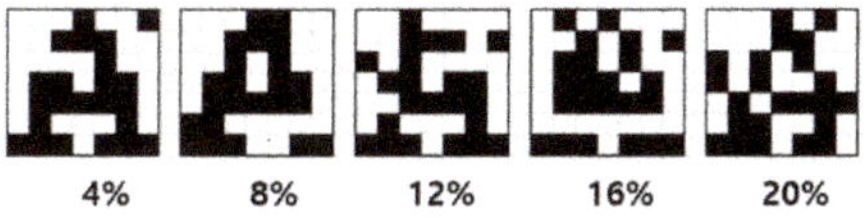

Figure 3. 7 × 7 inverted pixel "A" image with noise from 4% to 20%.

2.2. 3D VRRAM Synapse Operation Mechanism

For this paper, we actually simulated the 3D VRRAM structure as shown in Figure 1d, but a description of the behavior of the real structure would be very complex. Therefore, we will explain the operation of 3D VRRAM with a simple structure as shown in Figure 4.

Figure 4a,b shows a simple two-pixel image to illustrate the weight change in a 3D VRRAM synapse configured as shown in Figure 4c. To categorize an image, a spike should be generated at the corresponding output or neuron of the input image. This means that a spike will occur at the Out1 neuron when Figure 4a is an input, and it will appear at the Out2 neuron if Figure 4b is an input. To allow a 3D VRRAM to operate as synapse circuit, its 'Out1' current must be larger than its 'Out2' current when Figure 4a is the input image. Conversely, if Figure 4b is an input image, Out2 current should be larger than Out1 current.

The 3D VRRAM in Figure 4c has a total of 8 memristors between its pillars (Out1 and Out2) and odd word lines (positive word line; P1, P2) or even word lines (negative word line; N1, N2). The number of word lines indicates the number of pixels. The memristor is a two-terminal device, so the "P1-Out1" memristor existing between the P1 word line and the Out1 pillar or vertical bit line is controlled by the bias of P1 and Out1. Reduced resistance in the memristors connected to the positive word line results in an increase in pillar current, while increased resistance of the memristor connected to the negative word line reduces the pillar current.

There are various memristor models for circuit simulation [16–20]. We used the generalized memristor model for this work [16,17], and it was coded in Verilog-A for the HSPICE circuit simulator. Figure 4d is the nonlinear I-V characteristic and Figure 4e is the linearly modulated potentiation behavior of an experimentally measured Ta_2O_5 memristor device [21]. It shows that the experiment and simulation results using our model are qualitatively consistent.

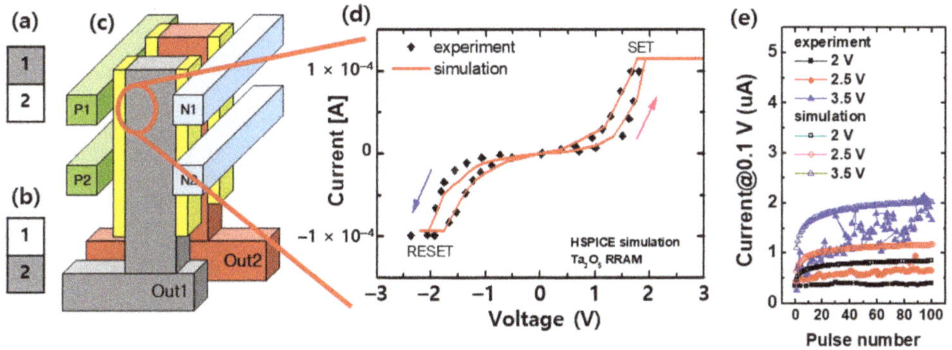

Figure 4. A two-pixel image where (**a**) pixel 1 is black and Out1 is "1"; (**b**) pixel 2 is black and Out2 is "1"; (**c**) 3D VRRAM synapse for a two-pixel image; (**d**) nonlinear I-V characteristic; and (**e**) linearly modulated potentiation behaviors of the Ta_2O_5 memristor device [21].

The memristor current is modeled by the hyperbolic sine function, as shown in Equation (1) [15,16]. Conductance is proportional to state variable x(t), which has a value between 0 and 1.

$$\mathrm{I(t)} = \left\{ \begin{array}{ll} a_1 x(t)\sinh(bV(t)), & V(t) \geq 0 \\ a_2 x(t)\sinh(bV(t)), & V(t) < 0 \end{array} \right\} \tag{1}$$

The change in the state variable over time is based on two different functions, $g(V(t))$ and $f(x(t))$.

$$\frac{dx}{dt} = g(V(t))f(x(t)) \tag{2}$$

$$g(V(t)) = \left\{ \begin{array}{c} A_p\left(e^{V(t)} - e^{V_p}\right),\ V(t) > V_p \\ -A_n\left(e^{-V(t)} - e^{V_n}\right),\ V(t) < -V_n \\ 0,\ -V_n \leq V(t) \leq V_p \end{array} \right\} \tag{3}$$

$$f(x(t)) = \left\{ \begin{array}{cc} e^{-\alpha_p(x-x_p)} w_p\left(x, x_p\right), & x \geq x_p \\ 1, & x < x_p \end{array} \right\} \tag{4}$$

$$f(x(t)) = \left\{ \begin{array}{cc} e^{\alpha_n(x+x_n-1)} w_n(x, x_n), & x \leq 1 - x_n \\ 1, & x > 1 - x_n \end{array} \right\} \tag{5}$$

$$w_p\left(x, x_p\right) = \frac{x_p - x}{1 - x_p} + 1 \tag{6}$$

$$w_n(x, x_n) = \frac{x}{1 - x_n} \tag{7}$$

where $g(V(t))$ is a function of a programming threshold on the memristor model and $f(x(t))$ was used to limit the motion of the state variable (x_p and x_n). The function w_p and w_n are developed to limit the range of the state variable between 0 and 1. The model parameters used in this study are listed in Table 1.

Table 1. Parameters used in the synapse guide model.

Symbol	Value	Symbol	Value
a_1	1×10^{-5}	A_n	1×10^{7}
a_2	1×10^{-5}	x_p	0.2
b	2.1	x_n	0.25
V_p	1 (V)	α_p	7
V_n	1 (V)	α_n	6
A_p	3×10^{6}	x_o	0.3

The memristor's conductance changes from a high-resistance state (HRS) to a low-resistance state (LRS) when subjected to a voltage higher than the set voltage (= 1.2 V). A lower voltage than the reset voltage (= −1.2 V) changes the conductance of the memristor from an LRS to an HRS. The weight of a synapse or the resistance of each memristor could be changed during the network's learning process but should be unchanged during the test process. To find the proper training voltage (Vtraining) and test voltage (Vtest), the change of resistance is simulated by applying various voltages to each memristor device. The voltage was applied from 0.5 V to 1.5 V or −0.5 V to −1.5 V at 0.25 V intervals. The unit pulse width is 10 ns and the rising and falling edge time is 0.5 ns. The line resistance of a vertical pillar is 3 Ω/cell with 20 nm class technology [8]. As shown in Figure 5a, the resistance changes only at 1.25 V and 1.5 V for five applied voltages because applying voltages greater than the set voltage (Vset) reduces resistance. Similarly, Figure 5b shows that the resistance changes at a voltage lower than the reset voltage (Vreset) but does not change at a higher voltage. Therefore, we set Vtraining = 1.5 V or −1.5 V, and Vtest = 1 V or −1 V considering the voltage drop in the crossbar array.

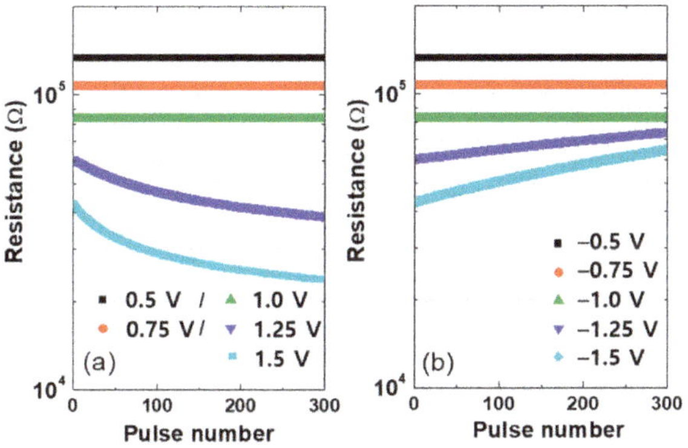

Figure 5. Resistance change of a memristor according to the (**a**) positive voltage and (**b**) negative voltage applied.

First, the sequence of 3D VRRAM synapse learning is as follows. Figure 6 shows the circuit diagram of Figure 4c. If the input image is Figure 4a or Figure 4b, a spike is generated at the Out1 or Out2 neuron, respectively. In this study, we adopted the "winner-take-all" method to determine the neurons in which spikes occur. Thus, a spike in Out1 means that the current flowing to this neuron is the largest among the output neuron currents. Referring to Figure 6, the current of the Out1 neuron should be larger than the current of Out2 when the input image is Figure 4a. In the guide training method, only black pixel data is used for neural network learning, changing the weight of the synapse, or the resistance of the memristor connected to the black pixel [15].

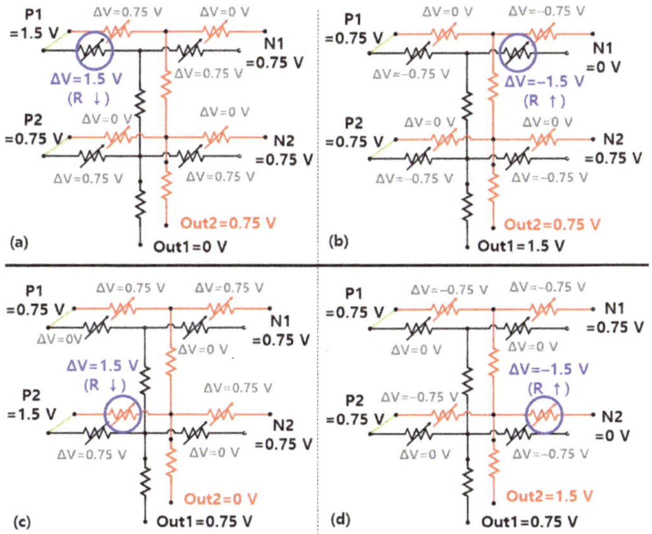

Figure 6. Simplified circuit diagrams of the 3D vertical synapse during the training procedure showing the voltages applied to (**a**) P1-Out1; (**b**) N1-Out1; (**c**) P2-Out2; and (**d**) N2-Out2 memristors when training Figure 4a,b.

Memristors connected to word lines P1 and P2 act as positive memristors that increase the weight of synapses. Increasing synaptic weights means that the resistance of the memristors is reduced, so Vtraining = 1.5 V is applied to P1 and P2 to increase the current flowing to Out1. In contrast, the memristor connected to N1 and N2 is a negative memristor that reduces the current in the Out1 neuron, and Vtraining = −1.5 V is applied to increase the resistance of the memristor. The number of positive and negative word line pairs matches the number of pixels. For example, P1 and N1 determine the characteristics of pixel 1 of the input image.

An example of training for Figure 4a is illustrated in Figure 6a,b. The goal of the synapse learning is to lower the weight of synapses connected to black pixels, increasing the Out1 line current. In principle, all memristor devices connected to the Out1 line (P1-Out1, P2-Out1, N1-Out1, N2-Out1), which is shown in black lines in Figure 6, affect the generation of a spike when Figure 4a is the input image. However, since only pixel 1 is black in Figure 4a, the resistance of P1-Out1 and N1-Out1 is changed to increase the current of Out1 as shown in Figure 6a,b. In other words, the current of Out1 becomes larger than Out2 only when pixel 1 is black. Therefore, the resistance of "P1-Out1" should be reduced and that of "N1-Out1" should be increased to generate a spike on the Out1 neuron or increase Out1 current.

The most important thing in the 3D vertical synapse learning process is that only the weights of the black pixel memristors change during learning, leaving other memristors unchanged. Therefore, to change the weight, a voltage greater than Vset is applied between the two electrodes of the P memristor, and a voltage less than Vreset is applied to its complementary N memristor. Figure 6a,b illustrates the training of the positive and negative memristors for the Figure 4a image and the Out1 neuron. During Out1 neuron training, Out2 remains at 0.75 V, and 0 V is applied to Out1 during positive memristor training and Vtraining (= 1.5 V) during negative memristor training. Basically, Vtraining (= 1.5 V) and 0 V are applied to the positive word line and negative word line, respectively, corresponding to the black pixels of the input image. The other four memristors (P1-Out2, P2-Out2, N1-Out2, N2-Out2), which are pictured with red lines in Figure 6, generate a spike on the Out2 neuron when the input is Figure 4b. Figure 6c,d shows the training procedure for Figure 4b like the training for the Out1 neuron.

The pillar of the 3D VRRAM connected to the Out1 neuron is used in common to train the positive and negative memristors. Therefore, the two processes should be done sequentially. The bias conditions for training and testing over time are shown in Figure 7. "Pos. for Out1" and "Neg. for Out1" represent the voltages that change the resistance of the positive and negative memristors. Since there are two pixels in Figure 4a,b, training occurs in a total of four sequences in Figure 7. The learning sequence increases in proportion to the number of pixels in the input image. The number of output neurons determines the number of test sequences. For example, if the input images are Figure 4a,b, we need two output sequences in this learning simulation.

Figure 8 shows the voltages in the simplified circuit diagrams of the 3D vertical synapses during the testing procedure. Unlike the learning process, the weight of the synapse (i.e., the resistance of the memristors), should not change during the testing process. Therefore, the test voltages are set to 1 V for the positive memristor and −1 V for the negative memristor, which are smaller than the set or reset voltages. During the learning process, the voltage applied to the memristor is determined by the difference between the voltage applied to the positive or negative word line and the voltage applied to the output line. During the test, however, the output line is held at 0 V and its current is determined only by the voltage applied to the word line. It means that 1 V and −1 V are respectively applied to the positive and negative word lines corresponding to black pixels. Therefore, when a voltage corresponding to Figure 4a is applied to the positive and negative word lines, the current of the Out1 neuron becomes larger than that of Out2 neuron, corresponding to the memristor resistances changed during the training process.

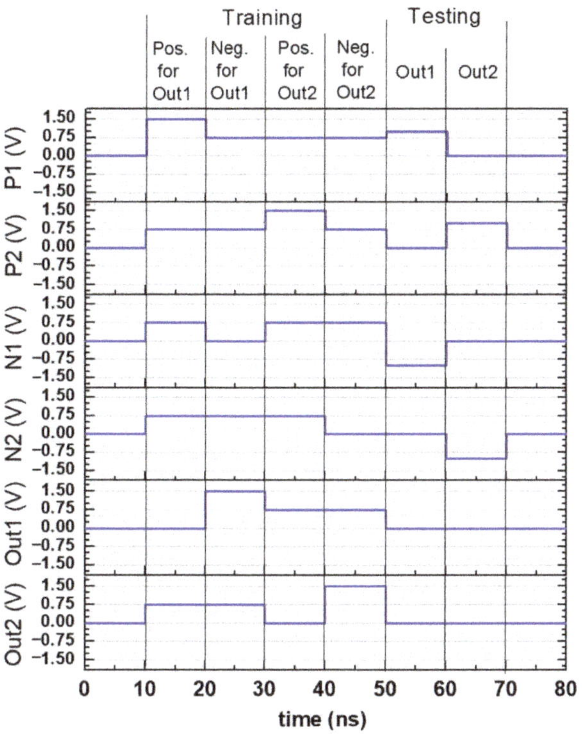

Figure 7. Input signal voltages at training and testing procedures.

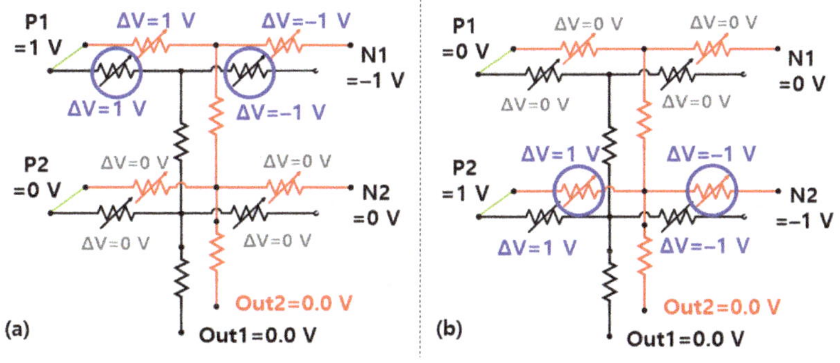

Figure 8. Simplified circuit diagrams of 3D vertical synapse during the testing procedure showing the test voltages applied to (**a**) the Out1 neuron and (**b**) the Out2 neuron.

3. Results

To evaluate the accuracy of the proposed 3D VRRAM synapses, a guide training algorithm was tested by classifying the alphabet in 7 × 7 letter images in an HSPICE simulation. The initial synaptic weights were randomized before the start of the new training event. The single data set of 26 images (Figure 2), one for each alphabet letter, was defined as 1 epoch. After training, testing was performed to classify 20 test image sets consisting of the original or inverted pixel images. For example, the noise 0% test set consisted of 520 original images, and the noise 4% test set consisted of 520 images with two randomly selected pixels inverted.

To confirm that the resistances were changed according to the training epoch, we applied the "S" image to the input and observed the synaptic change between the input neuron and the corresponding output neuron. Figure 9 shows the resistance change of the positive memristors according to the training epoch. There are 49 lines in the graph because the number of pixels or input neurons is 49. The training process enhances the synaptic weights of the input neurons associated with black pixels among the 49 pixels, and the enhancement of the synaptic weight means a decrease in resistance. The memristors with lowered resistance by training are shown by the red lines in Figure 9. In contrast to the positive memristors, the resistance of the negative memristors are increased by the training epoch. In Figure 10, as in Figure 9, only the memristors with increased resistance by training are shown in red.

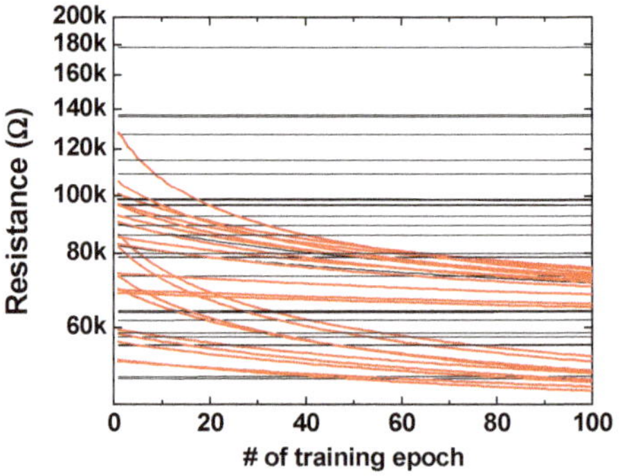

Figure 9. Resistance change of the positive memristors as a function of training epochs.

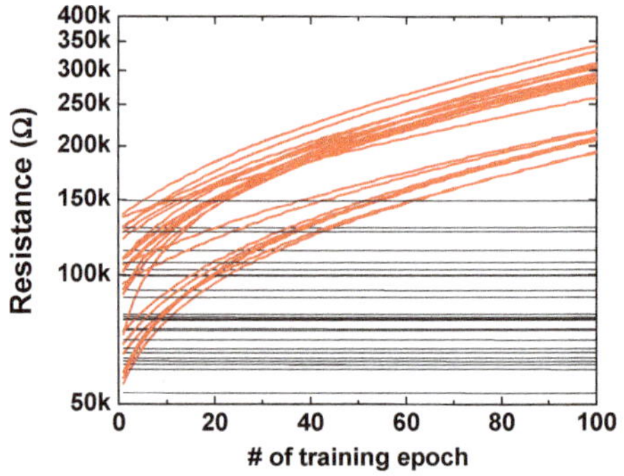

Figure 10. Resistance change of the negative memristors as a function of training epochs.

4. Discussion

In order to determine the appropriate number of training epochs, the learning accuracy was evaluated by varying the number of training epochs from 1 to 300. Figure 11a shows the accuracy of pattern classification according to the number of training epochs. Only the original image was used in the test, and the accuracy of the pattern classification increases as the number of training epochs increases. The accuracy of the training after 100 epochs, however, is almost unchanged. Thus, we set 100 epochs as the default for neural network training simulation.

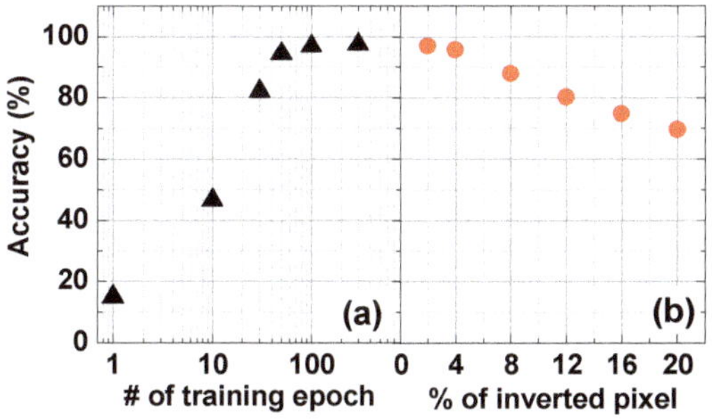

Figure 11. The accuracy of pattern classification after training according to (**a**) the number of training epochs and (**b**) the percentage of inverted pixels.

In order to verify how accurately the pattern classification can be performed even if noise is added to the input image, simulations were performed with an increasing number of inverted pixels as shown in Figure 11b. Obviously, as the noise increases in the input image, the accuracy of the pattern classification decreases. The simulation results, however, show 80% accuracy until the inverted pixel percentage increases to 12%. This means that 3D VRRAMs are usable as synapses in a neural network system. Therefore, using 3D VRRAM as the synapse structure of a neural network can greatly improve chip area utilization. In this study, we evaluated the accuracy of a neural network consisting only of input and output nodes with no hidden layers. A 3D VRRAM synapse with comb-shaped WLs structured with hidden layers is a subject for future work, and we will demonstrate the effects of 3D VRRAM synapses by performing simulations in a more diverse learning environment.

5. Conclusions

In this study, a 3D VRRAM structure was newly proposed as the synapse of a neural network system. It was concluded that 3D VRRAM implemented as synapses can increase the chip area efficiency and simplify the neuron circuits. This study investigates the operating principle of 3D VRRAM using comb-shaped WL synapses and proves that this structure has promise for a neural network system. The accuracy of a neural network with 3D VRRAM synapses was measured by classifying 7×7 alphabet letter images using a circuit simulator. The guide training algorithm was optimized for hardware implementation because it does not include a backpropagation algorithm. Therefore, the guide training algorithm and winner-take-all methods were used to validate the performance accuracy of the 3D VRRAM synapses in a HSPICE simulation. The simulation results showed 80% accuracy until the inverted pixel count reached 12%. This means that 3D VRRAMs are usable as synaptic mimic circuits in neural network systems. A 3D vertical synapse with an integrated 3D VRRAM structure will be a promising solution for a high-density neuromorphic chip.

Author Contributions: Conceptualization, W.S.; software, W.S., S.C., and B.K.; investigation, S.C., B.K., and J.P.; writing—original draft preparation, W.S.; writing—review and editing, W.S.; project administration, W.S.; funding acquisition, J.P.

Funding: This research was supported by the Basic Science Research Program through the National Research Foundation of Korea (NRF) funded by the Ministry of Education (grant numbers NRF-2016R1A6A3A11931998 and 2019R1I1A1A01040652).

Conflicts of Interest: The authors declare no conflict of interest.

References

1. Akopyan, F.; Sawada, J.; Cassidy, A.; Alvarez-Icaza, R.; Arthur, J.; Merolla, P.; Imam, N.; Nakamura, Y.; Datta, P.; Nam, G.-J.; et al. TruNorth: Design and Tool Flow of a 65 mW 1 Million Neuron Programmable Neurosynaptic Chip. *IEEE Trans. Comput. Aided Des. Integr. Circuits Syst.* **2015**, *34*, 1537–1557. [CrossRef]

2. Prezioso, M.; Merrikh-Bayat, F.; Hoskins, B.D.; Adam, G.C.; Likharev, K.K.; Strukov, D.B. Training and operation of an integrated neuromorphic network based on metal-oxide memristors. *Nat. Lett.* **2015**, *521*, 61–64. [CrossRef] [PubMed]
3. Park, Y.; Kwon, H.; Kim, B.; Lee, W.; Wee, D.; Choi, H.; Park, B.; Lee, J.; Kim, Y. 3-D Stacked Synapse Array Based on Charge-Trap Flash Memory for Implementation of Deep Neural Networks. *IEEE Trans. Electron. Device.* **2018**, *66*, 420–427. [CrossRef]
4. Burr, G.W.; Shelby, R.M.; Nolfo, C.; Jang, J.W.; Shenoy, R.S.; Narayanan, P.; Virwani, K.; Giacometti, E.U.; Kurdi, B.; Hwang, H. Experimental demonstration and tolerancing of a large-scale neural network (165,000 synapses), using phase-change memory as the synaptic weight element. In Proceedings of the IEEE International Electron Devices Meeting (IEDM), San Francisco, CA, USA, 15–17 December 2014; pp. 697–700.
5. Yu, S.; Gao, B.; Fang, Z.; Yu, H.; Kang, J.; Wong, H. A Neuromorphic Visual System Using RRAM Synaptic Devices with Sub-pJ Energy and Tolerance to Variability: Experimental Characterization and Large-Scale Modeling. In Proceedings of the IEEE International Electron Devices Meeting (IEDM), San Francisco, CA, USA, 10–12 December 2012; pp. 239–242.
6. Deng, Y.; Chen, H.-Y.; Gao, B.; Yu, S.; Wu, S.-C.; Zhao, L.; Chen, B.; Jiang, Z.; Liu, X.; Hou, T.-H.; et al. Design and Optimization Methodology for 3D RRAM Arrays. In Proceedings of the IEEE International Electron Devices Meeting (IEDM), Washington, DC, USA, 9–11 December 2013.
7. Choi, S.; Sun, W.; Shin, H. Analysis of Cell Variability Impact on a 3-D Vertical RRAM (VRRAM) Crossbar Array Using a Modified Lumping Method. *IEEE Trans. Electron. Device.* **2019**, *66*, 759–765. [CrossRef]
8. Choi, S.; Sun, W.; Shin, H. Analysis of Read margin and Write Power Consumption of a 3-D Vertical RRAM (VRRAM) Crossbar Array. *IEEE J. Electron. Devices Soc.* **2018**, *6*, 1192–1196. [CrossRef]
9. Wang, I.; Lin, Y.; Wang, Y.; Hsu, C.; Hou, T. 3D Synaptic Architecture with Ultralow sub-10 fJ Energy per Spike for Neuromorphic Computation. In Proceedings of the IEEE International Electron Devices Meeting (IEDM), San Francisco, CA, USA, 15–17 December 2014; pp. 665–768.
10. Piccolboni, G.; Molas, G.; Portal, J.M.; Coquand, R.; Bocquet, M.; Garbin, D.; Vianello, E.; Carabasse, C.; Delaye, V.; Pellissier, C.; et al. Investigation of the potentialities of Vertical Resistive RAM (VRRAM) for neuromorphic applications. In Proceedings of the IEEE International Electron Devices Meeting (IEDM), Washington, DC, USA, 7–9 December 2015; pp. 447–450.
11. Li, H.; Li, K.; Lin, C.; Hsu, J.; Chiu, W.; Chen, M.; Wu, T.; Sohn, J.; Eryilmaz, S.B.; Shieh, J.; et al. Four-Layer 3D Vertical RRAM Integrated with FinFET as a Versatile Computing Unit for Brain-Inspired Cognitive Information Processing. In Proceedings of the Symposium on VLSI Technology (SOVT), Honolulu, HI, USA, 14–16 June 2016.
12. Li, Z.; Chen, P.; Xu, H.; Yu, S. Design of Ternary Neural Network With 3-D Vertical RRAM Array. *IEEE Trans. Electron Device.* **2017**, *64*, 2721–2727. [CrossRef]
13. Gao, B.; Bi, Y.; Chen, H.; Liu, R.; Huang, P.; Chen, B.; Liu, L.; Liu, X.; Yu, S.; Wong, H.-S.P.; et al. Ultra-Low-Energy Three-Dimensional Oxide-Based Electronic Synapses for Implementation of Robust High-Accuracy Neuromorphic Computation Systems. *ACS Nano* **2014**, *8*, 6998–7004. [CrossRef] [PubMed]
14. Jo, S.; Sun, W.; Kim, B.; Kim, S.; Park, J.; Shin, H. Memristor Neural Network Training with Clock Synchronous Neuromorphic System. *Micromachines* **2019**, *10*, 384. [CrossRef] [PubMed]
15. Kim, B.; Jo, S.; Sun, W.; Shin, H. Analysis of the Memristor-Based Crossbar Synapse for Neuromorphic Systems. *J. Nanosci. Nanotechnol.* **2019**, *19*, 6703–6709. [CrossRef] [PubMed]
16. Yakopcic, C.; Taha, T.M.; Subramanyam, G.; Pino, R.E.; Rogers, S. A Memristor Device Model. *IEEE Electron. Device Lett.* **2011**, *32*, 1436–1438. [CrossRef]
17. Yakopcic, C.; Taha, T.M.; Subramanyam, G.; Pino, R.E. Generalized Memristive Device SPICE Model and its Application in Circuit Design. *IEEE Trans. Comput. Aided Des. Integr. Circuits Syst.* **2013**, *32*, 1201–1214. [CrossRef]
18. Yakopcic, C.; Taha, T.M.; Subramanyam, G.; Pino, R.E. Memristor SPICE model and crossbar simulation based on devices with nanosecond switching time. In Proceedings of the IEEE International Joint Conference on Neural Networks (IJCNN), Dallas, TX, USA, 4–9 August 2013.
19. Amirsoleimani, A.; Shamsi, J.; Ahmadi, M.; Ahmadi, A.; Alirezaee, S.; Mohammadi, K.; Karami, M.A.; Yakopcic, C.; Kavehei, O.; Al-Sarawie, S. Accurate charge transport model for nanoionic memristive devices. *Microelectron. J.* **2017**, *65*, 49–57. [CrossRef]

20. Pershin, Y.V.; Martinez-Rincon, J.; Di Ventra, M. Memory Circuit Elements: From Systems to Applications. *J. Comput. Theor. Nanosci.* **2011**, *8*, 441–448. [CrossRef]
21. Woo, J.; Padovani, A.; Moon, K.; Kwak, M.; Larcher, L.; Hwang, H. Linking Conductive Filament Properties and Evolution to Synaptic Behavior of RRAM Devices for Neuromorphic Applications. *IEEE Electron. Device Lett.* **2017**, *38*, 1220–1223. [CrossRef]

materials

Article

Multiscale Modeling for Application-Oriented Optimization of Resistive Random-Access Memory

Paolo La Torraca [1,*], Francesco Maria Puglisi [2], Andrea Padovani [3] and Luca Larcher [1,3]

[1] Dipartimento di Scienze e Metodi dell'Ingegneria, Università di Modena e Reggio Emilia, Via Amendola 2, 42122 Reggio Emilia, Italy; Luca_Larcher@amat.com
[2] Dipartimento di Ingegneria "Enzo Ferrari", Università di Modena e Reggio Emilia, Via P. Vivarelli 10/1, 41125 Modena, Italy; francescomaria.puglisi@unimore.it
[3] Applied Materials, Via Sicilia 32, 42122 Reggio Emilia, Italy; Andrea_Padovani@amat.com
* Correspondence: paolo.latorraca@unimore.it

Received: 31 July 2019; Accepted: 20 October 2019; Published: 23 October 2019

Abstract: Memristor-based neuromorphic systems have been proposed as a promising alternative to von Neumann computing architectures, which are currently challenged by the ever-increasing computational power required by modern artificial intelligence (AI) algorithms. The design and optimization of memristive devices for specific AI applications is thus of paramount importance, but still extremely complex, as many different physical mechanisms and their interactions have to be accounted for, which are, in many cases, not fully understood. The high complexity of the physical mechanisms involved and their partial comprehension are currently hampering the development of memristive devices and preventing their optimization. In this work, we tackle the application-oriented optimization of Resistive Random-Access Memory (RRAM) devices using a multiscale modeling platform. The considered platform includes all the involved physical mechanisms (i.e., charge transport and trapping, and ion generation, diffusion, and recombination) and accounts for the 3D electric and temperature field in the device. Thanks to its multiscale nature, the modeling platform allows RRAM devices to be simulated and the microscopic physical mechanisms involved to be investigated, the device performance to be connected to the material's microscopic properties and geometries, the device electrical characteristics to be predicted, the effect of the forming conditions (i.e., temperature, compliance current, and voltage stress) on the device's performance and variability to be evaluated, the analog resistance switching to be optimized, and the device's reliability and failure causes to be investigated. The discussion of the presented simulation results provides useful insights for supporting the application-oriented optimization of RRAM technology according to specific AI applications, for the implementation of either non-volatile memories, deep neural networks, or spiking neural networks.

Keywords: AI; neuromorphic computing; multiscale modeling; memristor; optimization; RRAM; simulation

1. Introduction

Artificial Neural Networks (ANNs) are possibly the most prominent computational model used in modern artificial intelligence (AI) applications. The computational scheme of ANN, loosely based on biological neural networks, comprises a collection of interconnected processing elements, referred to as artificial neurons, often organized in layers [1,2].

An ever-increasing effort has been devoted to the experimentation of different ANN architectures, which has led to the development of ANNs constituted by an extremely high number of neurons and layers [1,2], known as deep neural networks (DNNs). Thanks to their high flexibility and application-agnostic nature, DNNs have proved extremely effective in a variety of applications, such as image recognition [3,4] and speech recognition [5], easily outperforming other ANN architectures and machine learning techniques (i.e., Support Vector Machines, K-Nearest Neighbors).

However, the exceptional performance shown by the most advanced DNNs requires a heavy investment in terms of energy and hardware resources, during both the training of the network and the inference [6–8]. In fact, in most practical applications, DNNs are implemented in software and executed on von Neumann computer architectures that have to provide (i) sufficient computational power for fast training and inference, and (ii) a sufficiently large and fast memory for storing all the artificial neuron weights and any partial result. Nonetheless, the energy efficiency of training and inference must also be considered.

In order to achieve fast and efficient DNNs, computation has been progressively shifted from central processing units (CPUs) to optimized coprocessors, referred to as AI accelerators or Neural Processing Units (NPUs), that enable high parallelization by exploiting the DNN layered topology. Graphical Processing Units (GPUs) have readily been used as NPUs for their inherent capability to conduct efficient vector and matrix operations [9], followed by the development of the first Tensor Processing Units (TPUs), capable of efficient tensor operations and better data reuse [10]. Application-specific integrated circuits (ASICs) have recently been developed as special-purpose NPUs, co-designed with the desired DNN, exchanging a low flexibility for a higher energy efficiency, an optimized memory size and use, and a low area occupation [11–14].

Despite their steady improvements, even ASIC NPUs are now facing technological limits (i.e., the imminent end of Moore's law and the already broken Dennard scaling) and the intrinsic limits of the von Neumann architecture, mainly the so-called von Neumann bottleneck (i.e., the limited data transfer speed between the processor and memory, as well as the energy required for the data transfer itself). This is especially true in applications with strict volume, weight, and power constraints, such as automotive, battery-powered vehicles (i.e., drones); mobile devices; and Internet of Things (IoT) devices. In this context, memristor-based neuromorphic systems can potentially overcome the limitations posed by von Neumann architectures, not only to DNNs, but to AI in general.

Memristors are electronic passive devices characterized by a pinched hysteresis I-V curve, thus exhibiting a time-varying and non-volatile electrical resistance [15,16]. Ideally, the conductivity of a memristor can be arbitrarily modified by applying a proper electrical stimulus, indefinitely retaining the resistance state in the absence of external stimuli.

The peculiar memristor characteristics, combined with their extremely small size, have made them very appealing for the development of new non-volatile memories (NVMs), characterized by a low power, high density, and possibly multilevel data storage [17,18].

Even more importantly for AI applications, memristive crossbar arrays have been proposed as DNN accelerators, natively implementing an in-memory (typically analog) vector-matrix multiplication [18–20], which is the fundamental operation for the computation of a layer output in DNNs. By storing the weights of a DNN layer in the memristive array as conductance values, matrix-vector multiplication can be executed at once by only exploiting Ohm's and Kirchhoff's laws. The computation of a single DNN layer requires a single execution step and, moreover, it is performed at the data location, preventing the massive data transfer of weight values between the memory and processor required in von Neumann architectures.

Memristors are also finding applications in more biologically-plausible neural networks, such as Spiking Neural Networks (SNNs), in which the computation is performed by mimicking the actual operation of biological neurons (i.e., spatio-temporal coding of the information, synaptic plasticity, cell membrane V-I relationship, generation of action potentials, and intrinsically stochastic behavior) [18,19,21]. Different memristor-based artificial synapse implementations have been proposed, and have successfully exhibited both deterministic and stochastic spike-time-dependent plasticity (STDP) [21,22]. Their application to SNNs has highlighted the potential for supervised and unsupervised learning, and adaptation to input stimuli. A recent analysis on the Hodgkin–Huxley neuron model [23], known for being the most biologically-sound model of the neuron action potential, suggested that memristors are key components for its implementation [24]. Moreover, the intrinsic stochasticity of real memristors can be exploited for mimicking the probabilistic and noisy behavior of biological neurons [22], enabling more biologically-plausible artificial neuron implementations and overcoming the limits of the strictly deterministic CMOS implementations. Memristor-based SNNs thus have a huge potential, providing a new architectural and computational paradigm approaching a brain-like computation and circumventing the von Neumann bottleneck at once.

Since the fabrication of the first TiO_2 memristor in 2008 [25], many memristor technologies have been proposed [19,26]. In Resistive Random-Access Memories (RRAMs), the switching is induced by the formation of a conductive path in a dielectric material, controlled by an ion-based mechanism [27–31]. In Phase-Change Memories (PCM), the modulation of a chalcogenide material phase (i.e., amorphous and crystalline) through localized Joule heating allows the resistance switching [32–34]. In a Ferroelectric Tunnel Junction (FTJ), the tunneling electroresistance of a ferroelectric material is modulated by setting its internal polarization [35–37]. In a Magnetic Tunnel Junction (MTJ), the tunneling electroresistance of a thin insulator enclosed between two ferromagnetic layers is modulated by their magnetic polarization [38].

Although the proposed memristor technologies are characterized by a simple structure and are easy to fabricate, the physical principles underlying their analog resistance switching and, in general, the implications of the atomic material properties (i.e., defects, phase, morphology) on the electrical performances, are extremely complex and are still not comprehensively understood. This lack of knowledge is currently hampering the development of memristor-based systems.

In fact, all the memristor applications previously discussed ask for devices with different performance metrics, as summarized in Table 1. Memristors must thus be appropriately chosen, designed, and optimized to satisfy the performance requirements for each specific application. This, in turn, requires a deep knowledge of the physical mechanisms responsible for the resistance switching phenomena, their interplay, and how they are affected by the device materials and geometry. However, the partial comprehension of the physical mechanisms underlying memristor operation prevents the application-oriented design and tuning of the devices.

Table 1. Summary of desired performance metrics for memristors.

Metric	NVM [1] [26]	DNN [2] [39]	SNN [3] [40]
Feature size	<12 nm	<10 nm	-
Number of levels	≥2 (1 bit)	>100 (6.45 bits)	≥64 (6 bits)
Dynamic range (on/off ratio)	-	≥100	≥00
State retention	>1 year	>10 years	>10 years
Device endurance	>10^3 cycles	>10^9 cycles	>10^9 cycles
Energy consumption	<100 pJ/write	<10 fJ/programming pulse	<10 fJ/spike
Linearity	-	Yes	Yes
Symmetry	-	Yes	-
Switching time	<100 µS	<100 ns	-

[1] System level performance for replacing a NAND flash memory. [2] Performance for memristors in a deep neural network (DNN) accelerator with a crossbar memory array architecture. [3] Performance for memristors as a Spiking Neural Network (SNN) artificial synapse.

Physical multiscale modeling and simulation provide a powerful tool for investigating the physical mechanisms responsible for analog switching in memristors and to highlight the effects of the material properties (including defects) on the device performance. This information can then be used to further develop memristive technology, optimizing the properties of the devices (i.e., geometry and materials) to match the specifications required for the desired application (i.e., electric properties, data retention, variability, and noise), and strongly reducing its time-to-market.

In this paper, we use a multiscale modeling platform to simulate RRAM devices and investigate the physical mechanisms underlying their operation. The simulations are designed to highlight the effects of the device geometry, materials, forming conditions (i.e., temperature, current compliance, voltage stress mode), and programming. The discussion on the simulation results shows the relevance of the obtained insights for the different AI applications (i.e., non-volatile memories, deep neural networks, or spiking neural networks) and provides useful design principles for RRAM application-oriented design.

2. Materials and Methods

As highlighted in Section 1, the design of memristive devices requires complete knowledge of all the involved resistance switching phenomena, including the effects of the device geometry and materials.

In RRAMs, the fundamental mechanisms include (i) the interaction between the electronic and ionic transport, (ii) the effects induced by the applied electric field, and (iii) the influence of the microscopic material properties [41].

Due to the complexity of those mechanisms, exacerbated by their interplay, the physical modeling of RRAMs presented in this work is extremely advantageous, as it easily allows the following: (i) prediction of the device performance (i.e., switching time, endurance, and retention) from the material properties (which is one of the key novel aspects of this work, which allows the materials and the process conditions to be directly screened when targeting specific applications); (ii) investigation of the trade-off between the device scaling and variability; (iii) evaluation of the process effects on the device and its materials through the interpretation of electrical characterization data; and (iv) co-design of the device materials and geometries for satisfying the specific application requirements (see Table 1).

In this section, we first review the physical mechanism underlying the RRAM operation, and then present a multiscale modeling platform that includes all the presented effects and mechanisms.

2.1. RRAM Devices

In RRAMs, the analog resistance switching is controlled by a reversible, voltage-driven, and ion-based mechanism that allows the geometry of a conductive path within a dielectric layer to be modulated. Different switching mechanisms have been proposed for the implementation of RRAM [26,42,43], with each one requiring the comprehensive knowledge of different physical processes for being thoroughly understood.

In CBRAMs [44–46], a conductive filament (CF) is created (and dissolved) in a solid electrolyte by means of redox reactions. By applying a positive voltage to the "active" electrode (the anode), it releases metallic cations into the electrolyte that migrate towards the "inert" electrode (the cathode) pushed by the electric field. Once they reach the cathode, the cations are reduced, contributing to the formation of the CF and eventually connecting the two electrodes. Through reversing the redox process by applying a negative voltage to the anode, the CF is progressively dissolved.

Optimizing CBRAMs requires an understanding of the kinetics and interplay between the redox processes and the transport of metallic cations in solid electrolytes (i.e., drift and diffusion). Moreover, all the effects related to the material interactions and geometry must be considered.

In OxRAMs [47–51], a conductive path constructed of oxygen vacancies is formed in a high-k oxide layer (e.g., TiO_2, HfO_2, TaO_5), breaking the oxide atomic bonds (Figure 1a).

When applying a voltage to the oxide layer (Figure 1b), its lattice bonds are stretched. With a sufficiently high voltage, the bonds eventually break, generating a negatively charged oxygen ion and a positively charged oxygen vacancy (Frenkel pair). If no recombination of the pair occurs, the oxygen ion and vacancies migrate in opposite directions under the action of the electric field. However, due to their relatively high diffusion energy barrier [52], the oxygen vacancies experience little to no motion, locally increasing the electrical conduction and power dissipation in the material. The resulting temperature increment supports the creation of new oxygen ions/vacancies, leading to the rapid formation of a highly conductive path of oxygen vacancies between the two electrodes (Figure 1c). The conductive path can be broken by recombining the oxygen vacancies with the oxygen ions, i.e., bringing the oxygen ions near the oxygen vacancies by applying a negative voltage to the oxide layer (Figure 1d).

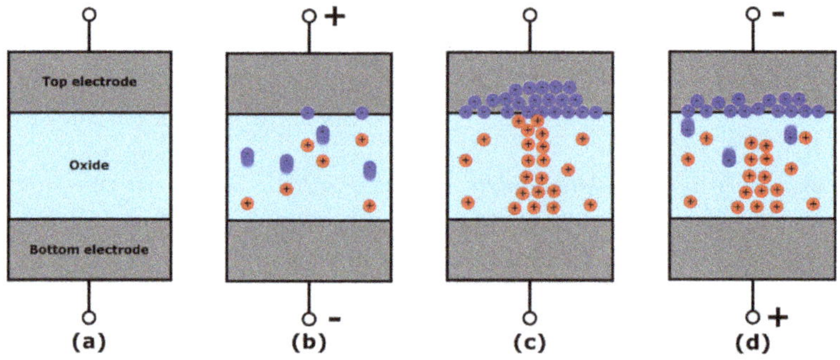

Figure 1. Structure and operation of a filamentary OxRAM device. (**a**) Device in pristine conditions. (**b**) Forming operation: a positive voltage is applied to the top electrode, generating oxygen ion/vacancy pairs. The ions (blue spheres) migrate under the effect of the electric field, leaving the oxygen vacancies (red spheres) behind. (**c**) Formed device with a conductive filament (CF) made of oxygen vacancies connecting the two electrodes. (**d**) Reset operation: a negative voltage is applied to the top electrode, bringing the oxygen ions near to the oxygen vacancies. The resulting recombination leads to partial dissolution of the CF and the formation of a dielectric barrier.

The analog resistance switching in OxRAMs relies on the modulation of a conductive path created during a forming process, consisting of a current-controlled breakdown of the dielectric. After the formation, only a thin portion of the formed conductive path is affected by the oxygen ion/vacancies generation and recombination processes. The conductance switching thus requires precise control of the geometrical properties of a thin insulating barrier.

Depending on the forming conditions (i.e., temperature, current compliance, voltage stress mode), the conductive path can assume either a uniform or filamentary shape. In the former [51], the dielectric conduction is uniformly modulated across its section and the resistance is thus controlled through the insulating barrier thickness only. In the latter [47–50], a CF is formed within the dielectric, enabling control of the resistance by both the barrier thickness and the CF diameter.

The design of OxRAMs requires an understanding of the complex processes of oxygen ions/vacancies generation, diffusion, and recombination under the action of an external electric field; their interplay with the charge transport in dielectrics; and the effects of the material properties and geometries on all those processes.

In this work, we focus on the multiscale simulation of OxRAM devices, and investigate the interplay between the physical mechanisms involved and their impact on the device performance, reliability, and variability. Specifically, we mainly consider OxRAM devices with a one-oxide-layer stack made of $TiN/HfO_x/TiO_y/TiN$ (where TiO_y is a parasitic layer). For comparison, we also consider a two-oxide-layer stack made of $TiN/Ta_2O_x/TiO_y/TiN$, showing the different properties enabled by such structural and material combination.

2.2. Multiscale Modeling of RRAMs

The multiscale modeling platform sketched in Figure 2 allows the RRAM devices to be thoroughly investigated. Starting from the key material properties, calculated using ab-initio methods [53–55], and the other device-specific properties (e.g., geometry and materials), the platform models the electrical device response considering all the complex physical mechanisms involved in the different RRAM operations, while accounting for all the resulting changes in the 3D electric and temperature fields, and in the material structure.

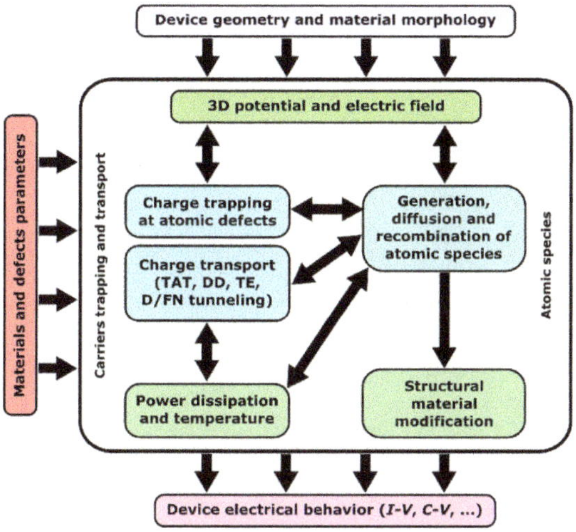

Figure 2. Multiscale modeling platform for RRAM devices. The device-level simulation engine includes three main modules: one for the simulation of charge transport; one for charge trapping; and one for the simulation of atomic species generation, diffusion, and recombination. The simulation requires the material parameters, calculated using ab-initio methods, and a definition of the device geometry. The modeling platform considers the 3D potential and electric field and how they are affected by localized trapped charge and power dissipation at defects. The results are the various characteristic curves describing the device electrical response.

The multiscale modeling platform comprises three main modules, addressing charge transport, charge trapping, and the generation/diffusion/recombination of atomic species (i.e., oxygen vacancies and interstitial ions), respectively.

For a comprehensive simulation of charge transport, many mechanisms are considered, including trap-assisted tunneling (TAT), thermo-ionic emission (TE), the Poole–Frenkel effect (PF), and Drift-Diffusion (DD) through conduction and valence bands, and through sub-bands originating from metal-rich regions formed within the oxide. Interestingly, in most RRAM devices, the TAT and DD phenomena dominate the charge transport dynamics, the first at low defect densities (i.e., the conduction in the oxide is mainly defect-assisted, typical of binary and ternary oxides [56–62]), and the latter for sufficiently high defect densities (i.e., a conductive path is present within the oxide). The TE and the PF phenomena are typically negligible in materials with a medium/high bandgap, such as transition metal oxides [63].

The TAT conduction is described using a multiphonon TAT model, inherently considering the electron-phonon coupling oxides by accounting for the atomic lattice rearrangement in the vicinity of the defect due to the presence of a trapped charge [56–58,64]. The TAT transport considered is fully described in [65]. This model requires knowledge of the relaxation energy, E_{REL}, associated with the atomic lattice relaxation process; the defect thermal ionization energy, E_T; and the defect density in the material, N_T. Both E_{REL} and E_T are calculated by means of ab initio methods (i.e., Density Functional Theory and Molecular Dynamics simulations). The DD conduction is best described by adopting the Landauer approach [66], which accounts for delocalized electron flow in the conductive path.

The defect-assisted charge transport naturally results in localized power dissipation at the defect sites, affecting the temperature distribution in the device. The power dissipation is self-consistently computed across the entire device volume by including the charge carrier's energy released at both the defects (at every charge trapping event) and the lattice (due to inelastic scattering mechanisms, i.e., optical and acoustic phonons). The temperature distribution in the device volume is calculated from the power dissipation by solving the Fourier's Law for heat conduction.

The charge transport dynamics are strongly coupled to the different phenomena related to atomic species in the oxide (i.e., generation, diffusion, recombination). Therefore, they must be consistently calculated to effectively model the structural material modifications occurring during RRAM operations (i.e., forming, setting, and resetting).

The generation of atomic species is described by a thermochemical bond breakage model [67], consisting of compact effective-energy formulas accounting for the microscopic material properties and the two main generation mechanisms: (i) the breakage of atomic bonds, enhanced by the local electric and temperature field profiles and locally favored by the possible presence of precursors [68] and other defects, and (ii) the redox reactions that occur at the interfaces, as well-favored by the local electric and temperature fields. The resulting generation rate is

$$G(x,y,z) = G_{0,G} \exp\left[-\frac{E_{A,G} - b \cdot F(x,y,z)}{k_B T(x,y,z)}\right], \quad (1)$$

where $b = p_0 \frac{2+k}{3}$ is the bond polarization factor related to the molecular dipole moment, p_0 is the bond breakage activation energy, k is the material dielectric constant, $G_{0,G}$ is the effective bond vibration frequency, $E_{A,G}$ is the bond breakage activation energy, $F(x,y,z)$ is the 3-D electric field, k_B is the Boltzmann's constant, and $T(x,y,z,)$ is the 3-D temperature field. The material-related parameters (i.e., the effective bond vibration frequency $G_{0,G}$, the molecular bond polarizability p_0, and the bond breakage activation energy $E_{A,G}$) are calculated using ab-initio methods [54,69].

The transport of atomic species is dominated by a DD mechanism, driven by the electric field and strongly accelerated by the local temperature, described by the equation

$$G_D(x,y,z) = G_{0,D} \exp\left[-\frac{E_{A,D} - \gamma \cdot E(x,y,z)}{k_B T(x,y,z)}\right], \quad (2)$$

where $G_{0,D}$ is the effective bond vibration frequency, $E_{A,D}$ is the diffusion activation energy, γ is the field acceleration factor, $F(x,y,z)$ is the 3-D electric field, k_B is the Boltzmann's constant, and $T(x,y,z,)$ is the 3-D temperature field.

However, both the electric and temperature fields are in turn affected by the presence of atomic species, implying a strong and complex coupling between the transport mechanism and the fields in the device. For correctly modeling the DD transport, the internal device conditions (e.g., current, trapped charge distribution, electric and temperature fields) are updated every time an individual defect is generated, recombined, or moved.

The stochastic nature of the mechanisms involved in RRAM is successfully accounted for by using a kinetic Monte Carlo approach, which allows a consideration of phenomena like the intrinsic variability of the forming, set, and reset processes, and the occurrence of Random Telegraph Noise [70–74], together with their dependence on the material properties and geometry, providing insights for their optimization.

The presented modeling platform successfully reproduces the RRAM electrical responses to arbitrary voltage and current inputs, allowing for the extraction of various characteristic curves of the device (I-V, C-V, and G-V). The parameters used in all the simulations are reported in Table 2.

Table 2. Simulation parameters.

Symbol	Quantity	Material		
		HfO_2	Ta_2O_5	TiO_2
	Material Parameters			
E_G	Band-gap (eV)	5.8	3.6	1.3
χ	Electron affinity (eV)	2.4	3.4	4.3
k	Relative dielectric permittivity	21	25	95
m_e^*	Electron tunneling effective mass	0.25 m_0	0.3 m_0	0.2 m_0
WF	TiN work function (eV)	4.57	4.57	4.57
	Defect Parameters			
E_T	Defect thermal ionization energy (eV)	1.7–2.7	0.8–1.2	0.1–0.5
E_{REL}	Defect relaxation energy (eV)	1.19	0.88	0.7
N_T	Defect density (cm^{-3})	5×10^{19}	5×10^{19}	5×10^{19}
	Metal-Oxygen Bond Breakage Parameters			
p_0	Polarizability (eÅ)	5.2	1.8	4
$E_{A,G}$	Activation energy (eV)	2.1	1.0	5.3
$G_{0,G}$	Effective bond vibration frequency (Hz)	4.5×10^{13}	4.5×10^{13}	4.5×10^{13}
	Oxygen Ion Diffusion Parameters			
Γ	Field acceleration factor (eÅ)	0.3	0.2	0.4
$E_{A,D}$	Activation energy (eV)—in x/y/z direction	0.8/0.8/0.7	1.2/1.2/1.0	1.0/1.0/0.75
$G_{0,D}$	Effective bond vibration frequency (Hz)	4.5×10^{13}	4.5×10^{13}	4.5×10^{13}

3. Results

The multiscale modeling platform presented in Section 2 combines all the most relevant physical mechanisms involved in RRAM operation, directly connecting the electrical performance of RRAM devices to their geometries and to the microscopic properties of the employed materials. Noticeably, thanks to the multiscale nature of the modeling platform, it can be used to gain insights into RRAM devices at different levels.

At the physical level, the modeling platform can be used to investigate the included physical mechanisms and the effects of their interplay on the generation of the conductive path. At the device level, it allows the whole conductance switching cycle (i.e., forming, set, and reset operations) to be simulated, and can therefore be used to predict the performance of RRAM devices. Moreover, its inherently stochastic implementation allows the device variability and reliability (retention and endurance) properties to be effectively investigated. Multiscale modeling thus provides a powerful tool for accelerating the further development and optimization of RRAM technology, focusing on the specific application (i.e., NVM, ANN, or SNN).

In this section, we use the presented multiscale modeling platform to perform multiscale simulations of RRAM devices. The different simulations are specifically designed to highlight the effects of the device geometry, materials, forming conditions (i.e., temperature, current compliance, voltage stress mode), and programming. The parameters used for the simulations are summarized in Table 2.

3.1. Conductance Switching Cycle

The presented multiscale modeling platform allows the whole conductance switching cycle to be simulated. Starting from a pristine device with specified geometries and materials, it is possible to investigate the device formation and the following conductance switching operations (SET and RESET) under different conditions. The electric and temperature fields and the location of atomic species in the device can also be monitored during simulations to gain insights into the involved switching mechanisms and their interplay.

As an example, Figure 3a shows the I-V characteristic curves of a simulated device made of a TiN/5 nm $HfO_x/TiO_y/TiN$ stack RRAM device, including the forming (solid red), the reset (dotted green), and set (dashed blue) operations. The simulations are performed by applying ramped voltages and a compliance current of 10 μA.

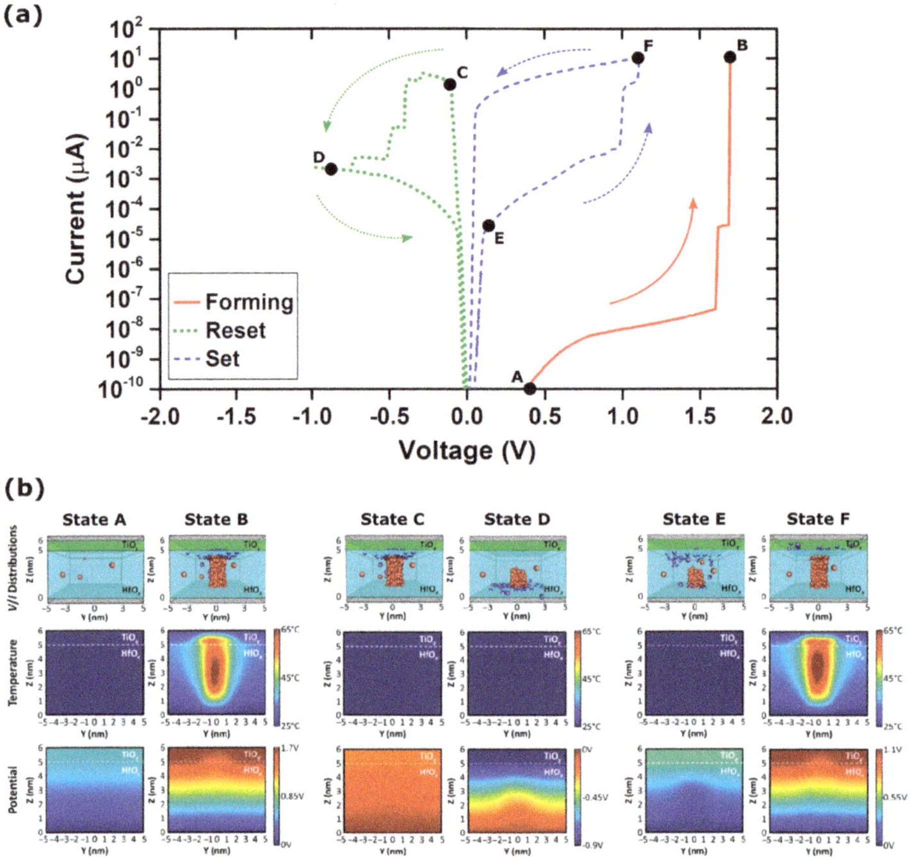

Figure 3. Simulation results of a TiN/5 nm $HfO_x/TiO_y/TiN$ stack RRAM device: (**a**) Current–Voltage characteristic during forming (solid red), reset (dotted green), and set (dashed blue) operations with a compliance current of 10 μA; (**b**) oxygen vacancy (red spheres) and ion (blue spheres) distribution, temperature profile, and potential profile of the simulated device at different operation stages (labeled A, B, C, D, E, and F in Figure 3a).

In the pristine state (state A), the conduction is dominated by the TAT through the relatively few preexisting defects in the material (i.e., oxygen vacancies accumulated at grain boundaries), which determines the very high initial resistance of the device. At a low voltage ($V < V_{FORM} = 1.7$ V in Figure 3), both the electric field and the power dissipation are too small to result in strong localized defect generation, leading to a very modest and uniform generation of defects across the whole volume of the device. Once the applied voltage exceeds V_{FORM}, the oxide bonds start to break under the effect of the increasing electric field, creating a significant number of atomic defects. Due to the different diffusion energy barriers, the oxygen ions generated drift towards the top electrode under the effect of the electric field, while the oxygen vacancies mostly remain in place. Noticeably, the oxygen ions accumulate at the TiO_x layer, creating the so-called "oxygen reservoir". The newly created oxygen vacancies support the TAT, locally increasing the current flow, power dissipation, and temperature, in turn assisting with the generation of new defects. A thermally-driven positive feedback process is thus established, leading to the rapid formation of a CF. After the formation (state B), the device is in a low resistance state. The conduction is dominated by DD in the vacancy-rich regions constituting the CF, while the oxygen ion counterparts are gathered at the top electrode.

The reset operation is simulated by the device configuration resulting from the described forming operation. This approach is advantageous since, in comparison to other approaches proposed in the literature [66,75], no a-priori assumptions of the CF structure and characteristics are required. Upon the application of a negative voltage ramp (state C), the oxygen ions gather in the oxygen reservoir during the forming drift towards the bottom electrode under the effect of the electric field. During their motion, the oxygen ions can recombine with the oxygen vacancy defects in the oxide, leading to the progressive formation of a thin dielectric barrier within the CF, causing resistive switching to the high resistance state (state D). Interestingly, this process is not associated with a large temperature increment in the device, suggesting that it is mostly driven by the electric field.

Lastly, the set operation is simulated by the device configuration obtained at the end of the reset operation. Upon the application of a positive voltage ramp (state E), the device experiences a process similar to that of forming, but confined to the thin dielectric barrier created during the reset process. Since the applied voltage drops almost completely across the thin dielectric barrier, the electric field required for the breaking of oxide bonds and the generation of new defects is easily exceeded at relatively low voltages ($V < V_{FORM}$). The restoration of the CF is thus initiated at lower voltages compared to the forming process. The same thermally-driven positive feedback described for the forming process is established, resulting in a quick restoration of the CF and the switch to a low resistance state (state F).

3.2. *Effects of Forming Conditions*

The presented multiscale modeling platform allows the effects of the forming condition (i.e., temperature, current compliance, voltage stress mode) on the performance and properties exhibited by the device after the forming process to be investigated.

The beneficial effects of a high-temperature forming process have been thoroughly reported in the literature, and have been associated with lower forming voltages and variability of the low resistance state, while improving the stability and reliability of the device [76–78]. The external temperature affects the forming process assisting the defect generation and promoting the oxygen ion diffusion in the device, leading to a lower density of oxygen ions near the conductive path after the forming process. The subsequent oxygen ion/vacancy recombination is strongly reduced, resulting in a higher stability and lower variability of the conductive path.

This is evidenced in Figure 4a, which shows the low state resistance distribution exhibited by TiN/5 nm HfO_x/TiO_y/TiN RRAM stacks after the forming process at two different external temperatures (i.e., 25 and 125 °C), using a ramped voltage and a 1 μA compliance current. In accordance with the literature [76], the experimental data (marked by the symbols in Figure 4a) show that the higher forming temperature leads to a tighter resistance distribution.

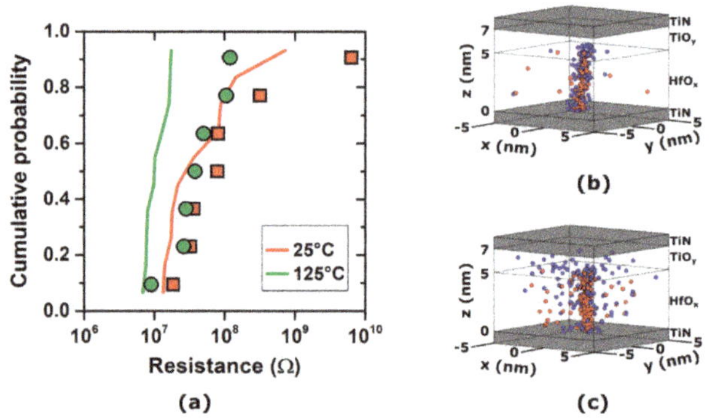

Figure 4. (**a**) Experimental (symbols) and simulated (lines) cumulative distributions of TiN/5 nm HfO_x/TiO_y/TiN RRAM stacks' low state resistances after forming at 25 and 125 °C. (**b**) Resulting oxygen ions/vacancies distribution in the device after forming at 25 °C. (**c**) Resulting oxygen ions/vacancies distribution in the device after forming at 125 °C. The forming process was performed using a ramped voltage and a 1 µA compliance current.

The effects of the forming temperature on the oxygen ions/vacancies generation and diffusion can be effectively investigated using the presented multiscale modeling platform. The simulations of the forming processes (shown by the lines in Figure 4), whilst not perfectly matching the measured samples, accurately reproduce the trend and order of magnitude of the experimental data, showing a tighter resistance distribution in the higher temperature forming case. The discrepancy between the experimental results and those of the simulation can be ascribed to several effects not considered in these simulations, mainly, the oxide thickness and area variations due to the fabrication process tolerances, and process-dependent interface effects between the oxide and the electrodes.

The microscopic differences caused by the higher forming temperature can be better appreciated in Figure 4b,c, which shows the simulated oxygen ions/vacancies distribution in the device after the forming process. At a low temperature (25 °C), the conductive path (in this case, a CF) made of oxygen vacancies is tightly surrounded by oxygen ions affecting its resistance and stability. Conversely, at a high temperature (125 °C), the oxygen ions are scattered in the device volume, affecting the CF to a lesser extent and leading to a tighter resistance distribution.

The platform can therefore be used to explore the best strategies to control the device-to-device variability of RRAMs for specific applications: for instance, high-temperature forming could reduce the variability for high-accuracy DNNs, while precisely controlling the temperature during the forming process could be used to obtain the desired variability level, optimizing the performance of stochastic learning networks.

The forming compliance current has a very strong impact on the morphology of the conductive path as it allows the defect generation processes in the device to be controlled by limiting the maximum current flow and power dissipation in the device. For example, in filamentary RRAMs, it has been observed that the magnitude of the compliance current allows the diameter of the CF to be controlled [57]. Moreover, it also greatly affects the low resistance state magnitude and variability: a sufficiently high compliance current allows the formation of a dense population of defects, forming low-resistance CFs with a similar morphology, while a low compliance current leads to a sparse population of defects, forming weak CF characterized by a larger variability. This is evidenced in Figure 5, which shows the low state resistance distribution exhibited by TiN/5 nm HfO_x/TiO_y/TiN RRAM stacks after the forming process at three different compliance currents (i.e., 1, 5, and 10 µA), using a ramped voltage and an external temperature of 25 °C.

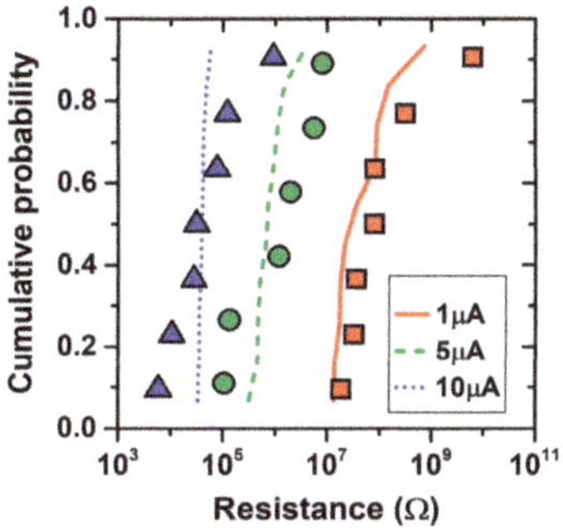

Figure 5. Experimental (symbols) and simulated (lines) cumulative distributions of TiN/5 nm HfO_x/TiO_y/TiN RRAM stacks' low state resistances after forming at 1, 5, and 10 μA. The forming process was performed using a ramped voltage and 25 °C external temperature.

The effects of the compliance current on the defect generation processes and the resulting device resistance magnitude and variability can be effectively investigated using the presented multiscale modeling platform. The simulations of the forming processes, shown in Figure 5, reproduce the trend found in the experiments, highlighting that the lower variability of the low resistance state is in fact related to the higher density of oxygen vacancies generated at higher compliance currents. The platform confirms its effectiveness for investigating the best strategies to control the device-to-device variability for specific applications, as previously mentioned.

In filamentary RRAM, the morphology of the CF is also strongly affected by the forming voltage stress mode (i.e., the time-varying profile of the forming voltage), as it determines different distributions of oxygen ions and vacancies in the device volume. Evaluating the effect of a specific voltage stress mode is highly desirable, since it allows the best strategy for a specific application to be identified. However, this task is extremely complex, as it requires the interplay between the (possibly) time-varying forming voltage, the defect generation processes driving the growth of the CF, and the oxygen ions diffusion to be considered. The presented multiscale modeling platform provides a powerful tool for such investigation.

Figure 6 shows the simulation of the oxygen ions/vacancies distribution in TiN/5 nm HfO_x/TiO_y/TiN RRAM stacks after the forming process using three different voltage stress modes (i.e., constant voltage, ramped voltage, and pulsed voltage), a compliance current of 1 μA, and an external temperature of 25 °C.

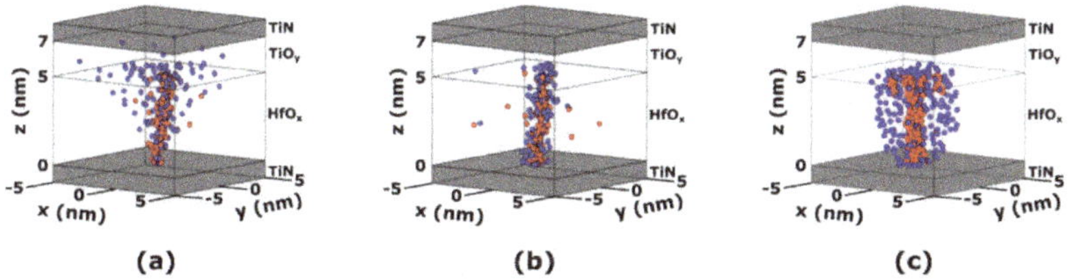

Figure 6. Simulated distributions of the oxygen ions (blue) and vacancies (red) in TiN/5 nm HfO_x/TiO_y/TiN RRAM stacks after forming with a (**a**) constant voltage, (**b**) ramped voltage, and (**c**) pulsed voltage. The forming process was performed using a 1 μA compliance current and 25 °C external temperature.

Noticeably, the oxygen ions distribution is significantly affected by the voltage stress mode. At constant voltage forming, the oxygen ions are mostly accumulated near the top electrode, while ramped and pulsed voltage forming results in a more uniform distribution. The pulsed voltage forming, however, leads to a higher radial diffusion of the oxygen ions compared to the constant voltage forming.

Comparing the oxygen ions and vacancies distribution shown in Figures 4 and 6, it can be noticed that the distribution corresponding to a low-temperature forming process (Figure 4b) is similar to the one of a ramped voltage forming process (Figure 6b). Conversely, the distribution corresponding to a high-temperature forming process (Figure 4c) is closer to that of a pulsed voltage forming process (Figure 6c). The similarity of the oxygen ions and vacancies suggests a similar behavior of the device. This is confirmed by experimental results [79], showing that pulsed voltage forming is associated with a tighter resistance distribution with respect to constant or ramped voltage forming.

The voltage stress mode can thus be exploited for optimization of the oxygen ions distribution in the formed device for achieving a tighter resistance distribution, similar to the previously discussed forming temperature. The platform can support such optimization, allowing for the fine tuning of RRAM device-to-device variability according to the specific application requirements.

3.3. *Analog Resistance Switching Optimization*

As previously discussed, the analog resistance switching in RRAM devices is driven by two different mechanisms. The switching from a high resistance state to a low resistance state is dominated by thermal positive feedback triggered by an electric field, leading to a mostly uncontrolled generation of oxygen vacancies and resulting in the abrupt formation of a conductive path. Conversely, the switching from a low resistance state to a high resistance state is determined by the recombination of oxygen ions/vacancies driven by the electric field, resulting in the new formation of a high-resistance dielectric barrier. The dielectric barrier formation, being unassisted by the temperature, is typically slower than the formation of the conductive path.

The differences between the two switching mechanisms cause strong asymmetry in the device characteristics, as evidenced in Figure 3, which has been recognized as detrimental for many applications (i.e., ANNs and SNNs). Moreover, the extremely fast formation of the conductive path prevents the fine control of analog resistance switching, potentially limiting both the number of distinguishable resistance levels (thus the number of bits per cell in NVM) and the device linearity.

A well-established method for mitigating the non-idealities exhibited by RRAM devices is pulsed programming, i.e., controlling the resistance switching by applying a sequence of voltage pulses to the device. Ideally, each set (reset) voltage pulse should decrease (increase) the device resistance by a small amount, according to the device's electrical characteristics, enabling fine tuning of the resistance [80].

In the simplest approach, the applied pulses are all identical in amplitude and width (with opposite signs in set and reset operations), allowing for better control of the conductive path formation. However, this is often not sufficient for the full compensation of RRAM non-idealities, requiring sequences of non-identical pulses and possibly a combination of positive and negative pulses for each set or reset operation [80]. Fine tuning of the pulse sequence shape, amplitude, and width is thus of paramount importance for exploiting the full potential of RRAM devices.

A combined design of the device geometries and materials can be beneficial for controlling the RRAM non-idealities and achieving linear resistance analog switching without using complex voltage pulse schemes [81]. A simple solution consists of using a two-layer RRAM stack made of two different dielectric materials, comprising a thin (~1–2 nm) low-k (LK) material and a thicker high-k (HK) material. The resulting distribution of the electric field across the device allows the switching mechanism to be controlled and gradual modulation of the device resistance to be produced. In such a configuration, the structural material changes responsible for the resistance switching (i.e., the conductive path and dielectric barrier formation) are confined to the LK layer, where the electric field is the highest, regardless of the layers' thickness. The confinement of these phenomena in the LK layer is the key factor that leads to a gradual change of the electrical resistance in the device, which is crucial to achieving precise and linear analog switching. Moreover, this two-layer structure allows for better control of the oxygen ions diffusion. The low electric field in the HK layer hinders the diffusion of oxygen ions coming from the LK layer, leading to the formation of an ion reservoir at the LK–HK interface. Having the oxygen ions reservoir near the conductive path contributes to smoothening the whole switching process and results in gradual modulation of the electrical resistance, with obvious benefits for applications requiring a linear and gradual conductance change, e.g., DNNs.

The presented multiscale modeling platform allows the devices' non-idealities and their effects on the device performance (i.e., symmetry, linearity, number of levels) to be evaluated. The retrieved information can then be exploited, supporting optimization of the device structure and materials, and the programming pulse sequence for achieving linear analog resistance switching.

Starting from a one-layer device, Figure 7 shows the experimental and simulated conductance evolution of TiN/6 nm $HfO_x/TiO_y/TiN$ RRAM stacks under the application of set pulse trains with an identical width (1 ms) and different voltage amplitudes (0.7, 0.8, 0.9, and 1 V). After each single set pulse, the conductance was read with a read pulse with 0.1 V amplitude and 1 ms width, which did not significantly influence the device resistance.

Noticeably, only pulse trains with amplitudes of 0.8 V and above induce a variation of the device conductance, mostly during the first few pulses (<5) of the sequence. The conductance quickly saturates, highlighting both the nonlinear characteristic of the device and the abrupt formation of the conductive path. These trends are accurately reproduced by the simulations. The fluctuation in conductance exhibited by the experimental results can be ascribed to the random nature of oxygen migration caused by the voltage pulses [82]. In fact, even after the conductance saturation, each pulse causes a small random motion of the oxygen ions in the RRAM stack, resulting in fluctuations of the conductance around a mean value.

Taking advantage of the RRAM stack's nonlinear and saturating behavior, it is possible to associate a set conductance value with a specific pulse voltage. Further simulations could support the optimization of pulse amplitudes for the best discrimination of conductance levels.

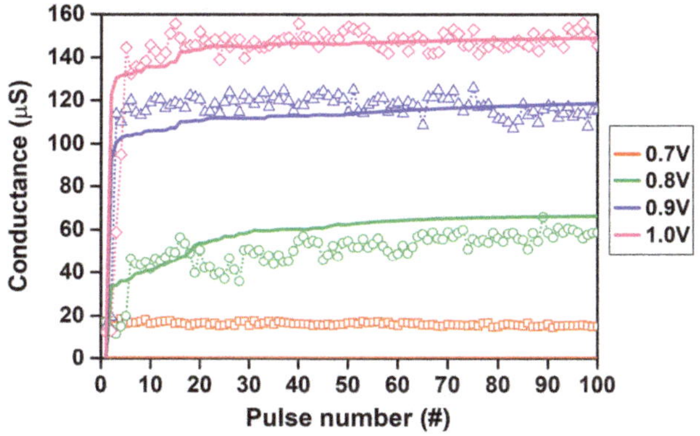

Figure 7. Experimental (symbols) and simulated (lines) conductance evolution of TiN/6 nm $HfO_x/TiO_y/TiN$ RRAM stacks under the application of set pulse trains with a 1 ms width and variable amplitude: (red) 0.7 V; (green) 0.8 V; (blue) 0.9 V; (magenta) 1.0 V. Initial forming was performed with a 100 μA compliance current.

Similar results are obtained by modulating the pulse width, as shown in Figure 8a, which depicts the experimental and simulated conductance evolution of the same device under the application of set pulse trains with an identical voltage amplitude (0.9 V) and different widths (10 μS, 100 μS, and 1 ms). As shown in Figure 8b, it is possible to take advantage of the nonlinear and saturating behavior exhibited by the considered RRAM stack to associate a set conductance value with a specific pulse width, which achieves six well-separated and recognizable resistance levels with an approximately linear characteristic. Finely tuning the programming pulse train for both set and reset processes allows a linear resistance update to be achieved for any specific RRAM device. The best combination of pulse amplitude, width, and sequence can be effectively investigated by the presented multiscale modeling platform, in order to optimize the synaptic behavior of the device. On the other hand, the platform could be useful for implementing design-circuit co-design strategies to enhance the device performance for multi-level memory applications, increasing the robustness and possibly reducing the bit error rate.

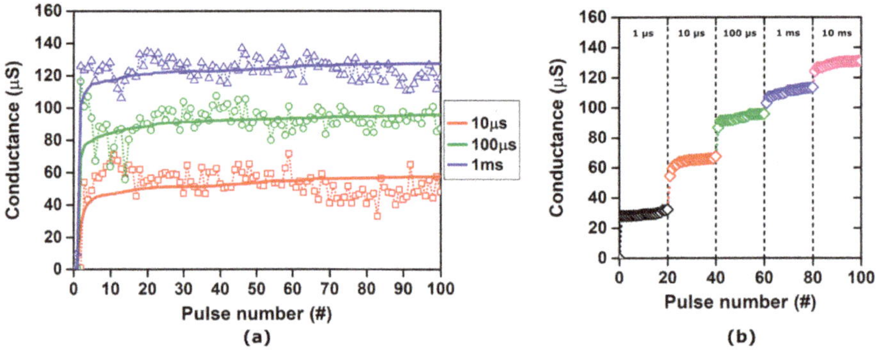

Figure 8. (**a**) Experimental (symbols) and simulated (lines) conductance evolution of TiN/6 nm HfO_x/TiO_y/TiN RRAM stacks under the application of set pulse trains with a 0.9 V amplitude and different widths: (red) 10 μS; (green) 100 μS; (blue) 1 ms. Initial forming was performed with a 100 μA compliance current. (**b**) Simulated conductance modulation obtained using set pulse trains with an increasing width: (black) 1 μS; (red) 10 μS; (green) 100 μS; (blue) 1 ms; (magenta) 10 ms.

Using a two-layer RRAM stack made of a thin LK layer (i.e., Ta_2O_5) and a thick HK layer (i.e., TiO_2), a linear conductance characteristic can be obtained. Figure 9 shows the experimental and simulated conductance evolution of TiN/2 nm Ta_2O_x/35-nm TiO_y/TiN RRAM stacks during both set and reset operations, under the application of pulse trains with an identical width (100 μS) and different voltage amplitudes. After each single pulse, the conductance was read with a read pulse with a 0.1 V amplitude and 1 ms width, which did not significantly influence the device resistance.

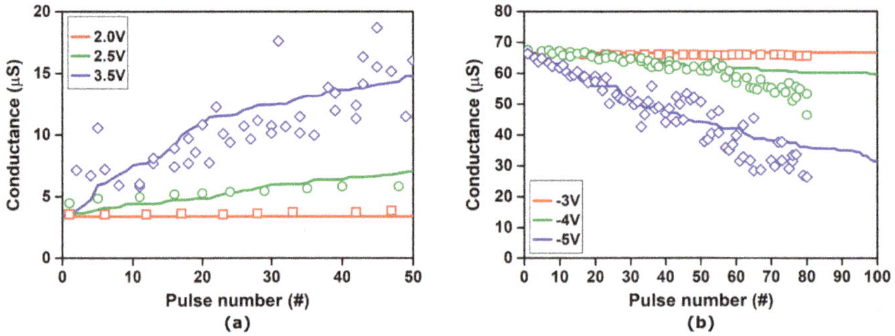

Figure 9. Experimental (symbols) and simulated (lines) conductance evolution of TiN/2 nm Ta_2O_x/35-nm TiO_y/TiN RRAM stacks under the application of set pulse trains with a 100 μS width and variable amplitude. (**a**) Set operation: (red) 2 V; (green) 2.5 V; (blue) −3.5 V. (**b**) Reset operation: (red) −3 V; (green) −4 V; (blue) −5 V.

Noticeably, the considered device exhibits an extremely linear behavior during both the set and reset operations, especially if compared with the characteristics of the one-layer device (Figures 7 and 8). However, the pulse voltage required for the switching to occur is considerably larger, starting at 2.5 V for the set process and requiring up to −4 V for the reset process. All these trends are accurately reproduced by the simulations.

While the two-layer stack structure allows for the fabrication of RRAM devices with an intrinsically linear characteristic, the lack of symmetry still prevents their use for ANN and SNN applications and could be detrimental in NVMs. The symmetry of the electrical characteristic can be pursued by further investigating the novel two-layer stack, using the presented modeling platform to optimize the materials and geometries combination, or by using specifically designed pulse sequences. Interestingly, the latter solution is relatively easy to implement: thanks to the intrinsic linearity of the set and reset characteristics, symmetry can be obtained by using different pulses (i.e., with different amplitudes) in the two operations.

3.4. Switching Reliability Optimization

The fundamental mechanism enabling analog resistance switching in RRAM devices is the diffusion of oxygen ions in the oxide layer. This process is greatly affected by the interaction of ions with the surrounding lattice, thus by the material's properties, and in turns affects many of the device's electrical properties. For example, as previously discussed, precise control of oxygen ion diffusion is key to achieving well-separated resistance levels. Even more importantly, the properties of the ion diffusion process are of paramount importance for evaluating the variability and endurance of RRAM devices [83]. In fact, precise switching between different resistance levels requires the dielectric barrier to be consistently modulated for the full lifespan of the device, with little to no variations between the cycles. Conversely, the newly proposed stochastic learning algorithms for SNNs can take advantage of device variability and non-uniformity. In both cases, the oxygen ion diffusion process must be thoroughly investigated for specific optimization of the devices. The presented multiscale modeling platform, fully accounting for the oxygen ion kinetics, can be used to investigate its effects on the reliability and variability of RRAMs.

The simulations of a TiN/5 nm HfO_x/TiO_y/TiN stack RRAM device, shown in Figure 10, reveal the high sensitivity of the device reset operation to the oxygen ion diffusion kinetics properties. Starting from a correctly formed device (Figure 10a), the reset operation was simulated considering slow and anisotropic (motion predominantly in the vertical direction) oxygen diffusion (Figure 10b), corresponding to well-performed reset operation. Then, starting from the same post-formed conditions, the simulation was performed for fast and anisotropic oxygen diffusion (Figure 10c), corresponding to an excessively high voltage reset process, and for slow and isotropic oxygen diffusion (Figure 10d). Interestingly, this last condition describes the diffusive motion of oxygen ions due to the sole temperature field.

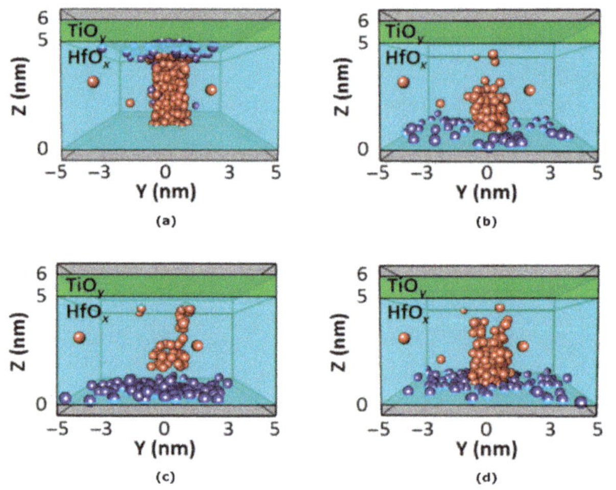

Figure 10. Simulated distributions of oxygen ions (blue) and vacancies (red) in TiN/5 nm HfO_x/TiO_y/TiN RRAM stacks: (**a**) after forming; (**b**) after the reset operation with slow and anisotropic oxygen diffusion, showing an efficient reset process; (**c**) after the reset operation with excessively fast and anisotropic oxygen diffusion, showing an inefficient reset process with the formation of a dielectric barrier near the bottom electrode; (**d**) after the reset operation with slow and isotropic oxygen diffusion (with significant motion in the radial direction), showing an inefficient reset process due to the excessive motion of the oxygen ions away from the CF.

An efficient reset operation was only obtained in the first case, where the oxygen ions are carried towards the CF in a mostly anisotropic way (some radial motion is beneficial) and are provided with enough time for recombination with the CF oxygen vacancies. In the case of fast diffusion of the oxygen ions (i.e., for an excessively high-voltage reset process), the latter condition is hindered: a significant portion of the oxygen ions are swept through the oxide, recombining along the CF length and eventually forming a dielectric barrier near the bottom electrode, as suggested in [52]. Finally, the slow and isotropic diffusion of oxygen ions leads to an inefficient reset of the device, as the excessive scattering of ions in the device volume prevents the formation of a fully dielectric barrier. The simulation results are in accordance with the experimental results showing thermally-driven oxygen ions diffusion from the "reservoir" to the CF [84].

The set operation is also affected by the diffusion of newly generated oxygen ions towards the TiO_x "reservoir" at the top electrode. Significant radial motion of the oxygen ions during the set operation would spread the ions in the "reservoir", not creating ion storage in sole proximity to the CF, leading to an increasingly ineffective reset operation and possibly to failure of the device. The cycling endurance of a device is clearly negatively affected by excessive radial motion of the oxygen ions induced by the diffusion. Therefore, convenient process recipes to optimize material properties can be implemented based on the results of these simulations to optimize the endurance and switching uniformity of RRAM devices, depending on the specific application target and its requirements.

4. Discussion

Memristors have an extremely high potential for revolutionizing both the memory and AI fields. In fact, memristors have been proposed for implementing high-density, high-speed, and low-power NVMs, and crossbar memory arrays supporting fast and efficient in-memory vector-matrix multiplication for DNN acceleration, and are finding applications in the development of SNNs, enabling the realization of artificial synapses exhibiting an STDP learning mechanism and biologically plausible artificial neurons (i.e., in accordance with the Hodgkin–Huxley model).

As illustrated in Table 1, each of the memristor applications poses different constraints for the performance metrics, demanding devices with rather different characteristics. However, the design and optimization of memristors is still difficult and, most of the time, impractical, due to the limited knowledge on the resistance switching phenomena, their interplay, and the effects of the device materials and geometry on such phenomena.

In this context, the described physical multiscale modeling and simulation provide an extremely powerful tool for the application-oriented optimization of RRAM-based memristors.

As shown in Section 3, the presented multiscale modeling platform allows the device properties, such as its macroscopic electrical properties, its resistance switching dynamics, and its microscopic properties (i.e., the oxygen ions and vacancies distribution), to be simultaneously extracted, and how such properties are affected by the device materials, geometry, and forming conditions to be investigated. Despite a few differences between the simulations and the experimental results, mainly evidenced in Figures 4 and 6, the platform proved capable of capturing the trends and fundamental relationships between the OxRAM devices' microscopic properties and their behavior.

The discrepancies shown by the simulations can be ascribed to several effects not considered by the platform, such as the oxide thickness and area variations due to the fabrication process tolerances, and process-dependent interface effects between the oxide and the electrodes. The platform can therefore be further improved by including the said effects. Moreover, it could be extended for simulating other memory devices, such as CBRAMs (i.e., including the chemical reaction phenomena at the device interfaces) and Phase Change Memories (PCMs) (i.e., accounting for the phase change in sub-regions of the device).

Nevertheless, the information obtained through the presented multiscale simulation can be effectively used to determine the best combination of OxRAM materials, geometry, forming conditions, and pulse schemes for the desired application, dramatically reducing the time required for its marked deployment.

The application of memristors to NVMs is less demanding performance-wise [26]. Noticeably, for binary NVM applications, the conductance update linearity and symmetry are not required, greatly relaxing both the device and pulse scheme design.

Even in this simple case, device optimization must account for its microscopic properties in order to satisfy the state retention and endurance constraints. In fact, as highlighted by the simulations presented in Section 3.4, the motion of oxygen ions in the device is of paramount importance for achieving an efficient and enduring resistance switching mechanism.

The multiscale simulations can effectively support the optimization of an RRAM-based memristor for NVMs. The device materials, geometry, forming condition, and pulse scheme can be optimized according to the energy consumption and switching time constraints, and the oxygen ions and vacancies distribution can be extracted at the same time. This information can then be used to discard the configurations exhibiting an instable conductive path, thus not satisfying the state retention and endurance constraints.

From the perspective of extending the number of levels of the memristive NVMs, the support of multiscale simulations is even more advantageous, as the higher number of levels requires a tighter resistance distribution of each level. As shown in Sections 3.1 and 3.2, the resistance variability of the devices can be precisely controlled by finely tuning the forming conditions (i.e., temperature, compliance current, and voltage stress), and the presented simulations allow the best forming condition to be explored.

It should be noted that a device with non-linear and/or non-symmetric resistance switching can still be used in multilevel applications if compensated for by designing a suitable pulse scheme [85–87], as shown in Section 3.3. With the support of the described multiscale simulations, the required pulse scheme can be co-designed with the device properties and optimized to achieve the required number of levels. However, linear and symmetric resistance switching would be highly desirable, as it allows for easier and more effective level control, without requiring complex pulse schemes.

As shown in Section 3.3, using a two-layer geometry RRAM allows linear resistance switching to be achieved. In this case, the interplay between the resistance switching phenomena of the two different dielectrics determines an extremely complex behavior, which can be effectively investigated through a multiscale simulation of the device. With the support of the extracted information, the two-layer structure (i.e., its materials and geometry) can be easily optimized to achieve the desired linear, and possibly symmetric, resistance switching.

The implementation of a DNN accelerator with a crossbar memory array architecture requires memristors with very different characteristics [39].

First, the number of levels is dictated by the weight precision required by the implemented DNN: a higher number of levels corresponds to a better learning capability, higher inference accuracy, and higher robustness. A precision as low as 6 bits (i.e., 64 levels) has been shown to be effective for both training and inference [88]. Moreover, the resistance switching must be absolutely linear and symmetric to avoid significant losses in the DNN accuracy [89]. This is especially true for online-trained DNNs, while for offline-trained DNNs, the non-ideal conductance update can be compensated for by suitable writing schemes.

For this application, a two-layer structure is clearly beneficial and, as stated before, the support of the described multiscale simulations allows a better understanding of the device's complex behavior and optimization of its structure to match the requirements.

Due to the high number of levels required, the dynamic range must increase in parallel with the weight precision to ensure a sufficient separation of the levels, while ensuring a sufficiently high resistance value of the low-resistance state in order to limit the inference energy consumption. The energy consumption of the training phase is instead determined by the programming energy, which must be limited. A related performance metric is the switching time, which must also be as low as possible to ensure both fast and energy-efficient training.

All of these metrics are interconnected and their relationship with the device geometry and materials, and their trade-offs cannot be easily appreciated and designed. The low-resistance state value and the variability of the resistance levels can be controlled by the forming conditions, as previously stated and as shown in Sections 3.1 and 3.2, but the effects on the required programming energy and switching time are not obvious. The multiscale simulation provides an extremely powerful tool to explore the possible solutions and possibly optimize the device materials, geometry, and forming conditions to match the requirements.

Finally, the reliability-related metrics (i.e., endurance and retention) are extremely demanding and critical: the training phase (or the weights set up in the case of offline training), requiring a large number of switching operations, can be stressful for the devices and the weight values must be retained (ideally) indefinitely. As for the NVM application, the stability of the conductive path in a specific device can be easily investigated though multiscale simulations, allowing for the recognition of unsuitable solutions.

The desired performance for memristors implementing SNN artificial synapses is extremely similar to that required for DNN accelerators [40], especially those concerning the number of levels and the reliability-related metrics (i.e., endurance and retention). This is reasonable, since SNNs also undergo a stressful training phase (or synaptic weight set up), requiring many switching operations. Moreover, the specific requirements for feature size and switching time can be reasonably assumed to be similar to those of DNN accelerators. Additionally, recent works suggest that artificial synapses with symmetric conductance updates allow for a better accuracy in SNNs [90].

Noticeably, the application-level effects of memristors' stochasticity, i.e., uniformity (or lack of thereof) and variability, are little discussed in the literature. In NVM applications, both the non-uniformity and high variability of the memory cell can be detrimental [39], posing a challenge for technology development. Neural network applications exhibit a good tolerance to device-to-device and cycle-to-cycle variations, especially if online training is used [88,89]. Interestingly, the exploitation of memristors' stochasticity has recently been proposed for implementing stochastic learning algorithms for SNNs [22,91]. In such a context, the device's variability, non-uniformity, and noise become key components of the learning algorithm, thus requiring a precise design. All those properties can also be investigated using multiscale simulations, e.g., as previously stated, the device's variability can be controlled and optimized by tuning the forming conditions.

5. Conclusions

We have shown that multiscale modeling and simulation can effectively support the application-oriented optimization of RRAM devices.

With the support of the presented multiscale modeling platform, we simulated the microscopic behavior of RRAMs and investigated the effects of the device geometry, materials, forming conditions (i.e., temperature, current compliance, voltage stress mode), and programming on the device performance. The multiscale simulations allowed the properties of RRAMs during their whole operation, from the forming process to the subsequent set-reset cycle, to be investigated, providing information about the device linearity, symmetry, dynamic range, and reliability.

The presented multiscale simulations provide useful design principles for RRAM technology optimization according to the specific AI application, for the implementation of non-volatile memories, deep neural networks, or spiking neural networks.

Moreover, the multiscale simulation allows the effects of different implementations of the device (i.e., different geometries or materials) to be explored, and both the forming conditions and the pulse scheme (i.e., amplitude, width, sequence) to be finely tuned for achieving the desired performance.

Author Contributions: Conceptualization, P.L.T. and F.M.P.; methodology, A.P.; software, A.P.; validation, L.L.; formal analysis, A.P. and L.L.; investigation, A.P. and F.M.P.; resources, L.L.; data curation, A.P.; writing—original draft preparation, P.L.T.; writing—review and editing, F.M.P. and L.L.; visualization, P.L.T.; supervision, L.L.; project administration, L.L.; funding acquisition, L.L.

Funding: This research received no external funding.

Conflicts of Interest: The authors declare no conflicts of interest.

References

1. Goodfellow, I.; Bengio, Y.; Courville, A. *The Deep Learning Book*; MIT Press: Cambridge, MA, USA, 2017; Volume 521, p. 785.
2. Geron, A. *Hands-on Machine Learning with Scikit-Learn, Keras, and TensorFlow: Concepts, Tools, and Techniques to Build Intelligent Systems*; O'Reilly Media, Inc.: Newton, MA, USA, 2019; ISBN 9781492032649.
3. Lecun, Y.; Bottou, L.; Bengio, Y.; Haffner, P. Gradient-based learning applied to document recognition. *Proc. IEEE* **1998**, *86*, 2278–2324. [CrossRef]
4. Kaensar, C. A Comparative Study on Handwriting Digit Recognition Classifier Using Neural Network, Support Vector Machine and K-Nearest Neighbor. *Adv. Intell. Syst. Comput.* **2013**, *209*, 155–163.
5. Imran, A.S.; Shahrebabaki, A.S.; Olfati, N.; Svendsen, T. A Study on the Performance Evaluation of Machine Learning Models for Phoneme Classification. In Proceedings of the 2019 11th International Conference on Machine Learning and Computing—ICMLC '19, Zhuhai, China, 22–24 February 2019; pp. 52–58.
6. Li, D.; Chen, X.; Becchi, M.; Zong, Z. Evaluating the Energy Efficiency of Deep Convolutional Neural Networks on CPUs and GPUs. In Proceedings of the 2016 IEEE International Conferences on Big Data and Cloud Computing (BDCloud), Social Computing and Networking (SocialCom), Sustainable Computing and Communications (SustainCom) (BDCloud-SocialCom-SustainCom), Atlanta, GA, USA, 8–10 October 2016; pp. 477–484.
7. Canziani, A.; Paszke, A.; Culurciello, E. An Analysis of Deep Neural Network Models for Practical Applications. *arXiv* **2016**, arXiv:1605.07678.2016.
8. Strubell, E.; Ganesh, A.; McCallum, A. Energy and Policy Considerations for Deep Learning in NLP. In Proceedings of the 57th Annual Meeting of the Association for Computational Linguistics, Florence, Italy, 28 July–2 August 2019.

9. Guzhva, A.; Dolenko, S.; Persiantsev, I. Multifold Acceleration of Neural Network Computations Using GPU. In *Computer Vision–ECCV 2012*; Springer Science and Business Media LLC: Berlin, Germany, 2009; Volume 5768, pp. 373–380.
10. Jouppi, N.P.; Borchers, A.; Boyle, R.; Cantin, P.-L.; Chao, C.; Clark, C.; Coriell, J.; Daley, M.; Dau, M.; Dean, J.; et al. In-Datacenter Performance Analysis of a Tensor Processing Unit. *ACM SIGARCH Comput. Arch. News* **2017**, *45*, 1–12. [CrossRef]
11. Chen, C.; Krishna, T.; Emer, J.; Sze, V. Eyeriss: An Energy-Efficient Reconfigurable Accelerator for Deep Convolutional Neural Networks "Eyeriss: An Energy-Efficient Reconfigurable Accelerator for Accessed Terms of Use. *Deep Convol. Neural Netw.* **2017**, *52*, 127–138.
12. Moons, B.; Uytterhoeven, R.; Dehaene, W.; Verhelst, M. 14.5 Envision: A 0.26-to-10TOPS/W subword-parallel dynamic-voltage-accuracy-frequency-scalable Convolutional Neural Network processor in 28nm FDSOI. In Proceedings of the 2017 IEEE International Solid-State Circuits Conference (ISSCC), San Francisco, CA, USA, 5–9 February 2017; Volume 60, pp. 246–247.
13. Bankman, D.; Yang, L.; Moons, B.; Verhelst, M.; Murmann, B. An always-on 3.8 μ J/86% CIFAR-10 mixed-signal binary CNN processor with all memory on chip in 28nm CMOS. *IEEE J. Solid-State Circuits* **2018**, *54*, 158–172. [CrossRef]
14. Moons, B.; Bankman, D.; Yang, L.; Murmann, B.; Verhelst, M. BinarEye: An always-on energy-accuracy-scalable binary CNN processor with all memory on chip in 28nm CMOS. In Proceedings of the 2018 IEEE Custom Integrated Circuits Conference (CICC), San Diego, CA, USA, 8–11 April 2018; Institute of Electrical and Electronics Engineers (IEEE): Piscataway, NJ, USA, 2018; pp. 1–4.
15. Chua, L. Memristor-The missing circuit element. *IEEE Trans. Circuit Theory* **1971**, *18*, 507–519. [CrossRef]
16. Chua, L. Resistance switching memories are memristors. *Appl. Phys. A* **2011**, *102*, 765–783. [CrossRef]
17. Wang, L.; Yang, C.; Wen, J.; Gai, S.; Peng, Y. Overview of emerging memristor families from resistive memristor to spintronic memristor. *J. Mater. Sci. Mater. Electron.* **2015**, *26*, 4618–4628. [CrossRef]
18. Zidan, M.A.; Chen, A.; Indiveri, G.; Lu, W.D. Memristive computing devices and applications. *J. Electroceramics* **2017**, *39*, 4–20. [CrossRef]
19. Burr, G.W.; Shelby, R.M.; Sebastian, A.; Kim, S.S.; Kim, S.S.; Sidler, S.; Virwani, K.; Ishii, M.; Narayanan, P.; Fumarola, A.; et al. Neuromorphic computing using non-volatile memory. *Adv. Phys.* X **2017**, *2*, 89–124. [CrossRef]
20. Ambrogio, S.; Narayanan, P.; Burr, G.W.; Tsai, H.-Y.; Shelby, R.M. Recent progress in analog memory-based accelerators for deep learning. *J. Phys. D Appl. Phys.* **2018**, *51*, 283001.
21. Ielmini, D. Brain-inspired computing with resistive switching memory (RRAM): Devices, synapses and neural networks. *Microelectron. Eng.* **2018**, *190*, 44–53. [CrossRef]
22. Sengupta, A.; Srinivasan, G.; Roy, D.; Roy, K. Stochastic Inference and Learning Enabled by Magnetic Tunnel Junctions. In Proceedings of the 2018 IEEE International Electron Devices Meeting (IEDM), San Francisco, CA, USA, 1–5 December 2019.
23. Hodgkin, A.; Huxley, A. A quantitative description of membrane current and its application to conduction and excitation in nerve. *Bull. Math. Boil.* **1990**, *52*, 25–71. [CrossRef]
24. Chua, L. Memristor, Hodgkin–Huxley, and Edge of Chaos. *Nanotechnology* **2013**, *24*, 383001. [CrossRef] [PubMed]
25. Strukov, D.B.; Snider, G.S.; Stewart, D.R.; Williams, R.S. The missing memristor found. *Nature* **2008**, *453*, 80–83. [CrossRef] [PubMed]
26. Chen, A.; Hutchby, J.; Zhirnov, V.; Bourianoff, G. *Emerging Nanoelectronic Devices*; Chen, A., Hutchby, J., Zhirnov, V., Bourianoff, G., Eds.; John Wiley & Sons Ltd.: Chichester, UK, 2014; ISBN 9781118958254.
27. Choi, S.J.; Lee, J.H.; Bae, H.J.; Yang, W.Y.; Kim, T.W.; Kim, K.H. Improvement of CBRAM Resistance Window by Scaling Down Electrode Size in Pure-GeTe Film. *IEEE Electron Device Lett.* **2009**, *30*, 120–122. [CrossRef]
28. Wang, S.Y.; Huang, C.W.; Lee, D.Y.; Tseng, T.Y.; Chang, T.C. Multilevel resistive switching in Ti/Cu_xO/Pt memory devices. *J. Appl. Phys.* **2010**, *108*, 114110. [CrossRef]
29. Rahaman, S.Z.; Maikap, S.; Das, A.; Prakash, A.; Wu, Y.H.; Lai, C.-S.; Tien, T.-C.; Chen, W.-S.; Lee, H.-Y.; Chen, F.T.; et al. Enhanced nanoscale resistive switching memory characteristics and switching mechanism using high-Ge-content Ge0.5Se0.5 solid electrolyte. *Nanoscale Res. Lett.* **2012**, *7*, 614. [CrossRef]

30. Padovani, A.; Woo, J.; Hwang, H.; Larcher, L. Understanding and Optimization of Pulsed SET Operation in HfO_x-Based RRAM Devices for Neuromorphic Computing Applications. *IEEE Electron Device Lett.* **2018**, *39*, 672–675. [CrossRef]
31. Sung, C.; Padovani, A.; Beltrando, B.; Lee, D.; Kwak, M.; Lim, S.; Larcher, L.; Della Marca, V.; Hwang, H. Investigation of I-V linearity in TaO_x-Based RRAM devices for neuromorphic applications. *IEEE J. Electron Devices Soc.* **2019**, *7*, 404–408. [CrossRef]
32. Wright, C.D.; Liu, Y.; Kohary, K.I.; Aziz, M.M.; Hicken, R.J. Arithmetic and Biologically-Inspired Computing Using Phase-Change Materials. *Adv. Mater.* **2011**, *23*, 3408–3413. [CrossRef] [PubMed]
33. Kuzum, D.; Jeyasingh, R.G.D.; Lee, B.; Wong, H.S.P. Nanoelectronic programmable synapses based on phase change materials for brain-inspired computing. *Nano Lett.* **2012**, *12*, 2179–2186. [CrossRef]
34. Ambrogio, S.; Ciocchini, N.; Laudato, M.; Milo, V.; Pirovano, A.; Fantini, P.; Ielmini, D. Unsupervised Learning by Spike Timing Dependent Plasticity in Phase Change Memory (PCM) Synapses. *Front. Mol. Neurosci.* **2016**, *10*, 384012. [CrossRef] [PubMed]
35. Chanthbouala, A.; Crassous, A.; Garcia, V.; Bouzehouane, K.; Fusil, S.; Moya, X.; Allibe, J.; Dlubak, B.; Grollier, J.; Xavier, S.; et al. Solid-state memories based on ferroelectric tunnel junctions. *Nat. Nanotechnol.* **2012**, *7*, 101–104. [CrossRef] [PubMed]
36. Wen, Z.; Li, C.; Wu, D.; Li, A.; Ming, N. Ferroelectric-field-effect-enhanced electroresistance in metal/ferroelectric/semiconductor tunnel junctions. *Nat. Mater.* **2013**, *12*, 617–621. [CrossRef] [PubMed]
37. Boyn, S.; Girod, S.; Garcia, V.; Fusil, S.; Xavier, S.; Deranlot, C.; Yamada, H.; Carrétéro, C.; Jacquet, E.; Bibes, M.; et al. High-performance ferroelectric memory based on fully patterned tunnel junctions. *Appl. Phys. Lett.* **2014**, *104*, 052909. [CrossRef]
38. Chappert, C.; Fert, A.; Van Dau, F.N. The emergence of spin electronics in data storage. *Nat. Mater.* **2007**, *6*, 813–823. [CrossRef]
39. Yu, S. Neuro-Inspired Computing with Emerging Nonvolatile Memory. *Proc. IEEE* **2018**, *106*, 260–285. [CrossRef]
40. Zhang, T.; Yang, K.; Xu, X.; Cai, Y.; Yang, Y.; Huang, R. Memristive Devices and Networks for Brain-Inspired Computing. *Phys. Status Solidi (RRL)-Rapid Res. Lett.* **2019**, *13*, 1–21.
41. Padovani, A.; Larcher, L.; Puglisi, F.M.; Pavan, P. Multiscale modeling of defect-related phenomena in high-k based logic and memory devices. In Proceedings of the 2017 IEEE 24th International Symposium on the Physical and Failure Analysis of Integrated Circuits (IPFA), Chengdu, China, 4–7 July 2017; Institute of Electrical and Electronics Engineers (IEEE): Piscataway, NJ, USA, 2017; pp. 1–6.
42. Puglisi, F.M.; Larcher, L.; Padovani, A.; Pavan, P. Bipolar Resistive RAM Based on HfO_2: Physics, Compact Modeling, and Variability Control. *IEEE J. Emerg. Sel. Top. Circuits Syst.* **2016**, *6*, 171–184. [CrossRef]
43. Puglisi, F.M.; Padovani, A.; Pavan, P.; Larcher, L. Advanced modeling and characterization techniques for innovative memory devices: The RRAM case. In *Advances in Non-Volatile Memory and Storage Technology*; Woodhead Publishing: Sawston, UK; Cambridge, UK, 2019; pp. 103–135.
44. Kund, M.; Beitel, G.; Pinnow, C.-U.; Rohr, T.; Schumann, J.; Symanczyk, R.; Ufert, K.; Muller, G. Conductive bridging RAM (CBRAM): An emerging non-volatile memory technology scalable to sub 20nm. In Proceedings of the IEEE InternationalElectron Devices Meeting, 2005. IEDM Technical Digest, Washington, DC, USA, 5 December 2005; pp. 754–757.
45. Nail, C.; Molas, G.; Blaise, P.; Piccolboni, G.; Sklenard, B.; Cagli, C.; Bernard, M.; Roule, A.; Azzaz, M.; Vianello, E.; et al. Understanding RRAM endurance, retention and window margin trade-off using experimental results and simulations. In Proceedings of the 2016 IEEE International Electron Devices Meeting (IEDM), San Francisco, CA, USA, 3–7 December 2016.
46. Goux, L.; Radhakrishnan, J.; Belmonte, A.; Witters, T.; Devulder, W.; Redolfi, A.; Kundu, S.; Houssa, M.; Kar, G.S. Key material parameters driving CBRAM device performances. *Faraday Discuss.* **2019**, *213*, 67–85. [CrossRef] [PubMed]
47. Lee, B.; Wu, Y.; Yu, S.; Wong, P. Low-power $TiN/Al_2O_3/Pt$ resistive switching device with sub-20 μA switching current and gradual resistance modulation. *J. Appl. Phys.* **2011**, *110*, 94104.
48. Yu, S.; Wu, Y.; Jeyasingh, R.; Kuzum, D.; Wong, H.-S.P. An Electronic Synapse Device Based on Metal Oxide Resistive Switching Memory for Neuromorphic Computation. *IEEE Trans. Electron Devices* **2011**, *58*, 2729–2737. [CrossRef]

49. Long, B.; Li, Y.; Jha, R. Switching Characteristics of Ru/HfO_2/TiO_{2-x}/Ru RRAM Devices for Digital and Analog Nonvolatile Memory Applications. *IEEE Electron Device Lett.* **2012**, *33*, 706–708. [CrossRef]
50. Matveyev, Y.; Egorov, K.; Markeev, A.; Zenkevich, A.; Matveyev, Y. Resistive switching and synaptic properties of fully atomic layer deposition grown TiN/HfO_2/TiN devices. *J. Appl. Phys.* **2015**, *117*, 044901. [CrossRef]
51. Wang, Y.-F.; Lin, Y.-C.; Wang, I.-T.; Lin, T.-P.; Hou, T.-H. Characterization and Modeling of Nonfilamentary Ta/TaO_x/TiO_2/Ti Analog Synaptic Device. *Sci. Rep.* **2015**, *5*, 10150. [CrossRef]
52. Bersuker, G.; Gilmer, D.C.; Veksler, D.; Kirsch, P.; Vandelli, L.; Padovani, A.; Larcher, L.; McKenna, K.; Shluger, A.; Iglesias, V.; et al. Metal oxide resistive memory switching mechanism based on conductive filament properties. *J. Appl. Phys.* **2011**, *110*, 124518. [CrossRef]
53. Foster, A.S.; Gejo, F.L.; Shluger, A.L.; Nieminen, R.M. Vacancy and interstitial defects in hafnia. *Phys. Rev. B* **2002**, *65*, 174117. [CrossRef]
54. Ramo, D.M.; Gavartin, J.L.; Shluger, A.L.; Bersuker, G. Spectroscopic properties of oxygen vacancies in monoclinic HfO_2 calculated with periodic and embedded cluster density functional theory. *Phys. Rev. B* **2007**, *75*, 205336. [CrossRef]
55. Robertson, J.; Gillen, R. Defect densities inside the conductive filament of RRAMs. *Microelectron. Eng.* **2013**, *109*, 208–210. [CrossRef]
56. Vandelli, L.; Padovani, A.; Larcher, L.; Southwick, R.G.; Knowlton, W.B.; Bersuker, G. A Physical Model of the Temperature Dependence of the Current through SiO_2/HfO_2 Stacks. *IEEE Trans. Electron Devices* **2011**, *58*, 2878–2887. [CrossRef]
57. Vandelli, L.; Padovani, A.; Larcher, L.; Broglia, G.; Ori, G.; Montorsi, M.; Bersuker, G.; Pavan, P. Comprehensive physical modeling of forming and switching operations in HfO_2 RRAM devices. In Proceedings of the 2011 International Electron Devices Meeting, Washington, DC, USA, 5–7 December 2011.
58. Larcher, L.; Padovani, A.; Pirrotta, O.; Vandelli, L.; Bersuker, G. Microscopic understanding and modeling of HfO_2 RRAM device physics. In Proceedings of the 2012 International Electron Devices Meeting, San Francisco, CA, USA, 10–13 December 2012.
59. Vandelli, L.; Padovani, A.; Larcher, L.; Bersuker, G. Microscopic Modeling of Electrical Stress-Induced Breakdown in Poly-Crystalline Hafnium Oxide Dielectrics. *IEEE Trans. Electron Devices* **2013**, *60*, 1754–1762. [CrossRef]
60. Padovani, A.; Larcher, L.; Bersuker, G.; Pavan, P. Charge Transport and Degradation in HfO_2 and HfO_x Dielectrics. *IEEE Electron Device Lett.* **2013**, *34*, 680–682. [CrossRef]
61. Padovani, A.; Larcher, L.; Pirrotta, O.; Vandelli, L.; Bersuker, G. Microscopic Modeling of HfO_x RRAM Operations: From Forming to Switching. *IEEE Trans. Electron Devices* **2015**, *62*, 1998–2006. [CrossRef]
62. Larcher, L.; Padovani, A.; Di Lecce, V. Multiscale modeling of neuromorphic computing: From materials to device operations. In Proceedings of the 2017 IEEE International Electron Devices Meeting (IEDM), San Francisco, CA, USA, 2–6 December 2017; Institute of Electrical and Electronics Engineers (IEEE): Piscataway, NJ, USA, 2017.
63. Larcher, L.; Padovani, A.; Puglisi, F.M.; Pavan, P. Extracting Atomic Defect Properties From Leakage Current Temperature Dependence. *IEEE Trans. Electron Devices* **2018**, *65*, 5475–5480. [CrossRef]
64. Zhang, M.; Huo, Z.; Yu, Z.; Liu, J.; Liu, M. Unification of three multiphonon trap-assisted tunneling mechanisms. *J. Appl. Phys.* **2011**, *110*, 114108. [CrossRef]
65. Larcher, L.; Padovani, A.; Pavan, P. Leakage current in HfO2 stacks: From physical to compact modeling. In Proceedings of the Workshop on Compact Modeling, San Jose, CA, USA, 18–21 June 2012.
66. Di Ventra, M. *Electrical Transport in Nanoscale Systems*; Cambridge University Press: Cambridge, UK, 2008; Volume 34, ISBN 9780511755606.
67. McPherson, J.; Kim, J.-Y.; Shanware, A.; Mogul, H. Thermochemical description of dielectric breakdown in high dielectric constant materials. *Appl. Phys. Lett.* **2003**, *82*, 2121. [CrossRef]
68. Padovani, A.; Gao, D.Z.; Shluger, A.; Larcher, L. A microscopic mechanism of dielectric breakdown in SiO_2 films: An insight from multi-scale modeling. *J. Appl. Phys.* **2017**, *121*, 155101. [CrossRef]
69. Foster, A.S.; Shluger, A.L.; Nieminen, R.M. Mechanism of Interstitial Oxygen Diffusion in Hafnia. *Phys. Rev. Lett.* **2002**, *89*, 225901. [CrossRef]
70. Puglisi, F.M.; Pavan, P.; Padovani, A.; Larcher, L.; Bersuker, G. RTS noise characterization of HfO_x RRAM in high resistive state. *Solid-State Electron.* **2013**, *84*, 160–166. [CrossRef]

71. Veksler, D.; Bersuker, G.; Vandelli, L.; Padovani, A.; Larcher, L.; Muraviev, A.; Chakrabarti, B.; Vogel, E.; Gilmer, D.C.; Kirsch, P.D. Random telegraph noise (RTN) in scaled RRAM devices. In Proceedings of the 2013 IEEE International Reliability Physics Symposium (IRPS), Anaheim, CA, USA, 14–18 April 2013; Institute of Electrical and Electronics Engineers (IEEE): Piscataway, NJ, USA, 2013.
72. Puglisi, F.M.; Pavan, P.; Vandelli, L.; Padovani, A.; Bertocchi, M.; Larcher, L. A microscopic physical description of RTN current fluctuations in HfO_x RRAM. In Proceedings of the 2015 IEEE International Reliability Physics Symposium, Monterey, CA, USA, 19–23 April 2015; IEEE: Piscataway, NJ, USA, 2015.
73. Puglisi, F.M.; Larcher, L.; Padovani, A.; Pavan, P. A Complete Statistical Investigation of RTN in HfO_2-Based RRAM in High Resistive State. *IEEE Trans. Electron Devices* **2015**, *62*, 2606–2613. [CrossRef]
74. Nminibapiel, D.M.; Veksler, D.; Shrestha, P.R.; Campbell, J.P.; Ryan, J.T.; Baumgart, H.; Cheung, K.P.; Kim, J.-H. Impact of RRAM Read Fluctuations on the Program-Verify Approach. *IEEE Electron Device Lett.* **2017**, *38*, 736–739. [CrossRef] [PubMed]
75. Ielmini, D. Modeling the Universal Set/Reset Characteristics of Bipolar RRAM by Field- and Temperature-Driven Filament Growth. *IEEE Trans. Electron Devices* **2011**, *58*, 4309–4317. [CrossRef]
76. Butcher, B.; Bersuker, G.; Young-Fisher, K.G.; Gilmer, D.C.; Kalantarian, A.; Nishi, Y.; Geer, R.; Kirsch, P.D.; Jammy, R. Hot forming to improve memory window and uniformity of low-power HfO_x-based RRAMs. In Proceedings of the 2012 4th IEEE International Memory Workshop, Milan, Italy, 20–23 May 2012; pp. 1–4.
77. Butcher, B.; Bersuker, G.; Vandelli, L.; Padovani, A.; Larcher, L.; Kalantarian, A.; Geer, R.; Gilmer, D. Modeling the effects of different forming conditions on RRAM conductive filament stability. In Proceedings of the 2013 5th IEEE International Memory Workshop, Monterey, CA, USA, 26–29 May 2013; pp. 52–55.
78. Traore, B.; Xue, K.-H.; Vianello, E.; Molas, G.; Blaise, P.; De Salvo, B.; Padovani, A.; Pirrotta, O.; Larcher, L.; Fonseca, L.R.C.; et al. Investigation of the role of electrodes on the retention performance of HfO_x based RRAM cells by experiments, atomistic simulations and device physical modeling. In Proceedings of the 2013 IEEE International Reliability Physics Symposium (IRPS), Anaheim, CA, USA, 14–18 April 2013.
79. Lorenzi, P.; Rao, R.; Irrera, F. Forming Kinetics in HfO_2-Based RRAM Cells. *IEEE Trans. Electron Devices* **2013**, *60*, 438–443. [CrossRef]
80. Chen, P.-Y.; Lin, B.; Wang, I.-T.; Hou, T.-H.; Ye, J.; Vrudhula, S.; Seo, J.-S.; Cao, Y.; Yu, S. Mitigating effects of non-ideal synaptic device characteristics for on-chip learning. In Proceedings of the 2015 IEEE/ACM International Conference on Computer-Aided Design (ICCAD), Austin, TX, USA, 2–6 November 2015; pp. 194–199.
81. Larcher, L.; Padovani, A.; Woo, J.; Hwang, H.; Pesic, M. RRAM synapse optimization: From material stack to device performance. *IEEE Trans. Electron Devices*. under review.
82. Gao, B.; Kang, J.; Zhou, Z.; Chen, Z.; Huang, P.; Liu, L. Metal oxide resistive random access memory based synaptic devices for brain-inspired computing. *Jpn. J. Appl. Phys.* **2016**, *55*, 4. [CrossRef]
83. Chen, B.; Lu, Y.; Gao, B.; Fu, Y.; Zhang, F.; Huang, P.; Chen, Y.; Liu, L.; Liu, X.; Kang, J.; et al. Physical mechanisms of endurance degradation in TMO-RRAM. In Proceedings of the 2011 International Electron Devices Meeting; Institute of Electrical and Electronics Engineers (IEEE), Washington, DC, USA, 5–7 December 2011.
84. Chen, Y.Y.; Komura, M.; Degraeve, R.; Govoreanu, B.; Goux, L.; Fantini, A.; Raghavan, N.; Clima, S.; Zhang, L.; Belmonte, A.; et al. Improvement of data retention in HfO_2/Hf 1T1R RRAM cell under low operating current. In Proceedings of the 2013 IEEE International Electron Devices Meeting, Washington, DC, USA, 9–11 December 2013.
85. Puglisi, F.M.; Wenger, C.; Pavan, P. A Novel Program-Verify Algorithm for Multi-Bit Operation in HfO_2 RRAM. *IEEE Electron Device Lett.* **2015**, *36*, 1030–1032. [CrossRef]
86. Belmonte, A.; Fantini, A.; Redolfi, A.; Houssa, M.; Jurczak, M.; Goux, L. Optimization of the write algorithm at low-current (10μA) in Cu/Al_2O_3-based conductive-bridge RAM. In Proceedings of the 2015 45th European Solid State Device Research Conference (ESSDERC), Graz, Austria, 14–18 September 2015; pp. 114–117.
87. Woo, J.; Moon, K.; Song, J.; Kwak, M.; Park, J.; Hwang, H. Optimized Programming Scheme Enabling Linear Potentiation in Filamentary HfO_2 RRAM Synapse for Neuromorphic Systems. *IEEE Trans. Electron Devices* **2016**, *63*, 5064–5067. [CrossRef]
88. Islam, R.; Li, H.; Chen, P.-Y.; Wan, W.; Chen, H.-Y.; Gao, B.; Wu, H.; Yu, S.; Saraswat, K.C.; Wong, H.-S.P.; et al. Device and materials requirements for neuromorphic computing. *J. Phys. D Appl. Phys.* **2019**, *52*, 113001. [CrossRef]

89. Burr, G.W.; Shelby, R.M.; Sidler, S.; Di Nolfo, C.; Jang, J.; Boybat, I.; Shenoy, R.S.; Narayanan, P.; Virwani, K.; Giacometti, E.U.; et al. Experimental Demonstration and Tolerancing of a Large-Scale Neural Network (165 000 Synapses) Using Phase-Change Memory as the Synaptic Weight Element. *IEEE Trans. Electron Devices* **2015**, *62*, 3498–3507. [CrossRef]
90. Boybat, I.; Le Gallo, M.; Nandakumar, S.R.; Moraitis, T.; Parnell, T.; Tuma, T.; Rajendran, B.; Leblebici, Y.; Sebastian, A.; Eleftheriou, E. Neuromorphic computing with multi-memristive synapses. *Nat. Commun.* **2018**, *9*, 2514. [CrossRef] [PubMed]
91. Yu, S.; Gao, B.; Fang, Z.; Yu, H.; Kang, J.; Wong, H.-S.P. Stochastic learning in oxide binary synaptic device for neuromorphic computing. *Front. Mol. Neurosci.* **2013**, *7*, 1–9. [CrossRef] [PubMed]

materials

MDPI

Article

Resistive Switching and Charge Transport in Laser-Fabricated Graphene Oxide Memristors: A Time Series and Quantum Point Contact Modeling Approach

N. Rodriguez [1,2,*], D. Maldonado [1], F. J. Romero [1,2], F. J. Alonso [3], A. M. Aguilera [3], A. Godoy [1,2], F. Jimenez-Molinos [1], F. G. Ruiz [1,2] and J. B. Roldan [1]

1 Department of Electronics and Computer Technology, Science Faculty, University of Granada, Av. Fuentenueva s/n, 18071 Granada, Spain; davidmaldonado@correo.ugr.es (D.M.); franromero@ugr.es (F.J.R.); agodoy@ugr.es (A.G.); jmolinos@ugr.es (F.J.M.); franruiz@ugr.es (F.G.R.); jroldan@ugr.es (J.B.R.)

2 Pervasive Electronics Advanced Research Laboratory, University of Granada, 18071 Granada, Spain

3 Department of Statistics and Operations Research, Science Faculty, University of Granada, Av. Fuentenueva s/n, 18071 Granada, Spain; falonso@ugr.es (F.J.A.); aaguiler@ugr.es (A.M.A.)

* Correspondence: noel@ugr.es

Received: 17 September 2019; Accepted: 10 November 2019; Published: 13 November 2019

Abstract: This work investigates the sources of resistive switching (RS) in recently reported laser-fabricated graphene oxide memristors by means of two numerical analysis tools linked to the Time Series Statistical Analysis and the use of the Quantum Point Contact Conduction model. The application of both numerical procedures points to the existence of a filament connecting the electrodes that may be interrupted at a precise point within the conductive path, resulting in resistive switching phenomena. These results support the existing model attributing the memristance of laser-fabricated graphene oxide memristors to the modification of a conductive path stoichiometry inside the graphene oxide.

Keywords: memristor; RRAM; variability; time series modeling; autocovariance; graphene oxide; laser

1. Introduction

Memristors have shown great potential in the context of neuromorphic circuits. Their operation, based on resistance modulation by means of ion transport and redox reactions, leads to the creation of regions of different conductivity mimicking neuronal synapses in a coherent and natural manner. Consequently, memristors are of most interest for the fabrication of optimized hardware that aims to design and implement artificial neural networks [1–3]. This potential, along with their intrinsic facet of non-volatility, poses the set of features needed by memristors to become the cornerstone for computation schemes beyond of the classical von Neumann paradigm, such as neuromorphic computing. This new focus will be essential to push forward the artificial intelligence challenges that the industry is facing currently [2,3].

From a more general perspective, the outstanding features of memristors make them also suitable for applications that run through non-volatile memories, Internet of Things (IoT) devices, 5G, etc. Among their promising characteristics, the following can be highlighted: fast read/write times for the set and reset processes, low power consumption, scalability and CMOS technology compatibility among others [3–7].

The physics behind memristors is strongly dependent on the materials employed and the details of their fabrication process. In this respect, there is a plethora of recent experimental, modeling and simulation studies on technologies that make use of transition metal oxides as the switching dielectric [4,5,8–15]. However, in the field of memristors based on 2D materials, the amount of studies and published manuscripts is much lower. In this context, the difficulties related to the creation of high quality metal contacts, the purity of the materials and the fabrication details pose extra difficulties for dealing with all of the facets of the study of these devices, and in particular, in regards to the physical simulation and modeling.

In the 2D material memristors landscape, there are h-BN based devices, memristors with a different number of graphene layers or other 2D materials that are employed for oxygen ion scavenging and other particular purposes [3,16,17]. Among all the 2D materials-based contenders, the laser fabrication of memristors based on graphene oxide (GO) was recently introduced [18]. GO is a highly functionalized form of polycrystalline nanographene that is decorated with oxygen-containing groups [19]. The use of GO as a memristive material takes advantage of its inherent 2D materials potential with respect to conduction and structural flexibility properties while simultaneously including its non-volatility and electrical plasticity [20], as expected in ideal memristors [21].

The implementation of a laser-assisted fabrication protocol provides the device with several attractive features for its potential industrial implementation: (i) the fabrication process is very simple, comprising a limited number of steps; (ii) there is no need for lithographic masks since the laser itself defines the geometry of the memristor; (iii) the devices do not require scarce or hazardous materials for their fabrication; (iv) the resistive switching behavior originates in the GO (and not in the electrodes) adding versatility from the contacting electrodes perspective and (v) the supporting substrate can be selected with versatility from a rigid surface to flexible polymers for conformal integration.

The novelty of the devices employed here results in a lack of studies linked to their resistive switching features, both from the physical modeling and experimental viewpoint. Therefore, the physics lying behind their operation has only had its surface scratched [18]. In this work, we intend to tackle this issue making use of well-established numerical techniques previously developed for more "conventional" memristors that are developed with 3D stacks of transitions metal oxides [13,15,22,23]. Therefore, in this manuscript, we specifically deal with the characterization and analysis of resistive switching processes and charge conduction in laser-fabricated graphene oxide (GO) memristors [18] from a statistical perspective. We do not focus this study on the digital performance of the devices; we consider instead their conductance variation in an analogic manner, as it is the proper approach for neuromorphic applications.

The device variability has also been considered in this study, specifically by using Time Series Statistical Analysis (TSSA) [24–27]. From the statistical viewpoint, information can be extracted that is related to the correlation of successive RS cycles and the inherent stochasticity of RS memristors operation. The quantum properties of conduction along the conductive filaments that short the electrodes have been scrutinized by means of the Quantum Point Contact (QPC) model as described in [15,22].

Therefore, the outline of this work is as follows: the fabricated devices and measurement process are described in Section 2, and the numerical procedure, the main results and the discussion are explained in Section 3. Finally, the conclusions are given in Section 4.

2. Device Fabrication and Measurement

The memristors fabricated for this study are fully based on the process described in [18] and summarized in Figure 1. The raw precursor material is a graphene oxide colloid (4 mg/mL) prepared following a modified version of Hummers and Offerman's method [28]. The GO colloid is deposited by drop-casting onto a PET (Polyethylene terephthalate, 3 M) film (0.5 mL/cm^2) and left on a 3D-shaker for 48 h until the water has completely evaporated (293 K, RH 50%). The CNC-driven laser is then applied in a rectangular pattern with the precise power that reduces the GO at the point where memristance is manifested ($P_{laser} \sim 70$ mW, $\lambda = 405$ nm) [18]. After the laser treatment, the volume of the reduced GO increases; the height difference between the GO film and the laser-treated GO is ~10 µm, determined using a DekTak XT profilometer from Bruker (Bruker Corporation, MA, USA). The devices were contacted using micro drops of conductive carbon-based paste (Bare Conductive Electric Paint, London, UK).

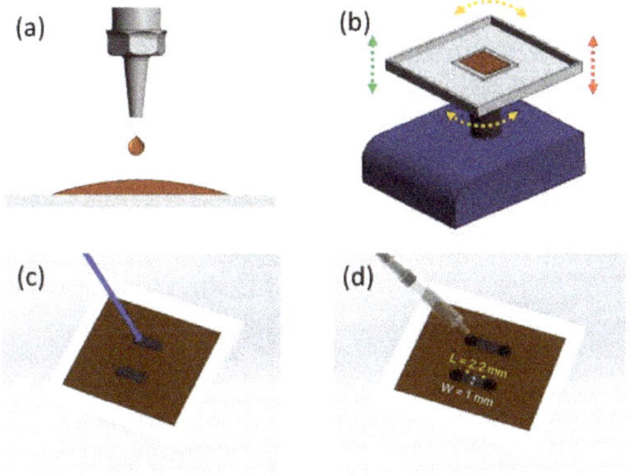

Figure 1. Schematic representation of the fabrication steps for graphene oxide memristors produced by laser. Graphene Oxide colloid is drop-casted on a PET substrate (**a**) and left 48 h on a 3D shaker for water evaporation (**b**). Then the laser diode is applied (70 mW) to partially reduce the GO resulting in the memristive structures (**c**). Finally, electrical contacts are created by depositing microdrops of organic bare conductive paint (**d**).

The electrical measurement experiments were performed with the support of a two-channel Keysight® B2902A (Keysight Technologies, Inc., CA, USA) precision source-measurement unit controlled by Easy-Expert® software (version 6.2.1927.7790, CA, USA). Figure 2a presents measured current–voltage characteristics showing two consecutive voltage cycles extracted from an L = 2.2 mm, W = 1 mm laser-fabricated graphene oxide memristor. These curves reveal the characteristic fingerprint of a memristor device that is determined by a pinched hysteresis loop closed in the origin of the current–voltage axis [29]. Figure 2b depicts the time evolution of the current when a −3 to 3 V symmetric voltage ramp is applied, illustrating the fast and abrupt transitions of the resistance.

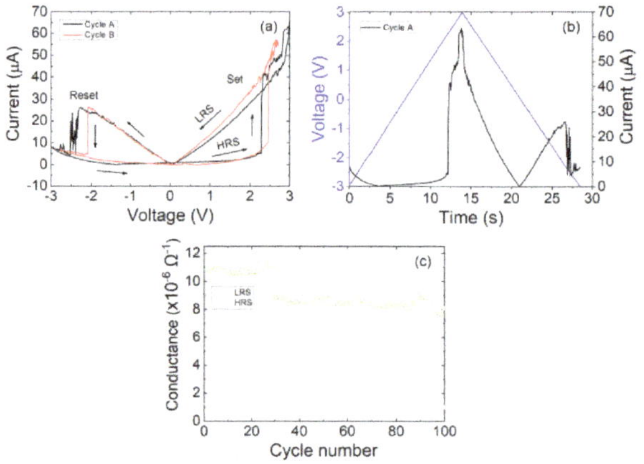

Figure 2. (**a**) Experimental current versus voltage for two different cycles within a resistive switching series. A ramped voltage with step of 10 mV was employed in the measurement process. (**b**) Voltage and current versus time for the cycle A shown previously. (**c**) Conductance values obtained during device cycling with limited compliance current [18]. The resistance was extracted in the range [−1,1] V of the current–voltage characteristics.

Figure 2c shows the device conductance extracted under successive device cycling from a laser-fabricated GO memristor. These measurements constitute the input of the Time Series Statistical Analysis discussed in Section 3. To avoid resistive switching degradation of the device, the current is limited to 20 μA [18]. As observed, the Low Resistance State (LRS) conductance presents a monotonic derivative, whereas the High Resistance State (HRS) conductance remains stable with cycling. The reader can notice the small conductance jump at cycle 28. This phenomenon is attributed to the defective nature of GO, which is heavily decorated with oxygen, hydroxyl and epoxy groups. Spontaneous movements of functional groups along the conductive path yields to local modification of the stoichiometry of the sample and, therefore, to the modification of its conductance [19]. Further structural and electrical details of Laser-Fabricated Graphene Oxide Memristors can be found in reference [18], including spectroscopic characterization, retention time and variability. The electrical results (average HRS/LRS ratio, 6; retention time, 10^4 s; endurance, 10^2 cycles [18]) can be considered to be promising given the early stage of development of this technology, and they are expected to become more attractive once advanced laser lithography tools are employed for the development of GO laser-fabricated memristors.

3. Numerical Analysis of Charge Conduction and Resistive Switching Mechanisms, Results and Discussion

3.1. Time Series Statistical Analysis (TSSA)

The TSSA has been employed to characterize the statistical features of the device operation variables through a long RS series [24]. In particular, the resistances in the LRS and HRS have been studied. The Autocorrelation (ACF) and Partial Autocorrelation functions (PACFs) have been calculated and represented in Figure 3 (see also Supplementary Materials). As can be observed, the degree of correlation between the measurements of previous cycles is very high with respect to other technologies (see, for instance, Reference [24] for other technologies with transition metal oxides as a dielectric).

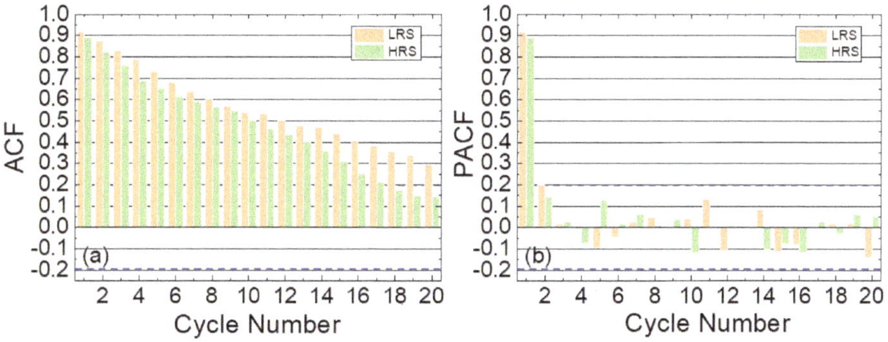

Figure 3. (**a**) ACF and (**b**) PACF versus cycle lag for the inverse of the values shown in Figure 2c. These functions show the ACF and PACFs versus cycle number that represent the distance apart in cycles within a RS series, see Reference [24]. The ACF and PACF minimum threshold bounds for the devices under study are ±0.195 for both plots (see the supplementary information for the information linked to the calculation of these threshold bounds), shown with dashed lines. We have considered 100 cycles in our series; this is a reasonable number to extract information on the correlation between the data and to extract a TSSA model.

It can be concluded that to obtain these results, the high conductivity region does not change much between different cycles; this feature is the main source of the correlation. This fact leads us to assume a filamentary-like conduction mechanism where a channel of high conductivity region is formed after a set process that shorts the electrodes. In addition, the high correlation suggests that the high conductivity path does not change much between cycles, keeping unaltered the main conduction properties. It is reasonable to assume that it is just a narrow region that changes in between two larger high conductivity regions that remain mostly unaltered. This narrowing is modified leading to the creation of a fully-formed high conduction path that shorts the electrodes or that isolates them in case the path is ruptured, leading to two large virtual electrodes (filaments remnants connected to the electrodes [6]).

We have employed TSSA to analytically describe the dependencies of the LRS and HRS resistances on previous cycles throughout the complete RS series (see in the Supplementary Material a summary of the steps needed to develop a TSSA model). The general expression employed was based on an Autoregressive (AR) approach [24], as seen in Equation (1):

$$R_{LRS/HRS(t)} = \Phi_1 \times R_{LRS/HRS(t-1)} + \Phi_2 \times R_{LRS/HRS(t-2)} + \ldots + \Phi_p \times R_{LRS/HRS(t-p)} + \varepsilon_t \quad (1)$$

where t stands for the cycle number within a long resistive switching series. In this modeling technique, the order (p) is linked to the physics governing RS process in these devices. No previous knowledge is assumed to extract the information from experimental data because the underlying technology details and physics mechanisms are "hidden" in the RS data collected. The TSSA models are empirical and determine the weights set (Φ_1, ..., Φ_p), and the model order is determined by p. The term ε_t is a residual that accounts for the model error (the difference between the measured and the modeled value). In this respect, we focus here on the statistical information of the measured data without any previous assumption linked to the underlying physics.

The resistance at the LRS can be modeled with an AR(2) approach, as seen in Equation (2).

$$R_{LRS(t)} = 4936.018 + 0.7306 \times R_{LRS(t-1)} + 0.229 \times R_{LRS(t-2)} + \varepsilon_t. \quad (2)$$

The HRS resistance works well with an AR(1), as described in Equation (3).

$$R_{HRS(t)} = 69955.16 + 0.9236 \times R_{HRS(t-1)} + \varepsilon_t. \quad (3)$$

The time series residuals that are left after a comparison with the experimental data show a white noise behavior; therefore, we can conclude that all the statistical information is included in the models described in Equations (2) and (3). It is important to highlight at this point that TSSA is an ideal tool used to analyze data in a series (such as a RS series); in this respect, it works well for cycle-to-cycle variability analysis if we consider parameters such as the set and reset voltages or LRS/HRS device resistances.

3.2. *Quantum Point Contact Modeled Conduction*

An analysis of the I–V curves in terms of second derivative dependencies has been performed following [22]. In this respect, it is important to highlight that a screening procedure was developed in [22] to detect charge conduction features that can be modeled with the QPC model. The results are shown in Figure 4.

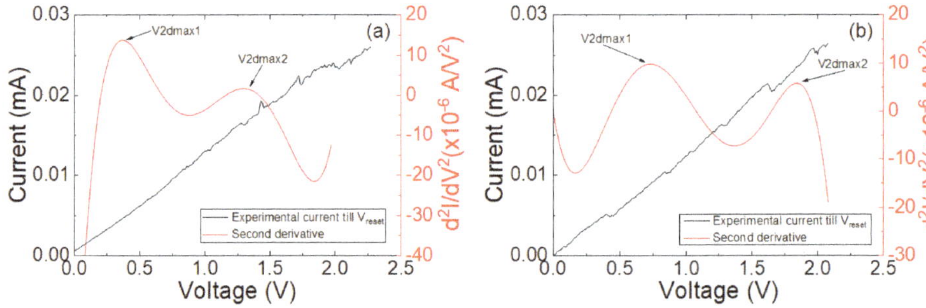

Figure 4. Experimental current versus applied voltage in the devices under study including the second derivative of the current versus voltage for cycle A (**a**) and cycle B (**b**) shown in Figure 2a. A pattern in agreement with the QPC model is seen in [22].

The characteristic one or two maxima in the current second derivative are seen in these devices. Following previous results [22], this behavior could be regarded as a footprint of the existence of QPC conduction. However, the fitting of the second derivative leads to an N parameter (number of channels in the QPC model [22]) lower than the unity, which is inconsistent with the QPC model. In this respect, a new representation is obtained assuming a series resistance of 5000 Ω (second numerical derivative of the corrected current, I, taking into account the series resistance is shown in Figure 5). This series resistance is reasonable considering the device resistance both at LRS and HRS, see Figure 2c. In this manner, the voltage on the constriction that leads to quantum effects can be obtained accurately.

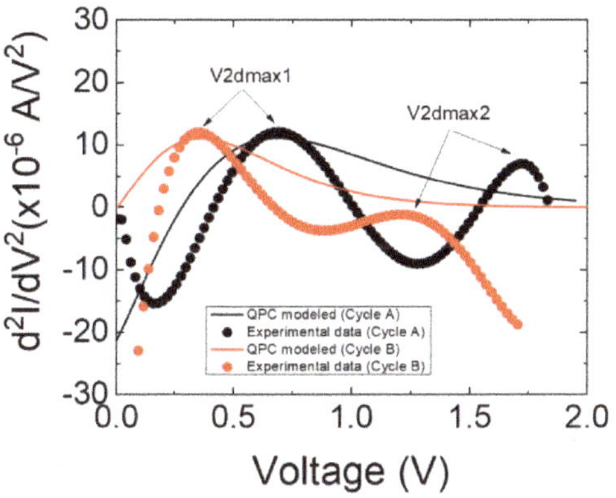

Figure 5. Second derivative of the experimental current (symbols) versus voltage in the device under study for the two reset curves shown in Figure 2. The analytically calculated QPC modeled current second derivative (solid lines) is also shown. The QPC model parameters employed for cycle A are the following: $\alpha = 6.5\ (\mathrm{eV})^{-1}$; $\beta = 0.4$; $\Phi = 0.13$ eV; N = 1; and for cycle B: $\alpha = 7.5(\mathrm{eV})^{-1}$; $\beta = 0.5$; $\Phi = 0.055$ eV; N = 1.

In both cases, there is only one channel for charge conduction, and this result corresponds to a low dimensional high conductivity region. Also, a low energy barrier is observed, suggesting an almost ohmic charge conduction regime, although in a low conductivity regime when compared with conventional memristors based on transition metal oxides.

The previous results support the existing model that attributes resistive switching in laser-reduced GO to the non-uniformity in the number and location of functional groups that create nanometric-size regions of different conductance [18]. The sp^2 regions present high-conductivity but they are interrupted by low-conductivity sp^3 domains at a nanoscale level that are responsible for a low current flow [30,31]. At certain locations within the structure, under the action of the voltage bias in the HRS, large electrostatic potential gradients are created in the nanometric-size low-conductivity regions, resulting in large localized electric fields. Assisted by Joule heating effects, these electric fields can trigger the drift of oxygen and oxygen-containing groups due to the low migration barrier in GO [32,33]. The group migration at a specific point within the structure establishes a continuity path of sp^2 domains, which was previously impeded by a nanometric sp^3 domain (quantum point contact as identified in this work) and leads to a LRS [18]. Finally, it is worth mentioning that the findings in this work, disclosing the filamentary nature of the conduction in laser fabricated GO memristors, open the path for scaling the devices down by using high precision laser scribing systems.

4. Conclusions

The origins of resistive switching in recently introduced laser-fabricated graphene oxide memristors have been studied by using statistical and numerical analysis tools. Time Series Statistical Analysis applied to the high and low resistance states of the devices has shown high correlation that supports the model of the formation of a conductive filament as the main source of the device internal resistance switching. Furthermore, the quantum point contact conduction method has pointed to the existence of a quantized point of conduction, which is formed and destroyed, connecting the electrodes by means of a conductive path. These results underpin the existing theory that attributes the memristance in GO to the formation of a highly reduced path in which stoichiometry is modified at a precise point leading to the resistive switching.

Supplementary Materials: The following are available online at http://www.mdpi.com/1996-1944/12/22/3734/s1.

Author Contributions: Conceptualization, N.R., F.G.R., F.J.M. and J.B.R.; Experiments, F.J.R. and N.R.; Analytical and numerical tools, D.M., F.J.A., A.M.A., J.B.R.; Figures, D.M., F.J.R.; Writing-original draft, N.R. and J.B.R; Writing-review and discussion A.G., F.J.M. and F.G.R.

Funding: The authors thank the support of the Spanish Ministry of Science, Innovation and Universities under projects TEC2017-89955-P, TEC2017-84321-C4-3-R, MTM2017-88708-P and project PGC2018-098860-B-I00 (MCIU/AEI/FEDER, UE), and the predoctoral grant FPU16/01451.

Conflicts of Interest: The authors declare no conflict of interest.

References

1. Yu, S.; Wu, Y.; Jeyasingh, R.; Kuzum, D.; Wong, H.S. An electronic synapse device based on metal oxide resistive switching memory for neuromorphic computation. *IEEE Trans. Electron Devices* **2011**, *58*, 2729–2737. [CrossRef]
2. Yu, S. *Neuro-Inspired Computing Using Resistive Synaptic Devices*; Springer: NY, USA, 2017; ISBN 978-3-319-54312-3.
3. Lanza, M.; Wong, H.-P.P.; Pop, E.; Ielmini, D.; Strukov, D.; Regan, B.C.; Larcher, L.; VillenaJ, M.A.; Yang, J.J.; Goux, L.; et al. Recommended methods to study resistive switching devices. *Adv. Electron. Mater.* **2019**, *5*, 1800143. [CrossRef]
4. Pan, F.; Gao, S.; Chen, C.; Song, C.; Zeng, F. Recent progress in resistive random access memories: Materials, switching mechanisms and performance. *Mater. Sci. Eng.* **2014**, *83*, 1–59. [CrossRef]
5. Ielmini, D.; Waser, R. *Resistive Switching: From Fundamentals of Nanoionic Redox Processes to Memristive Device Applications*; Wiley-VCH: Weinheim, Germany, 2017; ISBN 978-3-527-33417-9.
6. Waser, R.; Aono, M. Nanoionics-based resistive switching. *Nat. Mater.* **2007**, *6*, 833–840. [CrossRef] [PubMed]
7. Villena, M.A.; Roldan, J.B.; Jimienez-Molinos, F.; Miranda, E.; Suñe, J.; Lanza, M. SIM2RRAM: A physical model for RRAM devices simulation. *J. Comput. Electron.* **2017**, *16*, 1095–1120. [CrossRef]
8. Long, S.; Cagli, C.; Ielmini, D.; Liu, M.; Suñe, J. Reset statistics of NiO-based resistive switching memories. *IEEE Electron Device Lett.* **2011**, *32*, 1570–1572. [CrossRef]
9. Long, S.; Lian, X.; Ye, T.; Cagli, C.; Perniola, L.; Miranda, E.; Liu, M.; Suñe, J. Cycle-to-cycle intrinsic RESET statistics in HfO2-based unipolar RRAM devices. *IEEE Electron Device Lett.* **2013**, *34*, 623–625. [CrossRef]
10. Gonzalez-Cordero, G.; Roldan, J.B.; Jimenez-Molinos, F.; Suñé, J.; Long, S.; Liu, M. A new model for bipolar RRAMs based on truncated cone conductive filaments, a Verilog-A approach. *Semicond. Sci. Technol.* **2016**, *31*, 115013. [CrossRef]
11. Tsuruoka, T.; Terabe, K.; Hasegawaand, T.; Aono, M. Forming and switching mechanisms of a cation-migration-based oxide resistive memory. *Nanotechnology* **2010**, *21*, 425205. [CrossRef]
12. Padovani, A.; Larcher, L.; Pirrotta, O.; Vandelli, L.; Bersuker, G. Microscopic Modeling of HfO x RRAM Operations: From Forming to Switching. *IEEE Trans. Electron Device* **2015**, *62*, 1998–2006. [CrossRef]
13. Aldana, S.; Garcia-Fernandez, P.; Rodriguez-Fernandez, A.; Romero-Zaliz, R.; Gonzalez, M.B.; Jimenez-Molinos, F.; Campabadal, F.; Gomez-Campos, F.; Roldan, J.B. A 3D Kinetic Monte Carlo simulation study of Resistive Switching processes in Ni/HfO_2/Si-n^+-based RRAMs. *J. Phys. D Appl. Phys.* **2017**, *50*, 335103. [CrossRef]
14. Guy, J.; Molas, G.; Blaise, P.; Bernard, M.; Roule, A.; Carval, G.L.; Delaye, V.; Toffoli, A.; Ghibaudo, G.; Clermidy, F.; et al. Investigation of Forming, SET, and Data Retention of Conductive-Bridge Random-Access Memory for Stack Optimization. *IEEE Trans. Electron Devices* **2015**, *62*, 3482–3489. [CrossRef]
15. Villena, M.A.; Roldan, J.B.; Gonzalez, M.B.; Gonzalez-Rodalas, P.; Jimenez-Molinos, F.; Campabadal, F.; Barrera, D. A new parameter to characterize the charge transport regime in Ni/HfO_2/Si-n^+-based RRAMs. *Solid State Electron.* **2016**, *118*, 56–60. [CrossRef]
16. Hui, F.; Villena, M.A.; Fang, W.; Lu, A.-Y.; Kong, J.; Shi, Y.; Jing, X.; Zhu, K.; Lanza, M. Synthesis of large-area multilayer hexagonal boron nitride sheets on iron substrates and its use in resistive switching devices. *2D Mater.* **2018**, *5*, 031011. [CrossRef]
17. Shi, Y.; Liang, X.; Yuan, B.; Chen, V.; Li, H.; Hui, F.; Yu, Z.; Yuan, F.; Pop, E.; Wong, H.-S.P.; et al. Electronic synapses made of layered two-dimensional materials. *Nat. Electron.* **2018**, *1*, 458–465. [CrossRef]
18. Romero, F.J.; Toral-Lopez, A.; Ohata, A.; Morales, D.P.; Ruiz, F.G.; Godoy, A.; Rodriguez, N. Laser-Fabricated Reduced Graphene Oxide Memristors. *Nanomaterials* **2019**, *9*, 897. [CrossRef] [PubMed]

19. Dimiev, A.M.; Eigler, S. *Graphene Oxide: Fundamentals and Applications*; Wiley: NJ, USA, 2016; ISBN 978-1-119-06940-9.
20. Romero, F.J.; Toral-Lopez, A.; Ohata, A.; Morales, D.P.; Ruiz, F.G.; Godoy, A.; Rodriguez, N. Photothermically Lithographed Graphene-Oxide Memristors for Neuromorphic Applications. In Proceedings of the International Conference on Memristive Materials, Devices & Systems (MEMRISYS), Dresden, Germany, 8–11 July 2019.
21. Porro, S.; Accornero, E.; Pirri, C.F.; Ricciardi, C. Memristive devices based on Graphene oxide. *Carbon* **2015**, *85*, 383–395. [CrossRef]
22. Roldan, J.B.; Miranda, E.; Gonzalez-Cordero, G.; Garcia-Fernandez, P.; Romero-Zaliz, R.; Gonzalez-Rodelas, P.; Aguilera, A.M.; Gonzalez, M.B.; Jimenez-Molinos, F. Multivariate analysis and extraction of parameters in resistive RAMs using the Quantum Point Contact model. *J. Appl. Phys.* **2018**, *123*, 014501. [CrossRef]
23. Villena, M.A.; Gonzalez, M.B.; Roldan, J.B.; Campabadal, F.; Jimenez-Molinos, F.; Gomez-Campos, F.M.; Suñe, J. An in-depth study of thermal effects in reset transitions in HfO_2 based RRAMs. *Solid State Electron.* **2015**, *111*, 47–51. [CrossRef]
24. Roldan, J.B.; Alonso, F.J.; Aguilera, A.M.; Maldonado, D.; Lanza, M. Time series statistical analysis: A powerful tool to evaluate the variability of resistive switching memories. *J. Appl. Phys.* **2019**, *125*, 174504. [CrossRef]
25. Yule, G.U. On a method of investigating periodicities in disturbed series, with reference to Wolfer's Sunspot Numbers. *Philos. Trans. R. Soc. Lond.* **1927**, *226*, 267–298. [CrossRef]
26. Bisgaard, S.; Kulahci, M. *Time Series Analysis and Forecasting by Example*; Wiley: NJ, USA, 2011; ISBN 978-0-470-54064-0.
27. Brockwell, P.J.; Davis, R.A. *Introduction to Time Series and Forecasting*, 2nd ed.; Springer: NY, USA, 2002.
28. Romero, F.J.; Rivadeneyra, A.; Toral-Lopez, V.; Castillo, E.; Garcia-Ruiz, F.; Morales, D.P.; Rodriguez, N. Design guidelines of laser reduced graphene oxide conformal thermistor for IoT applications. *Sens. Actuators A Phys.* **2018**, *274*, 148–154. [CrossRef]
29. Chua, L. Resistance switching memories are memristors. *Appl. Phys. A* **2011**, *102*, 765–783. [CrossRef]
30. Qi, M.; Bai, L.; Xu, H.; Wang, Z.; Kang, Z.; Zhao, X.; Liu, W.; Ma, J.; Liu, Y. Oxidized carbon quantum dot–graphene oxide nanocomposites for improving data retention of resistive switching memory. *J. Mater. Chem. C* **2018**, *6*, 2026–2033. [CrossRef]
31. Abunahla, H.; Mohammad, B.; Homouz, D.; Okelly, C.J. Modeling Valence Change Memristor Device: Oxide Thickness, Material Type, and Temperature Effects. *IEEE Trans. Circuits Syst. I Regul. Pap.* **2016**, *63*, 2139–2148. [CrossRef]
32. Dai, Y.; Shuang, N.; Li, Z.; Yang, J. Diffusion and desorption of oxygen atoms on graphene. *J. Phys. Condens. Matter* **2013**, *25*, 405301. [CrossRef]
33. Zhou, S.; Bongiorno, A. Origin of the Chemical and Kinetic Stability of Graphene Oxide. *Sci. Rep.* **2013**, *3*, 2484. [CrossRef]

materials

MDPI

Article

Robust Memristor Networks for Neuromorphic Computation Applications

Dániel Hajtó [1,*] and Ádám Rák [2] and György Cserey [1,2]

[1] Faculty of Information Technology and Bionics, Pázmány Péter Catholic University, 1083 Budapest, Hungary; cserey.gyorgy@itk.ppke.hu

[2] StreamNovation Ltd., 1083 Budapest, Hungary; streamnovation@streamnovation.com

* Correspondence: hajto.daniel@itk.ppke.hu

Received: 30 September 2019; Accepted: 25 October 2019; Published: 31 October 2019

Abstract: One of the main obstacles for memristors to become commonly used in electrical engineering and in the field of artificial intelligence is the unreliability of physical implementations. A non-uniform range of resistance, low mass-production yield and high fault probability during operation are disadvantages of the current memristor technologies. In this article, the authors offer a solution for these problems with a circuit design, which consists of many memristors with a high operational variance that can form a more robust single memristor. The proposition is confirmed by physical device measurements, by gaining similar results as in previous simulations. These results can lead to more stable devices, which are a necessity for neuromorphic computation, artificial intelligence and neural network applications.

Keywords: memristor; neuromorphic computing; artificial intelligence; hardware-based deep learning ICs; circuit design

1. Introduction

Since the theoretical [1] and practical [2] discovery of memristors, they have been extensively studied [3–5] as elementary building blocks for artificial intelligence and neuromorphic computing applications.

The expected properties of memristors for such applications are wide and analog resistance range, low variance of device parameters and high device stability during long-term operation. Research has been done [6] to find optimal materials that satisfy these expectations, but even then there are other possibilities to further increase the capabilities of memristors.

In binary memory applications, three important properties should be considered. The first one is having two clearly distinguishable states and these state declarations should apply to every element in a memory array. The second one is having a fast switching speed between the states. To reach the performance of the current complementary metal–oxide–semiconductor (CMOS) technology's RAM the switching speed should be less than 10 ns. The third one is cycle endurance, which is the number of write–erase cycles without permanent device failure.

In crossbar-network applications, a certain amount of uniformity of the memristors is necessary. The programming voltage and current levels are the same for every element and thus one expects that they will behave similarly for the same input signals.

In the case of ANN applications, more deviance could be tolerated, but many state devices are needed, so the memristors developed for binary or multi-state memory purposes will not be sufficient.

The mass production of devices, which can reliably fulfill these requirements, is not trivial. If the production yield of single devices is less than 100 percent (as they are not functioning as memristors or they are outside of the accepted range of parameters), then they can also affect the access circuit and the encompassing parts of the neuromorphic system.

If the production yield of single devices is less than 100 percent (as they are not functioning as memristors or they are outside of the accepted range of parameters), then they can also affect the access circuit and the encompassing parts of the neuromorphic system.

In very large scale integration (VLSI) device manufacturing, it is often easier and tends to cause fewer faults to make the same device many times, and use it as a building block to emulate other devices, instead of creating fewer, but different devices [7]. The same approach can be applied to memristors, but one should take into consideration their special nonlinear behavior in the voltage–current domain. This idea is further supported by the fact that memristors as two-terminals, could be manufactured more easily on many layers on microchips [8] than transistors. However, with every extra layer, the probability of device defects could also increase.

In order to maintain or even improve the virtual yield of the production, interconnected structures of the memristor network are proposed. These circuits and the presented measurement results provide a response to the above mentioned challenges. Our proposed circuit constructions can be efficiently implemented on microchips, stacking the memristors of the circuit on top of each other. If a decent multilayer production technology arises with memristors, the disadvantage of the usage of several layers for the implementation of a single layer of memristor would be neglectable.

This paper is organized as follows: after the above problem proposal, the measurement environment is introduced and explanatory discussion is given about our circuitry. The third section contains the proposed circuits and the measurement results that are more detrimental to the yield. This circuitry effectively addresses the proposed task. In the fourth section, the results are summarized and analyzed. The article is closed with a brief summary of the results in the conclusion section.

2. Materials and Methods

2.1. Materials

The measured memristor devices are made of Ge_2Se_3 (germanium-selenide) and Ag (silver) based chalcogenide dielectric with W (Tungsten) conductors. The devices have a switching threshold, meaning that under a certain threshold voltage (0.1 V in our case), their state does not change. This feature makes the memristor implementation desirable for applications where reading the state should not change the state itself. On the other hand, usually it has very few metallic dendrites, which makes the characteristic very coarse. The memristors are current-controlled and the typical writing-erasing voltages are 2.5 V. One of the consequences of being current-controlled is that the erasing process is faster than the writing process.

The measurement setup consists of an amplifier circuit as a current–voltage converter and a current regulator resistor as it can be seen in Figure 1. The current regulator resistor helped to ensure that the current does not reach high values where the device could become faulty. The used signal generator and measurement device is an "NI ELVIS II+", controlled by LabView software (National Instruments, Austin, TX, United States). The sampling frequency is 500 kSample/s for every measurement. The state of every device has been set to an OFF state before every measurement.

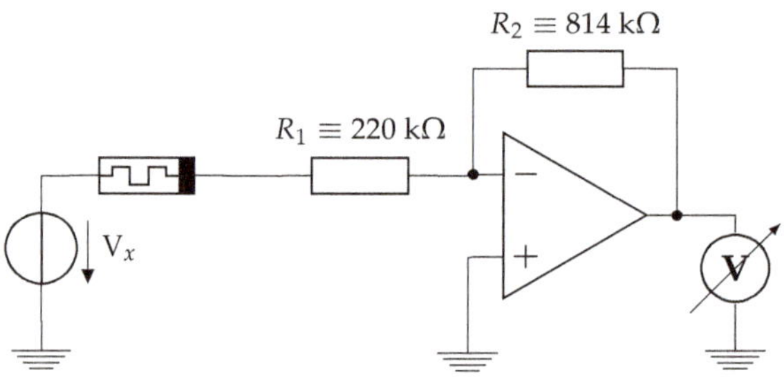

Figure 1. Measurement environment circuit. The measurement setup consists an amplifier circuit as a current controlled voltage source and a current regulator resistor. The used amplifier is a "TL082". The applied voltage V_x was strictly between −2.5 V and 2.5 V. The memristor symbol represents either a single memristor or a network of memristors depending on the measurement.

2.2. Methods

2.2.1. Metrics

First of all, it is important to differentiate two main types of memristors from a functional point of view. The first type is the analog purpose memristor (APM). It operates in the continuous domain, which means it can have any resistance (or conductance) value in its operational range. This might sound unrealistic as we know that at a very low scale, energy levels are quantized, but it can be interpreted as the memristor having so many states that can be considered as infinitely many. Another formal definition is that an APM can store any real value between the normalized range of zero and one.

The second type is the digital (or discrete) purpose memristor (DPM), which has several but countable states and the resistance value can only be one of these states. An important property is that these states should be clearly distinguishable from each other. This type can be used trivially as an n state memory unit based on the number of its possible states.

An extreme, but important case of the DPM is when only two states can be clearly distinguished, as they can be further classified as binary purpose memristors (BPM). With its reduced capabilities they lack applications beside their use as binary memory units supplementary to the CMOS based digital systems or implementing routing in logic gate arrays, like Field programmable gate arrays (FPGAs) [9].

In general, the mass production of BPMs is solved, there are manufacturers [10], who sell commercial devices for an affordable price. DPMs are existing in an early development state at research institutes [11]. APMs, which have practically an infinitely many numbers of states, are yet to be introduced and might even be impossible to produce due to physical limitations [12]; or it requires new quantum mechanical solutions, which are also under development [13]. In general, from an application point of view, digital memory technologies use BPMs, artificial neural networks need at least DPM complexity, and neuromorphic computation applications require APMs.

Our previously introduced circuit proposals [14] were intended to convert several DPMs into a single APM. This was tested through simulations, which showed that this circuit topology can achieve analog behavior when made from solely multi-state memristors. However, in this work real device measurement results are given, which proves that the same circuit can effectively convert several unreliable BPMs into a more reliable one.

The same control signal should produce the same result, both in the transient characteristics and the final state of the memristor. By reliability, we mean a low variance of the characteristics. Our aim was to avoid using a memristor model as an absolute reference, and be able to approximate the real memristors more accurately. Therefore, our analysis focuses on the mean and variance of characteristics of several measurements on the same device or network in a short period of time.

The index of dispersion has been used as the measure of unreliability. It formulates as the sum of the variance of the signal, normalized by the amplitude of the signal, due to the expectation that higher amplitude signals have naturally higher variance. This measure is valid only for positive data points. For this reason, the absolute value of the signal has been used:

$$u = \sum_{i}^{N} \frac{\sigma_i^2}{|\mu_i|}, \tag{1}$$

where u is the unreliability of the device, N is the number of measurement points, i is a measurement point of the measuring signal, σ_i^2 is the variance of a measurement point over the consecutive measurements and μ_i is the mean of a measurement point over the consecutive measurements.

The approximation of the yield of a production technology is highly dependent on the available number of samples of the given device. having a limited number of devices, this question can not be addressed, but it has been shown in a previous work [14] that the yield of a production technology can be increased with this method.

The planning and execution of the measurements have been carried out with consideration of previous related studies [15] on memristor measuring techniques.

2.2.2. Circuits

The measurements were carried out on four different memristor network circuit topologies of which two were introduced before [14] with corresponding simulation results. The H-fractal (Figure 2a) and checkerboard-like (Figure 2b) topology both gave comparably good results, which shows that verifying both cases with measurements is reasonable. During simulations with heavy defect probability, the checkerboard-like topology has given slightly better results.

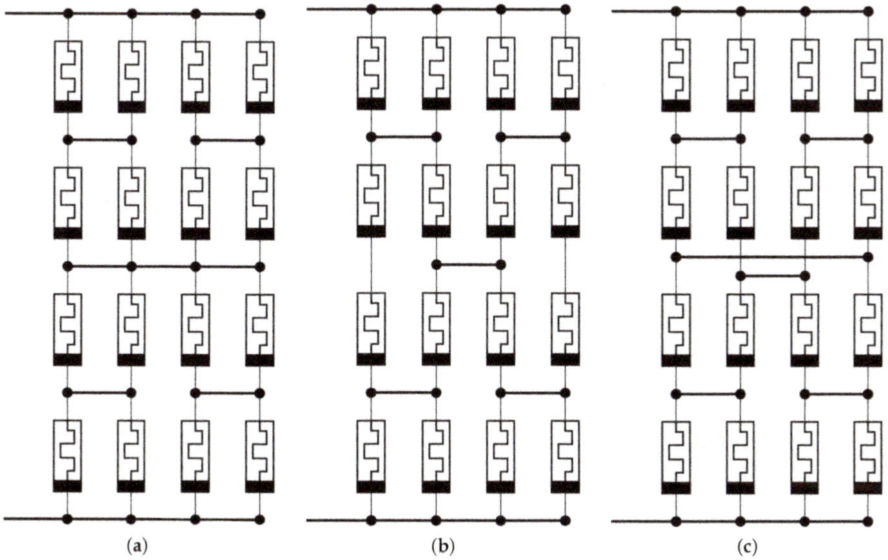

Figure 2. Measured general circuits. (**a**) H-fractal type of array. (**b**) Checkerboard type of array. (**c**) Our newly introduced array.

In this article a third general circuit design is proposed (Figure 2c), which can be implemented as a 2 × 2 × 4, three-dimensional grid structure on a multilayer carrier. A structure proposal can be seen in Figure 3a. This new circuit had a better compromise between open and short connection faults, but can only be constructed effectively in a three dimensional structure. The disadvantage is that since the height of the grid was even, and the top and bottom electrodes are aligned, they cannot form a crossbar network.

A workaround could be that this type of network can scale with the height of the 2×2 column, and it can be $2 \times 2 \times 3$ or $2 \times 2 \times 5$ sized. These new non-general networks result in different memristor parameters. The advantage of an odd height is that it can be realized in a crossbar network as it can be seen in Figure 3b.

Memristor networks that use binary memristors as building components will technically result in a discrete memory capacity as either component can be in the OFF or ON state. The overall resistance value can be calculated for every combination, which is a limited number of possible resistances. However, with sufficiently large grids, this effect can be neglected as the individual operational variances of the elements are also summing up, resulting in a complex macro-characteristics.

Another important property to consider is the used chip area. These networks should be implemented efficiently on a chip as a two dimensional crossbar network. The implementation of the previous networks was only possible using sixteen times more chip area for the emulation of a single device. The new network uses only four times more area with a similar reliability gain, as compared to a single memristor.

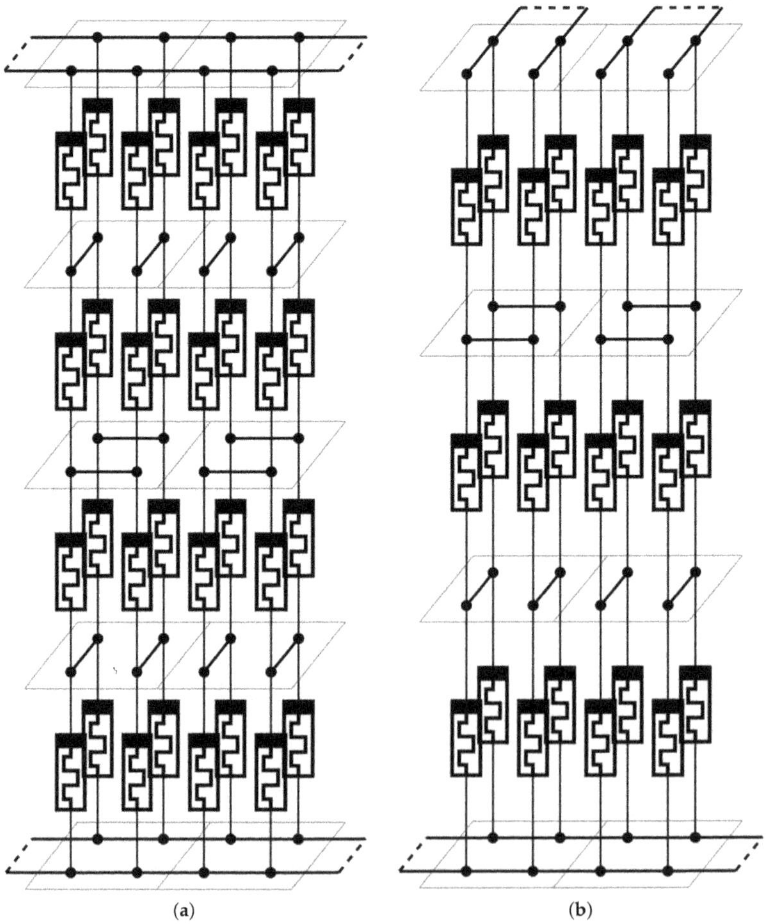

Figure 3. The proposed three dimensional cell structures. (**a**) Two emulated cells from a $2 \times 2 \times 4$ array. (**b**) Two emulated cells from a $2 \times 2 \times 3$ array.

3. Results

3.1. Single Memristor Measurements

First test measurements were prepared with a single memristor device. Here two types of signals were used. The first one was a single, 2.4 s long 2.5 V writing pulse, which shows some parameters of the device. The results can be seen in Figure 4. The average ON state was 57 kΩ, the average OFF state was 11.5 MΩ. The ON/OFF ratio is approximately 200.

The second type of signal is a sequence of a writing and an erasing signal. The writing pulse was 160 ms long, while the erasing one was shorter, 40 ms. The results can be seen in Figure 5. The writing process was faster and starts at a lower voltage level, but the switching was not as sharp as in the previous case (Figure 4). During the reading sequence, the small amplitude pulses did not change the state of the memristor.

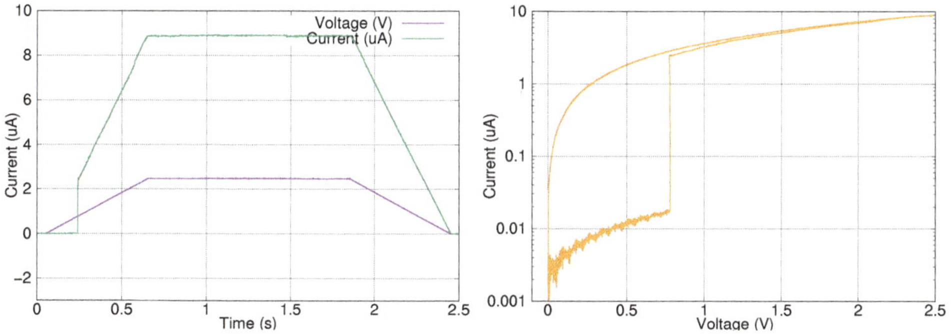

(**a**) (**b**)

Figure 4. Long timescale measurement on a single memristor device with focus on the writing characteristics. (**a**) The input signal and output response in the time domain. (**b**) Phase portrait of the measurement. Switching is very sharp and the ON/OFF ratio is at least 100.

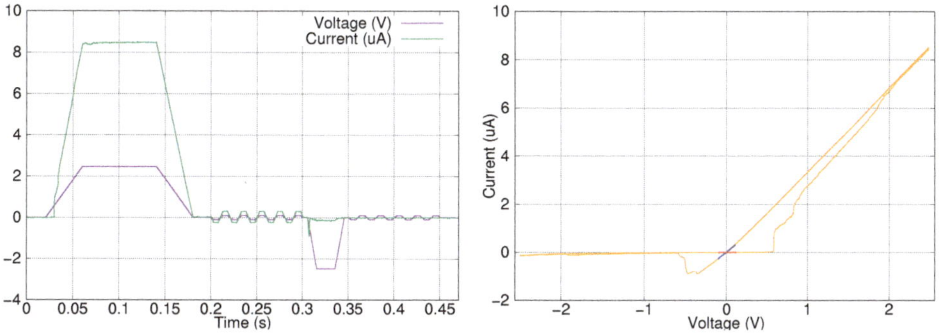

(**a**) (**b**)

Figure 5. Write-read-erase-read cycle measurement on a single memristor device. (**a**) The input signal and output response in the time domain. (**b**) Phase portrait of the measurement. The read sequence after the write and erase pulses are colored as blue and red, respectively.

3.2. Memristor Emulation Comparison Measurements

The following measurements were carried out on four different network types and on a single memristor for reference. The measuring signal is alternating write–erase sinusoidal pulses with a length of 23 ms in a sequence of 50 cycles.

This measurement is supposed to simulate a general training scenario, where an analogue memristor characteristic is expected and the training is done by several small pulses. According to this consideration, the writing pulses of the measurement have not enough energy to change the state of a single memristor into its ON state.

The results can be seen in Figures 6 and 7. Subfigures (**a**),(**c**) and (**e**) show the voltage–current diagram of the whole signal. Subfigures (**b**),(**d**) and (**f**) are the voltage–current diagrams of the average of all 50 write–erase signals with the current shown on a logarithmic scale.

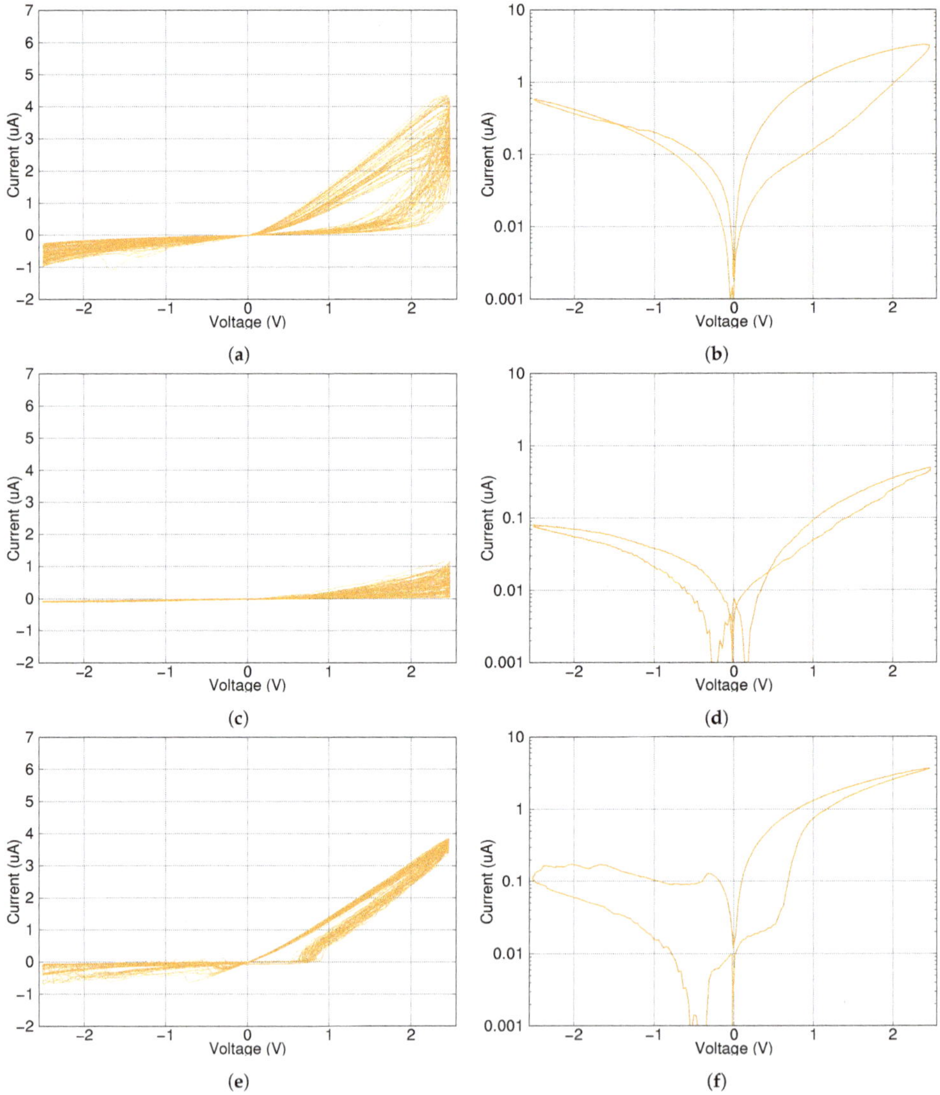

Figure 6. Short-time pulses on a single memristor, the checkerboard like and the H-fractal memristor network, respectively. (**a**,**c**) and (**e**) show the voltage–current diagram of the whole signal. (**b**,**d**,**f**) are the average of all 50 write–erase signals on a logarithmic scale.

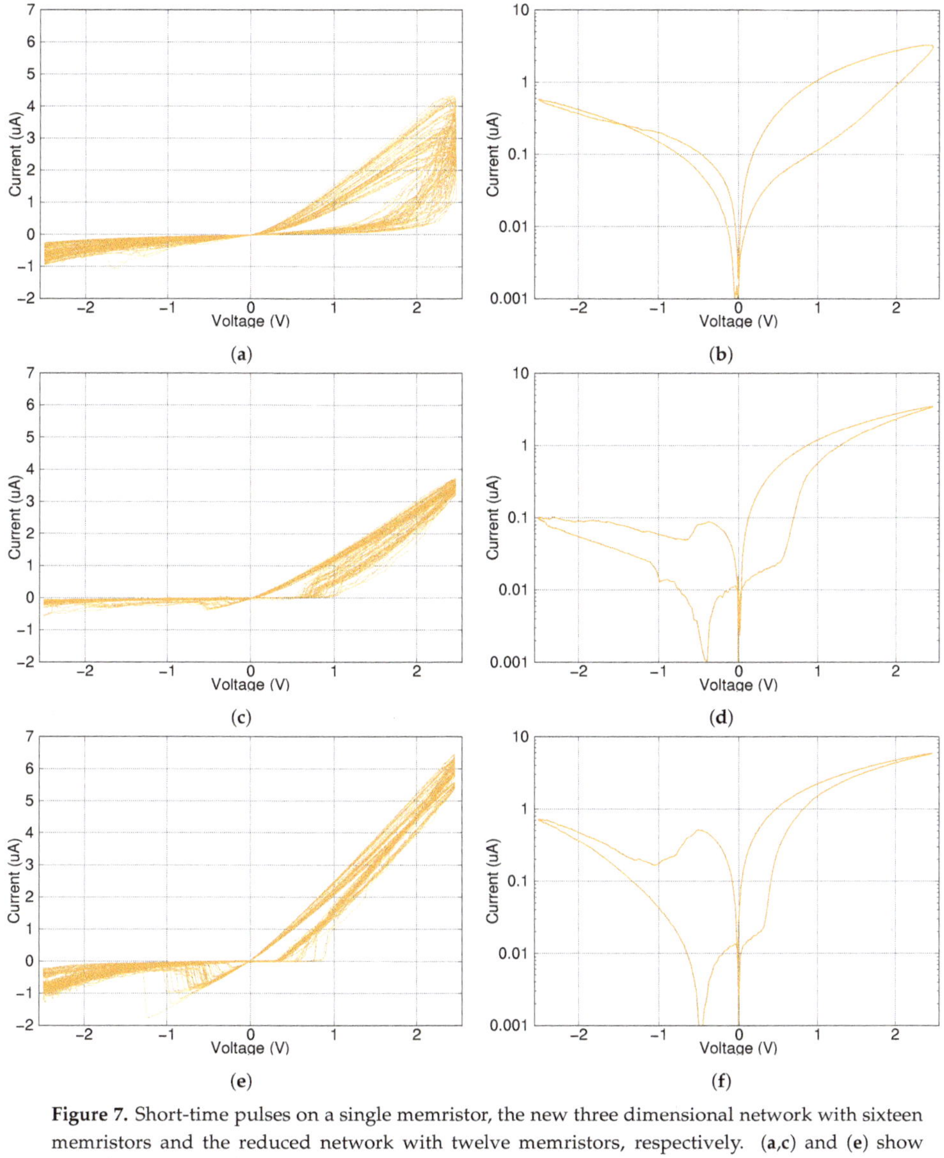

Figure 7. Short-time pulses on a single memristor, the new three dimensional network with sixteen memristors and the reduced network with twelve memristors, respectively. (**a**,**c**) and (**e**) show the voltage–current diagram of the whole signal. (**b**,**d**) and (**f**) are the average of all 50 write–erase signals on a logarithmic scale.

4. Discussion

The checkerboard type of network was practically unable to switch its state significantly compared to other solutions. This was probably due to the limited number of parallel connections in the network, which produced less possible routes to open. Higher control voltage could change its state, but the risk of device damage increases with the increased after-switch current. Longer pulses could also help, but it makes the writing process slower.

The results for the H-fractal type of network are very similar to the newly introduced network regarding the writing of the state into low resistance position. However, this type of network has problems with erasing the state into the OFF state and could get stuck at an in-between state.

The ON and OFF resistance values of the network with twelve memristors are lower than the other networks due to the reduced number of serial layers. However, when one compares it to a single memristor, it has lower ON resistance value and higher OFF resistance, meaning the network is more sensitive to control signals than only one memristor. In other words, a pulse with the same voltage level could make a clearer distinction between the initial and after states.

The previous simulation results suggested that the switching speed could decrease using memristor grids. Surprisingly, the switching speed did not decrease, but increased instead. The networks are approximately three times faster than a single memristor. This is fairly unexpected, as the control voltage stayed constant in both measurements, which means that the voltage on any single memristor in a network measurement had to be strictly lower than in the case of a single device measurement at any given time during measuring.

One explanation of this phenomenon could be the following: under the threshold voltage, the device behaves as a very small capacitor. As the metal flows into the dielectric matter to build up the filament, the partially charged capacitor discharges, causing a short-time high-energy electric current burst. The other devices are sensitive to fast current changes and the filament forming is starting in them as well. It can be seen as a "domino effect" with the consecutive memristors. If any of the OFF state memristors in a series switches to the ON state, the rest will automatically switch as well immediately after.

If any of the memristors which closes the source in the series, opens, the rest will automatically open immediately after.

Based on the above presented measurements the following parameter values were acquired, presented in Table 1. The resistance values are the average ON/OFF ratio values of the 50 cycle long measurement sequence.

Table 1. The table shows the main properties of emulating memristor networks. Higher ON/OFF ratio is considered better and the best values are indicated accordingly, namely the highest OFF resistance, the lowest ON resistance and the highest overall ON/OFF ratio. Lower dispersion is also considered better. The lowest is indicated.

Measured Object	OFF Resistance	ON Resistance	ON/OFF Ratio	Dispersion Index
Single memristor	5.7889 MΩ	0.7185 MΩ	8.0569	0.04553
H-fractal network	19.472 MΩ	0.6717 MΩ	28.990	0.02718
Checkerboard network	20.322 MΩ	5.4633 MΩ	3.7197	0.04921
3D $2 \times 2 \times 4$ network	**20.651 MΩ**	0.7072 MΩ	**29.201**	**0.01800**
3D $2 \times 2 \times 3$ network	9.3426 MΩ	**0.4194 MΩ**	22.276	0.02491

Another important feature of th networks to note is the stronger nanobattery effect [16]. This causes the visible shift of the zero current level after the erasing pulse. The nanobattery effect is undesired in most applications, but can be dealt with by an appropriate control voltage and timing. It can also be taken advantage of, in some scenarios.

5. Conclusions

Two new types of memristor networks have been introduced, which are able to emulate more reliable memristors. Measurements have been successfully carried out for both the previously presented networks and the new networks. The measurements provided new information about the macro-characteristics of memristor networks compared to the previous simulations. The increased switching speed of memristor networks should be further investigated. This solution can be used with existing devices to support the implementation of neuromorphic applications.

Author Contributions: Conceptualization, Á.R. and G.C.; methodology, D.H.; software, D.H.; validation, D.H., Á.R. and G.C.; formal analysis, Á.R.; investigation, Á.R.; resources, G.C.; data curation, D.H.; writing—original draft preparation, D.H.; writing—review and editing, Á.R. and G.C.; visualization, D.H.; supervision, G.C.; project administration, G.C.; funding acquisition, G.C.

Funding: This research was funded by the Hungarian Government grant number 2018-1.2.1-NKP-00008: Exploring the Mathematical Foundations of Artificial Intelligence. The Application Process Charge was funded by KAP19-1.1-ITK of the Pazmany Peter Catholic University

Acknowledgments: The authors gratefully acknowledge the support of grant 2018-1.2.1-NKP-00008 of the Hungarian National Research, Development and Innovation Office (NKFIH), the fund of KAP19-1.1-ITK of the Pazmany Peter Catholic University and the support of the Roska Tamás Doctoral School of Science and Technology.

Conflicts of Interest: The authors declare no conflict of interest. The funders had no role in the design of the study; in the collection, analyses, or interpretation of data; in the writing of the manuscript, or in the decision to publish the results.

Abbreviations

The following abbreviations are used in this manuscript:

VLSI	Very large scale integration
APM	Analog purpose memristor
DPM	Digital (or discrete) purpose memristor
BPM	Binary purpose memristor
CMOS	Complementary metal–oxide–semiconductor
RAM	Random access memory
FPGA	Field programmable gate array

References

1. Chua, L. Memristor-the missing circuit element. *IEEE Trans. Circuit Theory* **1971**, *18*, 507–519. [CrossRef]
2. Strukov, D.B.; Snider, G.S.; Stewart, D.R.; Williams, R.S. The missing memristor found. *Nature* **2008**, *453*, 80. [CrossRef] [PubMed]
3. Vaidyanathan, S.; Volos, C. *Advances in Memristors, Memristive Devices and Systems*; Springer: Berlin/Heidelberg, Germany, 2017; Volume 701.
4. Wang, Z.; Joshi, S.; Savel'ev, S.E.; Jiang, H.; Midya, R.; Lin, P.; Hu, M.; Ge, N.; Strachan, J.P.; Li, Z.; et al. Memristors with diffusive dynamics as synaptic emulators for neuromorphic computing. *Nat. Mater.* **2017**, *16*, 101. [CrossRef] [PubMed]
5. Indiveri, G.; Linares-Barranco, B.; Legenstein, R.; Deligeorgis, G.; Prodromakis, T. Integration of nanoscale memristor synapses in neuromorphic computing architectures. *Nanotechnology* **2013**, *24*, 384010. [CrossRef] [PubMed]
6. Magyari-Köpe, B.; Song, Y.; Duncan, D.; Zhao, L.; Nishi, Y. Research Update: Ab initio study on resistive memory device optimization trends: Dopant segregation effects and data retention in HfO_{2-x}. *APL Mater.* **2018**, *6*, 058102. [CrossRef]
7. Weste, N.H.; Eshraghian, K. Principles of CMOS VLSI design: A systems perspective. *NASA STI/Recon Tech. Rep. A* **1985**, *85* 554.
8. Lewis, D.L.; Lee, H.H.S. Architectural evaluation of 3D stacked RRAM caches. In Proceedings of the IEEE International Conference on 3D System Integration, San Francisco, CA, USA, 28–30 September 2009; pp. 1–4.
9. Cong, J.; Xiao, B. mrFPGA: A novel FPGA architecture with memristor-based reconfiguration. In Proceedings of the IEEE/ACM International Symposium on Nanoscale Architectures, Washington, DC, USA, 8–9 June 2011; pp. 1–8.
10. Knowm Inc. Homepage. Available online: https://knowm.org (accessed on 31 March 2019).
11. Stathopoulos, S.; Khiat, A.; Trapatseli, M.; Cortese, S.; Serb, A.; Valov, I.; Prodromakis, T. Multibit memory operation of metal-oxide bi-layer memristors. *Sci. Rep.* **2017**, *7*, 17532. [CrossRef] [PubMed]
12. Di Ventra, M.; Pershin, Y.V. On the physical properties of memristive, memcapacitive and meminductive systems. *Nanotechnology* **2013**, *24*, 255201. [CrossRef] [PubMed]

13. Xu, R.; Jang, H.; Lee, M.H.; Amanov, D.; Cho, Y.; Kim, H.; Park, S.; Shin, H.J.; Ham, D. Vertical MoS2 double layer memristor with electrochemical metallization as an atomic-scale synapse with switching thresholds approaching 100 mV. *Nano Lett.* **2019**, doi:10.1021/acs.nanolett.8b05140. [CrossRef] [PubMed]
14. Rák, Á.; Cserey, G. Emulation of analog memristors using low yield digital switching memristors. In Proceedings of the European Conference on Circuit Theory and Design (ECCTD), Dresden, Germany, 8–12 September 2013; pp. 1–4.
15. Lanza, M.; Wong, H.S.P.; Pop, E.; Ielmini, D.; Strukov, D.; Regan, B.C.; Larcher, L.; Villena, M.A.; Yang, J.J.; Goux, L.; et al. Recommended methods to study resistive switching devices. *Adv. Electron. Mater.* **2019**, *5*, 1800143. [CrossRef]
16. Valov, I.; Linn, E.; Tappertzhofen, S.; Schmelzer, S.; van den Hurk, J.; Lentz, F.; Waser, R. Nanobatteries in redox-based resistive switches require extension of memristor theory. *Nat. Commun.* **2013**, *4*, 1771. [CrossRef] [PubMed]

materials

MDPI

Article

A Parasitic Resistance-Adapted Programming Scheme for Memristor Crossbar-Based Neuromorphic Computing Systems

Son Ngoc Truong

Faculty of Electrical and Electronics Engineering, Ho Chi Minh City University of Technology and Education, Ho Chi Minh City 70000, Vietnam; sontn@hcmute.edu.vn; Tel.: +84-93-108-5929

Received: 10 October 2019; Accepted: 3 December 2019; Published: 8 December 2019

Abstract: Memristor crossbar arrays without selector devices, such as complementary-metal oxide semiconductor (CMOS) devices, are a potential for realizing neuromorphic computing systems. However, wire resistance of metal wires is one of the factors that degrade the performance of memristor crossbar circuits. In this work, we propose a wire resistance modeling method and a parasitic resistance-adapted programming scheme to reduce the impact of wire resistance in a memristor crossbar-based neuromorphic computing system. The equivalent wire resistances for the cells are estimated by analyzing the crossbar circuit using the superposition theorem. For the conventional programming scheme, the connection matrix composed of the target memristance values is used for crossbar array programming. In the proposed parasitic resistance-adapted programming scheme, the connection matrix is updated before it is used for crossbar array programming to compensate the equivalent wire resistance. The updated connection matrix is obtained by subtracting the equivalent connection matrix from the original connection matrix. The circuit simulations are performed to test the proposed wire resistance modeling method and the parasitic resistance-adapted programming scheme. The simulation results showed that the discrepancy of the output voltages of the crossbar between the conventional wire resistance modeling method and the proposed wire resistance modeling method is as low as 2.9% when wire resistance varied from 0.5 to 3.0 Ω. The recognition rate of the memristor crossbar with the conventional programming scheme is 99%, 95%, 81%, and 65% when wire resistance is set to be 1.5, 2.0, 2.5, and 3.0 Ω, respectively. By contrast, the memristor crossbar with the proposed parasitic resistance-adapted programming scheme can maintain the recognition as high as 100% when wire resistance is as high as 3.0 Ω.

Keywords: memristor; crossbar array; neuromorphic computing; wire resistance; synaptic weight; character recognition

1. Introduction

Neuromorphic computing was investigated by C. Mead in the late 1980s as a hardware-based approach for artificial intelligence [1]. The word "Neuromorphic" refers to an electronic circuit that is based on digital and analog components to mimic the neurobiological structures in nervous systems. Neuromorphic computing systems can be implemented on various VLSI (very-large scale integration) systems [2–6]. The prevailing VLSI technology today comprises mainly of CMOS (complementary-metal oxide semiconductor) devices. However, CMOS technology is approaching the end of their capabilities because scaling CMOS down faces several fundamental limiting factors stemming from electron thermal energy and quantum-mechanical tunneling [7,8]. The emerging memristive devices, termed memristors, have been considered a promising candidate for realizing the neuromorphic computing systems. Memristor was postulated by L. O. Chua in 1971 as the fourth fundamental passive circuit element and experimentally demonstrated by HP (Hewlett Packard) Labs in 2008 [9,10]. Memristors has been potentially used to implement the neuromorphic computing systems because the nonlinear relationship between magnetic flux and electric charge of memristors is very similar to the plasticity behavior of biological brain [11,12]. In biological brains, synapse is the connection between a presynaptic neuron and a postsynaptic neuron. The strength of a synapse is represented by a synaptic weight. According to the neuron activities including excitatory and inhibitory, synaptic weights can be positive or negative [13,14]. Synapses can be modeled by memristors as shown in Figure 1 [11]. The synaptic weight is represented by the conductance of memristor, which can increase or decrease according to the current flowing through the device.

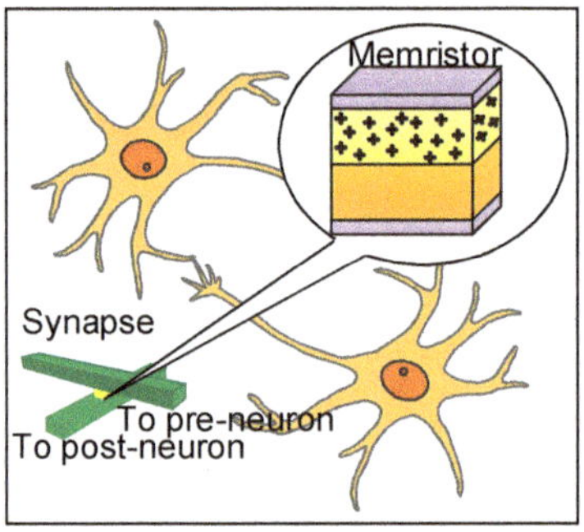

Figure 1. A conceptual diagram of a memristor-based synapse [11].

A memristor crossbar array is a fully connected mesh of perpendicular wires, in which any two crossing wires are connected by a memristor [15]. Neuromorphic computing systems employing crossbar architecture of memristors have gained more advantages in terms of the flexibility, power consumption, cost, and area [16–23]. Miao Hu et al. proposed a crossbar architecture of synaptic array composing of a plus and minus crossbar arrays representing plus- and minus-polarity connection matrices for analog neuromorphic computing [20]. To reduce the area and power consumption, S. N. Truong proposed a new memristor crossbar architecture, which is composed of a single memristor array and a constant-term circuit [21]. The proposed architecture can reduce the power consumption by 48% and the area by 50% [21]. The memristor crossbar has also applied to the applications of speech recognition and image recognition [22,23].

In a memristor crossbar array, some amount of voltage drop can be caused by parasitic resistance, also known as wire resistance along the row and the column lines [19,24–28]. Hereinafter "wire resistance" and "parasitic resistance" are used interchangeably. The impact of wire resistance becomes inevitable when the array size increases [22]. To mitigate the impact of wire resistance, several interesting schemes were proposed [25–28]. A design methodology has been proposed to reduce the impact of wire resistance in a one-selector-one resistive device (1S1R) crossbar array [27]. The proposed design methodology seems to be complicated since the physical specification of the devices must be considered [27]. Another approach to deal with the wire resistance is to use a dynamic reference scheme [25]. The read operation is performed with two steps associated with a special reading circuit. [25]. These proposed schemes are effective when they are applied to a memristor crossbar array, in which memristors are used as binary switches between two distinct high and low resistance states (HRS (High Resistance State) and LRS (Low Resistance State)). These solutions are mainly based on the additional techniques or circuits to compensate the variation of reading voltage caused by wire resistance. To the best of our knowledge, there is a lack of the techniques that can be applied to the programming process of crossbar circuit to lessen the impact of wire resistance in the inference process. In this work, we propose a parasitic resistance-adapted programming scheme for memristor crossbar-based neuromorphic computing systems, in which memristors are used as analog connections. An equivalent wire resistance is proposed for modeling wire resistance in crossbar circuit. The proposed equivalent wire resistance matrix is used to compensate wire resistance during the programming process. As the result, the impact of wire resistance in inference process is reduced significantly.

2. Materials and Methods

In neuromorphic computing systems, the synaptic weights obtained from the training process are either positive or negative according to they are excitatory synapses or inhibitory synapses [13,14]. The signal passing through these synaptic connections can be strengthened or weakened. When modeling biological synapses using memristors, it should be guaranteed that the synaptic weights could be negative values or positive values, consistent with the inhibitory or excitatory synapses. For doing this, the crossbar architecture with two memristor crossbar arrays for plus and minus connection matrices was proposed [20]. Figure 2a shows a conceptual diagram of crossbar architecture of an analog neuromorphic computing system [20]. Here plus-polarity and minus-polarity connection matrices are utilized to implement the synaptic array, in which synaptic weights can be programmed to be negative or positive. The circles in Figure 2a represent the memristors that connect the inputs and the columns. a_0 to a_n are additions, and s_0 to s_n are subtractions that produce the output voltages from V_0 to V_n. $g^+{}_{0,0}$ is the memristor's conductance value of the crossing point between the first row and the first column in M^+ array. Similarly, $g^-{}_{0,0}$ is the memristor's conductance in M- array, as shown in Figure 2a. The output voltage for the *i*th column can be calculated as

$$\begin{aligned} V_i &= \sum_{j=0}^{m} V_{in,j} g^+{}_{j,i} - \sum_{j=0}^{m} V_{in,j} g^-{}_{j,i} \\ V_i &= \sum_{j=0}^{m} V_{in,j} w_{j,i} \\ \textit{Here, } w_{j,i} &= (g^+{}_{j,i} - g^-{}_{j,i}) \end{aligned} \tag{1}$$

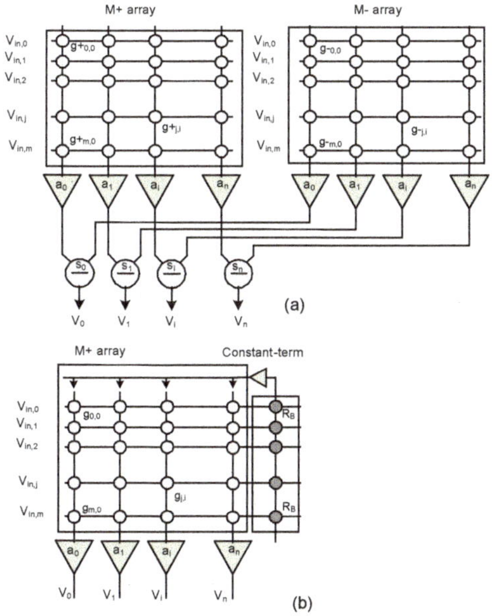

Figure 2. (**a**) The conceptual diagram of two crossbar arrays for implementing plus- and minus-polarity connection matrices [20] and (**b**) the optimized crossbar architecture, which employs only one memristor crossbar and a constant-term circuit for realizing negative and positive synaptic weights [21].

In Equation (1), the output voltage is a summation of inputs, which are weighted by the corresponding weights, $w_{j,i}$. The synaptic weight, $w_{j,i}$, is decided by the difference of two conductance values of memristors in two arrays; $g^{+}{}_{j,i}$ in the M^{+} array, and $g^{-}{}_{j,i}$ in M^{-} array. To reduce the power consumption and area, S. N. Truong proposed a new crossbar architecture, which employed only one crossbar array and a constant-term circuit [21]. The proposed crossbar architecture is conceptually shown in Figure 2b. There is only one memristor crossbar array instead of two memristor crossbar arrays for representing the signed synaptic array. The negative synaptic weight is generated using an additional column, which connects to the inputs through R_Bs, as shown in Figure 2b. Here, a constant-term circuit is used to replace a crossbar array without changing the functionality of the crossbar circuit [21].

In previous works, memristor crossbar circuits are simulated with ignoring the presence of wire resistance. However, the impact wire resistance in crossbar is inevitable. It becomes more serious as the array size increases [25]. Wire resistance is modeled by small-value resistors lying on the vertical lines and the horizontal lines, as shown in Figure 3. In Figure 3, if wire resistance is omitted, the output voltage of the ith column is calculated by Equation (2) [21].

$$
\begin{aligned}
V_{O,i} &= \sum_{j=0}^{m} V_{in,j} w_{j,i} \\
where,\ w_{j,i} &= R_0\left(\frac{1}{R_B} - \frac{1}{M_{j,i}}\right)
\end{aligned}
\tag{2}
$$

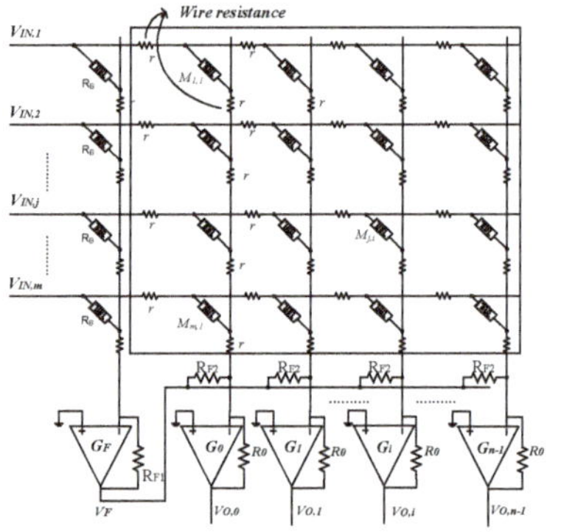

Figure 3. The schematic of memristor-based neuromorphic computing circuit with the presence of wire resistance. Wire resistance is modeled by small-value resistors on vertical lines and horizontal lines.

Equation (2) is used for calculating the output voltage of the ith column. The output of each column is a summation of the weighted inputs, hence each column works as a perceptron neuron. In Equation (2), $M_{j,i}$ is the memristance value of the crossing point between the jth row and ith column. R_B is a constant, the synaptic weight, $w_{j,i}$, can be decided to be either negative or positive by adjusting the memristance, $M_{j,i}$.

If wire resistance is not omitted, it can be modeled by small-value resistors along vertical and horizontal lines as shown in Figure 3. The ith column of crossbar is separated and shown in Figure 4. The output voltage of the ith column is calculated by applying Ohm's law and the Kirchhoff's current law to the node of V^{-} of the Op-amp, as presented in Equation (3).

$$
\begin{aligned}
V_{o,i} &= R_0 i_0 \\
where\ i_0 &+ \sum_{j=1}^{m} i_j = 0
\end{aligned}
\tag{3}
$$

To analyze the circuit in Figure 3, we can use the well-known superposition theorem. In particular, we isolate the circuit row by row as shown in Figure 4a. When we calculate the current for the jth row, we can assume that the inputs for other rows are zero, as shown in Figure 4b. Since the value of the resistor, r, is very small compared to the memristance values, the circuit in Figure 4b can be approximated by using the equivalent circuit, as illustrated in Figure 4c. In Figure 4c, the resistors, which the current i_1 passes through, can be approximately represented by an equivalent resistor $R_{1,i}$:

$$R_{1,i} = ir + mr \tag{4}$$

where $R_{1,i}$ is an equivalent wire resistance for cell $M_{1,i}$. In general, we can approximate the wire resistance for the cell $M_{j,i}$ as follows

$$R_{j,i} = ir + (m - j + 1)r \tag{5}$$

where, m is the number of rows in the crossbar circuit. r is wire resistance value.

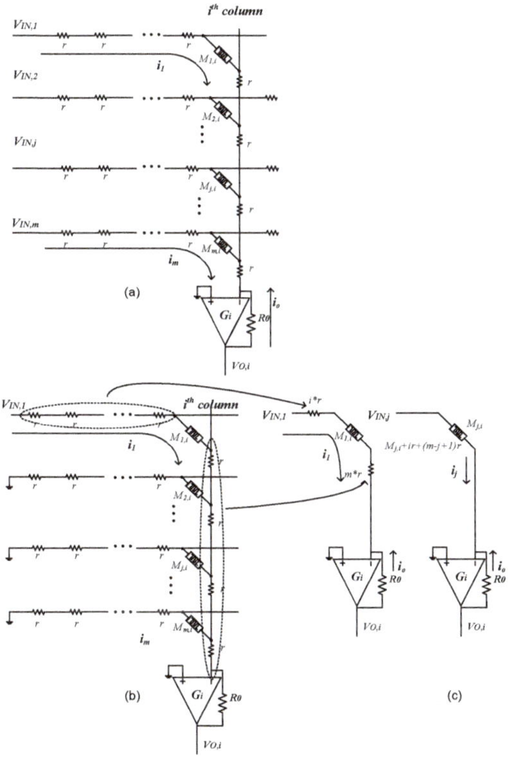

Figure 4. Analyzing the crossbar circuit using superposition method. (**a**) The schematic of the ith column with the presence of wire resistance; (**b**) analyzing the circuit using superposition method, and (**c**) the equivalent wire resistance for the cell $M_{j,i}$.

In this work, we proposed a wire resistance modeling method by using the proposed an equivalent wire resistance matrix for an m × n crossbar array, as illustrated in Figure 5. The elements in the proposed matrix are the equivalent resistance values of wire resistance on vertical line and horizontal line, which are calculated by Equation (5) for the corresponding cells.

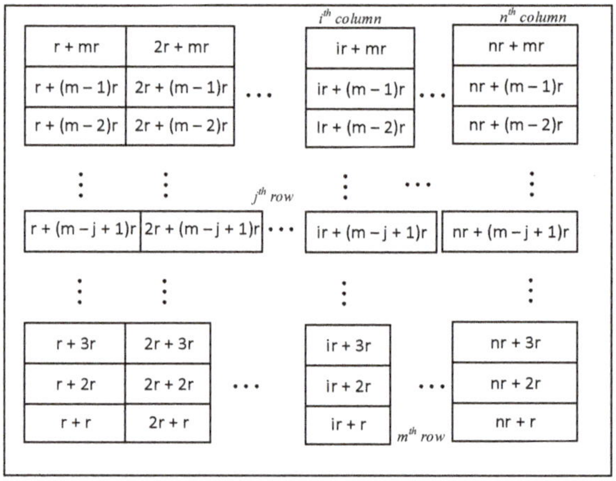

Figure 5. The proposed equivalent wire resistance matrix for modeling wire resistance in an m × n crossbar array. Here r is the value of wire resistance, m is the number of rows, and *n* is the number of columns.

The proposed equivalent wire resistance matrix was used to compensate the impact of wire resistance in crossbar array by adjusting the connection matrix according to the proposed equivalent wire resistance matrix. In particular, we proposed a parasitic resistance-adapted programming scheme to compensate wire resistance for a memristor crossbar-neuromorphic computing. The proposed scheme is conceptually shown in Figure 6b. Figure 6a shows a conventional programming scheme for a crossbar circuit. The synaptic weights that were obtained from the training process were converted to the values of memristance using Equation (2). The memristance values of the cells in crossbar form a connection matrix M as presented in Figure 6. For the conventional programming scheme, the cells in the crossbar array were programmed to the target values presented in the connection matrix M. Wire resistance was not considered during programming process and inference phase. To consider the presence of wire resistance, the connection matrix was updated before it is used to program the crossbar array. Specifically, the target memristance matrix was obtained by subtracting the proposed equivalent wire resistance matrix from the original connection matrix, as conceptually shown in Figure 6b. By updating the connection matrix with the proposed equivalent wire resistance matrix, wire resistance was compensated in the inference phase. The connection matrix is updated using the Equation (6)

$$\begin{aligned} M_{j,i} &= M_{j,i} - R_{j,i} \\ &= M_{j,i} - ir + (m - j + 1)r \end{aligned} \tag{6}$$

where, $M_{j,i}$ is memristance of the cell between the jth row the ith column. In the conventional programming scheme, the cell $M_{j,i}$ is programmed to have the memristance of $M_{j,i}$. In the proposed programming scheme, the cell $M_{j,i}$ is programmed to have the memristance of $M_{j,i} - ir + (m - j + 1)r$, where the amount of $ir + (m - j + 1)$r represents the equivalent wire resistance for the cell $M_{j,i}$. By doing this, wire resistance is compensated in the inference phase.

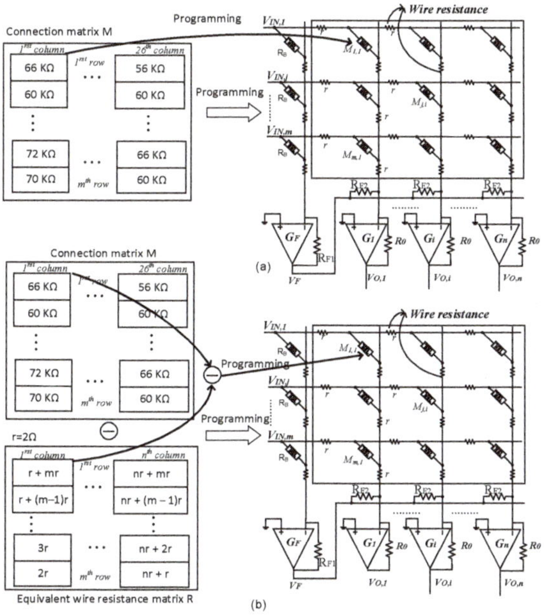

Figure 6. (**a**) The conventional programming scheme, in which the memristance values in connection matrix are used to program the corresponding cells in crossbar array and (**b**) the proposed parasitic resistance-adapted programming scheme, where the value of connection matrix is updated by subtracting the proposed equivalent wire resistance matrix from the original connection matrix. The updated connection matrix is then used to program the crossbar array. *R* is the proposed equivalent wire resistance matrix for an m × n crossbar array. *r* is the value of wire resistance, m is the number of rows, and n is the number of columns.

3. Results

The circuit simulations were performed to verify the proposed wire resistance modeling method and the parasitic resistance-adapted programming scheme for a memristor crossbar-based neuromorphic computing system. The simulations were performed using the SPECTRE circuit simulation provided by Cadence Design Systems Inc. [29]. Memristors were modeled using Verilog-A and CMOS technology is given by SAMSUNG 0.13 mm process technology [30,31]. Figure 7a shows a hysteresis behavior of a real memristor based on the film structure of Pt/$LaAlO_3$/Nb-doped $SrTiO_3$ stacked layer and a memristor model that can be used to describe various memristive behaviors [30,31]. The memristor model and parameters are presented in [30]. The crossbar circuit was used for the application of character recognition. Figure 7b shows eight × eight images of characters used in these simulations. Each character was composed of 64 black-and-white pixels. The crossbar circuit was schematically shown in Figure 7c for recognition of the characters from "A" to "Z". To recognize 26 characters, the memristor crossbar was composed of 26 columns and a constant-term of R_B as depicted in Figure 7c. The constant-term column connected to all inputs through R_B to generate the negative voltage as mentioned in the previous work [21]. The crossbar had 26 columns corresponding to 26 perceptron neurons for recognizing 26 characters from "A" to "Z". For example, the first column is trained to be activated with the input character "A" and the 26th column is trained to be activated with the input character "Z" [21]. Wire resistance was modeled by small-value resistors along vertical and horizontal lines, as shown in Figure 7c. Here R_B and R_0 were set to be 60 KΩ and 200 KΩ respectively. R_{F1} should be equal to R_{F2} as mentioned in previous work [21].

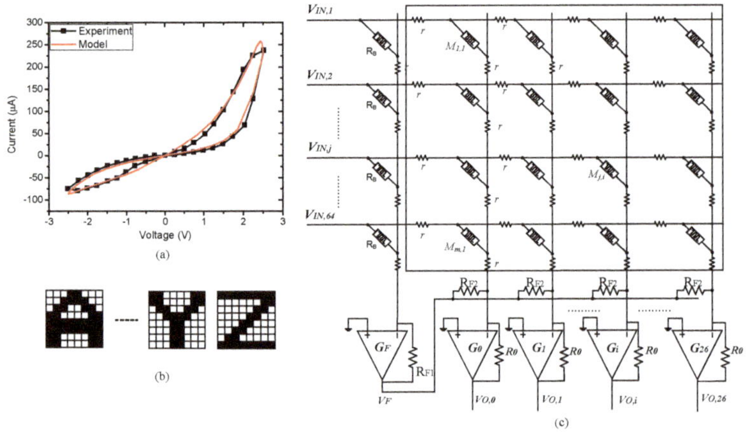

Figure 7. (**a**) The memristor's current–voltage characteristic measured from the real device and the memristor's behavior model; (**b**) the eight × eight images of characters used to test the proposed equivalent wire resistance modeling method and the parasitic resistance-adapted programming scheme; and (**c**) the schematic of crossbar circuit for the application of character recognition.

The proposed wire resistance modeling method using equivalent wire resistance matrix was verified by the simulation that was set up as presented in Figure 8a,b. The synaptic weights obtained from the training process were converted to the memristance values in connection matrix using Equations (2) and (6). For the conventional method, wire resistance was modeled by small-value resistors along vertical and horizontal lines, as shown in Figure 8a. The crossbar was programmed to the target memristance values presented in the connection matrix using the $V_{DD}/3$ write scheme [32]. For the proposed method, we calculated the equivalent wire resistance matrix as shown in Figure 5. The small-values resistors were not present in the crossbar circuit, the value of equivalent wire resistance matrix was added to the connection matrix instead, as conceptually shown in Figure 8b. In other words, the connection matrix was updated by adding corresponding elements of the connection matrix and the proposed equivalent wire resistance matrix. The crossbar was then programmed to the target memristance values presented in the updated connection matrix using $V_{DD}/3$ write scheme. In Figure 8c, the output voltages of 26 columns for recognizing 26 characters were measured when the vector of character "A" was applied to the inputs. Among the 26 columns, only the first column produced high voltage for recognizing character "A". When wire resistance was set to be 2.0 Ω, the voltage drop on wire resistance made the output voltages of columns increase, as shown in Figure 8c [33]. Since the voltage drop on wire resistance depends on the length of metal line, the column close to the first column had less change of voltage whereas the column far from the first column had much change of voltage, as demonstrated in Figure 8c [33]. The result obtained from the conventional method is represented by the square symbols and that one obtained from the proposed method with equivalent wire resistance matrix is represented by the round symbols. The discrepancy between the two methods was as low as 3%.

In Figure 8d, we calculated the percentage error, which is defined as the difference of the output voltages between the conventional wire resistance modeling method in Figure 8a and the proposed wire resistance modeling method in Figure 8b, in which wire resistance was modeled using the proposed equivalent wire resistance matrix. In these simulations, wire resistance was varied from 0.5 to 3.0 Ω. This range of wire resistance is commonly used and obtained from the International Technology Roadmap for Semiconductors [24,25,34–37]. When wire resistance was set to be 0.5 Ω, the percentage error was as low as 2.2%. The percentage error increased slightly when wire resistance increased, as shown in Figure 8d. On average, the discrepancy between the two methods was as low as 2.9%.

The simulation results indicate that wire resistance in crossbar circuit could be modeled using the proposed equivalent wire resistance matrix, which is presented in Figure 5.

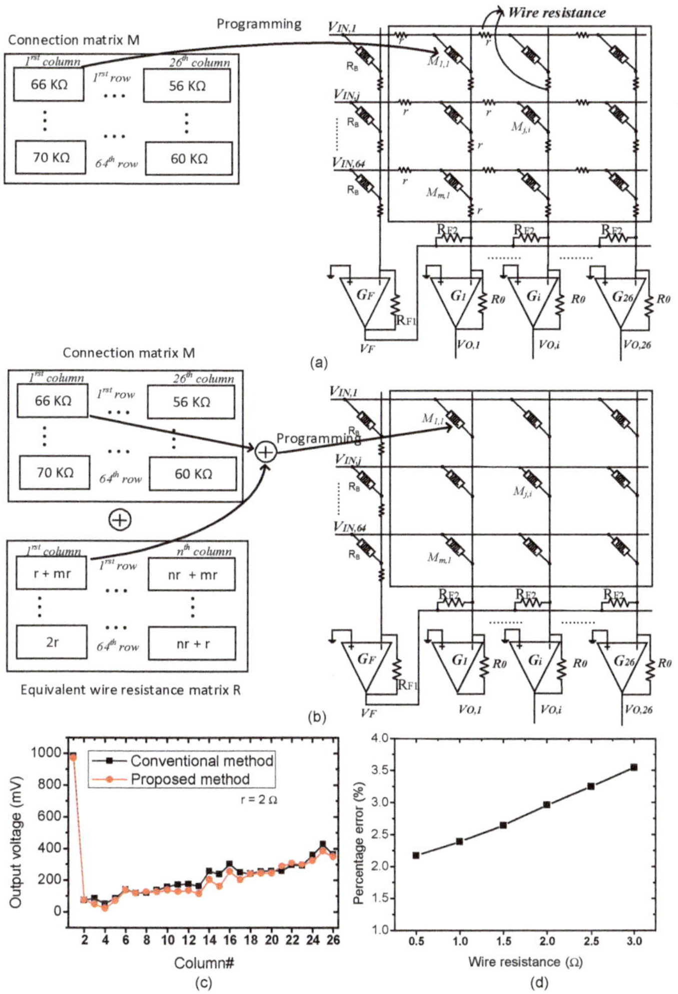

Figure 8. (**a**) The conventional method for the crossbar circuit simulation with taking the presence of wire resistance into account. Here wire resistance is modeled by small-value resistors along the vertical and horizontal lines; (**b**) the proposed method with equivalent wire resistance for the crossbar circuit simulation with considering the presence of wire resistance. Here, the small-value resistors are not present in the crossbar circuit, the connection matrix is updated by adding the equivalent wire resistance matrix to the connection matrix instead; (**c**) the output voltages of 26 columns for the input character "A" and (**d**) the percentage error with varying wire resistance from 0.5 to 3.0 Ω.

Figure 9 shows the comparison of the recognition rate of memristor crossbar array between the conventional programming scheme and the proposed parasitic resistance-adapted programming scheme for recognizing 26 characters when wire resistance was varied from 0.5 to 3.0 Ω. For the conventional programming scheme, the connection matrix obtained from the training process of memristor crossbar for recognition of 26 characters was used for the crossbar array programming. In the proposed parasitic resistance-adapted programming scheme, the connection matrix was updated by subtracting the proposed equivalent wire resistance matrix from the original connection matrix. The updated connection matrix was then used for the crossbar array programming. The recognition rate of the memristor crossbar with using conventional programming scheme declined dramatically when wire resistance increased. This was due to the fact that the synaptic weight is a nonlinear function of memristance as presented in Equation (2), the change of memristance caused by wire resistance makes the synaptic weight change remarkably. As a result, the recognition rate was degraded dramatically. In particular, the recognition rate of the memristor crossbar with using the conventional programming scheme was 99%, 95%, 81%, and 65% when the wire resistance was set to be 1.5, 2.0, 2.5, and 3.0 Ω, respectively, as indicated in Figure 9. The presence of wire resistance causes the output voltage increased as mathematically analyzed and experimentally demonstrated in previous work [33]. The last column had the large variation of output voltage caused by wire resistance [33]. Therefore, the increase of wire resistance caused the recognition rate to decrease significantly, as the shown in Figure 9. By contrast, the memristor crossbar with using the proposed parasitic resistance-adapted programming scheme could maintain the recognition as high as 100% when wire resistance was as high as 3.0 Ω. This was because the value of memristance in connection matrix was updated by subtracting the equivalent wire resistance matrix from the original connection matrix. By doing this, the wire resistance in crossbar circuit was compensated.

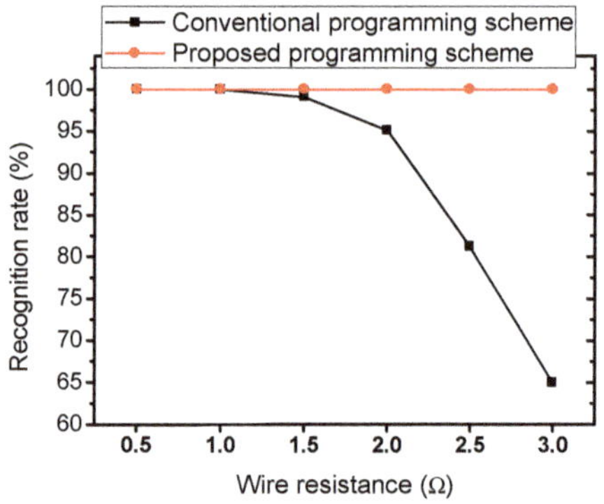

Figure 9. The comparison of recognition rate between the conventional programming scheme and the proposed parasitic resistance-adapted programming scheme when wire resistance is varied from 0.5 to 3.0 Ω.

Wire resistance degraded the performance of crossbar circuit dramatically. In this work, we tried to mitigate the impact of wire resistance by compensating wire resistance. It was done by adjusting the memristance values before they were used to program the crossbar array. In particular, the connection matrix was updated by subtracting the equivalent wire resistance matrix from the original connection matrix. By doing this, no additional circuits or components were required. The proposed parasitic resistance-adapted programming scheme was effective for memristor crossbar-based neuromorphic computing systems.

4. Conclusions

Wire resistance is one of the factors that degrade the performance of the crossbar circuits significantly. In this work, we proposed a parasitic resistance-adapted programming scheme to mitigate the impact of wire resistance in memristor crossbar array. Firstly, a wire resistance modeling method using equivalent wire resistance matrix was proposed. The equivalent wire resistance matrix was achieved by analysis the crossbar circuit using the superposition method. The connection matrix was updated before it was used as a target for memristor crossbar programming. The updated connection matrix was obtained by subtracting the proposed equivalent wire resistance matrix from the original connection matrix. The circuit simulations were performed to verify the proposed wire resistance modeling method and the parasitic resistance-adapted programming scheme. The simulation results showed that the discrepancy of the output voltages of the crossbar circuit between the conventional wire resistance modeling method and the proposed wire resistance modeling method was as low as 2.9% when wire resistance varied from 0.5 to 3.0 Ω. The recognition rate of the memristor crossbar with conventional programming scheme was 99%, 95%, 81%, and 65% when wire resistance was set to be 1.5, 2.0, 2.5, and 3.0 Ω, respectively. By contrast, the memristor crossbar with the proposed parasitic resistance-adapted programming scheme could maintain the recognition as high as 100% when wire resistance was as high as 3.0 Ω.

Funding: This research received no external funding.

Conflicts of Interest: The authors declare that they have no conflict of interest.

References

1. Mead, C. Neuromorphic electronic systems. *Proc. IEEE* **1990**, *78*, 1629–1636. [CrossRef]
2. Bartolozzi, C.; Indiveri, G. Synaptic dynamics in analog VLSI. *Neural Comput.* **2007**, *19*, 2581–2603. [CrossRef] [PubMed]
3. Mahowald, M.; Douglas, R. A silicon neuron. *Nature* **1991**, *354*, 515–518. [CrossRef] [PubMed]
4. Farquhar, E.; Hasler, P. A bio-physically inspired silicon neuron. *IEEE Trans. Circuits Syst.* **2005**, *52*, 477–488. [CrossRef]
5. Yu, T.; Cauwenberghs, G. Analog VLSI biophysical neurons and synapses with programmable membrane channel kinetics. *IEEE Trans. Biomed. Circuits Syst.* **2010**, *4*, 139–148. [CrossRef] [PubMed]
6. Indiveri, G.; Linares-Barranco, B.; Hamilton, T.J.; Van Schaik, A.; Etienne-Cummings, R.; Delbruck, T.; Liu, S.C.; Dudek, P.; Häfliger, P.; Renaud, S.; et al. Neuromorphic silicon neuron circuits. *Front. Neurosci.* **2011**, *5*, 73. [CrossRef] [PubMed]
7. Solomon, P.M. Device innovation and material challenges at the limit of CMOS technology. *Annu. Rev. Mater. Sci.* **2000**, *30*, 681–697. [CrossRef]
8. Brđanin, T.P.; Dokić, B. Strained silicon layer in CMOS technology. *Electronics* **2014**, *18*, 63–69.
9. Chua, L.O. Memristor—The missing circuit element. *IEEE Trans. Circuit Theory* **1971**, *18*, 507–519. [CrossRef]
10. Strukov, D.B.; Sinder, G.S.; Stewart, D.R.; Williams, R.S. The missing memristor found. *Nature* **2008**, *453*, 80–83. [CrossRef]
11. Jo, S.H.; Chang, T.; Ebong, I.; Bhadviya, B.B.; Mazumder, P.; Lu, W. Nanoscale memristor device as synapse in neuromorphic systems. *Nano Lett.* **2010**, *10*, 1297–1301. [CrossRef] [PubMed]
12. Passian, A.; Imam, N. Nanaosystems, Edge Computing, and Next Generation Computing Systems. *Sensors* **2019**, *19*, 4048. [CrossRef] [PubMed]
13. Abbott, L.F.; Regehr, W.G. Synaptic computation. *Nature* **2004**, *431*, 796–803. [CrossRef]
14. Lamprecht, R.; LeDoux, J. Structural plasticity and memory. *Nat. Rev. Neurosci.* **2004**, *5*, 45–54. [CrossRef] [PubMed]
15. Williams, R.S. How we found the missing memristor. *IEEE Spectr.* **2008**, *45*, 28–35. [CrossRef]
16. Zhang, X.; Huang, A.; Hu, Q.; Xiao, Z.; Chu, P.K. Neuromorphic Computing with Memristor Crossbar. *Phys. Status Solidi A* **2018**, *215*, 1–16. [CrossRef]
17. Sung, C.; Hwang, H.; Yoo, I.K. Perspective: A review on memristive hardware for neuromorphic. *J. Appl. Physic* **2018**, *124*, 1–13. [CrossRef]
18. Jeong, Y.; Lu, W.D. Neuromorphic Computing Using Memristor Crossbar Networks: A Focus on Bio-Inspired Approaches. *IEEE Nanotechnol. Mag.* **2018**, *12*, 6–18. [CrossRef]
19. Liang, J.; Wong, H.S.P. Cross-point memristor array without cell selector—Device characteristics and data storage pattern dependencies. *IEEE Trans. Electron. Device* **2010**, *57*, 2531–2538. [CrossRef]
20. Hu, M.; Li, H.; Wu, Q.; Rose, G.S.; Chen, Y. Memristor crossbar based hardware realization of BSB recall function. In Proceedings of the International Joint Conference on Neural Networks, Brisbane, Australia, 10–15 June 2012; pp. 1–7.

21. Truong, S.N.; Min, K.S. New memristor-based crossbar array architecture with 50-% area reduction and 48-% power saving for matrix-vector multiplication of analog neuromorphic computing. *J. Semicond. Technol. Sci.* **2014**, *14*, 356–363. [CrossRef]
22. Truong, S.N.; Ham, S.J.; Min, K.S. Neuromorphic crossbar circuit with nanoscale filamentary-switching binary memristors for speech recognition. *Nanoscale Res. Lett.* **2014**, *9*, 1–9. [CrossRef] [PubMed]
23. Truong, S.N.; Min, K. S New twin crossbar architecture of binary memristors for low-power image recognition with discrete cosine transform. *IEEE Trans. Nanotechnol.* **2015**, *14*, 1104–1111. [CrossRef]
24. Linn, E.; Rosezin, R.; Kügeler, C.; Waser, R. Complementary resistive switches for passive nanocrossbar memories. *Nat. Mater.* **2010**, *9*, 403–406. [CrossRef] [PubMed]
25. Shin, S.H.; Byeon, S.D.; Song, J.S.; Truong, S.N.; Mo, H.S.; Kim, D.J.; Min, K.S. Dynamic reference scheme with improved read voltage margin for compensating cell-position and back ground-pattern dependencies in pure memristor array. *J. Semicond. Technol. Sci.* **2015**, *15*, 685–694. [CrossRef]
26. Adeyemo, A.; Jabir, A.; Mathew, J. Minimising Impact of Wire Resistance in Low-Power Crossbar Array Write Scheme. *J. Low Power Electron.* **2017**, *13*, 649–660. [CrossRef]
27. Levisse, A.; Royer, P.; Giraud, B.; Noel, J.P.; Moreau, M.; Portal, J.M. Architecture, design and technology guidelines for crosspoint memories. In Proceedings of the IEEE/ACM International Symposium on Nanoscale Architectures (NANOARCH), Newport, RI, USA, 25–27 July 2017.
28. Giraud, B.; Makosiej, A.; Boumchedda, R.; Gupta, N.; Levisse, A.; Vianello, E.; Noel, J.-P. Advanced memory solutions for emerging circuits and systems. In Proceedings of the IEEE International Electron Devices Meeting (IEDM), San Francisco, CA, USA, 2–6 December 2017.
29. Spectre® Circuit Simulator User Guide. Available online: https://www.ee.columbia.edu/~{}harish/uploads/2/6/9/2/26925901/spectre_reference.pdf (accessed on 1 October 2019).
30. Truong, S.N.; Pham, K.V.; Yang, W.; Shin, S.; Pedrotti, K.; Min, K.S. New pulse amplitude modulation for fine tuning of memristor synapses. *Mircoelectron. J.* **2016**, *55*, 162–168. [CrossRef]
31. Yakopcic, C.; Taha, T.M.; Subramanyam, G.; Pino, R.E.; Rogers, S. A memristor device model. *IEEE Electron. Device Lett.* **2011**, *32*, 1436–1438. [CrossRef]
32. Ham, S.J.; Mo, H.S.; Min, K.S. Low-power $V_{DD}/3$ write scheme with inversion coding circuit for complementary memristor array. *IEEE Trans. Nanotechnol.* **2013**, *12*, 851–857. [CrossRef]
33. Truong, S.N. Compensating Circuit to Reduce the Impact of Wire Resistance in a Memristor Crossbar-Based Perceptron Neural Network. *Micromachines* **2019**, *10*, 671. [CrossRef]
34. International Technology Roadmap for Semiconductors. 2007. Available online: https://www.semiconductors.org/wp-content/uploads/2018/08/2007Interconnect.pdf (accessed on 1 October 2019).
35. Kim, S.; Zhou, J.; Lu, W.D. Crossbar RRAM arrays: Selector device requirements during wire operation. *IEEE Trans. Electron. Devices* **2014**, *61*, 2820–2826.
36. Schindler, G.; Steinlesberger, G.; Engelhardt, M.; Steinhögl, W. Electrical characterization of copper interconnects with end-of-roadmap feature sizes. *Solid State Electron.* **2003**, *47*, 1233–1236. [CrossRef]
37. Kohonen, T. *Self-organization and Associative Memory*; In Information Sciences; Springer: Berlin/Heidelberg, Germany, 1989.

materials

MDPI

Article

On the Application of a Diffusive Memristor Compact Model to Neuromorphic Circuits

Agustín Cisternas Ferri [1,†], Alan Rapoport [1,†], Pablo I. Fierens [2], German A Patterson [2,*], Enrique Miranda [3] and Jordi Suñé [3]

1 Departamento de Física, FCEyN, UBA, Pabellón 1, Ciudad Universitaria, Buenos Aires 1428, Argentina
2 Instituto Tecnológico de Buenos Aires, and National Scientific and Technical Research Council (CONICET), Buenos Aires 1437, Argentina
3 Departament d'Enginyeria Electrònica, Universitat Autònoma de Barcelona, 08193 Cerdanyola del Vallès, Spain
* Correspondence: gpatters@itba.edu.ar
† These authors contributed equally to this work.

Received: 30 May 2019; Accepted: 8 July 2019; Published: 13 July 2019

Abstract: Memristive devices have found application in both random access memory and neuromorphic circuits. In particular, it is known that their behavior resembles that of neuronal synapses. However, it is not simple to come by samples of memristors and adjusting their parameters to change their response requires a laborious fabrication process. Moreover, sample to sample variability makes experimentation with memristor-based synapses even harder. The usual alternatives are to either simulate or emulate the memristive systems under study. Both methodologies require the use of accurate modeling equations. In this paper, we present a diffusive compact model of memristive behavior that has already been experimentally validated. Furthermore, we implement an emulation architecture that enables us to freely explore the synapse-like characteristics of memristors. The main advantage of emulation over simulation is that the former allows us to work with real-world circuits. Our results can give some insight into the desirable characteristics of the memristors for neuromorphic applications.

Keywords: memristor; compact model; emulator; neuromorphic; synapse; STDP; pavlov

---

1. Introduction

Memristive elements or resistive switches are two-terminal components that exhibit a hysteretic relation between voltage and current [1–3]. Because they are highly nonlinear and have the property of non-volatility, there is a great interest in their use in the design of new applications in neuromorphic circuits [4–15], programmable logic [16–18] and chaotic circuits [19–21], as well as in the development of new memory technologies [22–25]. Unfortunately, it is not simple to come by samples of memristors. Moreover, each time a researcher desires to adjust a parameter to change their response, she needs to go through a laborious fabrication and testing process. The usual alternatives are to either simulate [26–30] or emulate [31–37] the memristive systems under study. Emulation has the additional advantage that it allows to test the interaction of memristors with real circuit components [38]. For this reason, we present a simple emulator, based on widely-available and low-cost hardware that can work with various numerical models of memristors.

Since synapses can be understood as two-terminal elements with variable conductance, there has been an increasing interest on the application of memristors as synaptic junctions [4–8,13]. In particular, it has been proposed to modulate memristors conductance by applying specific signals, namely action potentials, with shapes and time characteristics that define the response of the neuromorphic circuit such as in the case of the Spike-Timing-Dependent Plasticity (STDP) process [6,8]. STDP relates the change in connection strength between two neurons as a function of the temporal distance between pre and postsynaptic stimuli [39–41]. It has been observed that the synaptic strength increases (decreases) when the presynaptic cell fires before (after) the postsynaptic neuron.

In the literature, we find some sophisticated protocols and complex circuits that allow for qualitatively mimicking the behavior of synapses [4]. However, it has been recently shown that the response of memristors with diffusive dynamics is already very similar to that of a synaptic junction [29,42]. Thus, it is interesting to study the application of this type of memristors in neuromorphic computing systems.

Memristors have also been used as part of more complex neuromorphic circuits. Particularly, in those that mimic the classical learning rule known as Pavlovian conditioning [43–45]. In this learning procedure, a specific stimulus that provokes a given response is paired with a neutral stimulus and, as a result of this pairing, the neutral stimulus can later evoke a response in the absence of the specific stimulus [46].

Since memristors with diffusive dynamics are well-suited to mimic the behavior of a synapse, in this work, we focus on the study of such type of memristors in simple neuromorphic circuits that present STDP behavior and Pavlovian conditioning, and study their performance as a function of the memristive device response time. To this aim, we consider a compact model of memristor that accurately describes the behavior of actual memristive systems [47–49]. This memristor model was implemented in an emulation architecture based on a microcontroller and a digital potentiometer. An exhaustive characterization of the emulator device and preliminary results of the STDP process were presented in Ref. [50].

1.1. Compact Model of Memristive Behavior

In this section, we review a compact model for memristors with diffusive dynamics that we have already introduced and have shown to represent accurately the experimentally measured behavior of actual devices [47–49].

Memristive devices are usually modeled by two equations. While one of the equations describes the I–V characteristic, the other governs the evolution of a state variable on which the I–V characteristic depends on. Many experimental reports show that, as multiple conductive channels in the insulator are created or destructed, metal-insulator-metal devices exhibit more than two conductive states. For this reason, we developed a model whose state variable tracks the fraction of active conductive channels [47–49]. Assuming that the channel creation probability follows a threshold distribution $f^+(v)$, the dependence of the creation of conductive channels Γ^+ on the applied voltage v can be calculated as

$$\Gamma^+(v) = \int_{-\infty}^{+\infty} H(v-\xi) f^+(\xi) \mathrm{d}\xi \,, \tag{1}$$

where $H(x)$ is the Heaviside function. On the other hand, the destruction of conductive channels Γ^- can be obtained by considering the destruction threshold distribution $f^-(v)$. Both Γ^+ and Γ^- are used to define a recursive formula for the discretized-time evolution of active conductive channels as

$$\lambda(v(t)) = \min\left\{\Gamma^-(v(t)), \max\left[\lambda(v(t-h)), \Gamma^+(v(t))\right]\right\} \,, \tag{2}$$

where h is the integration time step. The evolution of λ is highly sensitive to the creation and destruction distributions $f^{\pm}(v)$. For instance, skewed distributions may be suitable to describe devices where transitions take place abruptly upon reaching a given threshold potential while bell-shaped distributions may be used to describe those devices with gentle transitions [51]. For the sake of simplicity, we consider the latter approach with $f^{\pm}(v)$ following logistic distributions. Thus, the $\Gamma^{\pm}$ functions are given by sigmoid functions

$$\Gamma^{\pm}(v) = \frac{1}{1+e^{-\alpha_{\pm}(v \mp \delta_{\pm})}} . \tag{3}$$

Parameters $\delta_{\pm}$ and $\alpha_{\pm}$ are positive constants that account for the positive and negative threshold potentials and transition rates, respectively. Figure 1 depicts voltage distributions $f^{\pm}$ and the corresponding $\Gamma^{\pm}$ functions. Equation (2) fixes the evolution of active channels λ between the region delimited by $\Gamma^{\pm}$. Conductive channels are neither aggregated nor dissolved instantaneously. Moreover, the response time depends on the magnitude of the driving signal. Experiments have shown that switching time and voltage are related by an exponential function. In order to account this phenomenon, the time evolution of active channels $w(t)$ is described by the differential equation

$$\tau_0 \exp\left(-\frac{|v(t)|}{v_0}\right)\frac{d}{dt}w(t) + w(t) = \lambda(v(t)), \tag{4}$$

where τ_0 is a characteristic response time, associated with a diffusive process, and v_0 a positive constant that weights the input stimuli.

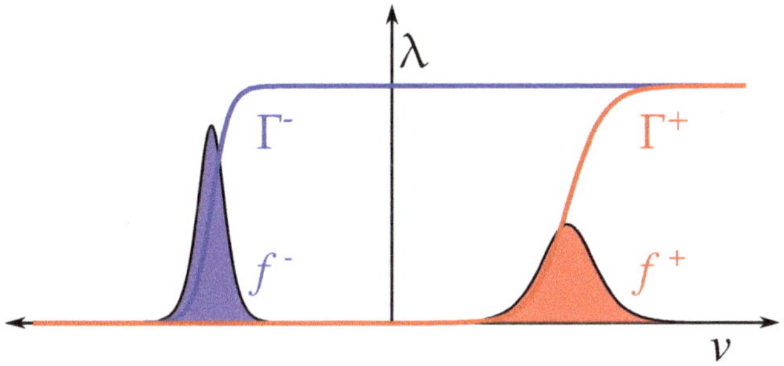

Figure 1. Threshold distributions $f^{\pm}$ are bell-shaped. The number of active channels λ is a function of the applied potential v and evolves within the region delimited by Γ^{+} and Γ^{-}.

The model is completed by specifying a relationship between $w(t)$ and the I–V characteristics of the device. In previous works, the I–V characteristic equation was a nonlinear relationship that resembled that of two identical opposite-biased diodes [52,53]. As the main goal is to study the dynamics of switching effect, we simplified the I–V relation to that of a linear variable resistance described by

$$R(t) = R_{\text{on}}w(t) + R_{\text{off}}\left(1 - w(t)\right), \tag{5}$$

where R_{on} and R_{off} are the low and high-resistance levels of the memristor, respectively. This simplified relation alleviates the computation burden of simulation and emulation processes, without changing the essence of the model.

1.2. Emulation Architecture

Many emulation architectures have been proposed [31–37]. Following the work of Olumodeji and Gottardi [36], we base our design on an Arduino board and a digital potentiometer. A schematic of the emulator design is shown in Figure 2. The analog-to-digital converters (ADCs) in the Arduino are used to measure the current that flows through the potentiometer. The microcontroller integrates the differential equations that model the behavior of the memristor and changes the resistance of the potentiometer. A description of the emulator architecture is given in Section 3.1. In Section 2.1, we present results that validate the correctness of the implemented emulator.

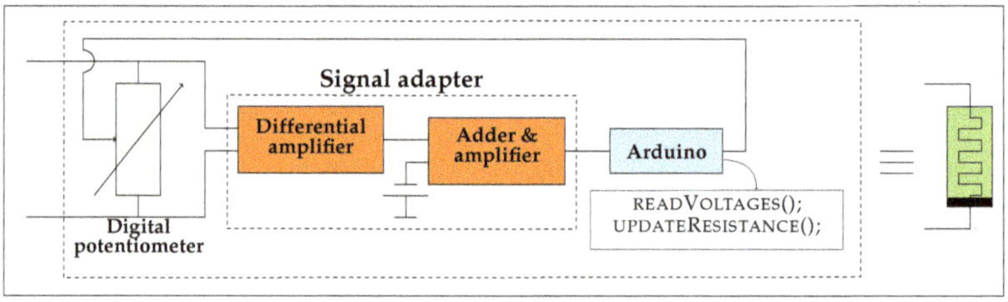

Figure 2. Schematic of the proposed emulator. An analog-to-digital converter (ADC) in the microcontroller measures the voltage on the digital potentiometer. The differential equations describing the memristor behavior are numerically integrated based on those measurements; then, the potentiometer resistance is changed accordingly. Signal conditioning is required to adapt the voltage to the microcontroller ADC input range.

1.3. Memristors for Neuromorphic Applications

There is a vast literature on the application of memristors for machine learning and computation (see, e.g., [54–58] and references therein). In particular, a review of the pertinent bibliography reveals a special interest on the use of memristors in neuromorphic circuits [4–15]. The focus of this paper is to study the possibility of using memristors as neuronal synapses and to characterize the role of the parameters that influence the dynamics of the memristive behavior.

A synapse is a biological structure that allows the communication of two neurons which is located, for example, in the junction of an axon with a dendrite of a different cell. The modulation of the synaptic strength plays a crucial role in learning and memory formation. By adjusting the weight of cells' connections, the neural network can be reconfigurated. The connection strength between network elements is adapted through processes known as learning rules. One type of these processes is the one described by the Hebbian theory where it is postulated that the synaptic modulation is driven by correlations between pre and postsynaptic neuronal activity. Spike-Timing-Dependent Plasticity (STDP) process [39–41,59] is one common protocol to analyze the adaptation of synaptic strength. The initial strength of connection is quantified by measuring the response of the postsynaptic neuron to the application of a measurement pulse to the presynaptic cell. Then, a periodic sequence of presynaptic and postynaptic stimuli, separated by a time Δt, is applied. The effect of such stimuli signals is evaluated by measuring the postsynaptic response to a new test pulse in the presynaptic neuron. STDP describes the dependence of the change of synaptic strength, before and after the treatment, on Δt. In Section 2.2, we review results of a series of experiments [50] with emulated memristors that mimic the STDP process of real biological synaptic junctions.

Classical conditioning is another type of learning theory that relates preceding stimuli and behavioral reactions in animals. Let us assume that there is an unconditioned stimulus (US) that provokes an unconditioned response (UR). There is also a neutral stimulus (NS) that initially does not provoke any response. If the neutral stimulus is presented to the subject simultaneously with the unconditioned stimulus in one or more opportunities, then an association is created and the NS becomes a conditioned stimulus (CS) that, even in the absence of the US, provokes a conditioned response (CR) like the unconditioned one. The typical example from Pavlov's original research is the physiological reaction of dogs in the presence of food [46]. A dog naturally salivates (UR) in the presence of food (US). If, for example, a dog is stimulated by the sound of a bell (NS), no reaction in the digestive system is found. However, if the food is accompanied by a bell sound in several opportunities, the dog learns to associate the bell to food. Then, the sound of the bell becomes a CS that provokes salivation in the absence of food (CR).

There are many examples of neuromorphic circuits involving memristors that appear to mimic Pavlovian learning [31,43–45,60,61]. Tan et al. [45] note that Pavlovian conditioning comprises three different behaviors: (1) acquisition of the association by training trials where NS and US are either simultaneous or close in time, (2) extinction of the association (forgetting) when CS is applied alone, and (3) recovery by a training process after the last extinction. According to Tan and colleagues, no previous works addressed all three features of classical learning.

Figure 3 shows a block diagram of the experimental setup identical to that in Hu et al. [43]. The unconditioned stimulus is fed into neuron 3 through synapse 1. Since the response to the US is innate and assumed to be unchangeable, synapse 1 is simply implemented as a constant resistor. The conditioned stimulus is fed into neuron 3 through synapse 2. Given that actual conditioning occurs in this synapse, its implementation is slightly more complex and it involves a memristor. Moreover, this synapse receives feedback from neuron 3. The output of the experimental setup is a simple comparator that gives a binary signal (salivation/no-salivation) based on the output of neuron 3. In Section 2.3, we show that the simplified model in Equations (2)–(5) is useful to reproduce the essence of classical conditioning when used to emulate the memristor in Figure 3. A detailed description of the experimental setup, including circuits schematics, is given in Section 3.2.

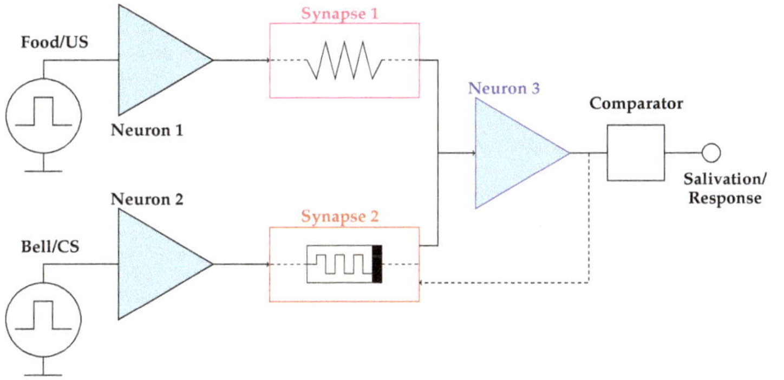

Figure 3. Block diagram of the system used to mimic Pavlovian learning [43].

2. Results and Discussion

2.1. Validation of the Emulation Architecture

We verified the correctness of the emulator design by implementing the memristor model introduced in Section 1.1 and comparing the resulting measurements with numerical simulations. The circuit schematic of the experimental setup and typical measurements are shown in Figure 4. The circuit under test, shown in Figure 4a, is comprised of an arbitrary wave generator that feeds the emulator device with a sinusoidal signal and an in-series measuring resistance that tracks the flowing current. Figure 4b shows experimental results for two driving frequencies. It can be seen that the rate at which the driving signal changes influences the apparent switching threshold [62]. In order to validate the memristor emulator, we solved Equations (2)–(5) numerically. These results are presented in Figure 4b showing a good agreement with the emulator results.

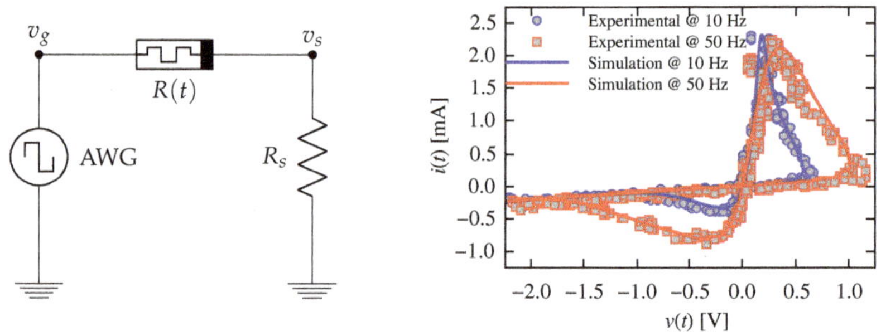

(**a**) Experimental setup

(**b**) Typical hysteresis cycles

Figure 4. Emulator results: (**a**) experimental setup. The circuit under test is driven by an arbitrary waveform generator (AWG). Current through the memristor is measured as a voltage drop on an in-series resistor $R_s = 1\ \text{k}\Omega$. (**b**) circuit current vs. memristor voltage: simulation (solid line) and measured emulator (points) results. The AWG provides a variable frequency sinusoidal signal with amplitude $A = 2.5$ V. The switching thresholds move towards higher voltage values when the input frequency increases. Parameters were set to $\alpha_\pm = 15\ \text{V}^{-1}$, $\delta_\pm = 0.2$ V, $R_{\text{on}} = 35\ \Omega$, $R_{\text{off}} = 9.5\ \text{k}\Omega$, $v_0 = 0.3$ V, and $\tau_0 = 0.01$ s.

2.2. Synapse Mimicking

Part of the material in this section was already presented in Ref. [50]. The main goal is to reproduce the STDP process by an appropriate pulsing experiment with the memristor playing the role of the synapse. We used a simple circuit comprising an arbitrary waveform generator, a resistor, and the memristor emulator as it is schematized in Figure 4a. We applied a 500 ms-period signal consisting of two stimulus pulses, one positive (the presynaptic stimulus) and one negative (the postsynaptic stimulus). The signal also included two measurement pulses, one of them 50 ms before the presynaptic pulse and the other 50 ms after the postsynaptic stimulus. While the stimuli were 50 ms-wide and had an absolute amplitude of 1.5 V, the measurement pulse was only 25 ms-wide and 200 mV high. Pulse duration was partly determined by the frequency limitations of the emulator circuit (see Section 3.1). The measurement pulse amplitude was chosen in order to avoid a significant resistance change. Figure 5 shows a particular example where two stimuli overlap for $\Delta t = 25$ ms. Figure 5 also shows results tracking the current flowing through the emulator. As expected, the transient response of the current corresponds to the resistance change of the emulator. Let us remark that the results in Figure 5, as well as the results in all the remaining figures of this work, were experimentally obtained on the basis of emulated memristors.

Having fixed the pulsing protocol, model parameters were chosen on a trial and error basis, aiming to obtain the desired synapse-like behavior: $\alpha_\pm = 30\ \text{V}^{-1}$, $\delta_\pm = 0.75$ V, $R_{\text{on}} = 1\ \text{k}\Omega$, $R_{\text{off}} = 5\ \text{k}\Omega$, and $v_0 = 0.2$ V. Since we are interested on the influence of the device's response time, τ_0 was varied. In order to understand the behavior of the memristor with the selected parameters, Figure 6 shows experimental results, measured on the emulator, for different values of τ_0. The experimental setup is the same as in Figure 4a, where a sinusoidal signal is applied. The frequency (1 Hz) and amplitude (1.5 V) were set to be commensurate to those in the pulsing experiment. It is interesting to compare the resulting curves in Figure 6 with those in Figure 4b. Whereas in the latter case R_{on} and R_{off} are attained in each cycle (as evidenced by the same extreme slopes for both driving frequencies), in the former case, the memristance changes between two intermediate values. Moreover, the two extreme resistance values depend on the response time τ_0.

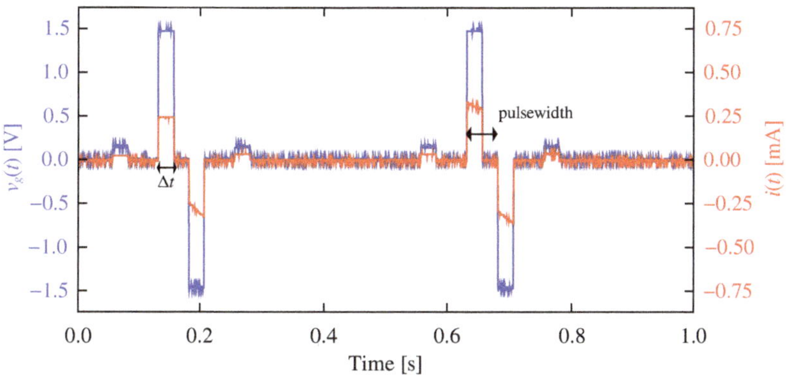

Figure 5. Driving signal v_g and current i flowing through the emulator. Two 50 ms-wide and 1.5 V-high stimulus pulses and two 25 ms-wide and 200 mV-high measurement pulses comprise each period. In this example, $\Delta t = 25$ ms and the pre and postynaptic stimuli overlap for 25 ms. Parameters: $\alpha_\pm = 30\ \text{V}^{-1}$, $\delta_\pm = 0.75$ V, $R_{\text{on}} = 1$ kΩ, $R_{\text{off}} = 5$ kΩ, $v_0 = 0.2$ V, and $\tau_0 = 10$ s.

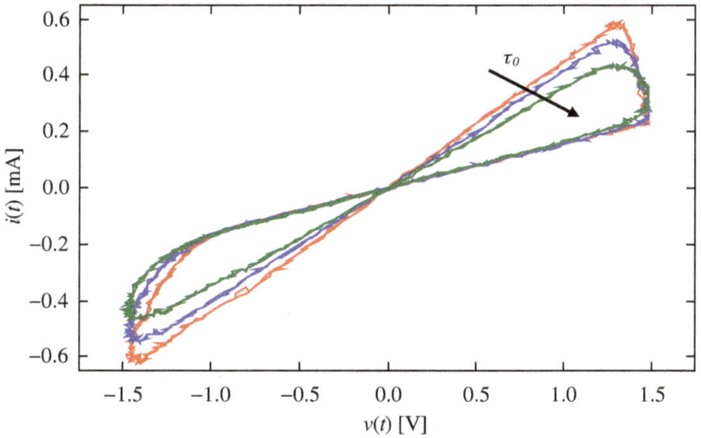

Figure 6. Circuit current vs. memristor voltage: measured emulator results. The AWG provides a 1 Hz sinusoidal signal with amplitude $A = 1.5$ V. Parameters were set to $\alpha_\pm = 30\ \text{V}^{-1}$, $\delta_\pm = 0.75$ V, $R_{\text{on}} = 1$ kΩ, $R_{\text{off}} = 5$ kΩ, and $v_0 = 0.2$ V. The device's response time was varied: $\tau_0 = 5, 10, 20$ s (red, blue, and green lines, respectively). Extreme memristance values depend on the value τ_0.

Let us now return to the pulsing protocol in Figure 5. For a fixed Δt, we applied a driving signal that was composed of several periods of the stimulus signal. In this way, we studied the relation between Δt and the resistive change of the device. Figure 7 shows the resistance behavior during the first eight periods for two Δt and a pair of different initial conditions. The figure shows that the final value of the resistance is sensitive to the delay Δt but not to the initial setting. We thoroughly characterized this behavior by exciting the memristor with 20 consecutive periods of the stimulus signal and changing the value of Δt. Figure 8 shows the relation between the final resistance and Δt. In particular, we show results for $\tau_0 = 5$, 10, and 20 s (see Equations (2)–(5)). As it can be seen, the behavior depends on whether Δt is smaller or greater than the pulsewidth (50 ms). Whenever there is destructive interference between the pre and postsynaptic stimuli ($|\Delta t| < 50$ ms), the final state exhibits a strong dependence on $|\Delta t|$. However, no such dependence is observed when $|\Delta t| > 50$ ms and only τ_0 influences the final resistance.

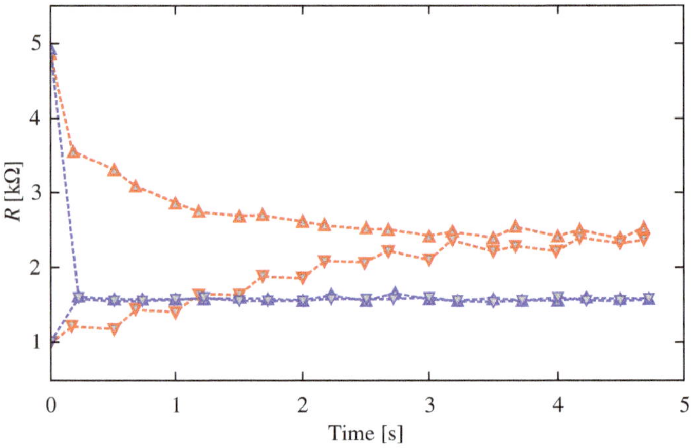

Figure 7. Behavior of the resistance. Initial conditions are indicated by the upside (=R_{off}) and downside (=R_{on}) triangles. Red and blue colors stand for Δt = 5 ms and Δt = 50 ms, respectively. All experimental parameters were as in Figure 5 except that τ_0 = 5 s.

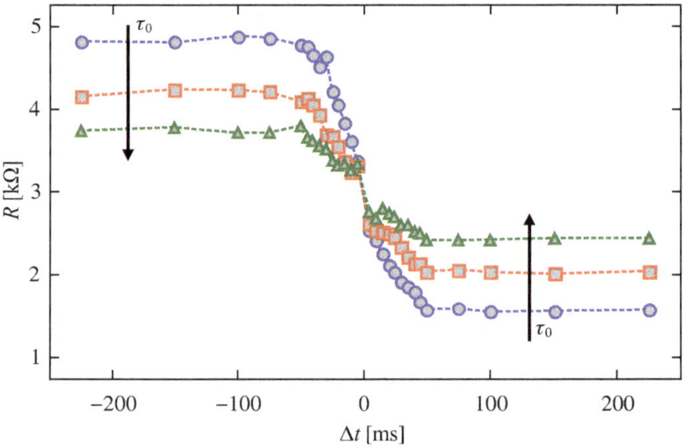

Figure 8. Influence of Δt on the emulator resistance for τ_0 = 5 (blue), 10 (red) and 20 s (green). The initial setting was 5 kΩ and the remaining experimental parameters were as in Figure 5.

Figure 9 shows the influence of Δt and τ_0 on the ratio of change of the resistance in relation to its final state. Since the measured behavior of the resistance as a function of Δt is qualitatively similar to that observed in real neurons, we believe that memristive devices that are modeled by this type of dynamic behavior are suitably to be used in neuromorphic circuits inspired by the STDP process. As the final state of resistance is affected by the parameter τ_0, it will affect the resistance change ratio. The change of resistance decreases as τ_0 increases.

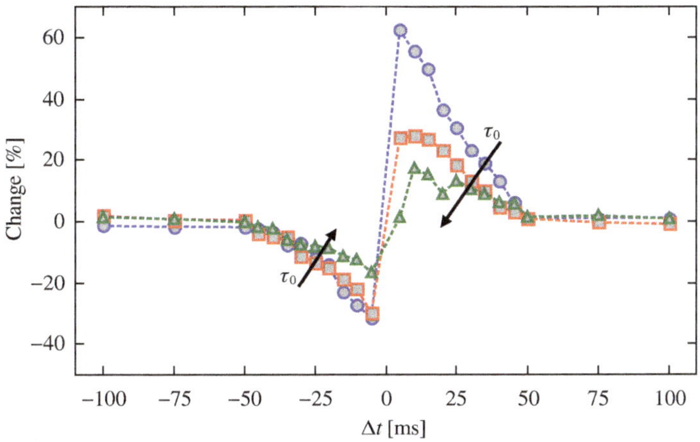

Figure 9. Percentage of change of the resistance vs. Δt for characteristics times $\tau_0 = 5$ (blue), 10 (red), and 20 s (green). The larger the τ_0, the weaker the learning rule.

2.3. Classical Conditioning

In this section, we show that the simplified model in Equations (2)–(5) is useful to reproduce the essence of classical conditioning. Figure 3 shows a block diagram of the experimental setup identical to that in Ref. [43]. Details of the experimental setup are given in Section 3.2.

Figure 10 shows typical results of our experimental setup for Pavlovian conditioning. Results are grouped into four blocks. In the first block, in the absence of association, the bell (signal V_b) is a neutral stimulus that does not provoke any response (no salivation in the last row). In the second block, the unconditioned stimulus (food, V_f) is accompanied by the unconditioned response. Although the bell follows immediately after the US has disappeared, no association is produced and there is no response to the neutral stimulus. In the third block, food and bell are simultaneous and the association is acquired: there is a conditioned response to the conditioned stimulus even after the unconditioned stimulus has disappeared. Moreover, after a lapse in which CS is applied alone, the association is forgotten. Finally, in the fourth block, the association is recovered. Note that the forgetting process takes longer than in the third block, which corresponds intuitively to the reinforcement of the association. In summary, all three features described by Tan et al. [45] as necessary for classical conditioning are present, viz. acquisition, extinction and recovery of the association.

One of the advantages of using an emulator instead of an actual memristor is the possibility of changing model parameters easily. It is this advantage that allows us to study the influence of the characteristic response time of the memristor τ_0 on learning time and memory persistence. Figure 11 shows results for the same experimental setup as in Figure 10. Memory persistence is measured as the number of input bell pulses, after the food stimulus has disappeared that produces a conditioned response. Since small random variations may produce changes in the measurements, Figure 11 presents results of ten experiments. Although it can be expected that, as τ_0 increases, the memory lasts longer, Figure 11 seems to exhibit a different picture. However, the fact is that, as τ_0 increases, it takes longer to produce a strong association between the conditioned stimulus (bell) and the conditioned response (salivation). Weaker association for larger memristor response time is reflected in shorter memory persistence. Even in Block 3, no association is learned when $\tau_0 = 20\,\mathrm{s}$. Longer memory persistence in Block 4 is due to the strengthening of association after a second round of training.

In order to evaluate memory persistence without the confounding element of learning time, we conducted a different set of experiments where the system departs from a strong association (low memristor resistance, $\sim$1 kΩ). At the beginning of each experiment, both the unconditioned and conditioned stimuli are present for five pulses. After this association-strengthening period, both stimuli are interrupted for a variable lapse (measured as number of absent stimulus pulses or blank spaces). Finally, only the conditioned stimulus is enabled again after the no-stimuli lapse. Memory persistence is measured as the number of CS pulses that produce a response in this final period of the experiment. Figure 12 shows a typical experiment and Figure 13 shows the results of five experiments. As it can be observed, the learned association persists longer as the characteristic time τ_0 increases, as it intuitively expected. Moreover, there is no significant evidence of a stronger forgetting process as the period without stimuli gets longer.

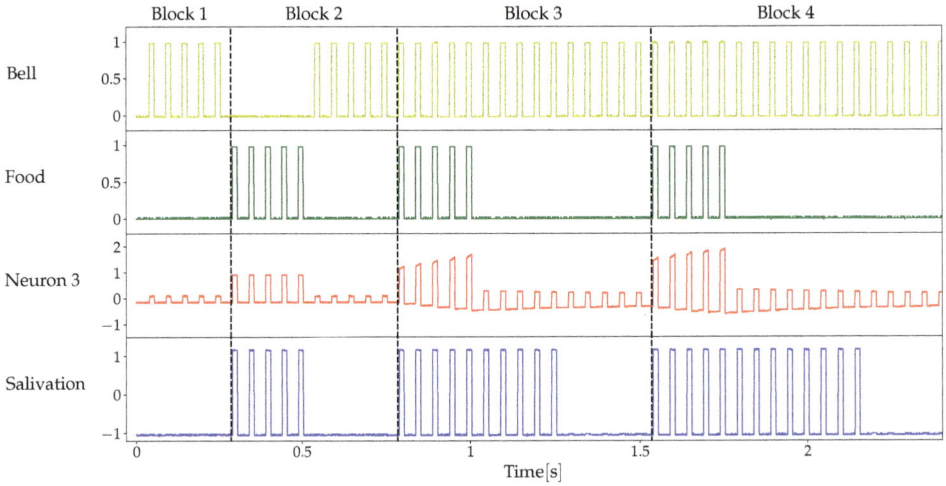

Figure 10. Pavlovian conditioning. When present, stimuli V_f (food) and V_b (bell) are represented 1 V-high square waves with a 20 Hz frequency and 30% duty cycle. Parameters of the memristor model: $v_0 = 0.2$ V, $\alpha_+ = 10$ V^{-1}, $\alpha_- = 5$ V^{-1}, $\delta_+ = 0.7$ V, $\delta_- = 0.6$ V.

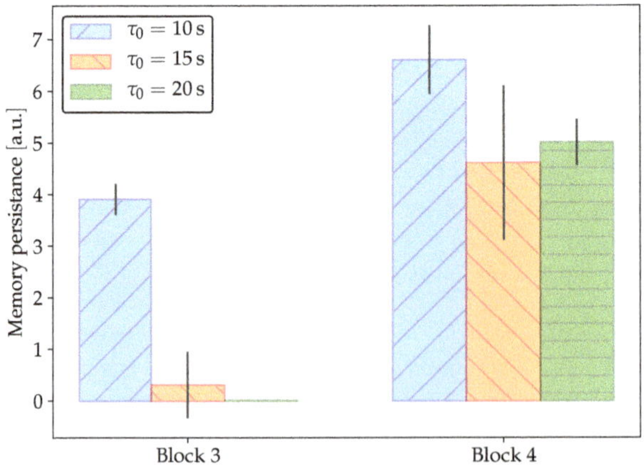

Figure 11. Memory persistence in Pavlovian conditioning. Results correspond to 10 experiments in the same conditions as in Figure 10. As the characteristic response time of the memristor, τ_0, increases, it takes longer to produce a strong association between the conditioned stimulus (bell) and the conditioned response (salivation).

The characteristic response time τ_0 varies between the different memristive systems. Amorphous silicon devices present τ_0 values of the order of 10^3 to 10^4 s [63,64], HfO_x/AlO_x structures of the order of 10^2 s [65], and Ti/HfO/Pt of the order of 1 s [66]. Moreover, many devices present a highly asymmetric behavior between ON/OFF switching times [67]. For these reasons, it is important to perform preliminary characterizations of the neuromorphic circuit to be implemented. Our results suggest that applications, where the information is to be retained for the longest time, should be based on devices with high τ_0 value. However, this has the disadvantage that the resulting learning rules are going to be weaker. On the other hand, in applications where the reconfiguration of the connections is dynamic and it is expected to obtain appreciable changes in short times, the design should be based on devices with low τ_0 where the learning rules are stronger.

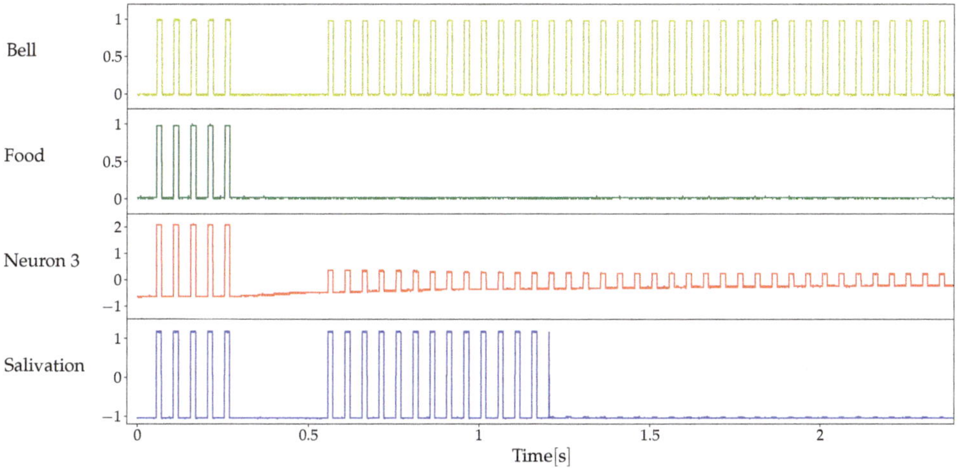

Figure 12. A typical example of the experiments to quantify memory persistence. After both stimuli are interrupted, only the conditioned stimulus (bell's sound) is re-enabled. In this case, there are five blank spaces (no-stimuli lapse) and the memory persistence is measured as 14. Model parameters are as in Figure 10, except for $\tau_0 = 20$ s.

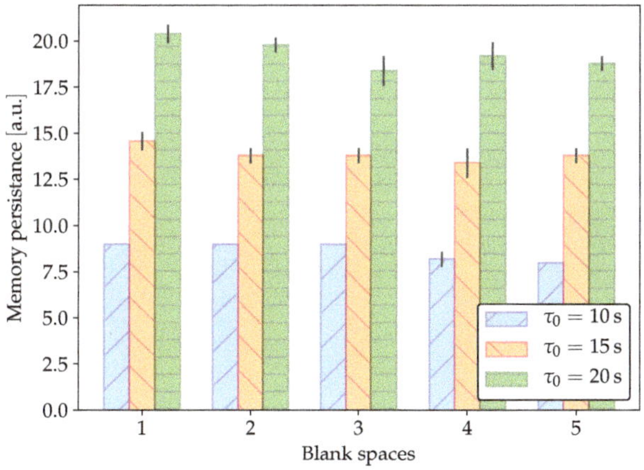

Figure 13. Memory persistence in Pavlovian conditioning. Results correspond to five experiments in the same conditions as in Figure 12.

3. Materials and Methods

3.1. Details of the Emulator Architecture

Figure 2 shows the schematic of the emulator design. A detailed description and analysis of the architecture of the emulator can be found in Ref. [50]. Time steps of the numerical integration algorithm are limited by the computation speed of the microprocessor. For this reason, we resorted to one of the fastest Arduino boards, the Arduino Due with an Atmel SAM3X8E processor running at 84 MHz [68]. The resulting integration time step was ∼400 µs and, hence, frequency of input signals are required to be $\ll$ 2.5 kHz.

We used a Renesas X9C103P [69] potentiometer that accepts bipolar voltage signals and has 100 possible resistance values between ∼35.0 Ω and ∼9.5 kΩ. Although we found this potentiometer adequate for our current implementation, it would be convenient to upgrade future designs with a higher resolution potentiometer.

The code used to interact with the digital potentiometer was developed by Timo Fager [70]. The X9C103P potentiometer is controlled by an external clock that sequentially changes the resistance by increment or decrement steps. The larger the change in resistance, the longer it takes to realize it due to this sequential programming feature, leading to larger integration time steps. Larger time steps, in turn, limit the highest admissible frequency of the input signals.

Analog-to-digital converters (ADCs) of the Arduino Due admit inputs only between 0.0 and 3.3 V. To prevent damage and malfunction of the microprocessor, there is a signal conditioner circuit to adapt the sensed voltage to adequate signal levels (see Figure 2). Essentially, the signal is buffered, attenuated and biased to comply with the ADC input range.

Measurement errors also limit the emulation accuracy. We found measurement errors much higher than the ADC resolution of the Atmel SAM3X8E microcontroller (12 bits, LSB < 1 mV) due to several noise sources, suggesting that a better noise-resistant circuit design is needed, especially in signal adaptation stage in Figure 2. One of the possible noise sources is due to digital clock feedthrough. Noise problems were somewhat alleviated with low pass filters.

The model described in Section 1.1 is implemented in Arduino Due using a semi-implicit Euler integration algorithm. Algorithm 1 shows the pseudocode of the main loop. Function SETRESISTANCE() uses the utilities in Ref. [70]. Function READVOLTAGES() reads the results from the microcontroller's ADCs and computes the voltage drop on the potentiometer on the basis of the signal adaptation circuit (see Figure 2). The remaining functions are explained in Algorithms 2 and 3.

Algorithm 1 Model implementation in Arduino Due: Main loop

```
while True do
    Δt = TIMEMEASURE()                  ▷ Computes the actual integration time step
    v = READVOLTAGES()                  ▷ Reads voltage adapted at the ADC's input
    R = UPDATERESISTANCE(v,Δt)          ▷ Integrates the differential equation of the model
    SETRESISTANCE(R)                    ▷ Sets the potentiometer resistance
end while
```

Algorithm 2 Model implementation in Arduino Due: Integration time step

```
function TIMEMEASURE
    t = micros()                        ▷ Read microcontroller's running time in microseconds
    Δt = t − t_old                      ▷ Time step
    t_old = t
    return Δt
end function
```

Algorithm 3 Model implementation in Arduino Due: Numerical Integration

function UPDATERESISTANCE(v,Δt)

$\Gamma^{+} = \frac{1}{1+e^{-\alpha_{+}(v-\delta_{+})}}$

$\Gamma^{-} = \frac{1}{1+e^{-\alpha_{-}(v+\delta_{-})}}$

$\lambda = \min\left\{\Gamma^{-}, \max\left[\lambda_{\text{old}}, \Gamma^{+}\right]\right\}$

$\tau = \tau_0 \exp\left(-\frac{|v|}{v_0}\right)$

$w = \frac{\tau w_{\text{old}} + \Delta t \lambda}{\Delta t + \tau}$

$R = R_{\text{on}} w + R_{\text{off}}(1 - w)$

$w_{\text{old}} = w$

$\lambda_{\text{old}} = \lambda$

return R

end function

3.2. Details of the Conditioned Learning Experiment

Figure 3 shows a block diagram of the experimental setup identical to that in Ref. [43] and Figure 14 shows a schematic of our implementation. We must note that Figure 14 shows only the outputs of neurons 1 and 2 in Figure 3: V_f is the response of neuron 1 to the unconditioned stimulus (i.e., food) and V_b is the response of neuron 2 to the conditioned stimulus (i.e., bell sound).

The unconditioned stimulus V_f is fed into neuron 3 through synapse 1. Since the response to the US is innate and assumed to be unchangeable, synapse 1 is simply implemented as a constant resistor R_{syn}. The conditioned stimulus V_b is fed into neuron 3 through synapse 2. Since actual conditioning occurs in this synapse, its implementation is slightly more complex and it involves an emulated memristor R_m instead of a constant resistor. Since the strength of the input to neuron 3 depends on the voltage divider formed by R_c and R_m, the input becomes stronger as R_m decreases. The constant voltage source V_{forget} tries to force the memristor in high resistance values. In this sense, V_{forget} acts as a forgetting drive that is always present. The state of R_m can also be altered by the feedback from the output of neuron 3, which is the actual source of association between salivation and the CS.

Simple calculations show that the voltage drop on the memristor is

$$V_m = \frac{R_s}{R_s + R_{\text{syn}}} V_f + V_b + V_{\text{forget}}. \tag{6}$$

Observe that V_m is independent of R_m and it depends only on the stimuli. This fact implies that the learning (or forgetting) process is independent of the state of the association between NS/CS and the response.

The output of neuron 3 is fed into a comparator in order to obtain a binary output (V_{out}) such that a high level corresponds to a (conditioned or unconditioned) response to stimuli.

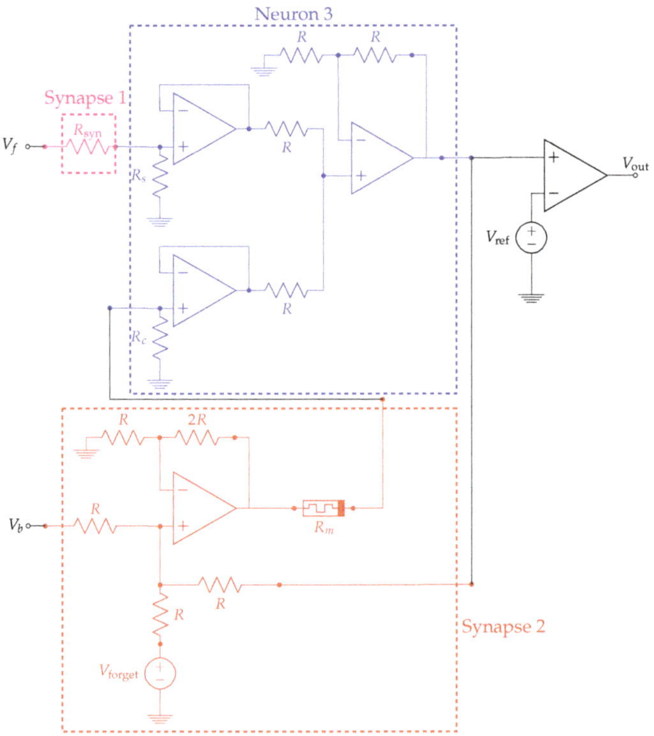

Figure 14. Circuit schematic of the system used to mimic Pavlovian learning. Only the output of the input neurons is represented: V_f is the response of neuron 1 to the unconditioned stimulus (i.e., food) and V_b is the response of neuron 2 to the conditioned stimulus (i.e., bell's sound)—cf. Figure 3. Resistance values: $R = 3.3\ \mathrm{k}\Omega$, $R_{\mathrm{syn}} = 220\ \Omega$, $R_s = 2.2\ \mathrm{k}\Omega$ and $R_c = 2\ \mathrm{k}\Omega$. Constant voltages: $V_{\mathrm{forget}} = 600\ \mathrm{mV}$, $V_{\mathrm{ref}} = 232\ \mathrm{mV}$.

4. Conclusions

It has been argued in the literature that diffusive memristor devices may mimic the behavior of synapses. In this work, we presented a computationally-efficient simplification of an accurate and compact model of such devices. We believe that this model can be very useful in the study of complex neuromorphic circuits and we present its application to two simple examples.

The proposed model was used in a memristor emulator composed of a digital potentiometer and a microprocessor. The main advantage of emulation over simulation is its ability to interact with real-world circuits. In order to validate the correct operation of the emulator, several numerical simulations of a very simple circuit were made under different conditions, finding a good agreement with the experimental results. Although the implemented emulation architecture is simple, it has some limitations. In particular, it is based on a microprocessor with relatively low computing capacity. Future work with more complex circuits or a larger number of emulated memristors will require a faster microprocessor.

The emulated memristor was shown to mimic the Spike-Timing-Dependent Plasticity behavior of synapses. Moreover, it was found that the response time parameter of the memristor, τ_0, affects the resistance change ratio in the STDP process. The larger τ_0, the lower the change of resistance.

Finally, we introduced a memristor-based neuromorphic circuit that exhibited the main characteristics of Pavlovian conditioned learning. We also explored the influence of the response time

τ_0 in learning and memory persistence. In general, the larger τ_0, the longer it takes the system to learn. However, once the conditioned response has been learned, a larger τ_0 leads to a longer memory persistence.

Author Contributions: Conceptualization, G.A.P., P.I.F., E.M. and J.S.; methodology, G.A.P., P.I.F., E.M. and J.S.; software, A.C.F. and A.R.; validation, E.M. and J.S.; formal analysis, A.C.F. and A.R.; investigation, A.C.F. and A.R.; resources, G.A.P. and P.I.F.; data curation, A.C.F. and A.R.; writing—original draft preparation, G.A.P. and P.I.F.; writing—review and editing, E.M. and J.S.; visualization, A.C.F. and A.R.; supervision, E.M. and J.S.; project administration, G.A.P. and P.I.F.; funding acquisition, E.M. and J.S.

Funding: The participation of E.M. and J.S. in this work has been developed within the WakemeUP project (EU-H2020-ECSEL-2017-1-IA), co-funded by grants from Spain (PCI2018-093107 grant from the Spanish Ministerio de Ciencia, Innovación y Universidades) and the ECSEL Joint Undertaking.

Conflicts of Interest: The authors declare no conflict of interest.

References

1. Chua, L. Memristor-the missing circuit element. *IEEE Trans. Circuit Theory* **1971**, *18*, 507–519. [CrossRef]
2. Chua, L.O.; Kang, S.M. Memristive devices and systems. *Proc. IEEE* **1976**, *64*, 209–223. [CrossRef]
3. Chua, L.O. The fourth element. *Proc. IEEE* **2012**, *100*, 1920–1927. [CrossRef]
4. Jo, S.H.; Chang, T.; Ebong, I.; Bhadviya, B.B.; Mazumder, P.; Lu, W. Nanoscale Memristor Device as Synapse in Neuromorphic Systems. *Nano Lett.* **2010**, *10*, 1297–1301. [CrossRef] [PubMed]
5. Querlioz, D.; Bichler, O.; Gamrat, C. Simulation of a memristor-based spiking neural network immune to device variations. In Proceedings of the 2011 International Joint Conference on Neural Networks, San Jose, CA, USA, 31 July–5 August 2011; pp. 1775–1781. [CrossRef]
6. Linares-Barranco, B.; Serrano-Gotarredona, T.; Camuñas-Mesa, L.; Perez-Carrasco, J.; Zamarreño-Ramos, C.; Masquelier, T. On Spike-Timing-Dependent-Plasticity, Memristive Devices, and Building a Self-Learning Visual Cortex. *Front. Neurosci.* **2011**, *5*, 26. [CrossRef]
7. Hu, S.G.; Wu, H.T.; Liu, Y.; Chen, T.P.; Liu, Z.; Yu, Q.; Yin, Y.; Hosaka, S. Design of an electronic synapse with spike time dependent plasticity based on resistive memory device. *J. Appl. Phys.* **2013**, *113*, 114502. [CrossRef]
8. Serrano-Gotarredona, T.; Masquelier, T.; Prodromakis, T.; Indiveri, G.; Linares-Barranco, B. STDP and STDP variations with memristors for spiking neuromorphic learning systems. *Front. Neurosci.* **2013**, *7*, 2. [CrossRef] [PubMed]
9. Bill, J.; Legenstein, R. A compound memristive synapse model for statistical learning through STDP in spiking neural networks. *Front. Neurosci.* **2014**, *8*, 412. [CrossRef] [PubMed]
10. Prezioso, M.; Merrikh-Bayat, F.; Hoskins, B.; Adam, G.C.; Likharev, K.K.; Strukov, D.B. Training and operation of an integrated neuromorphic network based on metal-oxide memristors. *Nature* **2015**, *521*, 61. [CrossRef]
11. Saïghi, S.; Mayr, C.G.; Serrano-Gotarredona, T.; Schmidt, H.; Lecerf, G.; Tomas, J.; Grollier, J.; Boyn, S.; Vincent, A.F.; Querlioz, D.; et al. Plasticity in memristive devices for spiking neural networks. *Front. Neurosci.* **2015**, *9*, 51. [CrossRef]
12. Covi, E.; Brivio, S.; Serb, A.; Prodromakis, T.; Fanciulli, M.; Spiga, S. Analog Memristive Synapse in Spiking Networks Implementing Unsupervised Learning. *Front. Neurosci.* **2016**, *10*, 482. [CrossRef]
13. Shen, J.X.; Shang, D.S.; Chai, Y.S.; Wang, S.G.; Shen, B.G.; Sun, Y. Mimicking Synaptic Plasticity and Neural Network Using Memtranstors. *Adv. Mater.* **2018**, *30*, 1706717. [CrossRef] [PubMed]
14. Kim, Y.; Kwon, Y.J.; Kwon, D.E.; Yoon, K.J.; Yoon, J.H.; Yoo, S.; Kim, H.J.; Park, T.H.; Han, J.W.; Kim, K.M.; et al. Nociceptive Memristor. *Adv. Mater.* **2018**, *30*, 1704320. [CrossRef] [PubMed]
15. Yoon, J.H.; Wang, Z.; Kim, K.M.; Wu, H.; Ravichandran, V.; Xia, Q.; Hwang, C.S.; Yang, J.J. An artificial nociceptor based on a diffusive memristor. *Nat. Commun.* **2018**, *9*, 417. [CrossRef] [PubMed]
16. Borghetti, J.; Li, Z.; Straznicky, J.; Li, X.; Ohlberg, D.A.; Wu, W.; Stewart, D.R.; Williams, R.S. A hybrid nanomemristor/transistor logic circuit capable of self-programming. *Proc. Natl. Acad. Sci. USA* **2009**, *106*, 1699–1703. [CrossRef] [PubMed]

17. Xia, Q.; Robinett, W.; Cumbie, M.W.; Banerjee, N.; Cardinali, T.J.; Yang, J.J.; Wu, W.; Li, X.; Tong, W.M.; Strukov, D.B.; et al. Memristor-CMOS hybrid integrated circuits for reconfigurable logic. *Nano Lett.* **2009**, *9*, 3640–3645. [CrossRef]
18. Gao, L.; Alibart, F.; Strukov, D.B. Programmable CMOS/memristor threshold logic. *IEEE Trans. Nanotechnol.* **2013**, *12*, 115–119. [CrossRef]
19. Itoh, M.; Chua, L.O. Memristor oscillators. *Int. J. Bifurc. Chaos* **2008**, *18*, 3183–3206. [CrossRef]
20. Muthuswamy, B.; Chua, L.O. Simplest chaotic circuit. *Int. J. Bifurc. Chaos* **2010**, *20*, 1567–1580. [CrossRef]
21. Muthuswamy, B. Implementing memristor based chaotic circuits. *Int. J. Bifurc. Chaos* **2010**, *20*, 1335–1350. [CrossRef]
22. Waser, R.; Dittmann, R.; Staikov, G.; Szot, K. Redox-based resistive switching memories–nanoionic mechanisms, prospects, and challenges. *Adv. Mater.* **2009**, *21*, 2632–2663. [CrossRef]
23. Waser, R.; Aono, M. Nanoionics-based resistive switching memories. In *Nanoscience in Addition, Technology: A Collection of Reviews from Nature Journals*; World Scientific: Singapore, 2010; pp. 158–165.
24. Gale, E. TiO_2-based memristors and ReRAM: Materials, mechanisms and models (a review). *Semicond. Sci. Technol.* **2014**, *29*, 104004. [CrossRef]
25. Lastras-Montaño, M.A.; Cheng, K.T. Resistive random-access memory based on ratioed memristors. *Nat. Electron.* **2018**, *1*, 466. [CrossRef]
26. Abdalla, H.; Pickett, M.D. SPICE modeling of memristors. In Proceedings of the 2011 IEEE International Symposium of Circuits and Systems (ISCAS), Rio de Janeiro, Brazil, 15–18 May 2011; pp. 1832–1835.
27. Kvatinsky, S.; Friedman, E.G.; Kolodny, A.; Weiser, U.C. TEAM: Threshold adaptive memristor model. *IEEE Trans. Circuits Syst. I Regul. Pap.* **2013**, *60*, 211–221. [CrossRef]
28. Volos, C.K.; Kyprianidis, I.M.; Stouboulos, I.N.; Tlelo-Cuautle, E.; Vaidyanathan, S. Memristor: A New Concept in Synchronization of Coupled Neuromorphic Circuits. *J. Eng. Sci. Technol. Rev.* **2014**, *8*, 157–173. [CrossRef]
29. Wang, Z.; Joshi, S.; Savel'ev, S.E.; Jiang, H.; Midya, R.; Lin, P.; Hu, M.; Ge, N.; Strachan, J.P.; Li, Z.; et al. Memristors with diffusive dynamics as synaptic emulators for neuromorphic computing. *Nat. Mater.* **2017**, *16*, 101. [CrossRef] [PubMed]
30. Xia, L.; Li, B.; Tang, T.; Gu, P.; Chen, P.; Yu, S.; Cao, Y.; Wang, Y.; Xie, Y.; Yang, H. MNSIM: Simulation Platform for Memristor-Based Neuromorphic Computing System. *IEEE Trans. Comput.-Aided Des. Integr. Circuits Syst.* **2018**, *37*, 1009–1022. [CrossRef]
31. Pershin, Y.V.; Ventra, M.D. Experimental demonstration of associative memory with memristive neural networks. *Neural Netw.* **2010**, *23*, 881–886. [CrossRef]
32. Kim, H.; Sah, M.P.; Yang, C.; Cho, S.; Chua, L.O. Memristor Emulator for Memristor Circuit Applications. *IEEE Trans. Circuits Syst. I Regul. Pap.* **2012**, *59*, 2422–2431. [CrossRef]
33. Ascoli, A.; Corinto, F.; Tetzlaff, R. A class of versatile circuits, made up of standard electrical components, are memristors. *Int. J. Circuit Theory Appl.* **2016**, *44*, 127–146. [CrossRef]
34. Yesil, A. A new grounded memristor emulator based on MOSFET-C. *AEU-Int. J. Electron. Commun.* **2018**, *91*, 143–149. [CrossRef]
35. Yu, D.S.; Sun, T.T.; Zheng, C.Y.; Iu, H.H.C.; Fernando, T. A Simpler Memristor Emulator Based on Varactor Diode. *Chin. Phys. Lett.* **2018**, *35*, 058401. [CrossRef]
36. Olumodeji, O.A.; Gottardi, M. Arduino-controlled HP memristor emulator for memristor circuit applications. *Integration* **2017**, *58*, 438–445. [CrossRef]
37. Ermini, M.A.; Dhanasekar, J.; Sudha, V. Memristor emulator using MCP3208 and digital potentiometer. *ICTACT J. Microelectron.* **2018**, *3*. [CrossRef]
38. Sánchez-López, C.; Mendoza-Lopez, J.; Carrasco-Aguilar, M.; Muñiz-Montero, C. A floating analog memristor emulator circuit. *IEEE Trans. Circuits Syst. II Express Br.* **2014**, *61*, 309–313.
39. Bi, G.q.; Poo, M.m. Synaptic Modifications in Cultured Hippocampal Neurons: Dependence on Spike Timing, Synaptic Strength, and Postsynaptic Cell Type. *J. Neurosci.* **1998**, *18*, 10464–10472. [CrossRef]
40. Bi, G.q.; Poo, M.m. Synaptic Modification by Correlated Activity: Hebb's Postulate Revisited. *Annu. Rev. Neurosci.* **2001**, *24*, 139–166. [CrossRef]
41. Dan, Y.; Poo, M.M. Spike Timing-Dependent Plasticity of Neural Circuits. *Neuron* **2004**, *44*, 23–30. [CrossRef]

42. Najem, J.S.; Taylor, G.J.; Weiss, R.J.; Hasan, M.S.; Rose, G.; Schuman, C.D.; Belianinov, A.; Collier, C.P.; Sarles, S.A. Memristive Ion Channel-Doped Biomembranes as Synaptic Mimics. *ACS Nano* **2018**, *12*, 4702–4711. [CrossRef]
43. Hu, S.G.; Liu, Y.; Liu, Z.; Chen, T.P.; Yu, Q.; Deng, L.J.; Yin, Y.; Hosaka, S. Synaptic long-term potentiation realized in Pavlov's dog model based on a NiOx-based memristor. *J. Appl. Phys.* **2014**, *116*, 214502. [CrossRef]
44. Wang, L.; Li, H.; Duan, S.; Huang, T.; Wang, H. Pavlov associative memory in a memristive neural network and its circuit implementation. *Neurocomputing* **2016**, *171*, 23–29. [CrossRef]
45. Tan, Z.H.; Yin, X.B.; Yang, R.; Mi, S.B.; Jia, C.L.; Guo, X. Pavlovian conditioning demonstrated with neuromorphic memristive devices. *Sci. Rep.* **2017**, *7*, 713. [CrossRef] [PubMed]
46. Pavlov, P.I. Conditioned reflexes: An investigation of the physiological activity of the cerebral cortex. *Ann. Neurosci.* **2010**, *17*, 136. [CrossRef] [PubMed]
47. Lorenzi, P.; Rao, R.; Irrera, F.; Suñé, J.; Miranda, E. A thorough investigation of the progressive reset dynamics in HfO2-based resistive switching structures. *Appl. Phys. Lett.* **2015**, *107*, 113507. [CrossRef]
48. Miranda, E.; Hudec, B.; Suñé, J.; Fröhlich, K. Model for the Current–Voltage Characteristic of Resistive Switches Based on Recursive Hysteretic Operators. *IEEE Electron Device Lett.* **2015**, *36*, 944–946. [CrossRef]
49. Patterson, G.A.; Suñé, J.; Miranda, E. Voltage-Driven Hysteresis Model for Resistive Switching: SPICE Modeling and Circuit Applications. *IEEE Trans. Comput.-Aided Des. Integr. Circuits Syst.* **2017**, *36*, 2044–2051. [CrossRef]
50. Cisternas Ferri, A.; Rapoport, A.; Fierens, P.I.; Patterson, G.A. Mimicking Spike-Timing-Dependent Plasticity with Emulated Memristors. In Proceedings of the 2019 Argentine Conference on Electronics (CAE), Mar del Plata, Argentina, 14–15 March 2019; pp. 58–64. [CrossRef]
51. Patterson, G.A.; Suñé, J.; Miranda, E. SPICE simulation of memristive circuits based on memdiodes with sigmoidal threshold functions. *Int. J. Circuit Theory Appl.* **2018**, *46*, 39–49. [CrossRef]
52. Miranda, E. Compact Model for the Major and Minor Hysteretic I–V Loops in Nonlinear Memristive Devices. *IEEE Trans. Nanotechnol.* **2015**, *14*, 787–789. [CrossRef]
53. Patterson, G.A.; Rodriguez-Fernandez, A.; Suñé, J.; Miranda, E.; Cagli, C.; Perniola, L. SPICE simulation of 1T1R structures based on a logistic hysteresis operator. In Proceedings of the 2017 Spanish Conference on Electron Devices (CDE), Barcelona, Spain, 8–10 Feburary 2017; pp. 1–4. [CrossRef]
54. Pershin, Y.V.; La Fontaine, S.; Di Ventra, M. Memristive model of amoeba learning. *Phys. Rev. E* **2009**, *80*, 021926. [CrossRef]
55. Pershin, Y.V.; Di Ventra, M. Memcomputing: A computing paradigm to store and process information on the same physical platform. In Proceedings of the 2014 International Workshop on Computational Electronics (IWCE), Paris, France, 3–6 June 2014; pp. 1–2. [CrossRef]
56. Pershin, Y.V.; Castelano, L.K.; Hartmann, F.; Lopez-Richard, V.; Di Ventra, M. A Memristive Pascaline. *IEEE Trans. Circuits Syst. II Express Br.* **2016**, *63*, 558–562. [CrossRef]
57. Jeong, D.S.; Kim, K.M.; Kim, S.; Choi, B.J.; Hwang, C.S. Memristors for Energy-Efficient New Computing Paradigms. *Adv. Electron. Mater.* **2016**, *2*, 1600090. [CrossRef]
58. Schuman, C.D.; Potok, T.E.; Patton, R.M.; Birdwell, J.D.; Dean, M.E.; Rose, G.S.; Plank, J.S. A Survey of Neuromorphic Computing and Neural Networks in Hardware. *arXiv* **2017**, arXiv:1705.06963.
59. Hebb, D.O. *The Organization of Behavior: A Neuropsychological Theory*; John Wiley & Sons Inc.: New York, NY, USA, 1949.
60. Kulkarni, M.S.; Teuscher, C. Memristor-based reservoir computing. In Proceedings of the 2012 IEEE/ACM International Symposium on Nanoscale Architectures (NANOARCH), Amsterdam, The Netherlands, 4–6 July 2012; pp. 226–232. [CrossRef]
61. Ziegler, M.; Soni, R.; Patelczyk, T.; Ignatov, M.; Bartsch, T.; Meuffels, P.; Kohlstedt, H. An Electronic Version of Pavlov's Dog. *Adv. Funct. Mater.* **2012**, *22*, 2744–2749. [CrossRef]
62. Rodriguez-Fernandez, A.; Cagli, C.; Perniola, L.; Suñé, J.; Miranda, E. Effect of the voltage ramp rate on the set and reset voltages of ReRAM devices. *Microelectron. Eng.* **2017**, *178*, 61–65. [CrossRef]
63. Jo, S.H.; Kim, K.H.; Lu, W. Programmable Resistance Switching in Nanoscale Two-Terminal Devices. *Nano Lett.* **2009**, *9*, 496–500. [CrossRef] [PubMed]
64. Gaba, S.; Sheridan, P.; Zhou, J.; Choi, S.; Lu, W. Stochastic memristive devices for computing and neuromorphic applications. *Nanoscale* **2013**, *5*, 5872–5878. [CrossRef] [PubMed]

65. Yu, S.; Wu, Y.; Wong, H.S.P. Investigating the switching dynamics and multilevel capability of bipolar metal oxide resistive switching memory. *Appl. Phys. Lett.* **2011**, *98*, 103514. [CrossRef]
66. Cao, M.G.; Chen, Y.S.; Sun, J.R.; Shang, D.S.; Liu, L.F.; Kang, J.F.; Shen, B.G. Nonlinear dependence of set time on pulse voltage caused by thermal accelerated breakdown in the Ti/HfO2/Pt resistive switching devices. *Appl. Phys. Lett.* **2012**, *101*, 203502. [CrossRef]
67. Strachan, J.P.; Torrezan, A.C.; Miao, F.; Pickett, M.D.; Yang, J.J.; Yi, W.; Medeiros-Ribeiro, G.; Williams, R.S. State Dynamics and Modeling of Tantalum Oxide Memristors. *IEEE Trans. Electron Devices* **2013**, *60*, 2194–2202. [CrossRef]
68. Atmel. *SMART ARM-Based MCU SAM3X/SAM3A Series*; Atmel: San Jose, CA, USA, 2015.
69. Renesas. *X9C102, X9C103, X9C104, X9C503. Digitally Controlled Potentiometer (XDCP)*; Renesas: Tokyo, Japan, 2009.
70. Fager, T. Arduino Library for Managing Digital Potentiometers X9Cxxx. Available online: https://sites.google.com/site/tfagerscode/home/digipotx9cxxx (accessed on 30 May 2019).

materials

MDPI

Article

Self-Organizing Neural Networks Based on OxRAM Devices under a Fully Unsupervised Training Scheme

Marta Pedró [1,*], Javier Martín-Martínez [1], Marcos Maestro-Izquierdo [2], Rosana Rodríguez [1] and Montserrat Nafría [1]

1 Departament d'Enginyeria Electrònica, Universitat Autònoma de Barcelona, 08193 Bellaterra, Spain; javier.martin.martinez@uab.es (J.M.-M.); rosana.rodriguez@uab.es (R.R.); montse.nafria@uab.es (M.N.)
2 Institut de Microelectrònica de Barcelona, IMB-CNM, CSIC, 08193 Barcelona, Spain; marcos.maestro@imb-cnm.csic.es
* Correspondence: marta.pedro@uab.es

Received: 9 September 2019; Accepted: 22 October 2019; Published: 24 October 2019

Abstract: A fully-unsupervised learning algorithm for reaching self-organization in neuromorphic architectures is provided in this work. We experimentally demonstrate spike-timing dependent plasticity (STDP) in Oxide-based Resistive Random Access Memory (OxRAM) devices, and propose a set of waveforms in order to induce symmetric conductivity changes. An empirical model is used to describe the observed plasticity. A neuromorphic system based on the tested devices is simulated, where the developed learning algorithm is tested, involving STDP as the local learning rule. The design of the system and learning scheme permits to concatenate multiple neuromorphic layers, where autonomous hierarchical computing can be performed.

Keywords: memristors; neuromorphic engineering; OxRAM; self-organization maps; synaptic device

1. Introduction

The implementation of electronic synapses is nowadays one of the challenges of hardware-based neuromorphic engineering, which aims to design electronic circuits with a similar architecture and behavior to the one found in biological brains. Within this context, the conductivity of an electronic device with memristive characteristics is identified as the weight or strength of a connection between two neurons (Figure 1), usually within a crossbar array which implements the synaptic matrix layer of an electronic neural network (Figure 2a). An analog behavior of the electronic synapse is desirable to improve the robustness of the network [1–3], showing a large window between its higher and lower conductivities and displaying many accessible conductivity levels in between. The conductivity of an analog synaptic device is then finely tuned according to some learning rule during the training stage of a learning algorithm. Among the different technologies that have been proved to be suitable for synaptic applications, the oxide-based resistive random access memory (OxRAM) technology stands out when analog conductivity changes are required [1–7].

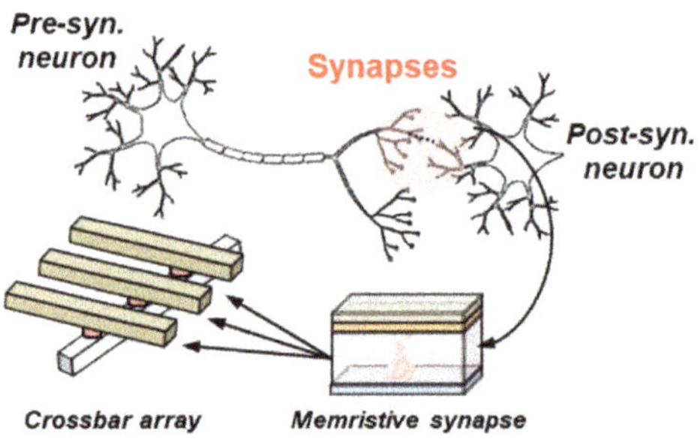

Figure 1. Electronic synapses can be implemented with memristive devices. The electronic neural network is implemented in a synaptic matrix layer.

1.1. Spike-Timing Dependent Plasticity (STDP) in Memristive Electronic Synapses

The synaptic weight updating process is therefore the basis for the application of any learning algorithm in a neural network, and is related to the capability of the synapse to adapt its conductivity through experience, namely its property of plasticity. In the case of electronic synapses, this feature involves the modulation of the conductivity (G) of an electronic device, where changes (ΔG) can be induced by applying the appropriate voltage drop between its two terminals (Figure 2b). These updates in the conductivity of the device are applied according to the recent activity of the neurons it connects. For instance, temporal correlations and causality between the recent activity of the input and output neurons can determine the magnitude and direction of the relative synaptic weight change, $\Delta G/G$. The so-called spike-timing dependent plasticity (STDP) has been reported in biological systems [8–16], and is a popular bio-inspired learning rule implemented in artificial neural networks and computational neuroscience [10–15], where $\Delta G/G$ is described as a function of the time delay Δt between the pre (input) and post-synaptic (output) neurons spike firing, respectively (Figure 2c). The nature of the synaptic change is what depends on the causality between the input and output neurons activations.

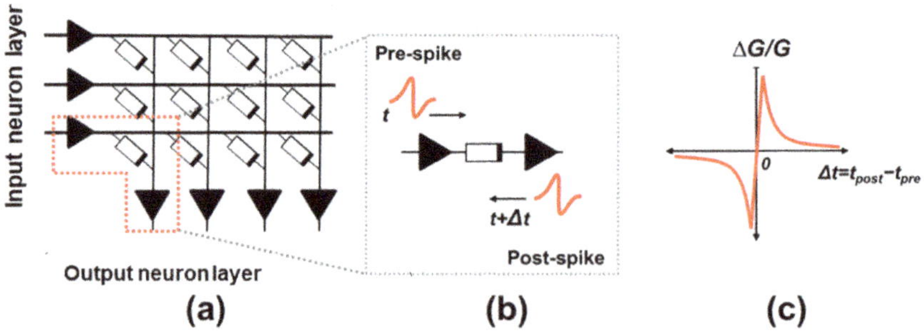

Figure 2. (**a**) Neuromorphic memristive array. Each node within the crossbar corresponds to the weighted connection (synapse) between two neurons, implemented with a memristor. (**b**) The conductivity of the device can be changed according to the activity of the neurons it connects. (**c**) STDP function.

In order to demonstrate the plasticity property of memristive devices, the input and output activities are assumed to be in the form of voltage pulses, and the significant change in $\Delta G/G$ occurs when these pulses meet at the terminals of the synaptic device, overlapping in time, causing a significant voltage drop (Figure 2b). In this case, the STDP function (Figure 2c) can be tuned by changing the shape of the input and output neuron pulses [12–15]. The most popular shape of the STDP, resembling the one reported in a biological culture by Bi and Poo [16] (Figure 2c shows the average of the experimental data), has already been reported in many electronic devices [12,13,17–21]. However, the possibility to tune the STDP function shape, concerning the electronic synapse electrical characteristics, is often skipped. Variety in STDP functions appears in biological synapses [8,12–15]. This variety extends the application of the STDP as a local learning rule in artificial intelligence learning schemes [12], especially in those based on unsupervised techniques.

1.2. Unsupervised Learning and Self-Organizing Neural Networks

Unsupervised learning involves a methodology where the training stage does not require the calculation of any error made by the system for a certain input, in order to improve its performance. That is, both user and system are not meant to know the actual solution of the problem entered to the network, nor detailed information about the input dataset properties, in contraposition with supervised learning techniques. Unsupervised learning implementation would be beneficial for neuromorphic architectures, since on the one hand, it does not rely on the error computation and correction as the supervised learning techniques do, so extra circuitry specialized for this purpose could be avoided. Furthermore, unsupervised learning models, such as the above mentioned STDP learning rule, are considered to be biologically plausible. By reverse engineering simple and primitive biological nervous systems as a first approach, the neuromorphic community would take advantage and inspiration because of the simplicity of their design, compared to the ones found in artificial deep learning neural networks, which present an extremely high density of synapses, neural layers and complex pathways and dynamics. Applications of unsupervised learning algorithms are related to classification, symbolic representation, and associative tasks, usually by extracting the relevant statistical features of the input dataset. Examples of bio-inspired unsupervised learning implementations based on memristive devices for image recognition tasks can be found in [17–21]. However, the hardware-based implementation of other unsupervised learning applications remains unexplored.

A particular example of bio-inspired unsupervised learning is the self-organizing map (SOM), also called Kohonen network [22]. Applications of SOM extend to financial predictions, medical diagnosis, or data mining, among others [22–24]. The aim of this learning algorithm consists in mapping the input dataset onto a regular and usually two-dimensional grid, which corresponds to the output layer, under an unsupervised and competitive learning scheme. A diagram of a Kohonen network is depicted in Figure 3a. In here, the input layer is unidimensional and consists of three nodes (input neurons). The output layer is bidimensional, and each node corresponds to an output neuron. Output neurons can communicate to their immediate neighbors. All of the input nodes have a weighted connection (synapse) with every output node. The weight of the synapse determines how strong an output neuron responds to the activation of a particular input. These neural networks are inspired in the topological maps found in the sensory-processing areas of the brain (Figure 3b), where neurons that respond to similar inputs are spatially located very close. The key of this algorithm consists in evaluating the similarity between the set of weights of an output neuron and the input data, which is fed to the system as a vector. The original software algorithm consists in the sequential execution of the following steps, parting from a network with randomly initialized weights. For randomly chosen input from a particular dataset, the Euclidean distance between the input and the weights of every output neuron must be computed, in order to determine which is the output neuron whose weights are closer to the input. This element is identified as the best matching unit (BMU) and its weights are updated in order to slightly reduce its distance with the input data.

Once trained, these networks present topographical organization such as the one found in sensory processing areas of the brain, such as the tonotopic map found in the primary auditory cortex, in charge of processing sound (Figure 3b). In here, the neurons that respond to similar sound frequencies are grouped in clusters, which appear in a frequency-ordered fashion. In this way, similar inputs activate neurons in the output layer which are found close to each other, whereas dissimilar ones affect distant regions [22,25–27]. The output layer neurons in a trained SOM appear organized in clusters, whose relative size and location provides statistical information of its corresponding input data item characteristics. It is actually the presence or absence of an active response of an output neuron cluster, and not so much the exact input–output signal transformation or magnitude of the response, that provides an interpretation of the input information [22–24].

Many methods are derived from the SOM algorithm, where the neural system is built with SOMs as basic blocks or layers, such as the multi-layer or hierarchical SOM (HSOM) [22]. In the latter case, the network is constituted by concatenating SOMS in a feed-forward way (cascade), where one SOM layer is trained by receiving as input the outputs of another previous SOM. The advantage of HSOMs is that they require less computational effort than a standard SOM to perform certain tasks or problems that present a hierarchical or thematic structure, and moreover, HSOMs provide a simpler representation of the results, which leads to an easier interpretation because they allow the user to check what clustering has been performed at each level of the hierarchy.

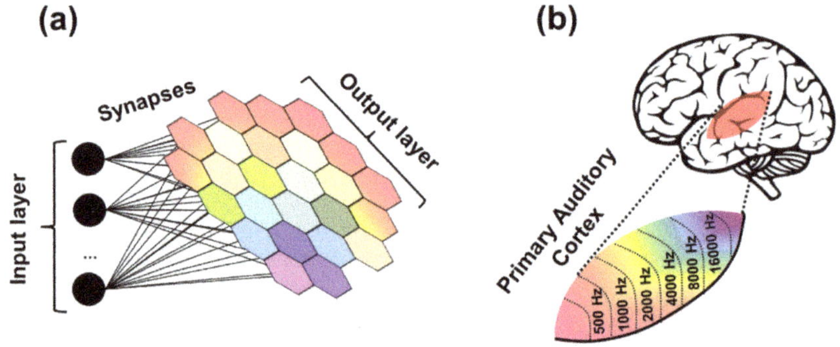

Figure 3. (**a**) Example of a self-organizing map. (**b**) An example of a topological map in the human brain, corresponding to the tonotopic map of the primary auditory cortex.

In this work, we propose an unsupervised hardware adaptation of the SOM algorithm to be implemented in an on-line learning neuromorphic OxRAM-based crossbar array, by means of bio-inspired unsupervised learning methods, being the first of its kind, to the best of our knowledge. There is another work related to the electronic implementation of the SOM algorithm: [28] is also a simulation work, and is based upon the previous calculation of the desired synaptic weight update, hence not being an unsupervised learning algorithm. In contrast, in our work we provide a fully unsupervised learning algorithm, in which the weight updating process relies on the STDP property of the employed memristive devices. For the sake of simplicity, a very simple input dataset is used as an example, for which a color identification task is provided. First of all, a model from a previous work [29] is used to analyze the plasticity property of the tested devices, which is further verified experimentally. A methodology for tuning the STDP function, which is a key element to control the learning process, is proposed. The obtained STDP curves are used as the local learning rules within the adapted SOM algorithm, for which a fundamental application is demonstrated. The learning mechanisms introduced in this work can concatenate multiple SOMs without extra circuitry, providing a step towards the implementation of hardware-based hierarchical computing systems.

2. Materials and Methods

2.1. Electrical Characterization and Device Modeling

The devices employed in this study are TiN/Ti-HfO_2-W metal–insulator–metal (MIM) structures. They were fabricated on silicon wafers either with an oxide isolation scheme or as a single crossbar on a thermally grown 200 nm-thick silicon dioxide. The 10 nm-thick HfO_2 layer was deposited by atomic layer deposition at 225 °C using TDMAH and H_2O as precursors, and N_2 as carrier and purge gas. The top and bottom metal electrodes were deposited by magnetron sputtering and patterned by photolithography. The bottom electrode (BE) consists of a W layer and the top electrode (TE) of TiN on a 10 nm-Ti layer acting as oxygen getter material. The fabricated devices are square cells with an area of $5 \times 5\ \mu m^2$. Figure 4a shows a scanning electron microscope (SEM) (IMB-CNM (CSIC), Barcelona, Spain) image of the tested structures, where the TE and BE are indicated. More details on the electrical behavior and fabrication process of these samples can be found in [30,31].

(a)

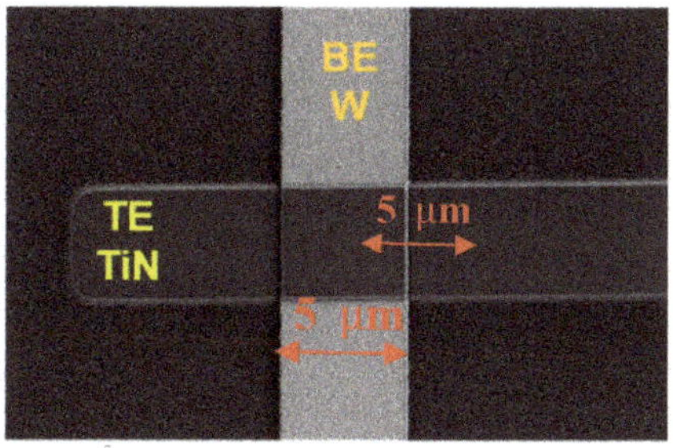

(b)

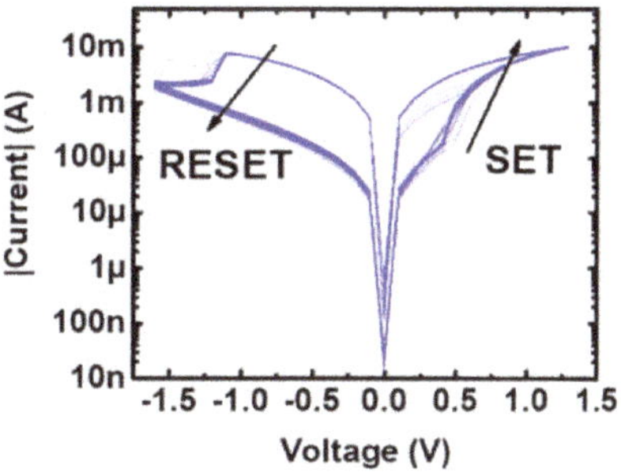

Figure 4. (**a**) SEM image of the tested structure (**b**) Experimental I-V characteristics of the analyzed devices [29]. A voltage limit for the RESET process was set to −1.6V, whereas for the SET process, the conductivity-controlling parameter was the maximum current driving the device (current compliance, I_c) set by the user.

In Figure 4b, a few examples of experimental I–V curves are shown, where it can be noted that the tested devices display a bipolar resistive switching behavior, consisting in transitions from high (HRS) to low (LRS) resistance states and vice versa. These transitions are identified as the SET and RESET processes, respectively. The main results of a previous work [30] show that small changes in the conductivity at the low resistance state (LRS) can be induced by means of controlling the maximum current driving the devices during the SET process, proving their plasticity property, and thus indicating that the tested devices are suitable to play the synaptic role in a neuromorphic crossbar-array. In [29], a pulse-programming setup was proposed, with the aim of analyzing in which ways fine changes in the conductivity of the device can be induced by the application of single pulses. The proposed setup allowed obtaining the experimental G–V characteristics of the tested devices, by means of the application of increasing and decreasing amplitude single pulses with a fixed pulse-width over time. Results from [29] are shown in Figure 5, where the pulse amplitude and the conductivity measured after every single applied pulse (in G_o units, being $G_o = 77.5\ \mu S$ the quantum of conductance unit) are plotted against the number of applied pulses. The conductivity state G was measured after the application of every pulse (Figure 5a, red pulses), by means of applying 50mV (Figure 5b, gray pulses) and reading the current flowing through the device. In the analyzed voltage range, conductivity can take values between ~10 Go and 30 Go.

By means of representing the obtained experimental conductivity as a function of the applied voltage, the experimental the G–V characteristics can be fitted according to the compact model of [32]. In here, the so-called hysteron function is used to describe a time-independent conductivity window as a function of the applied voltage in non-linear memristive devices. An example of an ideal hysteron function of a non-linear memristive device is depicted in Figure 6a. The normalized internal state λ is represented as a function of voltage drop at the memristor. The top and bottom boundaries are identified as the maximum (g_{max}) and minimum (g_{min}) conductivity states. In order to increase (decrease) the conductivity state of the device, a positive (negative) voltage has to be applied so that λ shifts towards g_{max} (g_{min}), describing the Γ^+ (Γ^-) trajectories. The pair of logistic ridge functions Γ^+ and Γ^- can be modeled with two cumulative distribution functions (cdf) [29], related to the pulse amplitudes applied to the non-linear memristive device, being V^+, σ^+ and V^-, σ^- the average and standard deviation values of the cdf related to Γ^+ (for $dV/dt > 0$) and Γ^- ($dV/dt < 0$) curves, respectively.

Both of them define the boundaries of the possible conductivities of the device within a range limited by the minimum and maximum conductivity states, g_{min} and g_{max}, respectively.

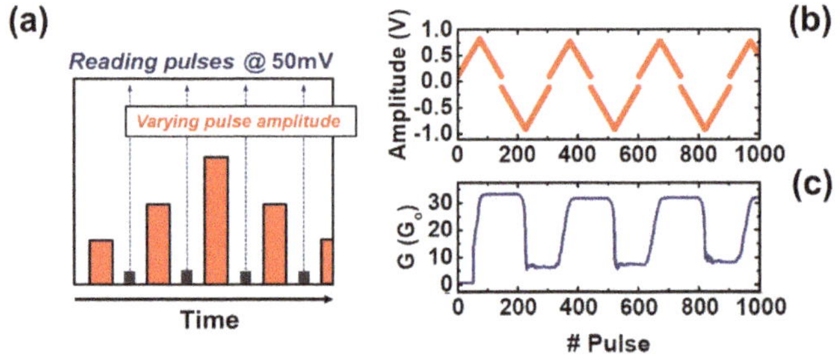

Figure 5. (**a**) Stair-case pulse-programming scheme used in [29] for obtaining the G–V characteristics of a memristive device. (**b**) The pulse amplitude was increased and decreased over time to change the device conductivity. (**c**) Conductivity G as a function of the applied pulses.

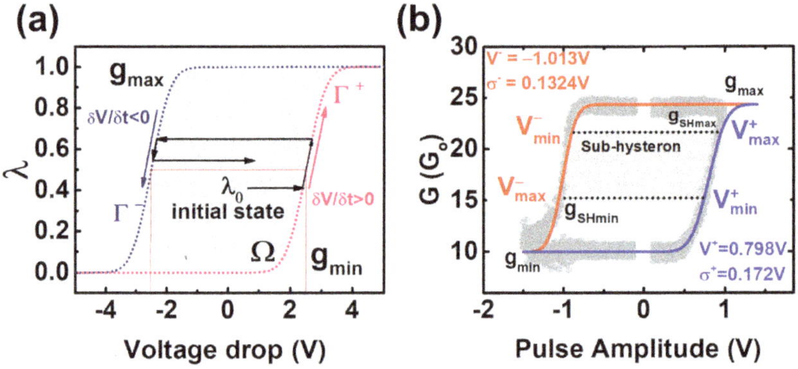

Figure 6. (**a**) Ideal hysteron function of a non-linear memristive device [31]. (**b**) Examples of experimental (gray dots) and an example of a fitted particular case (blue and red lines) G–V characteristics. The fitting parameters $V^{\pm}$ and $\sigma^{\pm}$ are also indicated at the top left and bottom right parts of the figure.

In Figure 6b, examples of the experimental G–V characteristics of the tested device are shown, alongside an example of a fitted curve (continuous lines). In here, a conductivity state sub-space is identified as a sub-hysteron (gray area). The main parameters which allow confining the conductivity of a device within the g_{SHmax} and g_{SHmin} conductivity boundaries as the top and bottom limits of the identified sub-hysteron are $V^{\pm}{}_{max}$ and $V^{\pm}{}_{min}$. Asymmetry of the obtained G–V characteristics can be noted by comparing the mean value on the two cdf, V^{+} and V^{-}, which were used to fit the experimental data to the logistic ridge functions Γ^{+} and Γ^{-}. The obtained time-independent empirical model allows computing the conductivity change of the employed devices when single pulses with varying amplitude are applied, such as the ones required for studying the STDP property of electronic synapses.

2.2. STDP as a Learning Rule

For this application, the experimental STDP windows obtained in [33] were fitted using the above described model. The experimental STDP measurements were obtained by means of applying identical pre and post-synaptic waveforms with a spike width of 1 ms and a maximum voltage of $|0.7V_{peak}|$ (Figure 7a), which corresponds to the voltage required to set the conductivity state of the device at g_{SHmin} ~$15G_o$ (Figure 6b). Two examples of the experimental and modeled STDP functions are shown in Figure 7b. In here, a bias towards synaptic depression is observed. This biasing is related to the asymmetry observed in the G–V characteristics shown in Figure 6b. Also, saturation of the synaptic weight update is observed for small and negative Δt. This occurs mainly because the voltage drop applied to the device is so large in magnitude, that the reached conductivity state after its application is its lowest value g_{min}, so the dependence of Δg with Δt is lost for −0.5 ms < Δt < 0 ms.

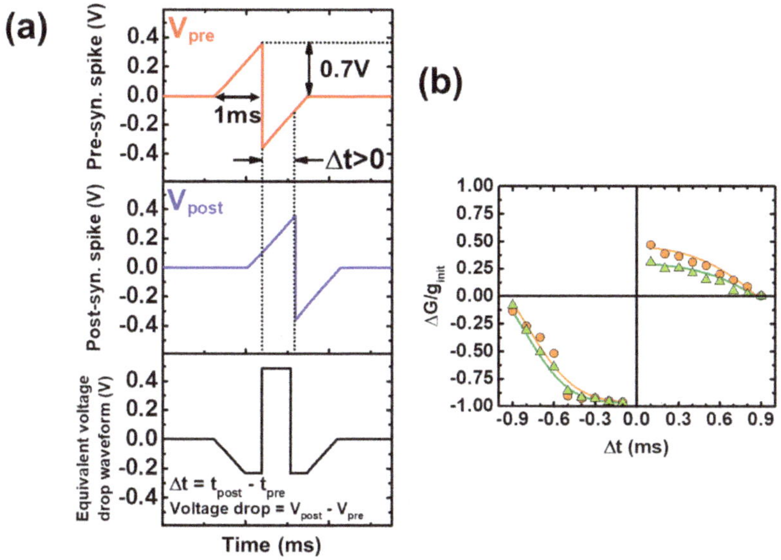

Figure 7. (**a**) Identical pre (red) and post-synaptic (blue) waveforms are applied to the tested samples, which result in an equivalent voltage drop waveform (black) showing a dependence on the time delay Δt. (**b**) Experimental [33] (dots) and modeled (line) STDP functions.

In order to get symmetrical STDP functions, instead of using identical pre and post-synaptic waveforms, we propose using the pair of synaptic pulse shapes shown in Figure 8a (pre) and Figure 8b (post), so the STDP function can be easily tuned in terms of biasing, according to the desired working regime of the employed devices. The resulting equivalent voltage drop applied to the simulated device is depicted in Figure 8c. The maximum and minimum voltage drops at the synaptic device are defined as the $V^{\pm}_{max}$ and $V^{\pm}_{min}$ parameters, respectively (see Figure 6b). By using the proper $V^{\pm}_{max}$ and $V^{\pm}_{min}$ values, a linear operation regime can be achieved (gray area identified as a sub-hysteron in Figure 6b), where the conductivity state can be finely updated according to the STDP rule, and the saturation of ΔG is withdrawn. Moreover, the stochasticity related to the RESET process is avoided. In our case, the following parameters were employed: $V_{pre}^{+} = 0.7$ V, $V_{pre}^{-} = -0.225$ V, $V_{post}^{+} = 0.875$ V and $V_{post}^{-} = -0.25$ V. With these voltages, the conductivity is kept within a sub-hysteron region, in this case ranging from $g_{SHmin} = 0.33$ (13 G_o) to $g_{SHmax} = 0.8$ (22 G_o).

This procedure allows implementing the balanced STDP functions shown in Figure 8e (simulation), where multiple cases involving different initial conductivity values (g_{init}) within the sub-hysteron region are shown. Since there is a dependence on the STDP function shape and g_{init}, the symmetry in the induced conductivity changes has to be checked at the normalized conductivity state of g_{init} ~0.5 within the sub-hysteron region, corresponding to g_{init} ~17.5 G_o in our case. These results support that symmetrical conductivity changes can be induced by using the proposed pre and post-synaptic waveforms, this symmetry being a key factor for increasing the neural network performance [6].

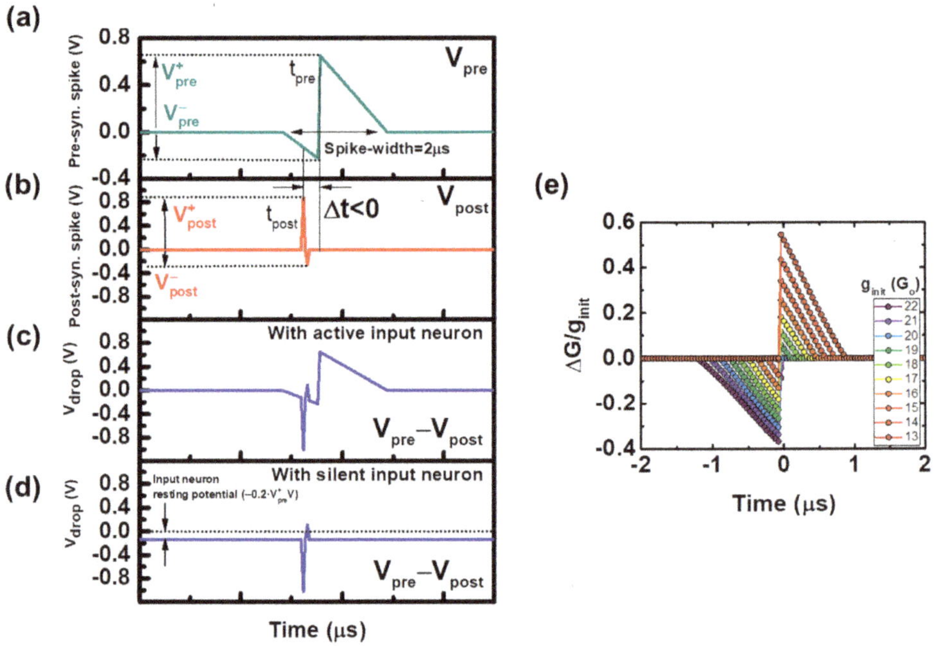

Figure 8. Pair of proposed pre (**a**) and post-synaptic (**b**) waveforms. Resulting voltage drop waveform applied to the sample for an active (**c**) and silent (**d**) pre-synaptic (input) neuron. (**e**) Balanced STDP function. Each curve corresponds to a different initial conductivity state of the same device.

2.3. *Self-Organizing Neural Networks Based on OxRAM with Fully-Unsupervised Learning Training*

The obtained symmetric STDP function in Figure 8e is used as a local learning rule in a proposed electronic implementation of a unidimensional self-organizing map (SOM). The simulated system consists in a single memristive synaptic layer, which is implemented by an OxRAM-based crossbar array. Input and output neurons share the same structure and functionality, so that the neuron layer roles can be interchanged, and multiple synaptic layers can be concatenated without adding extra circuitry.

The neurons are considered to be integrate-and-fire neurons: the received charge is accumulated, which causes the neuron to depolarize along its membrane (membrane potential), until a certain threshold potential is reached. This process is analogous to a capacitor being charged. Finally, due to this depolarization, the neuron is able to transmit an electrochemical signal towards its synapses, thus communicating with post-synaptic (output) neurons. A schematic of the proposed electronic neuron is shown in Figure 9a. It has six input/output terminals: terminals In1 and In4 receive current signals from the previous and following synaptic arrays, respectively. These signals polarize the neuron and update its accumulated charge, related to the membrane potential. The depolarization is monitored by means of comparing the accumulated charge to a charge threshold, Q_{thr}. In the case of an output neuron, when this threshold is reached, the neuron is discharged (its accumulated charge is reset to 0). Then, it triggers a voltage pulse backwards through Out1 and forwards via terminal Out4, towards its synapses. Lastly, I/O2 and I/O3 are communication ports related to the neuron neighbor's activity signaling, providing communication with the neuron immediate neighbors. For instance, if a neuron fires a pulse, its terminal I/O2 and I/O3 flags will be activated, so its neighbors are warned and will consequently trigger a pulse, which is independent of its actual accumulated charge. When this event occurs, the accumulated charge of the neighbors is also reset. The system depicted in Figure 9b is a simple example of a 2 × 2 crossbar array, showing all of the above mentioned connections. The system consists in two neural layers behaving as the input and output layers. The input and output layers are connected through the 2 × 2 memristive crossbar array, where every intersection corresponds to a weighted connection between an input and an output neuron, provided by a memristor. Adjacent neurons within the neuron layers are connected (black wide line) in order to provide lateral interaction, which is one of the key aspects of the proposed hardware-adapted learning algorithm.

For simplicity, a system with a single synaptic layer is considered in this work. The neuron behavior was included mathematically. Implementations of the designs of electronic neurons based in CMOS technology can be found in [34,35]. In the case of a single synaptic layer system, such as the one depicted in Figure 9b, the input neurons of the system are in charge of triggering voltage pulses through terminal Out4 according to the input dataset (signaled via In1), sourcing or draining current from/to the synaptic layer, and have the integrate function disabled, as well as the neighbor interaction. Output neurons integrate the received current through terminal In1, which corresponds to the summation of each of the input neurons voltage pulse, weighted by its connection weight or device conductivity. These output neurons fire a post-synaptic pulse backwards, as a response to the input neurons activity if their accumulated charge reaches the charge threshold, and also communicate with their immediate neuronal neighbors within the output layer via terminals I/O2 and I/O3. Its activity is measured through Out4. Finally, its terminal In4 is left unconnected.

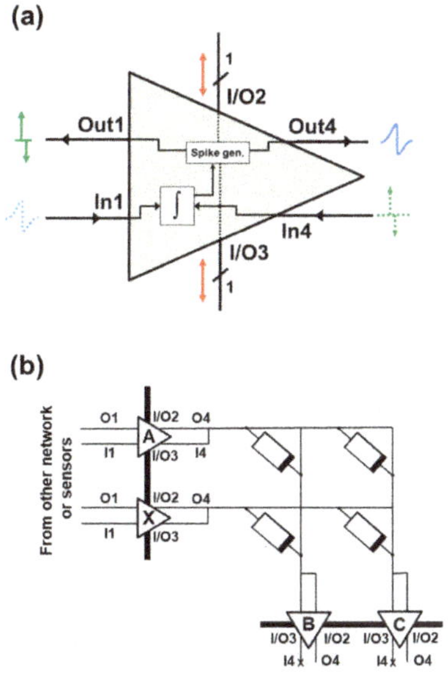

Figure 9. (**a**) Schematic of the proposed electronic neuron, which can play both input and output neuron roles. (**b**) A simplified scheme of the proposed self-organizing neuromorphic network.

A few aspects concerning the learning algorithm are worth to be highlighted: lateral neural neighbor interaction and vertical inhibition within a synaptic column. Lateral neighborhood interaction is one of keys regarding the self-organizing property of the network. According to T. Kohonen in [22], "it is crucial to the formation of ordered maps that the cells doing the learning are not affected independently of each other but as topologically related subsets, on each of which a similar kind of correction is imposed". This means that when one output neuron receives a signal from a neighbor, which has recently fired a voltage pulse, it is also meant to trigger an identical pulse, both to its own connections with the input layer, and also to its other output neuron neighbor. In other words, the output activity of a particular output neuron propagates through the output neuron layer, leading to the activation of its neighbors. The number of affected neighbors can be defined externally, as well as the shape of the neighborhood interaction function.

The implementation of a neighborhood interaction function whose amplitude decays laterally is often used in the software versions of the self-organizing networks (Figure 10). This is motivated by both anatomical and physiological evidence of the way neurons in nervous system interact laterally. The most popular choices for this function include a rectangular (abrupt) interaction function, Gaussian (a soft transition) or the so-called Mexican hat function, which consists in a soft transition involving the inhibition of the outermost neurons within the neighborhood. In our case, the decaying amplitude of the neighborhood interaction function is inherent to our system, because of the implementation of the above described STDP function as a local learning rule. Despite the neighbors of the maximally responding output neuron are intended to fire an identical pulse, this pulse will be delayed in comparison with the response of the main responding neuron (center of the neighborhood). With increasing Δt, the induced $\Delta G/G$ will also decay with increasing lateral distance, as shown in Figure 10. The radius or number of affected neighbors can be set externally by controlling the time delay: the whole neighborhood activity can be delayed (all delayed, AD), and the propagation delay (PD) between immediate neighbors.

In Figure 10, different neighbor interaction functions are depicted as examples considering different types of delay, where ND states for "not delayed". The ND curve corresponds to a function where minimum delays are considered: the main firing output neuron B is firing with an accumulative delay AD of one time unit with respect to the last pre-synaptic pulse sent by neuron A, and the PD is also of one time unit. Therefore, the time delay in which a neuron C within the neighborhood fires a pulse after the main responding neuron A has triggered one, as an answer to an input neuron, corresponds to AD + PD·(N+1), being N the number of neurons which separate neurons B and C. In Figure 10, the distance between neurons B and C is none, thus N = 0. The AD/NPD and AD/PD curves present a delay of AD = 5 time units, so that all the conductivity changes in the neighborhood are diminished equally. The difference between these two functions relies on the propagation delay: AD/NPD has the minimum PD, whereas AD/PD has a PD of two time units. As seen in Figure 10, increasing PD results in a narrower function, reducing the number of affected neurons.

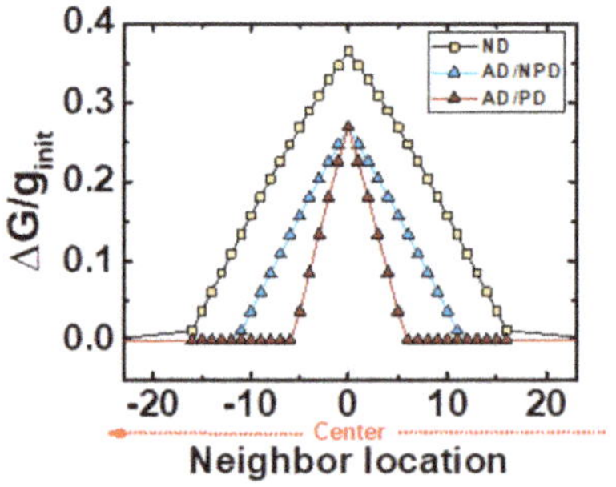

Figure 10. Neighborhood interaction functions based on the STDP rule. The ND curve (yellow squares) shows an example where any delay is considered. AD/NPD curve (blue triangles) consists in a delayed response from the main spiking neuron, but minimum propagation delay. The AD/PD curve is an example of the presence of both delays.

Another important aspect is the inhibition of the synapses within the synaptic column of an active neuron. The synaptic column comprises all of its synapses, some of them connecting the neurons with inactive input neurons. For our system, both potentiation of the synapse, relating the firing neuron with the active inputs, and the depression of its synaptic weights which connect it with the inactive inputs, are mandatory to efficiently group or cluster the output neurons, so that a complete correction of the synaptic weights (and thus, of its neighborhood) is performed. This means that if a particular OxRAM conductivity is increased as a result of applying the STDP rule, the other OxRAMs in that synaptic column, connecting the same output neuron with the inactive input neurons, shall be depressed (i.e., their conductivity is decreased). We refer to this process as synaptic inhibition, which leads to an increase of the sensitization of an output neuron to a single input neuron, facilitating clusters specialization to a specific input property. In order to implement this feature electronically, the silent input neurons at a particular time are not actually silent, but rather applying a small and negative voltage through terminal Out4 to their synapses, in analogy with the biological neurons' resting potential. When an output neuron is firing a pulse backwards, the induced voltage drop at the synapses connecting to a silent input neuron will cause a decrease in their conductivity states. In this case, there is no direct relationship with the STDP rule, since the induced voltage drop at the synapses is not related to any time correlation between the pre and post-synaptic activities.

A sketch of the operation of the 2 × 2 crossbar array with active and silent neurons, where all of these signals are indicated, is shown in Figure 11. In here, the arrows indicate the current flow in the system. The accumulated charge of the output neurons is also depicted. The input neuron layer consists on neurons A and X, whereas the output neuron layer consists on neurons B and C. In Figure 11a, input neuron X fires a pulse through Out4, and input neuron A remains silent. These signals update the accumulated charge of the output neurons B and C. In Figure 11b, input neuron A fires a pulse, and output neuron B accumulated charge reaches the charge threshold, Q_{thr}. In Figure 11c, the accumulated charge of B is reset, and B fires a pulse delayed by a certain delay AD with respect to the firing time of input neuron A. The voltage drop at the synapses within the B column causes a change in their synaptic weights. Then, neuron B communicates with its neighbors (only neuron C is depicted). Finally, in Figure 11d, neuron C triggers a pulse with increased time delay with respect to the firing time of A, AD + PD, and its accumulated charge is reset. Because its pulse presents a larger time delay, the magnitude of the change of its synapses will be smaller, according to the induced STDP function.

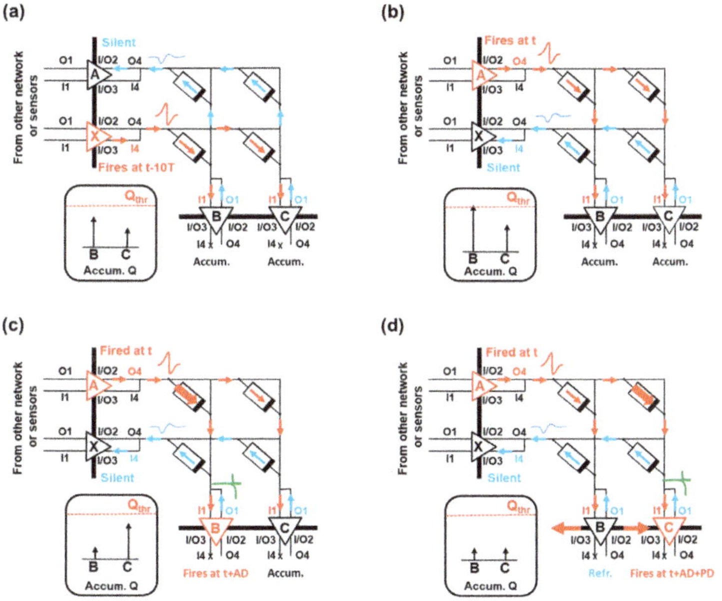

Figure 11. Sketch of the 2 × 2 crossbar array operation. (**a**) Input neuron X fires a pulse through Out4, and input neuron A remains silent. (**b**) Input A fires a pulse, and output neuron B accumulated charge reaches the charge threshold, Q_{thr}. (**c**) The accumulated charge of B is reset, and B fires a pulse delayed by AD with respect to the firing time of A. (**d**) Neuron B communicates with its neighbors (only C is depicted). Neuron C triggers a pulse delayed AD + PD with respect to the firing time of A, and its accumulated charge is reset.

Lastly, the methodology suggested for the unsupervised self-organization process to arise is discussed. The synaptic layer is randomly initialized, that is, the conductivity state of each RRAM device is set randomly between the g_{SHmin} and g_{SHmax} values defined previously in Figure 6b. In order to amplify the initial differences between each output neuron synaptic weight values, the threshold potential has to be set large enough, so that the first post-synaptic firing occurs after the presentation of at least 100 pre-synaptic pulses in the case of our electronic synapses. This value takes into account the initial conductivity state values of the employed synaptic devices, and the voltages required to induce the conductivity change according to the STDP function (Figure 8e).

The active input neurons provide current (red arrows) to the output neuron layer, whereas silent input neurons drain current (blue arrows) from the system because of the polarity of its resting potential. In this way, active inputs depolarize the neurons increasing their membrane potential, whereas silent inputs decrease it (Figure 11a,b). The identification of the best matching unit by means of calculating the Euclidean distance of the whole set of synaptic columns is avoided, which simplifies the electronic implementation of the learning algorithm compared to the original Kohonen's self-organizing learning algorithm, despite a larger number of iterations being required in order to execute this step. On the other hand, if a neuron has recently fired a spike, it will present a refractory period, meaning that it will not be able to fire again after some time, because its accumulated charge has been reset. By doing this, the output neurons which have not fired recently are encouraged to do it. We do not explore the effects of dynamically changing the threshold potential of the output layer. However, a dynamic threshold could improve the performance in terms of convergence time of learning algorithms [36].

The whole training stage is summarized in the flow diagram depicted in Figure 12. Initially, all of the devices are assumed to have a random conductivity around 15–18G_o in our case. The output neurons membrane potentials are also initialized to zero. The input dataset is then fed to the system through the input neurons, which are triggering the pre-synaptic voltage waveform depicted in Figure 8a if active, or applying their resting potential (small negative voltage) to the synaptic array, if silent (as shown in the sketches of Figure 11a,b). The output neurons potentials increase as the output neurons integrate the pulses of the input neurons that they receive, which are weighted by the conductivity of the synaptic devices. That is, the output neurons are receiving a charge whose magnitude is related to the input activity and the weight of the connections between each of them and the input layer. Eventually, one of the output neurons potential will reach the defined charge threshold Q_{thr}. At this point, the weight updating process occurs: the output neuron resets its accumulated potential to zero, and triggers the post-synaptic voltage waveform from Figure 8b backwards, affecting its synapses (Figure 11c). The maximum voltage drop given by this post-synaptic voltage pulse and the active input neuron corresponds to the sum of V^{+}_{pre} and V^{-}_{post} (positive Δt), so this particular synapse is strengthened. On the other hand, the synapses with silent input neurons are depressed, being their voltage drop equal to the sum of V^{+}_{pre} and the input neurons resting potential, which is a DC voltage of $0.2 \cdot V^{+}_{pre}$ V. Therefore, the induced conductivity change in these synapses has a smaller magnitude in comparison with the one induced to the synapse that connects the winning output neuron with the active input neurons. After the weight updating of the main neuron has been executed, its activity is propagated through the output layer, affecting its immediate neighbors. These other output neurons trigger a voltage pulse with the same amplitude, but with a certain accumulated delay (Figure 11d). That is, the magnitude of the change in the strengthened synapses will be decreasing as the output signal propagates through the output layer, until reaching a non-significant synaptic change, following the neighbor interaction function of Figure 10. The affected neighbors will also reset their output potential to zero.

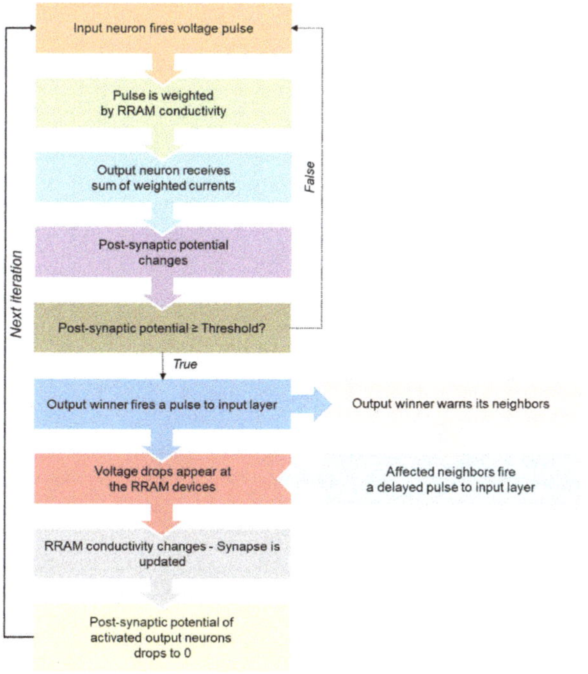

Figure 12. Flow diagram of the self-organizing algorithm based on STDP.

In order to reach a convergence state of the map, the maximum synaptic change is diminished by increasing the firing neuron time delay over the iterations. Also, the size of the neighborhood is naturally decreasing over time, since the neighbor firings are consequently delayed. At the end of this training stage, the crossbar weights are organized in clusters, which present overlapped areas. In this way, nearby output neurons will be prompt to react to the same input, whereas distant output neurons will be sensitized to other inputs, as occurs in the software version of the Kohonen map.

3. Application

A fundamental application of the proposed autonomous SOM is shown as an example. In here, a single synaptic layer system of 150 OxRAM synapses is simulated. The synapses are distributed in a 3×50 array, 3 being the size of the neuron input layer, and 50 the length of the output neuron layer. The input of the system are the red (R), green (G), and blue (B) color components of a pixel of an image. During the training stage, only one of these components is shown at each time, that is, only one input neuron is firing a pre-synaptic pulse (Figure 8a) with the V_{pre}^{+} value as the one shown above (V_{pre}^{+} = 0.7 V), i.e., is active at each time. The silent input neurons resting potential is set to a DC voltage of $-0.2 \cdot V_{pre}^{+} = -0.14$V. These voltage waveforms are weighted by the synaptic devices conductivities, which are randomly initialized between 15 G_o and 18 G_o. The accumulated charge threshold of the output neurons has to be set in a way that only one output neuron reaches this threshold after a certain time. In the case of the simulated system, the accumulated charge threshold is set to Q_{thr} = 1 mC, so that initially only one output neuron fires a post-synaptic spike. This firing is delayed initially by seven time units (being in our case a time unit t = 0.05 μs, so that initially, AD = 0.35 μs) with respect to the pre-synaptic pulse, so that the maximum relative conductivity change magnitude of a 10% according to the STDP function depicted in Figure 8e. The propagation delay PD is kept constant at five time units = 0.025 μs.

Through the iterations, the system is able to self-organize in an autonomous way, without any intervention, being a fully-unsupervised training scheme. After the training stage, the memristors in the column of every neuron within the output layer have a different synaptic weight combination, according to the conductivity states found in the memristors' column of the output neuron. An example of the obtained topographical pattern is depicted in Figure 13. In particular, Figure 13a displays the gray-scale used to represent the synaptic weights of Figure 13b, which are normalized according to the maximum and minimum conductivity values found in the sub-hysteron region of Figure 6b. The highest conductivity states, depicted in white, correspond to $21G_o$, whereas the lowest ones in black correspond to 13.5 G_o, being within the defined range of g_{SH} (13–22G_o). Figure 13b is a representation of the simulated crossbar array after the training, where the synaptic weights are depicted according to the above mentioned gray-scale. The size of this matrix is of 3×50 (3 rows and 50 columns), corresponding to the number of input and output neurons, respectively, which are not shown in this representation. It can be seen that, in each of the three rows of the matrix, the synaptic weights increase and decrease gradually. The synapses with the highest synaptic weights of the three rows are located in different regions of the crossbar array, corresponding to the 24th and 50th output neurons in the case of the first row, to the 15th for the second row, and lastly, to the 46th for the third row. The first row of synapses was connected to an input neuron representing the red color component, whereas the second and the third rows were connected to input neurons representing the green and the blue color components, respectively. Then, nearby output neurons appear to have similar colors components assigned, as expected. Hence, groups of output neurons sensitive to one of the primary colors used during the training stage can be identified.

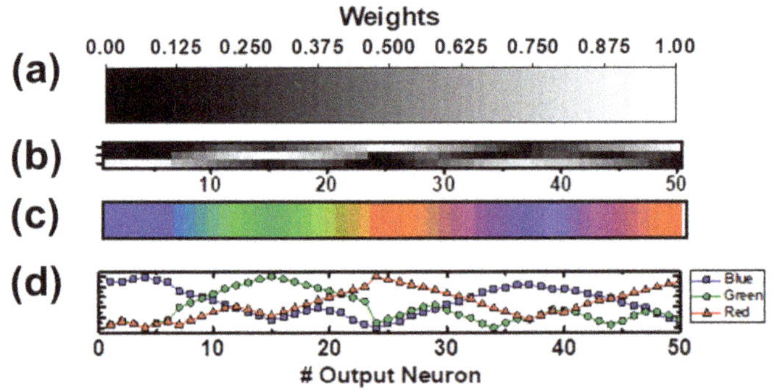

Figure 13. (**a**) Gray-scale used to represent the synaptic weights of the crossbar array. (**b**) 3×50 crossbar array displaying the normalized conductivity states of the simulated OxRAM devices after the learning stage. (**c**) Output neuron layer color assignation. The system shows a topographical or spatial organization of the RGB color components. (**d**) Activation response of the output neurons when a red (red line with diamonds), green (green dotted line), or blue (blue line with triangles) color is presented as an input.

The synaptic weights from every output neuron are related to a RGB coded color, and each of the RGB components is represented by one or two groups of output neurons. The system shows a topographical or spatial organization of the RGB color components. According to Figure 13b, there are output neurons that have a synapse with a large synaptic weight connecting to only one of the three input neurons, whereas their other synapses have a low synaptic weight. This means that these neurons will increase its accumulated charge rapidly, if the input neuron that they are tightly related to shows a strong activity (it fires many pulses in a brief period of time), i.e. these neurons are highly connected to an input neuron, and thus, are highly specialized to a certain color component. Some output neurons, such as the ones found between the 7th and the 13th output neurons, have two synapses with medium synaptic weights, whereas the third one has an extremely low weight. These neurons have a significant relationship with two input neurons, and will respond equally to both of them. If these two input neurons are firing at the same time, because a color consisting of a mixture of green and blue is being used as an input to the system, the output neurons with the two medium-weight synapses will show a stronger response, compared to their response given when only one input neuron is active.

The specialization of the output neurons to a certain input neuron or to a combination of them can be represented by computing the resulting color given by the linear combination of the synaptic weights, relating each of the output neurons to each of the input neurons. The output neuron layer color assignation is represented in Figure 13c, where the color which each of the output neurons is specialized to is depicted. The output neurons' specialization to a certain color component or its combinations can also be checked by plotting their activation pattern, that is, the change in their accumulated charge due to a certain input activity. Examples of activation patterns of the simulated crossbar caused by single input activity, meaning that only one input neuron is active at a certain time, are shown in Figure 13d, consisting in the increment of the output neurons' accumulated charge when a red (red line with diamonds), green (green dotted line), or blue (blue line with triangles) color is presented as an input. By means of comparing the output neurons activation as a response of the input data, the system is able to map and classify any combination of the presented colors to the most similar color cluster (i.e., the one showing the highest activation), behaving as a simple self-organizing neural network, such as the software version of the self-organizing map neural network. It is the activation of a particular region of the output neuron layer, corresponding to a certain cluster of output neurons, which gives the information of which input color is being fed to the system. Since the mapping relies on the activation of a group of neurons, redundancy is actually being added to the system. For instance, if one neuron or some synapse is damaged or has an unexpected behavior, the system performance is not going to be affected by it. In a previous work [37], the training reliability of the proposed algorithm was checked. To do so, in [37], different cycle-to-cycle variability levels were considered, and it was proved that the training algorithm presents a significant tolerance to noise and synaptic variability.

The training stage time can be computed in terms of the number of applied pulses and the time scale of the implemented STDP function. The crossbar array after the training shown in Figure 13b was developed within two presentations of the whole input dataset, consisting of 10^6 pulses of a defined total spike-width T = 2 μs (see Figure 8a), being the time between the input pulses of 10T, which corresponds to a total training time $t_T = 24$ s. The design of the proposed self-organizing map is based on the fact that there is no difference in the electronic design and behavior between the input and output neurons. Because the training scheme is based on hardware-adapted unsupervised learning techniques and the neurons are designed to be able to implement both pre and post-synaptic roles simultaneously (Figure 9a), it is possible to concatenate multiple crossbar arrays, where information flows in a bidirectional manner.

By means of adding computing layers to a self-organizing neural network such as the one presented in this work, hierarchical computation can be achieved. Figure 14 displays an example of a hierarchical SOM system, where the first synaptic layers are constituted by SOMs, such as the color-mapping SOM presented in this work (Layer 1.1), which can also be trained with audio data (Layer 1.2) as to classify the sounds of English vowels. This primary level of the hierarchy (Level 1) pre-processes the information to be fed to higher-order levels, where an associative process between colors and sounds takes place in another SOM, located in Level 2. In other words, the hierarchy permits to develop more complex data structures involving not only the self-organizing property, but also associative learning, which can be summarized as the ability to correlate different memories to the same fact or event [38]. This would represent a step forward towards reproducing complex neural processes and biologically-plausible learning mechanisms in neuromorphic architectures [38].

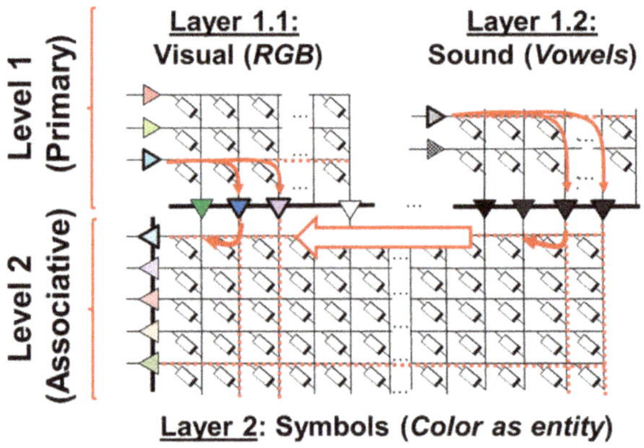

Figure 14. Basic hierarchical computing architecture where the first level (primary) is composed of two memristive synaptic layers, which pre-process the information following the unsupervised algorithm introduced in this work. The output of these layers is fed as the input data of a layer within a higher-order of computation level, where associative learning takes place.

4. Conclusions

Neuromorphic engineering takes inspiration from the biological neural networks learning models, especially when unsupervised techniques are preferred. The most popular learning rule related to unsupervised learning in electronic synapses is the STDP, because it can be easily induced in analog memristive devices, such OxRAM. In this work, a methodology to obtain a symmetrical STDP function in terms of conductivity changes is proposed. It is further applied in the first hardware-adapted version of the self-organizing map (SOM) learning algorithm, which includes other bio-inspired mechanisms in order to achieve topological organization in an autonomous way. This algorithm is performed in a simulated single-layer crossbar array based on the tested devices, for which a fundamental color-mapping application is shown. The introduced system can be potentially used as the basic building block of a multi-layer neuromorphic system, in which hierarchical computing can be achieved without modifying the training algorithm or adding extra circuitry.

Author Contributions: Conceptualization, M.P., J.M.-M.M., and M.N.; Measurements and data analysis, M.P. and M.M.-I.; Validation, J.M.-M.; Writing—original draft preparation, M.P.; Writing—review and editing, M.N. and R.R.; Project administration, and funding acquisition, R.R. and M.N.

Funding: The participation of M.N. and R.R in this work has been developed within the Spanish MINECO and ERDF (TEC2016-75151-C3-1-R). The participation of M.M-I. in this work has been developed within the Spanish MINECO and ERDF TEC2017-84321-C4-1-R. The participation of M.P., E.M and J.M.-M. in this work has been developed within the WakemeUP project (EU-H2020-ECSEL-2017-1-IA), co-funded by grants from Spain (PCI2018-093107 grant from the Spanish Ministerio de Ciencia, Innovación y Universidades) and the ECSEL Joint Undertaking. This work has made use of the Spanish ICTS Network MICRONANOFABS.

Conflicts of Interest: The authors declare no conflict of interest.

References

1. Bill, J.; Legenstein, R. A compound memristive synapse model for statistical learning through STDP in spiking neural networks. *Front. Neurosci.* **2014**, *8*, 412. [CrossRef] [PubMed]
2. Garbin, D.; Vianello, E.; Bichler, O.; Rafhay, Q.; Gamrat, C.; Ghibaudo, G.; DeSalvo, B.; Perniola, L. HfO_2-based OxRAM devices as synapses for convolutional neural networks. *IEEE Trans. Electron Devices* **2015**, *62*, 2494–2501. [CrossRef]
3. Lee, D.; Park, J.; Moon, K.; Jang, J.; Park, S.; Chu, M.; Kim, J.; Noh, J.; Jeon, M.; Hun , B.; et al. Oxide based nanoscale analog synapse device for neural signal recognition system. In Proceedings of the IEEE International Electron Devices Meeting (IEDM), Washington, DC, USA, 4–7 December 2015.

4. Jo, S.H.; Chang, T.; Ebong, I.; Bhadviya, B.B.; Mazumder, P.; Lu, W. Nanoscale memristor device as synapse in neuromorphic systems. *Nano Lett.* **2010**, *10*, 1297–1301. [CrossRef] [PubMed]
5. Prezioso, M.; Merrikh-Bayat, F.; Hoskins, B.D.; Adam, G.C.; Likharev, K.K.; Strukov, D.B. Training and operation of an integrated neuromorphic network based on metal-oxide memristors. *Nature* **2015**, *521*, 61–64. [CrossRef] [PubMed]
6. Burr, G.W.; Shelby, R.M.; Sebastian, A.; Kim, S.; Kim, S.; Sidler, S.; Virwan, K.; Ishii, M.; Narayanan, P.; Fumarola, A.; et al. Neuromorphic computing using non-volatile memory. *Adv. Phys.* **2017**, *X 2.1*, 89–124. [CrossRef]
7. Indiveri, G.; Linares-Barranco, B.; Legenstein, R.; Deligeorgis, G.; Prodromakis, T. Integration of nanoscale memristor synapses in neuromorphic computing architectures. *Nanotechnology* **2013**, *24*, 384010. [CrossRef]
8. Feldman, D.E. The spike-timing dependence of plasticity. *Neuron* **2012**, *75*, 556–571. [CrossRef]
9. Stijn, C.; Laurent, G. Hebbian STDP in mushroom bodies facilitates the synchronous flow of olfactory information in locusts. *Nature* **2007**, *448*, 709.
10. Rudy, G.; VanRullen, R.; Thorpe, S.J. Neurons tune to the earliest spikes through STDP. *Neural Comput.* **2005**, *17*, 859–879.
11. Carlson, K.D.; Carlson, K.D.; Richert, M.; Dutt, N.; Krichmar, J.L. Biologically plausible models of homeostasis and STDP: stability and learning in spiking neural networks. In Proceedings of the IEEE International Joint Conference on Neural Networks (IJCNN), Dallas, TX, USA, 1–8 August 2013.
12. Kuzum, D.; Jeyasingh, R.G.; Lee, B.; Wong, H.S.P. Nanoelectronic programmable synapses based on phase change materials for brain-inspired computing. *Nano. Lett.* **2011**, *12*, 2179–2186. [CrossRef]
13. Linares-Barranco, B.; Serrano-Gotarredona, T. Exploiting memristance in adaptive asynchronous spiking neuromorphic nanotechnology systems. In Proceedings of the 9th IEEE Conference on Nanotechnology (IEEE-Nano), Genoa, Italy, 26–30 July 2008.
14. Linares-Barranco, B.; Serrano-Gotarredona, T. Memristance can explain STDP in neural synapses. Available online: hdl.handle.net/10101/npre.2009.3010.1 (accessed on 10 May 2019).
15. Zamarreño-Ramos, C.; Serrano-Gotarredona, T.; Camuñas-Mesa, L.A.; Perez-Carrasco, J.A.; Zamarreño-Ramos, C.; Masquelier, T. On STDP, memristive devices, and building a self-learning visual cortex. *Front. Neurosci.* **2011**, *5*, 26.
16. Bi, G.; Poo, M. Synaptic modifications in cultured hippocampal neurons: dependence on spike timing, synaptic strength, and postsynaptic cell type. *J. Neurosci.* **1998**, *18*, 10464–10472. [CrossRef] [PubMed]
17. Ambrogio, S.; Ciocchini, N.; Laudato, M.; Milo, V.; Pirovano, A.; Fantini, P.; Ielmini, D. Unsupervised learning by spike timing dependent plasticity in phase change memory (PCM) synapses. *Front. Neurosci.* **2016**, *10*, 56. [CrossRef] [PubMed]
18. Ambrogio, S.; Balatti, S.; Milo, V.; Carboni, R.; Wang, Z.Q.; Calderoni, A.; Ramaswamy, N.; Ielmini, D. Neuromorphic learning and recognition with one-transistor-one-resistor synapses and bistable metal oxide RRAM. *IEEE Trans. Electron Devices* **2016**, *63*, 1508–1515. [CrossRef]
19. Serb, A.; Bill, J.; Khiat, A.; Berdan, R.; Legenstein, R.; Prodromakis, T. Unsupervised learning in probabilistic neural networks with multi-state metal-oxide memristive synapses. *Nat. Commun.* **2016**, *7*, 12611. [CrossRef]
20. Ambrogio, S.; Balatti, S.; Milo, V.; Carboni, R.; Wang, Z.; Calderoni, A.; Ramaswamy, N.; Ielmini, D. Novel RRAM-enabled 1T1R synapse capable of low-power STDP via burst-mode communication and real-time unsupervised machine learning. In Proceedings of the IEEE Symposium on VLSI Technology (VLSI), Honolulu, HI, USA, 1–2 June 2016.
21. Covi, E.; Brivio, S.; Serb, A.; Prodromakis, T.; Fanciulli, M.; Spiga, S. Analog memristive synapse in spiking networks implementing unsupervised learning. *Front. Neurosci.* **2016**, *10*, 482. [CrossRef]
22. Kohonen, T. The self-organizing map. *Proc. IEEE* **1990**, *78*, 1464–1480. [CrossRef]
23. Barbalho, J.M.; Duarte, A.; Neto, D.J.A.F.; Costa, J.A.; Netto, M.L. Hierarchical SOM applied to image compression. In Proceedings of the International Joint Conference on Neural Networks (IJCNN), Washington, DC, USA, 15–19 July 2001.
24. Yuan, J.; Zhou, Z.H. SOM ensemble-based image segmentation. *Neural Process. Lett.* **2004**, *20*, 171–178.
25. Lamour, Y.; Dutar, P.; Jobert, A. Topographic organization of basal forebrain neurons projecting to the rat cerebral cortex. *Neurosci. Lett.* **1982**, *2*, 117–122. [CrossRef]
26. Kaas, J.H. Topographic maps are fundamental to sensory processing. *Brain Res. Bull.* **1997**, *44*, 107–112. [CrossRef]

27. Sirosh, J.; Miikkulainen, R. Topographic receptive fields and patterned lateral interaction in a self-organizing model of the primary visual cortex. *Neural Comput.* **1997**, *9*, 577–594. [CrossRef] [PubMed]
28. Choi, S.; Sheridan, P.; Lu, W.D. Data clustering using memristor networks. *Sci. Rep.* **2015**, *5*, 10492. [CrossRef] [PubMed]
29. Pedro, M.; Martin-Martinez, J.; Rodriguez, R.; Gonzalez, M.B.; Campabadal, F.; Nafria, M. A Flexible Characterization Methodology of RRAM: Application to the Modeling of the Conductivity Changes as Synaptic Weight Updates. *Solid-State Electron.* **2019**, *159*, 57–62. [CrossRef]
30. Pedro, M.; Martin-Martinez, M.; Gonzalez, M.B.; Rodriguez, R.; Campabadal, F.; Nafria, M.; Aymerich, X. Tuning the conductivity of resistive switching devices for electronic synapses. *Microelectron. Eng.* **2017**, *178*, 89–92. [CrossRef]
31. Poblador, S.; Gonzalez, M.B.; Campabadal, F. Investigation of the multilevel capability of TiN/Ti/HfO_2/W resistive switching devices by sweep and pulse programming. *Microelectron. Eng.* **2018**, *187–188*, 148–153. [CrossRef]
32. Miranda, E. Compact Model for the Major and Minor Hysteretic I–V Loops in Nonlinear Memristive Devices. *IEEE Trans. Nanotechol.* **2015**, *14*, 787–789. [CrossRef]
33. Maestro, M.M.; Gonzalez, M.B.; Campabadal, F. Mimicking the spike-timing dependent plasticity in HfO_2-based memristors at multiple time scales. *Microelectron. Eng.* **2019**, *215*, 111014. [CrossRef]
34. Indiveri, G. A low-power adaptive integrate-and-fire neuron circuit. In Proceedings of the International Symposium on Circuits and Systems (ISCAS), Beijing, China, 4 May 2013.
35. Poon, C.S.; Zhou, K. Neuromorphic silicon neurons and large-scale neural networks: challenges and opportunities. *Front. Neurosci.* **2011**, *5*, 108. [CrossRef]
36. Anderson, J.R. *Language, Memory, and Thought*; Psychology Press: London, UK, 2013.
37. Pedro, M.; Martín-Martínez, J.; Miranda, E.; Rodríguez, R.; Nafria, M.; Gonzalez, M.B.; Campabadal, F. Device variability tolerance of a RRAM-based Self-Organizing Neuromorphic system. In Proceedings of the 2018 IEEE International Reliability Physics Symposium (IRPS), San Francisco, CA, USA, 4–5 March 2018.
38. Pershin, Y.V.; Di Ventra, M. Experimental demonstration of associative memory with memristive neural networks. *Neural Netw.* **2010**, *23*, 881–886. [CrossRef]

materials

MDPI

Article

Memristor-CMOS Hybrid Circuit for Temporal-Pooling of Sensory and Hippocampal Responses of Cortical Neurons

Tien Van Nguyen, Khoa Van Pham and Kyeong-Sik Min *

School of Electrical Engineering, Kookmin University, Seoul 02707, Korea; tiennv@kookmin.ac.kr (T.V.N.); khoapv@kookmin.ac.kr (K.V.P.)

* Correspondence: mks@kookmin.ac.kr

Received: 24 February 2019; Accepted: 13 March 2019; Published: 15 March 2019

Abstract: As a software framework, Hierarchical Temporal Memory (HTM) has been developed to perform the brain's neocortical functions, such as spatial and temporal pooling. However, it should be realized with hardware not software not only to mimic the neocortical function but also to exploit its architectural benefit. To do so, we propose a new memristor-CMOS (Complementary Metal-Oxide-Semiconductor) hybrid circuit of temporal-pooling here, which is composed of the input-layer and output-layer neurons mimicking the neocortex. In the hybrid circuit, the input-layer neurons have the proximal and basal/distal dendrites to combine sensory information with the temporal/location information from the brain's hippocampus. Using the same crossbar architecture, the output-layer neurons can perform a prediction by integrating the temporal information on the basal/distal dendrites. For training the proposed circuit, we used only simple Hebbian learning, not the complicated backpropagation algorithm. Due to the simple hardware of Hebbian learning, the proposed hybrid circuit can be very suitable to online learning. The proposed memristor-CMOS hybrid circuit has been verified by the circuit simulation using the real memristor model. The proposed circuit has been verified to predict both the ordinal and out-of-order sequences. In addition, the proposed circuit has been tested with the external noise and memristance variation.

Keywords: memristor-CMOS hybrid circuit; temporal pooling; sensory and hippocampal responses; cortical neurons; hierarchical temporal memory; neocortex

1. Introduction

The neocortex occupying most of the brain's surface area has been believed to perform the most human-like functions such as intelligence, cognition, etc. among all human organs. It is just 2.5-mm thick and is composed of six layers [1–3]. All six neocortical layers have the same columnar architecture, where the neocortical neurons are connected in both the vertical and horizontal directions to form various feedback and feedforward paths to communicate with each other. Anatomical experiments have observed the columnar architecture consistently through the entire neocortex [4,5]. This fact may hint that there is a canonical neural circuitry that can describe various neocortical functions with one model [6].

In this paper, we try to develop a memristor-CMOS hybrid circuit that can emulate the neocortex's canonical neural circuitry by combining nanoscale memristor crossbars with CMOS peripheral circuits. Memristors have been studied intensively for many years for their possible use of neuromorphic hardware since the first experimental demonstration [7,8]. This is because the memristive behavior seems very similar with the biological synaptic plasticity, where the synaptic connection can be strengthened and weakened dynamically according to the sensory stimulus [9]. The ionic dynamics of memristors can also be used in implementing the reservoir computing hardware, where the cognitive function can be processed simply by applying the time-domain signals to the memristor-based reservoir [10]. Moreover, the memristor crossbars can be built in a 3-dimensional architecture by a CMOS-compatible fabrication process, where the 3-dimensionality is very similar to the anatomical view of the real biological neuron-synapse connections in the neocortex [11,12]. Also, the memristor crossbar can perform a bitwise parallel operation which has been thought as one of the key aspects of energy-efficient computing of the human brain's cognition, compared to modern state-of-the-art computers [13,14].

As a software framework for modeling the neocortical function, Hierarchical Temporal Memory (HTM) has been developed recently [15–20]. Figure 1a shows a functional block diagram of HTM that is composed of the Spatial Pooler (SP) and Temporal Memory (TM). SP receives the sensory information to learn the cortical representation. As a result, SP generates Sparse Distributed Representation (SDR) [16]. SDR is a mathematical description for representing the cortical neurons that may be activated or deactivated in response to the sensory information from the cochlea, retina, etc. Actually, SP was proposed as a software algorithm in the HTM software framework [15–20]. To realize the spatial pooling with hardware, we developed the spatial-pooling memristor crossbar circuit in a previous work, where the circuit could convert the sensory information to the SDR that meant the representation of cortical neurons [21].

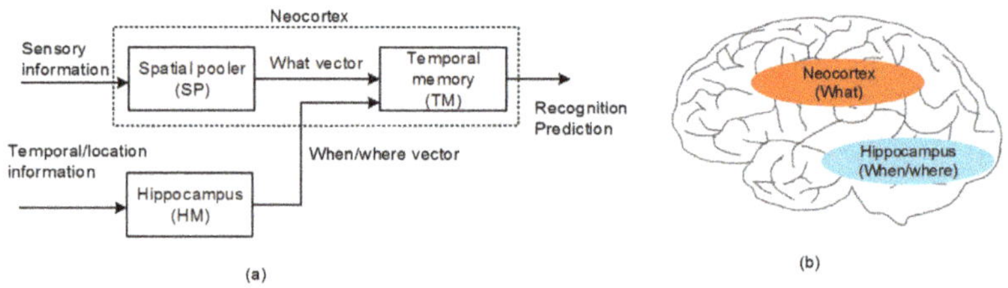

Figure 1. (**a**) The functional block diagram of Hierarchical Temporal Memory (HTM): The spatial pooler receives the sensory information from various sensory organs and forms the Sparse Distributed Representation (SDR) output representing the collective cortical neurons activated in response to the sensory information. The temporal memory learns the sequence of items that are represented by the SDR vectors by combining the sensory information with the temporal information. (**b**) The cross-sectional view of the human brain: Here, the neocortex and hippocampus regions are shown for processing the "what" and "when/where" information, respectively.

The temporal memory (TM) in Figure 1a puts together the "what" and "when/where" vectors that come from the spatial pooler and hippocampus model, respectively [22,23]. By combining the "what" with "when/where", the temporal memory can perform both the spatial recognition and the temporal prediction. For the temporal prediction, the representation of temporal succession ("when") should be segregated from the representation of the content ("what"), as shown in Figure 1a [24,25]. From the experimental observations, the hippocampus has been known to play a central role in encoding the information of ordinal sequences ("when") [25,26], whereas the representation of the content ("what") has been known to come from the neocortex, as indicated in Figure 1b.

The representation of the temporal sequence ("when") can be extended to the spatial sequence ("where") [27,28]. For example, the order of the words during reading depends on where one is looking ("where"). However, the order of the words during listening can be interpreted as the temporal sequence ("when"'). Actually, every principal neuron in the hippocampus can work as either a "place cell" or "time cell" [29]. By doing so, the hippocampus can model both the temporal ("when") and spatial ("where") information with the same kinds of representation. Thus, we can think that the spatial sequence of location information is one case of the temporal sequence [26].

Though HTM has been developed as the software framework for performing the neocortex's cognition, it should be realized with hardware not only to mimic the neocortex's function but also to exploit its architectural benefit. One reason for this need of a hardware version is the demand of the edge-computing devices in the Internet of Things (IoT) era [30–32]. For the near-sensor processing and computing of IoT devices, the speed and power benefit due to the bitwise parallel-processing of memristor crossbars can be very important in terms of the possibility of real-time and on-chip cognitive functions for various edge-computing applications [32]. Thus, the neocortex's cognitive function combined with the crossbar's architectural merit can accelerate the transition from the HTM software framework to its hardware emulator [30].

To implement HTM by hardware not software, in this paper, we propose a new memristor-CMOS hybrid circuit for realizing the temporal-pooling function of the human brain, which is composed of the input and output layers, to mimic the temporal prediction of neocortical neurons. In the hybrid circuit, the input layer has proximal and basal/distal dendrites to combine the sensory information with the temporal/location information. The output layer composed of the same circuitry with the input layer can perform a prediction by integrating the temporal information through the basal/distal dendrites. In this paper, the input and output layers realized with the memristor-CMOS hybrid circuit are verified to perform the temporal recognition and prediction that are the same functions within the human brain's neocortex.

2. Proposed Methods

Memristor crossbars are thought to be very suitable in mimicking the anatomical and functional architecture of neocortex. Memristive behaviors seem similar with the synaptic plasticity of biological neurons. Moreover, the 3-D connectivity of crossbars can be useful in realizing the real neuronal 3-D architecture of the neocortex. Also, the crossbars can perform a bitwise parallel computation, as the pyramidal neurons do in the neocortical layers. To develop the neocortex-mimicking memristor crossbar, first, we need to understand the functional model of neocortical columns and layers [33,34].

Figure 2a shows the conceptual model of temporal memory composed of input-layer and output-layer neurons [23]. From previous experimental observations, the HTM theory deduced a couple of rules to describe the neocortex's operation. First, it is assumed that the input-layer neurons receive the sensory information though the single proximal dendrite [23]. The synapses connected to this proximal dendrite are involved in only local signal-processing, as shown in Figure 2a. They do not communicate with the neurons outside the local region. The proximal dendrite is more likely to form short-distance vertical connections to receive the sensory information. On the contrary, the basal/distal dendrite is responsible for long-distance horizontal communication [23]. The dendrite can receive information from distantly located regions such as the hippocampus. One thing to note is that one neocortical neuron is allowed to have only single proximal dendrite. However, the basal/distal can have multiple.

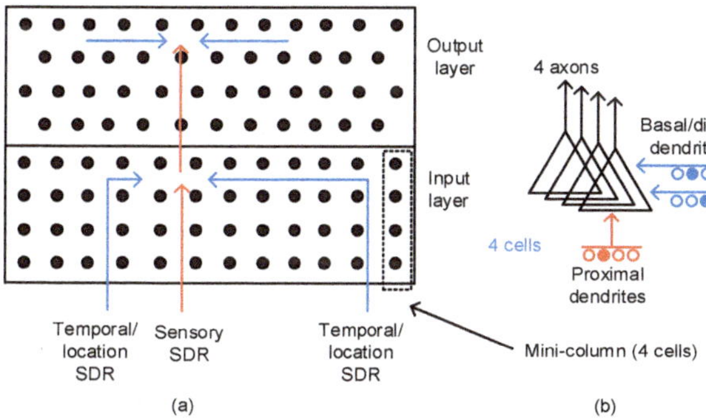

Figure 2. (**a**) The conceptual model of temporal memory architecture: The red and blue lines represent the proximal and basal/distal dendrites, respectively. (**b**) The schematic of a pyramidal neuron with a single proximal dendrite and multiple basal/distal ones. The number of output axons can be multiple too. Here, we showed 4 axons to constitute one mini-column with 4 cells. The pyramidal neurons are known as the majority of neocortical neurons.

Figure 2a also shows the output-layer neurons that are basically the same as the input-layer ones. The proximal dendrite is for short-and-direct connections from the input-layer neurons. The output-layer neurons can receive long-distance information horizontally through multiple basal/distal dendrites for the temporal integration of "when" vectors. The two-layer model is regarded as a general feature of the neocortex and can be used as an elemental unit in realizing the memristor-based temporal-pooling crossbar [23].

Figure 2b shows the schematic of a pyramidal neuron that incorporates the axonal and dendritic connections. The proximal dendrite receives the direct feed-forward inputs from the sensory organs. The basal/distal dendrite can be driven by the long-distance signals from far away regions, such as the hippocampus.

Figure 3 shows the conceptual schematic of the temporal-pooling memristor crossbar composed of input-layer and output-layer neurons. The input-layer neurons receive sensory SDR and temporal/location SDR from the spatial pooler and hippocampus model, respectively. The sensory SDR vectors are connected with the proximal dendritic synapses. The basal/distal dendrites of the input-layer neurons receive hippocampal responses that contain the temporal and location information.

The output-layer neuron in Figure 3 has the same circuitry as the input-layer neuron, as shown in Figure 2b. The proximal connection of the output-layer neuron comes from the axonal output of an input-layer neuron. The basal/distal dendrite can make the output-layer neuron a predicted state by depolarizing its body. If the body is depolarized enough by the previous basal/distal dendritic inputs, it can fire spikes sooner than the other output-layer neurons, if they are not in the predicted state. If the output-layer neuron is not in the predicted state, it cannot fire spikes, even though it receives the same feedforward input as the predicted-state neuron. Only the predicted-state neuron which is depolarized already can fire spikes in response to the proximal dendritic input.

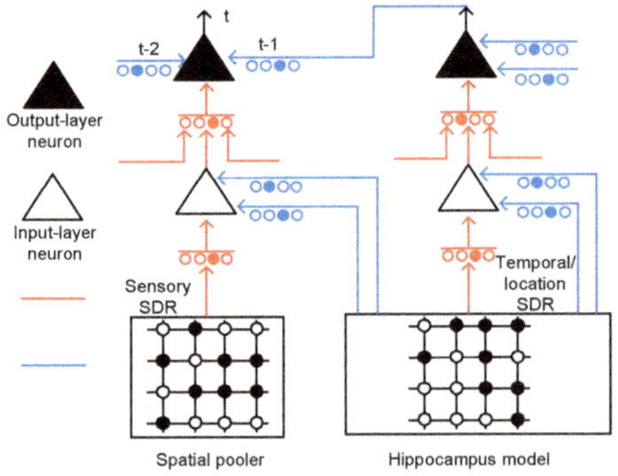

Figure 3. The conceptual schematic of a temporal-pooling memristor crossbar composed of input-layer and output-layer neurons: The input-layer neuron receives sensory SDR and temporal/location SDR from the spatial pooler and hippocampus model, respectively. The sensory and temporal/location SDR are generated from the spatial-pooling memristor crossbar that was developed in a previous work [21]. The output-layer neuron can perform a prediction by integrating the temporal information through multiple basal/distal dendrites.

In Figure 4a, we propose a memristor-CMOS hybrid circuit that has the input and output layers for the temporal-pooling of sequences such as words, sentences, etc. Here, the sensory SDR vectors enter the proximal dendrites of m_0, m_1, m_2, etc. The temporal/location SDR vectors are connected to the basal/distal dendrites of m_3, m_4, m_5, etc. One thing to note in Figure 4a is that each neuron is allowed to have only a single proximal dendrite. However, for the basal/distal ones, the neuron can have multiple dendrites, as explained in Figure 2. The sensory SDR and temporal/location SDR are collectively received by the input-layer neurons. The column current of the sensory SDR "A" is delivered to C_0, where the column current is converted to a voltage and then compared with the threshold. The detailed schematic of C_0 is shown in Figure 4b. Similarly, the column current of "B"' is delivered to C_1. The temporal/location SDR vectors of "#1", "#3", and "#2" generate the row currents which are delivered to C_2, C_3, and C_4, respectively. A_0, A_1, and A_2 are the AND gates that combine the sensory information of "A"' with the temporal/location SDRs of "#1", "#3", and "#2", respectively. The outputs of A_0, A_1, and A_2 are represented with i_0, i_1, and i_2, respectively. They enter the pulse-type set-reset latches of L_0, L_1, and L_2, respectively. The pulse-type set-reset latch is shown in Figure 4c. L_0 can be set if the SDR "A" and SDR "#1" are recognized at the same time. L_1 is set for "A" and "#3". L_2 is switched to the SET state for "A" and "#2". Similarly, L_3, L_4, and L_5 can respond to the input SDR of "B#1", "B#3", and "B#2", respectively. The set-reset latch in Figure 4c is reset by the delayed version of the "EOW_P" pulse from the delay line τ. Here, "EOW_P" means the pulse indicating the end of the word. "EOW_P" is generated when the word ends.

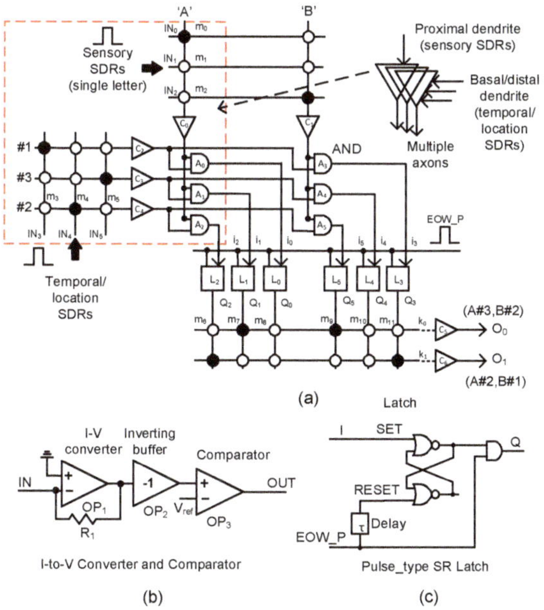

Figure 4. (**a**) The schematic of the proposed memristor-CMOS hybrid circuit for the temporal pooling of sequences such as words, sentences, etc: The input layer is composed of the memristor crossbars for sensory and temporal/location SDRs, the current-to-voltage converters, comparators, the AND gates, etc. The output layer is composed of the memristor crossbars, converters, comparators, latches, etc. (**b**) The schematic of the current–voltage converter and comparator and (**c**) the schematic of the pulse-type set-reset latch.

As mentioned earlier, if the sensory SDR of letter "A" and the location SDR of "#3" are applied to the input-layer neuron, Q_1 is activated. Similarly, when the sensory SDR of "B" and the location SDR of "#2" are recognized, Q_5 becomes high. When "EOW_P" is activated, the two latches of L_1 and L_5 keep Q_1 and Q_5 high, respectively, until the reset. Assuming that the dendritic synapses of the output neuron O_0 are already put in the predicted state with "A#3" and "B#2", m_7 and m_9 are already programmed LRSs (Low Resistance States) as a result of crossbar training. Here, the solid and open circles represent LRS and HRS (High Resistance State), respectively. At end-of-word, if the row current of k_0 is larger than the output-layer neuron's threshold, O_0 becomes high. Actually, we can think that the k_0 current represents the integration of temporal responses to the sensory/location SDRs of "A#3" and "B#2" because "A#3" and "B#2' were already recognized at the previous time. Similarly, if "A#2" and "B#1" are recognized one by one, the row current k_1 becomes larger than the threshold and can activate O_1.

Figure 5a shows a current–voltage relationship of the measured memristor that was obtained by a Keithley-4200 (Semiconductor Characterization System, Tektronix, Inc., Beaverton, OR, USA) [35]. The measured memristor's film is a Pt/$LaAlO_3$/Nb-doped $SrTiO_3$ stacked layer [35]. Here, the LRS and HRS were measured as 10 kΩ and 1 MΩ, respectively. The black line in Figure 5a represents the behavioral model of memristors [35]. The measured data are represented with the red line. The behavioral model described by Verilog-A was used in the circuit simulation of the hybrid circuits of memristors and CMOS in this paper. Here, the circuit simulation was performed using CADENCE SPECTRE (Cadence Design Systems, Inc., San Jose, CA, USA) and SAMSUNG 0.13-µm circuit simulation parameters [36]. The mathematical equations of the Verilog-A model of memristors were explained in a previous publication in detail [35].

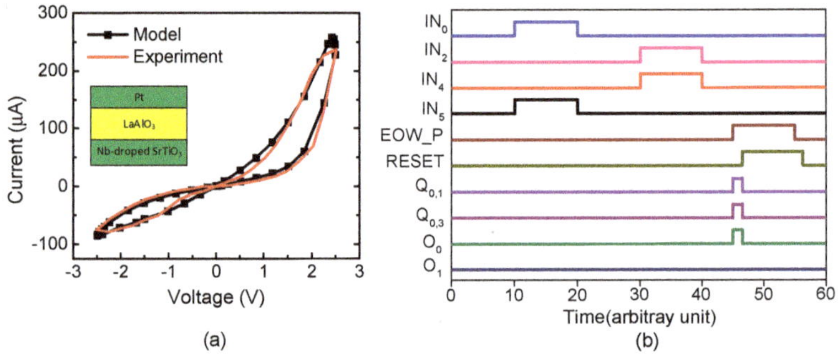

Figure 5. (**a**) The current–voltage relationships of memristors for the measurement and Verilog-A model: The black line represents the Verilog-A model of memristors used in the circuit simulation in this paper [35]. The red line is for the measurement [35]. The details of the measurement and the Verilog-A model were explained well in a previous publication [35]. (**b**) The waveforms of the proposed memristor-CMOS hybrid circuit for temporal pooling shown in Figure 4.

Figure 5b shows the waveforms of Figure 4 obtained from the CADENCE (Cadence Design Systems, Inc., San Jose, CA, USA) circuit simulation with the memristor's Verilog-A model in Figure 5a and the SAMSUNG 0.13-µm SPICE parameters. First, we assumed the sensory SDR of letter "A" and the location SDR of "#3" are generated by the spatial pooler. As a result, the IN_0 and IN_5 pulses are high, while the others are low in Figure 5b. By doing so, Q_1 becomes high. Second, if the spatial pooler generates the sensory SDR of letter "B" and the location SDR "#2", Q_5 becomes high. At end-of-word, the pulse of "EOW_P" is enabled and the output neuron O_0 becomes active. Here, the output neuron is already put in the predicted state by the previous signals of Q_1 and Q_5. After the output neuron O_0 fires a pulse, O_0 returns to low, as the typical integrate-and-fire neuron acts. To do so, the "EOW_P" pulse goes through the delay line τ and its delayed pulse resets the set-reset latches. The integrate-and-fire operation is realized very simply using the digital CMOS gates and the memristor crossbar, as shown in Figure 4a–c.

3. Results

In this paper, we tested the proposed memristor-CMOS hybrid circuit of temporal pooling in Figure 4a with an EMNIST (Extension of Modified National Institute of Standards and Technology) data-set of handwritten letters [37]. For training the memristor crossbar to recognize EMNIST handwritten letters, we applied the simple Hebbian learning to 26 EMNIST letters from "a" to "z". The operational steps of simple Hebbian learning of memristor crossbars is shown in Figure 6. Here, first, we initialized the memristor crossbar. Second, we calculated the amount of overlap between the input vector and the crossbar's column or row. If the crossbar's column or row has an overlap larger than the threshold, the column or row is activated. In this case, the permanence values of matched and unmatched memristor cells belonging to the activated column or row are increased and decreased according to the predetermined parameter Δ, respectively. If the permanence value becomes larger than 1 or less than 0, the memristor corresponding to the permanence is strengthened or weakened according to the memristor programing circuit. Here, we used the typical $V_{DD}/2$ scheme for programming memristors. One thing to note is that the memristor programming based on Hebbian learning does not need the complicated backpropagation calculation [21]. By doing so, the proposed memristor-CMOS hybrid circuit can be very suitable to online learning because the hardware complexity of Hebbian learning is much simpler than that of a backpropagation-based system.

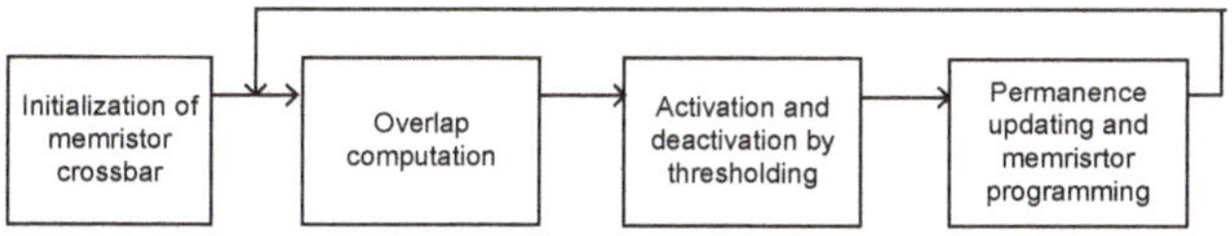

Figure 6. The operational steps of simple Hebbian learning of memristor crossbars: initialization, overlap computation, activation and deactivation by thresholding, and permanence updating and memristor programming. Here the memristor programming based on Hebbian learning does not need the complicated backpropagation calculation.

In this test, the 26 EMNIST letters have 60,000 training vectors. Each image is composed of 20 × 20 gray pixels. To estimate the recognition rate, we tested 10,000 execution vectors of an EMNIST letter. The first row in Figure 7 shows 4 images of EMNIST letters. They are "c", "o", "m", and "e", respectively. EMNIST vectors are randomized first and then applied to the spatial-pooling memristor crossbar proposed in a previous work [21]. The second row in Figure 7 shows the randomized version of the EMNIST vectors. It should be noted that the memristor-CMOS hybrid circuit does not need to use the complicated random number generation circuit. Once we decided the randomization function, we applied the same function to all the test vectors without changing it for every vector [21]. Thus, we did not use the random number generator circuit in a previous work [21].

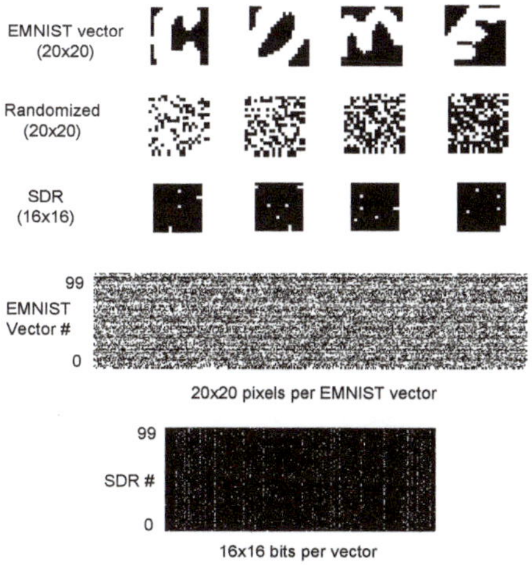

Figure 7. The first row shows the EMNIST handwritten letters of "c", "o", "m", and "e", respectively. The second row shows randomized images of EMIST handwritten letters. The third row are the SDRs that are obtained from the spatial-pooing memristor crossbar for the randomized images of "c", "o", "m", and "e". The fourth row shows 100 EMNIST input vectors. Each EMNIST vector is composed of 20 × 20 pixels. The fifth row shows 100 SDRs with 16 × 16 bits which are obtained from 100 EMNIST input vectors with 20 × 20 pixels. Among the 16 × 16 bits, only 2% of the bits become active to maintain the sparsity ratio around 2% by spatial-pooling for EMNIST vectors [21].

If we perform the spatial pooing with 256 columns, we can obtain 16 × 16 SDRs from 20 × 20 EMNIST input vectors. The third row in Figure 7 shows the SDRs that are obtained from the spatial-pooing memristor crossbar for the randomized images of "c", "o", "m", and "e", respectively. The fourth row in Figure 7 shows the pixel map of 100 EMNIST test vectors. The average sparsity of the EMNIST test vectors is as high as 55.8%; that means 55.8% of the pixels can be white. On the contrary, the SDRs from the spatial-pooling crossbar have a sparsity as low as 2%. The fifth row shows 100 SDRs with 16 × 16 bits. Among the 16 × 16 bits of each SDR, only 2% of the bits become active by the spatial-pooling of the 20 × 20-pixel EMNIST vector. This low sparsity of SDRs is very useful in cognitive computations such as union, pattern matching, etc. [38]. In addition, the small number of active bits can reduce the number of LRS cells in a memristor crossbar. By doing so, the power consumption and sneak-leakage problem can be improved much in the spatial-pooling crossbar [39].

To test the temporal-pooling memristor-CMOS hybrid circuit in Figure 4a, we put together EMNIST handwritten letters to form arbitrary words. Figure 8 shows the recognition rate of the proposed temporal-pooling circuit for the 40 words tested in this paper. The recognition rate of words is estimated as high as 95.6%, 99.1%, and 99.3% for 256-bit SDRs, 1024-bit SDRs, and 4096-bit SDRs, respectively. One thing to note is that the recognition rate of words is much better than the recognition rate of EMNIST letters. This is because the temporal-pooling circuit interprets both sensory and temporal/location information together, as indicated in Figure 2. Combining the sensory SDRs with the location SDRs makes the recognition of words better than the recognition of letters. Figure 8 also shows the recognition rate of sentences as high as the rate of words. The recognition rate of sentences is simulated 96.5%, 99.3%, and 99.7% for 256-bit SDRs, 1024-bit SDRs, and 4096-bit SDRs, respectively. Here, the number of sentences tested in Figure 8 is 10.

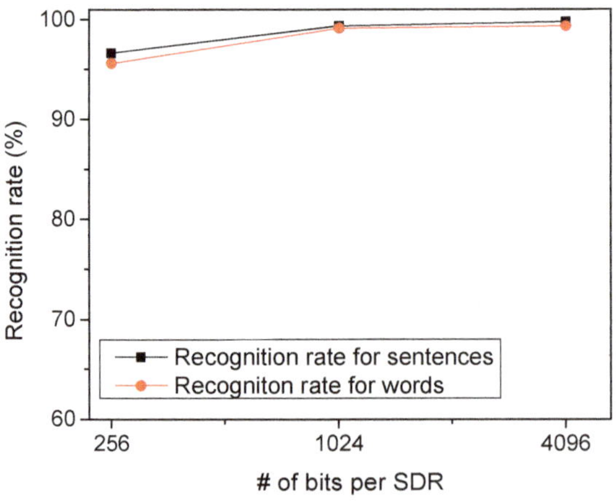

Figure 8. The recognition rate of words and sentences with varying the number of bits per SDR.

Figure 9 shows the recognition rate by varying the amount of noise added to SDRs. The noise is added by randomly flipping a fraction of the active bits to inactive, and vice versa so that the sparsity can be maintained constant. As shown in Figure 4a, the temporal-pooling circuit receives both the sensory and location SDRs from the spatial pooler. Here, the red circles represent the recognition rate for the noise added to the sensory SDRs. The black boxes are for the noise added to the location SDRs. From this figure, the noise added to the location SDRs seems more critical in terms of recognition rate. If a noise as large as 40% is added to the location SDRs, the recognition rate becomes as low as 45.3%. However, the rate can be as high as 92.5% for the same amount of noise added to the sensory SDRs.

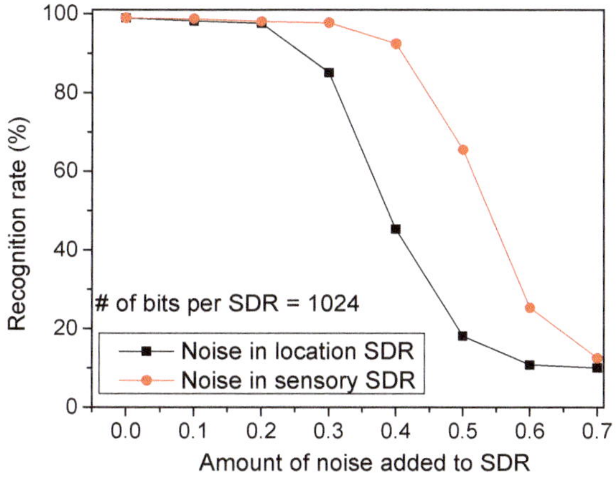

Figure 9. The recognition rate of words by varying the amount of noise added to location SDRs and sensory SDRs: The red circles represent the recognition rate for the noise added to the sensory SDRs. The black boxes are for the noise added to the location SDRs.

In Figure 10, we assumed the statistical distribution of LRS and HRS with the memristance variation = 10%, as shown in the inset figure. Here, the main figure shows the recognition rate by varying the amount variation in memristance from 0% to 15%. Here, the median values of HRS and LRS are assumed as 1 MΩ and 10 KΩ, respectively. Though the variation is as large as 15%, the recognition rate is still as high as 85.9%. The loss of recognition rate for the variation = 15% is only as small as 13.2% compared to the variation = 0%.

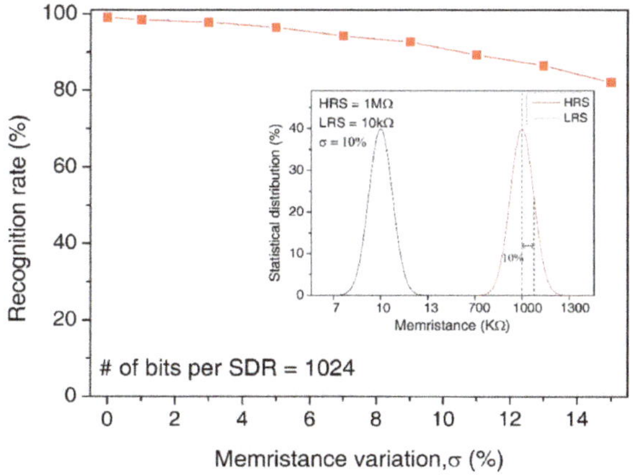

Figure 10. The recognition rate of words by increasing the percentage variation in memristance from 0% to 15%: The inset figure shows the statistical distribution of LRS and HRS for the memristance variation = 10%.

Figure 11 shows the prediction rate of sentences by increasing the number of words sensed in the tested sentence. Here, we tested two cases of sequences which are ordinal and out-of-order sequences, respectively. First, let us explain the ordinal sequence. Assume that we try to recognize two sequences of "'A-B-C-D-E" and "A-B-C-E-D". Here, the first three SDRs are "A-B-C" which are the same for both sequences. Also, the fourth and fifth SDRs are different each other. If the first SDR of "A" comes to the memristor crossbar, it cannot distinguish the two sequences. Similarly, for the second SDR of "B", the crossbar circuit also cannot make a judgement between "A-B-C-D-E" and "A-B-C-E-D". However, if the fourth SDR is given to the crossbar, it can predict if the fifth SDR will be "E" or "D" according to the fourth SDR information. This is called the ordinal prediction in Figure 11, where the temporal-pooling circuit can predict the ordinal sequence of SDRs. Figure 11 shows the prediction rate of ordinal sentences. The prediction rate starts from zero. This means the crossbar can predict nothing at the starting time of prediction. If the first SDR is given, the crossbar starts to predict the rest words of the tested sentence. As the crossbar receives more words from the spatial pooler, the prediction becomes more accurate, as shown in Figure 11. When the crossbar receives the final SDR at the end of sentence (period symbol), the prediction rate in Figure 11 becomes equal to the recognition rate of sentences in Figure 8.

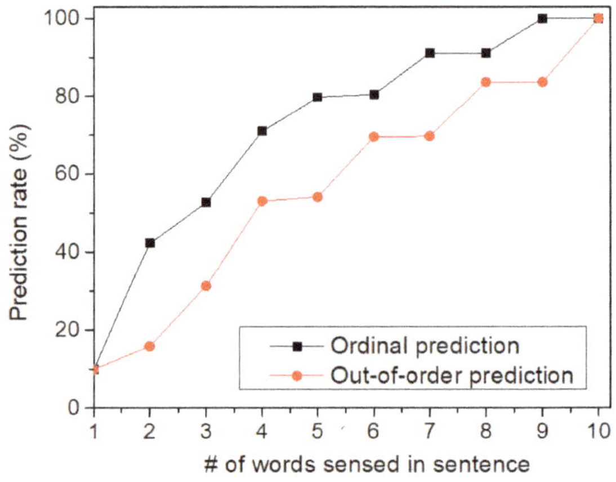

Figure 11. The prediction rate of sentences by increasing the number of words sensed for recognizing the sentences: Here, both the ordinal and out-of-order sequences can be recognized by the temporal-pooling memristor crossbar circuit proposed in this paper.

We also tested the prediction for out-of-order sequences in Figure 11. In the out-of-order prediction, the sequence of SDRs are out of order. In spite of the out-of-order sequence, the crossbar can accumulate the information of the sensed words over time. By doing so, the temporal-pooling circuit can guess what word should come next. This out-of-order prediction is exactly the same case as the crossword puzzle problem. In solving the crossword puzzle, we predict the word by accumulating the information of letters in the out-of-order sequence over time. When the temporal-pooling circuit is given only half words in the tested sentence, Figure 11 indicates that the crossbar can predict the ordinal and out-of-order sentences as accurate as 79.8% and 54.2%, respectively.

4. Discussion

In this section, we compare the proposed memristor-CMOS hybrid circuit with the previous sequential memristor crossbar [40] in terms of the memristor crossbar area, power consumption, and prediction of the ordinal and out-of-order sequences. The previous sequential memristor crossbar was designed not to consider the concept of location SDR in the crossbar, unlike the proposed temporal-pooling hybrid circuit in this paper [40]. Thus, the previous sequential scheme can recognize only the ordinal not the out-of-order sequence [40]. This is a very big disadvantage of the previous sequential scheme. For the power consumption, we had to program memristor cells of the serial chain one by one in the previous sequential crossbar to recognize the ordinal sequences [40]. This results in a large amount of programming power consumption in the previous scheme. On the contrary, the proposed temporal-pooling hybrid circuit does not demand the memristor programming in recognizing both the ordinal and out-of-order sequences. By doing so, the power consumption of the proposed temporal-pooling circuit can be almost as small as 1/29 of the previous scheme, as indicated in Table 1. One more thing to note is the CMOS peripheral circuit in Figure 4a consumes only a negligible amount of the power than the memristor crossbar. Actually, most of the power is consumed in the LRS cells in the crossbar. Thus, minimizing the number of LRS cells in the memristor crossbar is very critical not only for alleviating the sneak leakage problem but also for reducing the power consumption [21]. Comparing the memristor crossbar's area between the previous and proposed schemes indicates the number of memristors of the proposed temporal-pooling hybrid circuit is estimated almost the same with that of the previous scheme, as shown in Table 1.

Table 1. A comparison of the memristor crossbar area, power consumption, and prediction of the ordinal and out-of-order sequences.

Scheme	The Previous Sequential Memristor Crossbar [40]	The Proposed Memristor-CMOS Hybrid Circuit of Temporal Pooling
The number of memristors (Memristor crossbar area)	17556	17027
The amount of power consumption (LRS = 1 MΩ, HRS = 100 MΩ)	151.5 μW	5.24 μW
Prediction of ordinal sequences	O	O
Prediction of out-of-order sequences	X	O

Finally, we discuss here the practical applications of Hebbian-based HTM algorithm. Actually, if we compare the Hebbian-based HTM algorithm with the previous deep-learning ones such Convolutional Neural Networks, etc. for recognizing the benchmark image data-set, the deep learning outperforms the Hebbian-based HTM [21]. However, according to Numenta Inc. that developed HTM algorithm, the biologically inspired HTM can work best with data that meets the following characteristics: streaming data rather than batch data files, data with time-based patterns, many individual data sources where hand crafting separate models is impractical, subtle patterns that cannot always be seen by humans, and data for which simple techniques such as thresholds yield substantial false positives and false negatives [41]. This means that the Hebbian-based HTM algorithm can be more suitable to the area of Human-like sensory information such as the streaming data composed of anomaly patterns, as we showed in the case of the out-of-order prediction in Figure 11. On the contrary, for a static image data-set such as MNIST, CIFAR, etc., the conventional deep learning techniques can be better than HTM [21]. The real practical applications of the Hebbian-based HTM algorithm were explained in detail in previous publications [41,42]. In addition, the experimental results of memristor crossbars with Hebbian learning were shown in previous publications [43,44], where memristor's conductance was trained by the Hebbian algorithm for various neuromorphic applications.

5. Conclusions

As a software framework, Hierarchical Temporal Memory (HTM) has been developed to perform the brain's neocortical functions such as spatial and temporal pooling in software. However, it should be realized with hardware not software not only to mimic the neocortex's function but also to exploit its architectural benefit. To do so, in this paper, we proposed the memristor-CMOS hybrid circuit to realize the temporal-pooling function of human brain, which is composed of the input and output layers to mimic the neocortical neurons. In the hybrid circuit, the input layer has proximal and basal/distal dendrites to combine the sensory information with the temporal/location information caused from the brain's hippocampus. Using the same crossbar architecture, the output layer can perform predictions by integrating the temporal information through the basal/distal dendrites. For training the memristor-CMOS hybrid circuit, we used only simple Hebbian learning, not the complicated backpropagation algorithm. Due to the simple hardware of Hebbian learning, the hybrid circuit can be thought very suitable to online learning.

The proposed memristor HTM circuit was verified by the circuit simulation using memristor's Verilog-A model obtained from the measurement. The proposed crossbar circuit was tested to recognize words and sentences that are composed of EMNIST data-set of handwritten letters. The recognition rate for sentences was estimated as high as 96.5% for 256-bit Sparse Distributed Representation (SDR). In addition, the proposed circuit was tested with the external noise and memristance variation. The proposed temporal-pooling circuit also was verified to perform both the ordinal and out-of-order predictions. When the proposed circuit was given only half words in the tested sentence, it could predict the ordinal and out-of-order sequences with the accuracy of 79.8% and 54.2%, respectively.

Author Contributions: All authors contributed to the submitted manuscript of the present work. K.S.M. defined the research topic. T.V.N. and K.V.P. performed the simulation and measurement. K.S.M. wrote the manuscript. All authors read and approved the submitted manuscript.

Funding: The work was financially supported by NRF-2015R1A5A7037615, MOTIE/KEIT (10052653), and ETRI grant (18ZB1800).

Acknowledgments: The CAD tools were supported by the IC Design Education Center (IDEC), Daejeon, Korea. The authors are very grateful for the device fabrication by Yeon Soo Kim, Chansoo Yoon, Sanik Lee, and Bae Ho Park, Konkuk University, Seoul, Korea.

Conflicts of Interest: The authors declare that they have no competing interests.

References

1. Hawkins, J.; Blakeslee, S. *On Intelligence: How a New Understanding of the Brain Will Lead to the Creation of Truly Intelligent Machines*; Henry Holt & Company: New York, NY, USA, 2004.
2. Horton, J.C.; Adams, D.L. The cortical column: A structure without a function. *Philos. Trans. R. Soc. Lond. B Biol. Sci.* **2005**, *360*, 837–862. [CrossRef] [PubMed]
3. Thomson, A.M. Neocortical layer 6, a review. *Front. Neuroana* **2010**, *4*, 13. [CrossRef] [PubMed]
4. Hensch, T.K.; Stryker, M.P. Columnar architecture sculpted by GABA circuits in developing cat visual cortex. *Science* **2004**, *303*, 1678–1681. [CrossRef] [PubMed]
5. Muir, D.R.; Cook, M. Anatomical constraints on lateral competition in columnar cortical architectures. *Neural Comput.* **2014**, *26*, 1624–1666. [CrossRef] [PubMed]
6. Douglas, R.J.; Martin, K.A.C.; Whitteridge, D. A canonical microcircuit for neocortex. *Neural Comput.* **1989**, *1*, 480–488. [CrossRef]
7. Chua, L.O. Memristor-the missing circuit element. *IEEE Trans. Circuit Theory* **1971**, *18*, 507–519. [CrossRef]
8. Strukov, D.B.; Snider, G.S.; Stewart, D.R.; Williams, R.S. The missing memristor found. *Nature* **2008**, *453*, 80–83. [CrossRef] [PubMed]
9. Jo, S.H.; Chang, T.; Ebong, I.; Bhadviya, B.B.; Mazumder, P.; Lu, W. Nanoscale memristor device as synapse in neuromorphic systems. *Nano Lett.* **2010**, *10*, 1297–1301. [CrossRef] [PubMed]
10. Du, C.; Cai, F.; Zidan, M.A.; Ma, W.; Lee, S.H.; Lu, W.D. Reservoir computing using dynamic memristors for temporal information processing. *Nat. Commun.* **2017**, *8*, 2204. [CrossRef] [PubMed]
11. Kügeler, C.; Meier, M.; Rosezin, R.; Gilles, S.; Waser, R. High-density 3D memory architecture based on the resistive switching effect. *Solid State Electron.* **2009**, *53*, 1287–1292. [CrossRef]
12. Shulaker, M.M.; Wu, T.F.; Pal, A.; Zhao, L.; Nishi, Y.; Saraswat, K.; Wong, H.-S.P.; Mitra, S. Monolithic 3D integration of logic and memory: Carbon nanotube FETs, resistive RAM, and silicon FETs. In Proceedings of the IEEE International Electron Devices Meeting, San Francisco, CA, USA, 15–17 December 2014; pp. 638–641.
13. Truong, S.N.; Shin, S.H.; Byeon, S.D.; Song, J.S.; Min, K.S. New twin crossbar architecture of binary memristors for low-power image recognition with discrete cosine transform. *IEEE Trans. Nanotechnol.* **2015**, *14*, 1104–1111. [CrossRef]
14. Truong, S.N.; Ham, S.J.; Min, K.S. Neuromorphic crossbar circuit with nanoscale filamentary-switching binary memristors for speech recognition. *Nanoscale Res. Lett.* **2014**, *9*, 1–9. [CrossRef] [PubMed]
15. Hawkins, J.; Ahmad, S.; Dubinsky, D. *Hierarchical Temporal Memory Including HTM Cortical Learning Algorithms*; Tech. Rep.; Numenta, Inc.: Palo Alto, CA, USA, 2011.
16. Cui, Y.; Ahmad, C.; Hawkins, J. The HTM spatial pooler—A neocortical algorithm for online sparse distributed coding. *bioRxiv* **2016**. [CrossRef] [PubMed]

17. Ahmad, S.; Hawkins, J. Properties of sparse distributed representations and their application to hierarchical temporal memory. *arXiv*, 2015; arXiv:1503.07469.
18. Ahmad, S.; Hawkins, J. How do neurons operate on sparse distributed representations? A mathematical theory of sparsity, neurons and active dendrites. *arXiv*, 2016; arXiv:1601.00720.
19. Cui, Y.; Ahmad, C.; Hawkins, J. Continuous online sequence learning with an unsupervised neural network model. *arXiv*, 2015; arXiv:1512.05463.
20. Pietroń, M.; Wielgosz, M.; Wiatr, K. Formal analysis of HTM Spatial Pooler performance under predefined operation conditions. *arXiv*, 2016; arXiv:1607.00791v1.
21. Truong, S.N.; Pham, K.V.; Min, K.S. Spatial-pooling memristor crossbar converting sensory information to sparse distributed representation of cortical neurons. *IEEE Trans. Nanotechnol.* **2018**, *17*, 482–491. [CrossRef]
22. Hawkins, J.; Ahmad, S. Why neurons have thousands of synapses, a theory of sequence memory in neocortex. *arXiv*, 2016; arXiv:1511.00083.
23. Hawkins, J.; Ahmad, S.; Cui, Y. A theory of how columns in the neocortex enable learning the structure of the world. *Front. Neural Circuits* **2017**, *11*, 81. [CrossRef] [PubMed]
24. Zeki, S.; Shipp, S. The functional logic of cortical connections. *Nature* **1988**, *335*, 311–317. [CrossRef] [PubMed]
25. Ungerleider, L.G.; Mishkin, M. Two cortical visual system. In *Analysis of visual Behavior*; Goodale, M.A., Ingle, D.J., Mansfield, R.J., Eds.; MIT Press: Cambridge, MA, USA, 1982; pp. 549–586.
26. Friston, K.; Buzáki, G. The functional anatomy of time: What and when in the brain. *Trends Cogn. Sci.* **2016**, *20*, 500–511. [CrossRef] [PubMed]
27. Fortin, N.J.; Agster, K.L.; Eichenbaum, H. Critical role of the hippocampus in memory for sequences of events. *Nat. Neurosci.* **2002**, *5*, 458–462. [CrossRef] [PubMed]
28. Ergorul, C.; Eichenbaum, H. The hippocampus and memory for "what," "where," and "when". *Learn. Mem.* **2004**, *11*, 397–405. [CrossRef] [PubMed]
29. Moser, E.I.; Kropff, E.; Moser, M.B. Place cell, gird cells, and the brain's spatial representation system. *Annu. Rev. Neurosci.* **2008**, *31*, 69–89. [CrossRef] [PubMed]
30. Krestinskaya, O.; Dolzhikova, I.; James, A.P. Hierarchical temporal memory using memristor networks: A survey. *IEEE Trans. Circuits Syst.* **2018**, *2*, 380–395. [CrossRef]
31. Wijesinghe, P.; Ankit, A.; Sengupta, A.; Roy, K. An all-memristor deep spiking neural computing system: A step toward realizing the low-power stochastic brain. *IEEE Trans. Emerg. Top. Comput. Intell.* **2018**, *2*, 345–358. [CrossRef]
32. Krestinskaya, O.; James, A.P.; Chua, L.O. Neuro-memristive circuits for edge computing: A review. *arXiv* **2018**, arXiv:1807.00962.
33. Shipp, S. Structure and function of the cerebral cortex. *Curr. Biol.* **2007**, *17*, R443–R449. [CrossRef] [PubMed]
34. Douglas, R.J.; Martin, K.A. Neuronal circuits of the neocortex. *Annu. Rev. Neurosci.* **2004**, *27*, 419–451. [CrossRef] [PubMed]
35. Truong, S.N.; Pham, K.V.; Yang, W.S.; Shin, S.H.; Pedrotti, K.; Min, K.S. New pulse amplitude modulation for fine tuning of memristor synapses. *Microelectron. J.* **2016**, *55*, 162–168. [CrossRef]
36. *Virtuoso Spectre Circuit Simulator User Guide*; Cadence Design System Inc.: San Jose, CA, USA, 2011.
37. Cohen, G.; Afshar, S.; Tapson, J.; Schaik, A.V. EMNIST: And extension of MNIST to handwritten letters. *arXiv* **2017**, arXiv:1702.05373.
38. James, A.P.; Fedorova, I.; Ibrayer, T.; Kudithipudi, D. HTM spatial pooler with memristor crossbar circuits for sparse biometric recognition. *IEEE Trans. Biomed. Circuits Syst.* **2017**, *11*, 640–651. [CrossRef] [PubMed]
39. Shin, S.H.; Byeon, S.D.; Song, J.S.; Truong, S.N.; Mo, H.S.; Kim, D.J.; Min, K.S. Dynamic reference scheme with improved read voltage margin for compensating cell-position and back ground-pattern dependencies in pure memristor array. *J. Semicond. Technol. Sci.* **2015**, *15*, 685–694. [CrossRef]
40. Truong, S.N.; Pham, K.V.; Yang, W.; Min, K.S. Sequential memristor crossbar for neuromorphic pattern recognition. *IEEE Trans. Nanotechnol.* **2016**, *15*, 922–930. [CrossRef]
41. The Numenta Anomaly Benchmark: The First Temporal Benchmark Designed for Anomaly Detection in Streaming Data, Whitepaper. Numenta, Inc., 2015. Available online: https://numenta.com/assets/pdf/numenta-anomaly-benchmark/NAB-Business-Paper.pdf (accessed on 25 February 2019).
42. Lavin, V.; Ahmad, S. Evaluating real-time anomaly detection algorithms–the Numenta anomaly benchmark. In Proceedings of the IEEE 14th International Conference on Machine Learning and Applications (ICMLA), Miami, FL, USA, 9–11 December 2015; pp. 38–44.

43. Ziegler, M.; Riggert, C.; Hansen, M.; Bartsch, T.; Kohlstedt, H. Memristive Hebbian Plasticity Model: Device Requirements for the Emulation of Hebbian Plasticity Based on Memristive Devices. *IEEE Trans. Biomed. Circuits Syst.* **2015**, *9*, 197–206. [CrossRef] [PubMed]
44. Hansen, M.; Zahari, F.; Kohlstedt, H.; Ziegler, M. Unsupervised Hebbian learning experimentally realized with analogue memristive crossbar arrays. *Sci. Rep.* **2018**, *8*, 8914. [CrossRef] [PubMed]

materials

Article

Hybrid Circuit of Memristor and Complementary Metal-Oxide-Semiconductor for Defect-Tolerant Spatial Pooling with Boost-Factor Adjustment

Tien Van Nguyen, Khoa Van Pham and Kyeong-Sik Min *

School of Electrical Engineering, Kookmin University, Seoul 02707, Korea
* Correspondence: mks@kookmin.ac.kr; Tel.: +82-2-910-4634

Received: 17 June 2019; Accepted: 29 June 2019; Published: 1 July 2019

Abstract: Hierarchical Temporal Memory (HTM) has been known as a software framework to model the brain's neocortical operation. However, mimicking the brain's neocortical operation by not software but hardware is more desirable, because the hardware can not only describe the neocortical operation, but can also employ the brain's architectural advantages. To develop a hybrid circuit of memristor and Complementary Metal-Oxide-Semiconductor (CMOS) for realizing HTM's spatial pooler (SP) by hardware, memristor defects such as stuck-at-faults and variations should be considered. For solving the defect problem, we first show that the boost-factor adjustment can make HTM's SP defect-tolerant, because the false activation of defective columns are suppressed. Second, we propose a memristor-CMOS hybrid circuit with the boost-factor adjustment to realize this defect-tolerant SP by hardware. The proposed circuit does not rely on the conventional defect-aware mapping scheme, which cannot avoid the false activation of defective columns. For the Modified subset of National Institute of Standards and Technology (MNIST) vectors, the boost-factor adjusted crossbar with defects = 10% shows a rate loss of only ~0.6%, compared to the ideal crossbar with defects = 0%. On the contrary, the defect-aware mapping without the boost-factor adjustment demonstrates a significant rate loss of ~21.0%. The energy overhead of the boost-factor adjustment is only ~0.05% of the programming energy of memristor synapse crossbar.

Keywords: memristor-CMOS hybrid circuit; defect-tolerant spatial pooling; boost-factor adjustment; memristor crossbar; neuromorphic hardware

1. Introduction

The human brain's neocortex covers the brain's surficial area, which is known to carry out the most intelligence functions. The thickness of neocortex has been observed as thin as 2.5 mm, where six layers are stacked one-by-one [1–3]. The six neocortical layers seem to be columnar, in which the complicated vertical and horizontal synaptic connections are intertwined among neurons to form the 3-dimensional neuronal architecture [4,5]. The neocortical neurons collectively respond to human's sensory information from retina, cochlea, and olfactory organ [6]. The collective activation of neocortical neurons are trained over and over with respect to time, by changing the synaptic connection's strength according to the sensory stimuli. The neuronal activation and synaptic plasticity can be thought of as a fundamental aspect of human perception and cognition, which are computed in a different way from the conventional Von Neumann machines.

As a software framework, Hierarchical Temporal Memory (HTM) has been developed to model the cognitive functions of neocortex [7–11]. By doing so, HTM can recognize and interpret various spatiotemporal patterns, mimicking how the human brain's neocortex understands human's sensory stimuli. The software framework of HTM is divided into two functional blocks: Spatial Pooler (SP) and Temporal Memory (TM). The role of SP is receiving and learning the sensory information. In SP, the sensory information is transformed into the collective activation of neocortical neurons. From the biological experiments, the neocortical neurons have been observed to be activated sparsely, not densely, in response to human sensory stimuli. The sparse activation of neocortical neurons is mathematically described as Sparse Distributed Representation (SDR) in HTM [1]. After SP learning the spatial features of the sensory stimuli, TM responds to the temporal sequences of SDR patterns generated from SP. By learning the temporal sequences of SDR patterns, TM can perform recognition and prediction for them.

Figure 1a shows a conceptual diagram of SP operation, where the input-space neurons are mapped to the SP neurons [8]. Here, the input-space and SP neurons refer to the neurons of sensory organ and neocortex, respectively. The sensory stimuli generated from the input-space neurons are connected with the neocortical neurons, as indicated in Figure 1a. The lines between the input and the SP spaces represent the synaptic connections. Synaptic weights of the connections are trained according to Hebbian learning rule in HTM [8]. If an SP neuron becomes active, in response to an input-space stimulus, the synaptic weights belonging to this neuron are strengthened, and weakened otherwise [8]. The circle zone in the SP space represents a local inhibition area, within which only few neurons are allowed to be active. In HTM, the size of inhibition zone in the SP space can be decided to control the sparsity of neuronal activation. It has been known that the percentage of neuronal activation is as sparse as 2% on average in the brain's neocortex. This low sparsity of neuronal activation may have something to do with high energy-efficiency of neocortical cognitive operation.

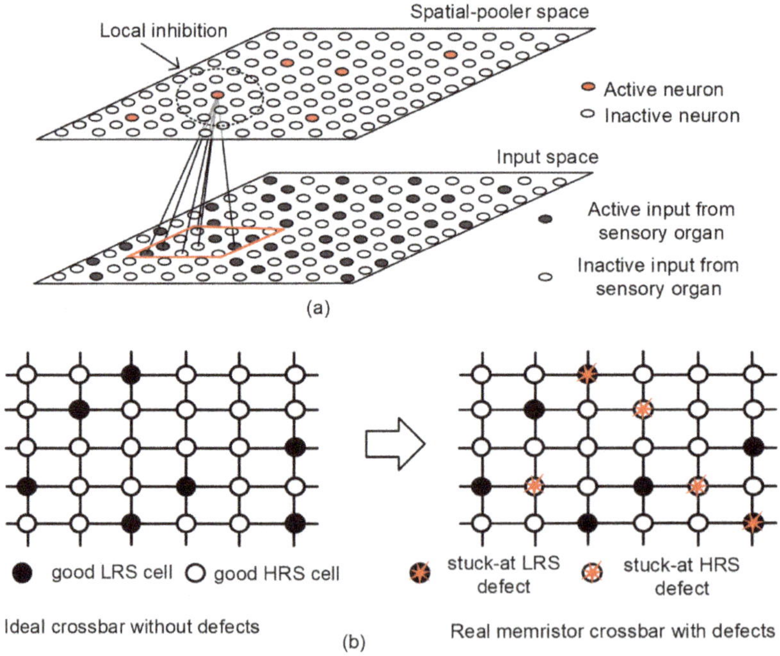

Figure 1. (**a**) The conceptual diagram of Spatial Pooler (SP) operation, where the input-space neurons are mapped to the SP neurons; and (**b**) the comparison of the ideal crossbar without defects and the real crossbar with defects. LRS and HRS mean Low Resistance State and High Resistance State, respectively.

In the previous publications, we developed hybrid CMOS-memristor circuits for implementing HTM, which was developed as the software framework originally, as mentioned earlier [12,13]. Memristors have been studied intensively for many years for their potential in neuromorphic hardware, since the first experimental demonstration [14,15]. This is because the memristive behaviors seem very similar with the experimental synaptic plasticity observed from biological neurons. From the biological experiments, the synaptic connections have been observed to be strengthened or weakened dynamically by electrical spiking signals applied to them [16].

Moreover, memristors can be fabricated to build 3-dimensional crossbar architecture using the CMOS-compatible Back-End-Of-Line (BEOL) process [17,18]. The 3-dimensional connectivity of memristor-synapses is very similar to the anatomical structure of the biological neocortex. In terms of cognitive functions, the memristor crossbar can perform vector-matrix multiplications in parallel, which can be considered very important in implementing energy-efficient computing like human brain's cognition, unlike the state-of-the-art Von Neumann based computers [19,20].

One important thing to consider in the memristor crossbar is defects, as shown in Figure 1b. In the real memristor crossbar, there are stuck-defects, such as stuck-at-0, stuck-at-1, etc. [21]. In addition, variation-related defects can also be considered, where each memristor can have different LRS and HRS values due to process variations [22]. Here, LRS and HRS mean Low Resistance State and High Resistance State, respectively. Figure 1b compares the ideal crossbar (without defects) and the real one (with defects). The solid and open red circles with stars represent stuck-at-LRS and stuck-at-HRS defects, respectively. For the memristor defects such as stuck-at-faults and variations, these defects may be caused from the random nature of filamentary current path which can be formed or erased by the applied current and voltage to the memristor. The filamentary current path created or erased during the memristor programming can have statistical distributions like FLASH memory. Various statistical distributions by device-to-device, wafer-to-wafer, lot-to-lot, and process-to-process lead to the variations in memristance and stuck-at-faults [21].

To minimize a loss of recognition rate due to these memristor defects, we can consider the defect-tolerance scheme based on the conventional defect-aware mapping [21]. To explain the previous defect mapping scheme, the following logic function is assumed, $f = X_1X_2 + X_2X_3 + X_3X_1 + /X_1/X_2/X_3$ is implemented in the crossbar [21].

In the logic function, $/X_1$ means the inversion of X_1. Figure 2a shows the real memristor crossbar (with defects). Here, I_1, I_2, etc. represent input columns. O_1, O_2, etc. are output rows. The gray circle indicates a good memristor cell, which can be programmed with HRS or LRS. The solid and open red circles represent stuck-at-1 and stuck-at-0 defects, respectively. Figure 2b shows the direct mapping without considering the defect map. P_1, P_2, P_3, and P_4 indicate the first, second, third, and fourth partial products in the target logic function. P_1 calculates X_1X_2. However, P_2 calculates $X_1X_2X_3$, not X_2X_3 defined in the logic function, because of the stuck-at-1 fault on the crossing point between X_1 and P_2. P_4 also calculates the wrong partial product. The stuck-at-0 fault is found at the crossing point between $/X_2$ and P_4. By doing so, P_4 calculates $/X_1/X_3$ instead of the target product of $/X_1/X_2/X_3$.

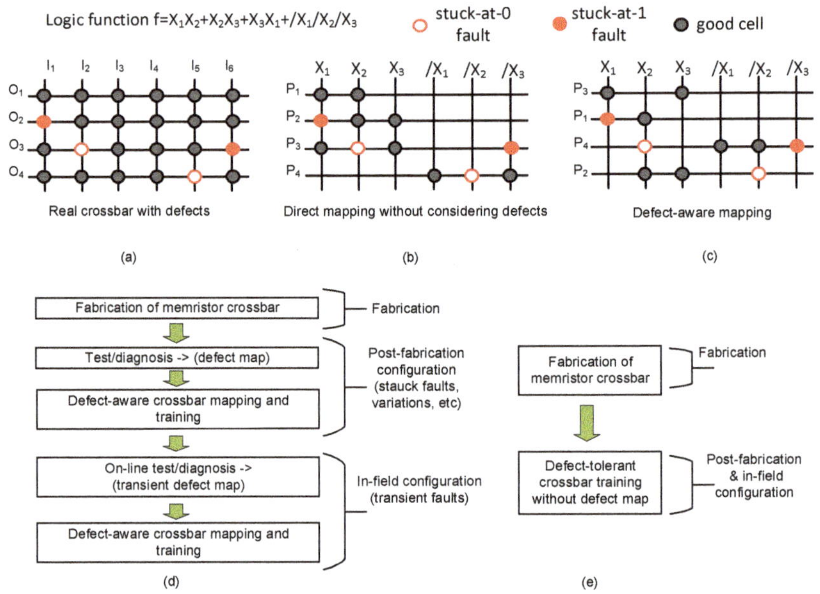

Figure 2. (**a**) The real crossbar with defects; (**b**) the direct mapping of the logic function without considering the defect map; (**c**) the defect-aware mapping of the logic function with considering the defect type and location; (**d**) the flowchart of crossbar training using the conventional defect-aware mapping [21]; and (**e**) the proposed flowchart of the defect-tolerant crossbar training without using the defect map.

Figure 2c shows the defect-aware mapping, where the defects can be used in implementing the logic function according to the defect type and location. To do so, the crossbar's rows in Figure 2c are reordered to consider the defect type and location in calculating the partial products. For example, the first row in Figure 2c is assigned to P_3, not P_1. P_1 is assigned to the second row to calculate X_1X_2. The stuck-at-1 fault on the second row can be used in calculating $P_1 = X_1X_2$. Similarly, the stuck-at-1 fault on P_4 can be employed to calculate $P_4 = /X_1/X_2/X_3$. Moreover, the stuck-at-0 faults on P_2 and P_4 do not cause a wrong result for the calculation of partial products of P_2 and P_4. As shown in Figure 2c, the defects can be employed in implementing the target logic function according to the defect type and location. However, the defect-aware mapping scheme demands very complicated circuits, such as memory, processor, controller, etc., to be implemented in hardware.

Figure 2d shows the flowchart of crossbar training using the conventional defect-aware mapping. After fabricating the memristor crossbar, the defect map should be obtained by measuring the crossbar. As a post-fabrication configuration, the trained synaptic weighs can be transferred to the crossbar using the defect-aware mapping, as explained in Figure 2c. To do so, however, the complicated digital circuits, such as memory, controller, processor, etc., are needed for implementing the defect-aware mapping in hardware, as mentioned earlier.

Not using the defect-aware mapping, in this paper, we propose a simple memristor-CMOS hybrid circuit of defect-tolerant spatial-pooling, which does not need the complicated circuits of memory, controller, processor, etc., as shown in Figure 2e, where, unlike in Figure 2d, the crossbar's defect map is not used. For developing the hybrid circuit of memristor-CMOS, we first show that the spatial-pooling based on Hebbian learning can be defect-tolerant, owing to the boost-factor adjustment, in Section 2. Additionally, we propose a new memristor-CMOS hybrid circuit, where the winner-take-all circuit is implemented not using capacitors occupying large area. In Section 3, the proposed hybrid circuit is verified to be able to recognize well Modified subset of National Institute of Standards and Technology (MNIST) hand-written digits, in spite of memristor defects such as stuck-at-faults, variations, etc. In Section 4, we discuss and compare the following three cases: (1) Spatial-pooling without both the boost-factor adjustment and the defect-aware mapping, (2) spatial-pooling with the defect-aware mapping, and (3) spatial pooling with the boost-factor adjustment, in terms of hardware implementation, energy consumption, and recognition rate. Finally, in Section 5, we summarize this paper.

2. Materials and Methods

To develop a memristor-CMOS hybrid circuit for realizing HTM's SP function by hardware, memristor defects such as stuck-at-faults and variations should be considered. To consider the memristor defects in developing the hybrid circuit of the SP function, we explain the memristor fabrication and its behavioral model in the following sub-section of 'a. Materials'. Then, we describe the boost-factor adjustment in HTM's SP operation can make it defect-tolerant, because the false activation of defective columns in the crossbar are suppressed, in the sub-section of 'b. Methods (scheme)'. In the sub-section of 'c. Method (circuit)', we propose the memristor-CMOS hybrid circuit by explaining its schematic and operation in detail. The hybrid circuit with the boost-factor adjustment is discussed and compared with the previous techniques without the boost-factor adjustment, later in this paper. The simulation result and comparison indicates that the memristor-CMOS hybrid circuit with the boost-factor adjustment can improve the recognition rate by more than ~20%, than the previous defect-map-based technique. This hybrid circuit can be very useful for energy-efficient computing in future IoT systems, where many IoT sensors are connected to a cloud of centralized data processing, as explained later.

a. Materials

Figure 3a shows a cross-sectional view of the fabricated memristor in this paper. The fabricated memristor has a film structure made of a Pt/$LaAlO_3$/Nb-doped $SrTiO_3$ stacked layer [23]. A microscope picture of the measured device is shown in Figure 3b, where the top electrode area is 100 µm × 100 µm [24]. The top and bottom electrodes were formed by Platinum (Pt) and SrTiO3, in the measured device, respectively [23].

Figure 3c shows current–voltage relationships of the fabricated memristor and the Verilog-A model, respectively [23]. The measurement was performed by Keithley-4200 (Semiconductor Characterization System, Tektronix, Inc., Beaverton, OR, USA) [23]. Here, the HRS/LRS ratio in Figure 3c was observed as large as 100. The black and red lines in Figure 3c represent the behavioral model of memristors and the measured data, respectively. The behavioral model described by Verilog-A in Figure 3c was used in the circuit simulation of the memristor-CMOS hybrid circuit in this paper.

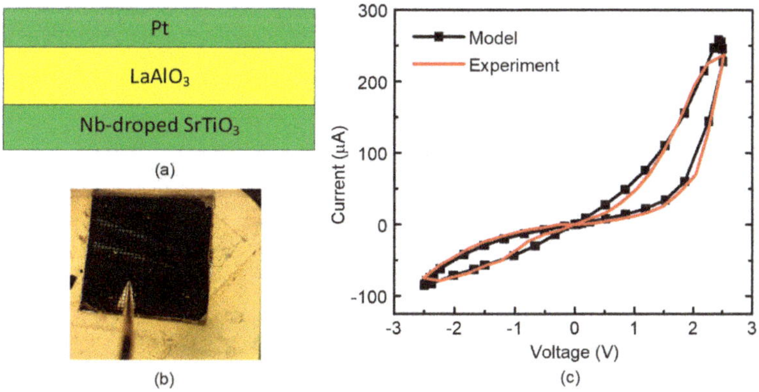

Figure 3. (**a**) The cross-sectional view of the measured memristor [23]; (**b**) the microscope picture of the measured memristor [24]; and (c) the memristor's current–voltage relationships of the measurement and Verilog-A model [23].

b. Methods (scheme): boost-factor adjustment scheme for defect-tolerant spatial-pooling

The spatial-pooling in HTM software framework is composed of initialization, overlap computation, inhibition, and learning, as shown in Figure 4a [8,12]. After the initialization step (Phase 1), three steps: Overlap computation (Phase 2), inhibition (Phase 3), and learning (Phase 4), are repeated sequentially [8,12]. In Phase 1, random sets of inputs are selected from the input space, as indicated in Figure 1a. The number of random sets of inputs per training vector is the same with the number of crossbar's columns. Each input in this random set can be connected to an output neuron in the SP via a synapse [8,12]. In Phase 2, an amount of overlap of each output neuron with the chosen set of inputs from the input space is calculated [8,12] The amount of overlap of each neuron in the SP can be calculated with the number of the connected synapses with the active inputs, multiplied by each column's boost factor. In Phase 3, we decide which columns can be winners within the inhibition radius [8,12]. By doing so, the sparsity regarding the percentage of activation in the neocortical neurons can be controlled to not exceed a certain limit. In the case of the human brain's neocortex, only 2% of neocortical neurons have been observed to be activated in response to human sensory stimuli. In Phase 4, Hebbian learning is performed to strengthen and weaken synaptic connections [8,12]. For the winners chosen in Phase 3, the synaptic permanence values for the active inputs are increased by p+. For the inactivate inputs, the permanence values are decreased by p-. p+ and p- represent the increment and decrement of synaptic permanence, respectively. The permanence value is allowed to vary between 0 and 1. If it reaches 1 or 0, the synaptic weight is changed to LRS or HRS, respectively.

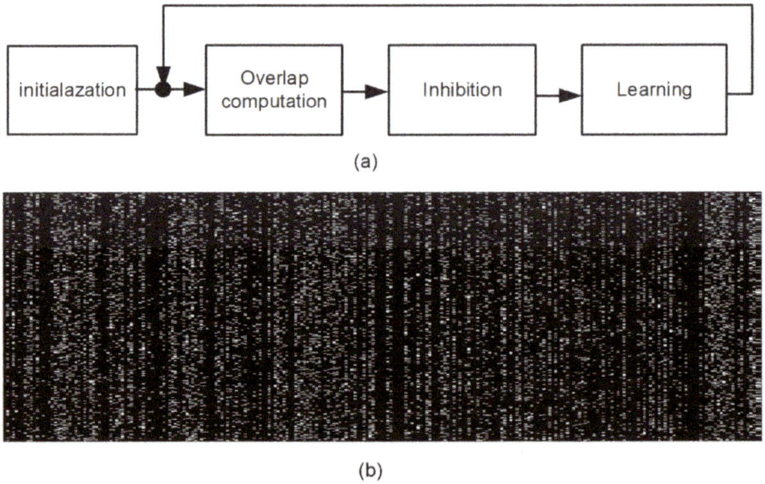

Figure 4. (**a**) The spatial-pooling algorithm composed of initialization, overlap computation, inhibition, and learning [8,12]; and (**b**) the defect map of a memristor crossbar with 10% random defects. Here the numbers of rows and columns of the crossbar are 400 and 256, respectively. The random defects are stuck-at-LRS and stuck-HRS defects.

One more parameter needed to be updated after the activation of each neuron is a boost factor. The boost factor can be defined with the following inverse relationship with the activity ratio [8]:

$$b_i = e^{-\beta(a_i - \langle a_{i,neighbor} \rangle)} \quad (1)$$

Here, b_i means the boost factor of column, i. β is a positive parameter that controls the strength of the adaptation effect. a_i is the activity ratio of column i, and $< a_{i,\ neighbor} >$ means the average activity ratio of the column's neighborhood. For given M test vectors, the activity ratio of column, i, can be calculated with

$$a_i = \frac{1}{M}\sum_{j=1}^{M}(activation(column, i)). \quad (2)$$

Here, a_i is the activity ratio of column i. M is the number of test vectors. The activation function defined with 'activation(column, i)' in Equation (2) becomes one, if the column, i, is activated. If the column is not activated, the activation function should be zero. For a neuron activated very frequently, its boost factor should be adjusted to be very small to lower the probability of activation. On the contrary, if a neuron is chosen very rarely, its boost factor should be increased. As explained just earlier, by adjusting each column's boost factor according to each column's activity ratio, the number of activations can be distributed more evenly for all columns in the crossbar.

We now discuss how each column's activity ratio can be affected by memristor defects. Figure 4b shows a defect map of 400 × 256 memristor crossbar. Here, we assume random defects = 10% in the crossbar. The random defects can be stuck-at-HRS and stuck-at-LRS. Because the HRS defects do not cause erroneous activation of neurons, we focus on the LRS defects here.

In Figure 5a, the number of defects per column is ranked from the largest to the smallest. The number of columns in the crossbar is assumed to be 256 in Figure 5a. Each column is assumed to have 400 cells. Among the 400 cells per column, the most defective column has almost ~90 defects. The smallest number of defects per column is ~0. Figure 5b and c compare the simulated boost factors of the crossbars without and with the boost-factor adjustment, respectively. In Figure 5b, all 256 columns have the same boost factor, fixed by 50. On the contrary, in Figure 5c, each column's boost factor is adjusted between 0 and 100, according to each column's activity ratio.

Figure 5d and e compare the activity ratios of the crossbars without and with the boost-factor adjustment. Here, each column's activity ratio is shown on the y-axis with respect to the ranked column number according to the number of defects. Figure 5d clearly indicates that a large number of defects in a defective column causes frequent activation of the column. The small number of defects results in the rare activation of the column. The frequent activation due to the defective column is very likely to be false and should be suppressed not to happen. Figure 5e shows that the frequent activation of the defective columns can be suppressed, by decreasing the boost factor of the defective columns lower than the neighbors. By doing so, we can reduce the false activation of the defective columns. Thus, the recognition rate loss due to the defective columns can be minimized by the boost-factor adjustment.

In Figure 5f, the crossbar's entropy is compared without and with the boost-factor adjustment. The entropy of the crossbar with N columns is calculated with Equation (3) [8].

$$\text{Entropy} = \sum_{i=1}^{N}\left[-a_i \log_2 a_i - (1-a_i)\log_2(1-a_i)\right] \quad (3)$$

In Equation (3), 'Entropy' means the calculated amount of entropy. N is the number of columns in the crossbar. a_i is the activity ratio of column i. 'log' means the logarithmic function. Figure 5f indicates that the crossbar with the boost-factor adjustment shows much larger entropy than the crossbar without the boost-factor adjustment. The better entropy can result in a better recognition rate, as shown later in this paper.

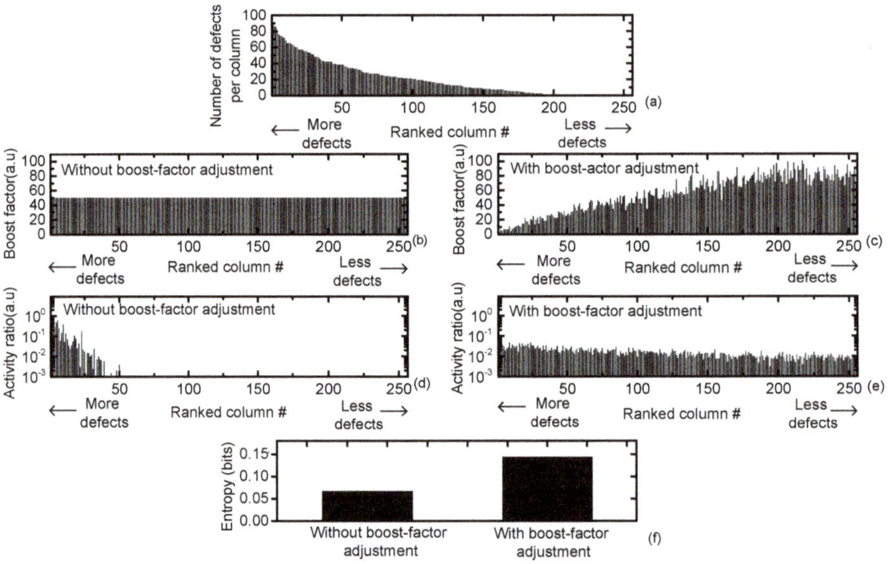

Figure 5. (**a**) The number of defects per column ranked from largest (left) to smallest (right); (**b**) the simulated boost factor of the crossbar without the boost-factor adjustment; (**c**) the simulated boost factor of the crossbar with the boost-factor adjustment; (**d**) the simulated activity ratio of the crossbar without the boost-factor adjustment; (**e**) the simulated activity ratio of the crossbar with the boost-factor adjustment; and (**f**) the comparison of crossbar entropy without and with the boost-factor adjustment.

c. Methods (circuit): memristor-CMOS hybrid circuit of defect-tolerant spatial pooling

Figure 6a shows a schematic of the memristor-CMOS hybrid circuit of defect-tolerant spatial pooling, where each column's boost factor can be adjusted to make each column's activity ratio more even. The memristor crossbar is composed of 400 rows and 256 columns for recognizing the MNIST hand-written digits. The 400 rows can receive 20 × 20 input pixels of each MNIST test vector. The 256 columns correspond to the 256 output neurons of the SP. In Figure 6a, X_0 and X_1 are the first and second row, respectively. $g_{0,0}$ means memristor's conductance of row #0 and column #0. Similarly, $g_{1,0}$ means memristor's conductance of row, #1, and column, #0. I_0 and I_1 represent the currents of columns, #0 and #1, respectively. I_0 and I_1 enter the current–voltage converters of B_0 and B_1, respectively, where each column's boost factor can be adjusted according to each column's activity ratio. Here, V_0 and V_1 are the converted voltages of columns #0 and #1, respectively. The converted voltages, V_0 and V_1, enter the comparators of C_0 and C_1, respectively, where V_0 and V_1 are compared with V_{REF}. V_{REF} is obtained from the maximum output voltage among the neighbors using the diode-connected MOSFETs of M_0, M_1, etc. If we assume the diode 'ON' voltage is very small, V_{REF} can be very similar with the maximum voltage among all the output voltages such as V_0, V_1, etc. If V_0 or V_1 is very close to V_{REF}, then column #0 or column #1 will be activated as a winner, inhibiting the neighboring columns from being activated. One thing to note here is that the V_{REF} for selecting the winner columns is obtained dynamically by extracting the largest output voltage among the neighbors. If a new input vector is applied to the crossbar, the output voltages are changed, too. Thus, we can obtain a new maximum voltage for the new input vector dynamically. Comparing each column's output voltage with the new maximum, we can choose the next winner columns that are very close to the new maximum voltage. Y_0 and Y_1 refer to the output SDR bits for columns #0 and #1, respectively.

The circuit proposed in this paper does not use any capacitor for realizing the winner-take-all function, as shown in Figure 6a. This is different from the previous publications [12,20], where the capacitor was used to integrate the column current over time to accumulate the charge. The accumulated charge can be represented by the capacitor's voltage. If one column's voltage reaches a certain level at the earliest time, then that column is chosen as the winner [12,20]. Instead of capacitors occupying a very large area, the diode-connected MOSFETs are used here to obtain the maximum voltage among all output voltages, as shown in Figure 6a. The winning column can be chosen by comparing each column's output voltage with the maximum voltage extracted from the diode-connected MOSFETs. The diode-connected MOSFETs in Figure 6a can occupy a much smaller area than the capacitors used in the previous publications [12,20].

One problem with the winner-take-all circuit using the diode-connected MOSFETs in Figure 6a is that the winner may be multiple, not single, in some cases. To investigate the number of winning columns per input vector, the statistical sparsity distribution is compared between the previous winner-take-all and the proposed circuit in Figure 6a. To do so, the average and variance of sparsity distribution are calculated for the previous winner-take-all and the proposed circuit in Figure 6a. The average sparsity of the previous winner-take-all and the proposed circuit in Figure 6a, are 2.2% and 2.3%, respectively. The calculated variance values are 0.09 and 0.11, respectively. The small difference in variance between the previous and proposed indicates that the winner-take-all can be implemented with the diode-connected MOSFETs and voltage comparators, not using the capacitors occupying a very large area.

Figure 6b shows a detailed schematic of the current-to-voltage converter, B_0, with the boost-factor adjustment. OP_1 and OP_2 are OP amplifiers. The column current, I_0, goes though R_1. The node voltage, N_1, becomes–$I_0 \times R_1$. The converted voltage from I_0 is given to R_2. Thereby, the current though R_2 goes to $M_{b,0}$ and is finally converted to V_0. V_0 is the output voltage of the current–voltage converter. Here, we used $R_1 = 5$ kΩ and $R_2 = 100$ MΩ, respectively. For the boost-factor adjustment, $M_{b,0}$ should be changed according to the activity ratio of column #0, with respect to the activity ratios of the neighbors. S_1, S_2, and S_3 are the switches controlled by SW_0. SW_0 is applied by the boost-factor adjustment controller. V_P means the memristor programming pulse. V_P is applied to $M_{b,0}$, through S_1 and S_2, to change the memristor's conductance. V_P is applied to the boost-factor memristor for the boost-factor adjustment, when SW_0 is high. On the contrary, when SW_0 is low, S_3 becomes 'ON' and V_0 is compared with the other output voltages such as V_1, V_2, etc.

Figure 6c shows the operational diagram of the proposed memristor-CMOS hybrid circuit illustrated in Figure 6a,b. As indicated in Figure 6c, the crossbar performs the overlap calculation, in which the input voltage is multiplied with the memristor's conductance. Then, each column's current can be calculated by summating all the cell currents belonging to the column. The column current enters the current-to-voltage converter. The converted voltage from each column is delivered to the winner-take-all, where the winning column is chosen. Based on the winning column, the learning controller adjusts each column's boost factor and the permanence values of the cells belonging to the column, according to Hebbian rule. The steps indicated in the operational diagram in Figure 6c are repeated again, when a new input vector is applied to the crossbar.

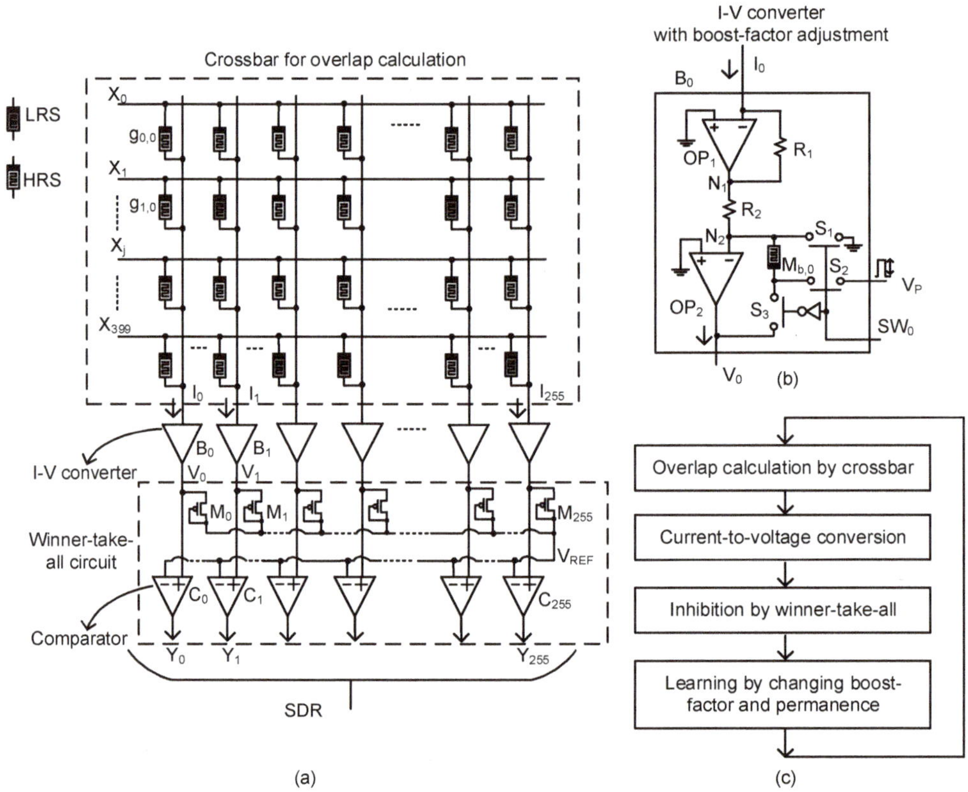

Figure 6. (**a**) The detailed schematic of the memristor-CMOS (Complementary Metal-Oxide-Semiconductor) hybrid circuit of defect-tolerant spatial pooling. The hybrid circuit is composed of the memristor crossbar, the current–to-voltage (I–to-V) converters with the boost-factor adjustment, and the winner-take-all circuit with the diode-connected Metal-Oxide-Semiconductor Field-Effect Transistors (MOSFETs) and comparators; (**b**) the detailed schematic of the voltage-converter circuit with the boost-factor adjustment; and (**c**) the operational diagram of the memristor-CMOS hybrid circuit.

The simulated waveforms in Figure 7 demonstrate the operation of the proposed memristor-CMOS hybrid circuit with the boost-factor adjustment. Here, the circuit simulation was performed using CADENCE SPECTRE (Cadence Design Systems, Inc., San Jose, CA, USA) and SAMSUNG 0.13-µm circuit simulation parameters [25]. The mathematical equations of the Verilog-A model of memristors used in the circuit simulation were explained in-detail in a previous publication [23]. In the simulation, we assumed the memristor crossbar of SP with 400 rows and 256 columns. The number of synaptic memristors per column is 25 among 400 cells. It means the 25 cells can be activated at the maximum among 400 cells per column in the crossbar. The increment and decrement of permanence are +0.01 and −0.01, respectively. The initial permanence values are assumed to be random between 0 and 1. The minimum amount of overlap between the input-space and spatial-pooler space can start from zero. The amount of overlap can be calculated by multiplying the input voltages with the memristor synaptic weights. The size of inhibition circuit zone is 64 columns in the crossbar. The number of winning columns is allowed not to exceed 2 among 64 columns. Thereby, the sparsity in Figure 6a can be controlled within 2%, as the brain's neocortex does.

In Figure 7, during the crossbar training time, each column's activity ratio is calculated by counting the number of activation of each column. If column #0 becomes activated, Y_0 becomes high. Similarly, if column #1 becomes activated, Y_1 is high. After the crossbar training time, the boost factor can be adjusted according to each column's activity ratio, as described in Equation (1). The more frequent activation of column #0 leads to decrease the boost factor more. The less frequent activation of column #1 reduces the boost factor little, as shown in Figure 7. For adjusting the boost factors of columns #0 and #1, the pulse widths of SW_0 and SW_1, respectively, are modulated. $M_{b,0}$ can be decreased more than $M_{b,1}$ by many programming pulses of V_P, because SW_0 is high for a longer time than SW_1. On the contrary, $M_{b,1}$ is changed little, due to the fact that SW_1 is high only for a very short time. The pulse modulation of SW_0 and SW_1 can be controlled very easily by counting the number of activations of each column during the crossbar training time.

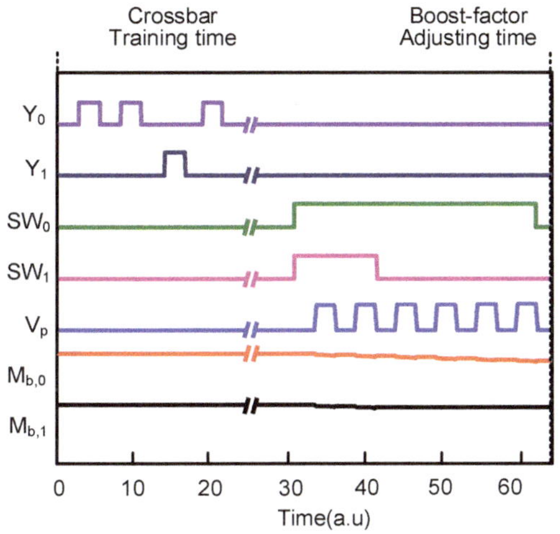

Figure 7. The simulated waveforms of the proposed memristor-CMOS hybrid circuit with the boost-factor adjustment.

3. Simulation Results

For calculating the recognition rate, we tested MNIST vectors [26,27] with the proposed memristor-CMOS hybrid circuit. To reflect the real crossbar with non-ideal effects, we considered source resistance, neuron resistance, wire resistance, etc., in the recognition-rate simulation [22]. Figure 8a shows a schematic of memristor crossbar that includes these non-ideal parasitic effects. Here, R_S and R_N represent source resistance and neuron resistance, respectively [2]. R_W represents wire resistance from metal layers. In the non-ideal crossbar, R_N and R_S are assumed to be 0.27% of HRS and 0.067% of HRS, respectively [22]. R_W is assumed to be ~1Ω per cell in this paper. These R_S and R_N, which are 0.27% of HRS and 0.067% of HRS, respectively, are the worst-case values of the source and neuron resistance observed from the fabricated real crossbars [22]. In Figure 8a, V_0, V_1, and V_n represent the input voltages. I_0, I_1, and I_m represent the column currents.

We now explain the crossbar architecture for recognizing the MNIST vectors. Here, the number of rows in the crossbar should be 400, which should be the same with the number of input voltages. Each MNIST vector is composed of 20 × 20 = 400 pixels. Thus, the number of input voltages is 400 for recognizing the MNIST vector. For the number of columns of the SP crossbar, 256, 1024, and 4096 columns are used in Figure 8b, c, and d, respectively. It is known that having more SP columns can result in a better recognition rate [12]. This is because each SP column can store a specific feature of tested vectors. If the number of SP columns becomes larger, then more features can be stored in the columns. Thereby, the recognition rate for the tested images can be improved with increasing the number of SP columns. The number of SP columns = 256 is the same condition for the memristor-implemented Convolutional Neural Network, where the testing image has 20 × 20 pixels, the kernel size is 5 × 5, and the number of kernels = 1. Similarly, the number of SP columns = 1024 is the same condition of Convolutional Neural Network, with 20 × 20 image, 5 × 5 kernel, and the number of kernels = 4. The number of SP columns = 4096 is the same condition of Convolutional Neural Network, with 20 × 20 image, 5 × 5 kernel, and the number of kernels = 16. In this simulation, we did not simulate the crossbars with SP columns more than 4096, because we do not use the number of kernels more than 16 for recognizing the MNSIT vectors, in Convolutional Neural Network.

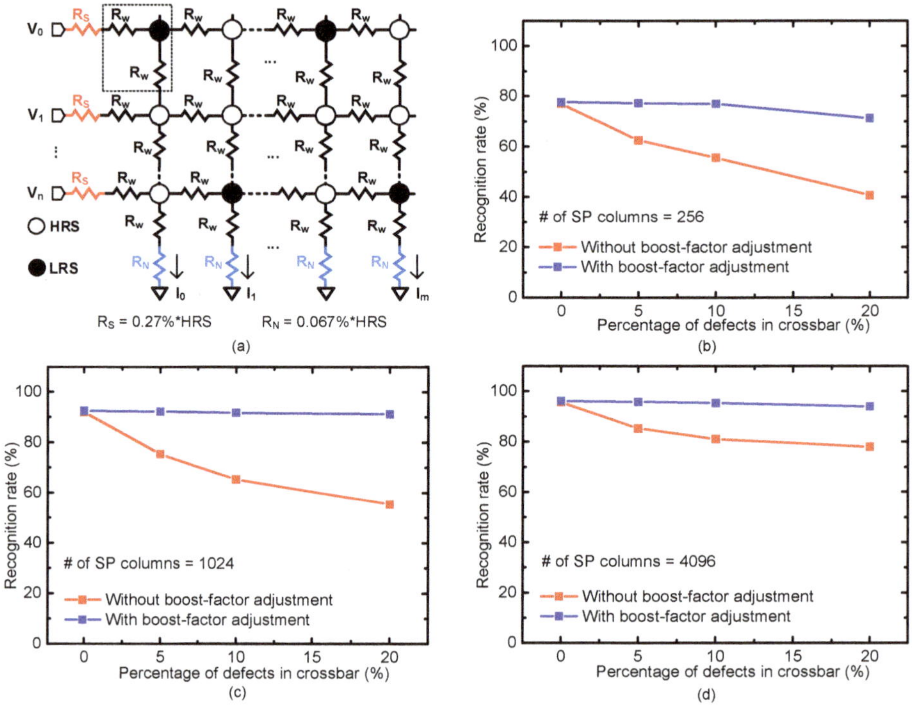

Figure 8. (**a**) The memristor crossbar with the non-ideal effects of R_S, R_N, and R_W. Here R_S = 0.27%*HRS and R_N = 0.067%*HRS.; (**b**) the MNIST recognition rate of the non-ideal crossbar with 256 SP columns. Here, SP means Spatial Pooler. The percentage σ of memristance variation of HRS and LRS is assumed to be 0% in Figure 8.; (**c**) the MNIST recognition rate of the non-ideal crossbar with 1024 SP columns. Here the percentage σ of memristance variation of HRS and LRS is 0%; and (**d**) the MNIST recognition rate of the non-ideal crossbar with 4096 SP columns. The percentage σ of memristance variation in HRS and LRS is assumed 0%.

Figure 8b shows MNIST recognition rate of the memristor crossbar with SP columns = 256. Here, the percentage of defects in the crossbar is changed from 0% to 20%. The percentage σ of memristance variation of HRS and LRS is assumed to be zero. For the percentage of defects = 0%, the crossbars without and with the boost-factor adjustment show the recognition rates of 77.3% and 77.6%, respectively. When the percentage of defects is very small, the boost-factor adjustment affects the recognition rate very little. However, if the percentage increases, the boost-factor adjustment plays an important role to keep the recognition rate as high as the rate of defects = 0%, as shown in Figure 8b. For the defects = 20%, the boost-factor adjustment can show the recognition rate better by as much as 30.6%, compared to the crossbar without the boost-factor adjustment.

Figure 8c is for the SP columns = 1024. As mentioned earlier, the crossbar with the SP columns = 1024 recognizes MNIST vectors better than the SP columns = 256. For the percentage of defects = 0%, the recognition rates of 256 and 1024 SP columns are 77.6% and 92.5%, respectively. As indicated in Figure 8b, the boost-factor adjustment in Figure 8c can maintain this good recognition rate, even though the percentage of defects is increased to 20%. For the percentage = 20%, the gap of recognition rates without and with the boost-factor adjustment is as much as 35.9%.

Figure 8d is for the SP columns = 4096. If the percentage of defects is 0%, the recognition rate of the crossbar is as high as 96.2%. In spite of the percentage of defects = 20%, the boost-factor adjustment can keep the rate as high as 94%, whereas the crossbar without the boost-factor adjustment is as low as 78%.

Figure 9a shows the statistical distributions of HRS and LRS, where the percentage σ of memristance variation is assumed to be 30%. Figure 9 b, c, and d are for the SP columns = 256, 1024, and 4096, respectively. As indicated in Figure 9, the more SP columns can result in the better recognition rate. In Figure 9b, the percentage of defects is changed from 0% to 20%. For the percentage of defects = 0%, the boost-factor adjustment affects the recognition rate very little. However, if the percentage of defects is increased to 20%, the boost-factor adjustment can improve the recognition rate significantly compared to the crossbar without the boost-factor adjustment. Similarly, in Figure 9c with the SP columns = 1024, the recognition rates without and with the boost-factor adjustment are 54% and 87%, respectively, when the defects = 20%. In Figure 9d with the SP columns = 4096, the recognition rates without and with the boost-factor adjustment are 74% and 93.9%, respectively, when the defects = 20%.

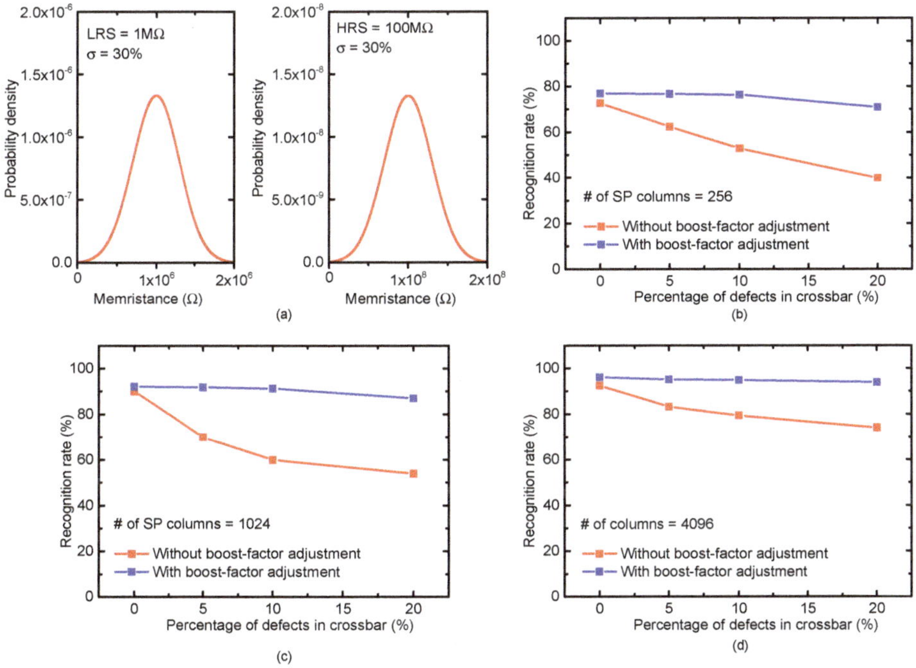

Figure 9. (**a**) The statistical distributions of LRS and HRS with the percentage σ of memristance variation = 30% in the simulation; (**b**) the MNIST recognition rate of the non-ideal crossbar with 256 SP columns and the percentage σ of memristance variation = 30%. Here, SP means Spatial Pooler.; (**c**) the MNIST recognition rate of the non-ideal crossbar with 1024 SP columns and the percentage σ of memristance variation = 30%; and (**d**) the MNIST recognition rate of the non-ideal crossbar with 4096 SP columns and the percentage σ of memristance variation = 30%.

4. Discussion

In this session, to understand the benefit of the proposed circuit exactly, we discuss and compare the following three SP schemes in Table 1: (1) Spatial-pooling without both the boost-factor adjustment and the defect-aware mapping, (2) spatial-pooling with the defect-aware mapping, and (3) spatial-pooling with the boost-factor adjustment.

Table 1. Comparison of possibility of hardware implementation, energy consumption for the crossbar programming, and MNIST recognition rate for the three SP schemes. Here, SP means Spatial Pooler. Energy consumption is calculated during the training time of 10,000 MNIST vectors.

	Possibility for Hardware Implementation	Energy Consumption of the Crossbar Programming (SP Column = 256)	MNIST Recognition Rate		
			# of SP Columns	Rate (%) Defects = 0%	Rate (%) Defects = 10%
(1) Spatial-pooling without the boost-factor adjustment and the defect-aware mapping	Able to be implemented with hardware	3.9 mJ for the crossbar programming	256	77.3	55.6
			1024	92	65.4
			4096	95.7	81.1
(2) Spatial-pooling with the defect-aware mapping	The defect-aware mapping in Figure 2d demands the very complicated hardware of memory, processor, controller, etc.	3.9mJ for the crossbar programming	256	77.3	56.3
			1024	92	66.5
			4096	95.7	82.4
(3) Spatial- pooling with the boost-factor adjustment	Able to be implemented with hardware	3.9 mJ for the crossbar programming, +2uJ for the boost-factor adjustment (Energy overhead due to boost-factor adjustment: ~0.05%)	256	77.6	77
			1024	92.5	91.8
			4096	96.2	95.4

First, we discuss the possibility of hardware implementation in Table 1. As mentioned earlier, (1) and (3) can be implemented in hardware. However, the defect-aware mapping of (2), as indicated in Figure 2d, demands very complicated circuits such as memory, processor, controller, etc.

Second, the energy consumptions of the crossbar programming are compared among (1), (2), and (3) in Table 1. The amount of programming energy is simulated during the training time of 10,000 MNIST vectors (1) and (2) consume 3.9 mJ for programming the crossbar with HRS and LRS, according to Hebbian learning rule, as explained in Figure 4a. The energy overhead due to the boost-factor adjustment is less than ~0.05% of the crossbar programming energy. This is because each column has only one memristor for the boost-factor adjustment, compared to 400 cells per column for Hebbian learning.

For the recognition rate, in Table 1 (1), without the boost-factor adjustment and defect-aware mapping, shows MNIST recognition rates of 77.3% and 55.6%, when the defects = 0% and 10%, respectively. Similarly, (2), with only the defect-aware mapping, shows the rates of 77.3% and 56.3%, when the defects = 0% and 10%, respectively. Without the boost-factor adjustment, the defective columns necessarily become activated frequently. The frequent activation of defective columns degrades the recognition rate significantly, as shown in (2) in Table 1. On the contrary, (3) with the boost-factor adjustment shows the rates of 77.6% and 77%, when the defects = 0% and 10%, respectively. It has very little loss of the recognition rate, in spite of the defects = 10%. The gap between the defects = 0% and 10% is negligibly small for the crossbar with the boost-factor adjustment.

We now discuss the relationship of this work to the previous works performed in HTM hardware realization. Actually, as a previous works of this paper, we developed the memristor crossbar circuits for performing the SP and TM operations of HTM, respectively [12,13]. However, in the previous works, we did not consider the memristor defects, which should be taken into account in the real memristor crossbar having defects of stuck-at-faults and variations. Thus, the SP hardware implemented with the real defective memristor crossbar can be an essential part of future HTM's hardware system. Additionally, as a further work, we try to fabricate the crossbar having more than 100 memristors and combine the fabricated crossbar with the CMOS circuit to verify the SP operation by hardware, for testing the MNSIT vectors.

Finally, we discuss possible applications of the memristor-CMOS hybrid circuit of HTM's hardware. As Internet of Things (IoT) sensors become more popular in human life and environment, an amount of data generated from the sensors becomes enormous [28–30]. To handle this huge amount of data from the physical world, we can think of the integration of IoT sensors and memristor-CMOS hybrid circuit into one chip [31,32]. By doing so, the unstructured data from the sensors can be pre-processed and interpreted near the sensors by the integrated memristor-CMOS hybrid circuit of HTM hardware. If we deliver all the data generated from the IoT sensors to the cloud, without any pre-processing of the unstructured data near the IoT sensors, an amount of computing energy demanded at the cloud may be huge [33]. Thus, the memristor-CMOS hybrid circuit that can perform the pre-processing of the unstructured data from the IoT sensors can be very useful for energy-efficient computing in future.

5. Conclusions

The SP of HTM has been known as the software framework to model human brain's neocortical operation such as recognition, cognition, etc. However, mimicking the brain's neocortical operation by hardware rather than software is more desirable, because the hardware not only describes the neocortical operation, but also employs the brain's architectural advantages such as high energy efficiency, extreme parallel-computation, etc.

To realize HTM's SP by hardware, in this paper, we developed the memristor-CMOS hybrid circuit. One thing important for hardware implementation is that memristor defects such as stuck-at-faults, memristance variations, etc., should be considered in developing the memristor-CMOS hybrid circuit of SP.

For considering memristor defects in hardware implementation, first, we showed that the boost-factor adjustment can make HTM's SP defect-tolerant, because the false activation of defective columns can be suppressed. Second, we proposed the memristor-CMOS hybrid circuit with the boost-factor adjustment for realizing the defect-tolerant spatial-pooling in hardware. The proposed circuit does not rely on the conventional defect-aware mapping scheme, which cannot avoid the false activation of defective columns in spatial-pooling. For the MNIST data-set, the boost-factor adjusted crossbar with the defects = 10% was verified to have a rate loss as low as ~0.6%, compared to the ideal crossbar with the defects = 0%. On the contrary, the defect-aware mapping without the boost-factor adjustment demonstrated a significant rate loss, as much as ~21.0%. The energy overhead of the boost-factor adjustment was estimated to be as little as ~0.05% of the programming energy of the memristor synapse crossbar.

Author Contributions: All authors have contributed to the submitted manuscript. K.-S.M. defined the research topic. T.V.N. and K.V.P. performed the simulation and measurement. K.-S.M. wrote the manuscript. All authors read and approved the submitted manuscript.

Funding: The work was financially supported by NRF-2015R1A5A7037615, MOTIE/KEIT (10052653), ETRI grant (18ZB1800), and Samsung Electronics under Project Number SRFC-IT1701-07.

Acknowledgments: The CAD tools were supported by IC Design Education Center (IDEC), Daejeon, Korea.

Conflicts of Interest: The authors declare that they have no competing interests.

References

1. Hawkins, J.; Blakeslee, S. *On intelligence: How a New Understanding of the Brain Will Lead to the Creation of Truly Intelligent Machines*; Henry Holt & Company: New York, NY, USA, 2004.
2. Horton, J.C.; Adams, D.L. The cortical column: A structure without a function. *Philos. Trans. R. Soc. Lond. B Biol. Sci.* **2005**, *360*, 837–862. [CrossRef] [PubMed]
3. Thomson, A. Neocortical layer 6, a review. *Front. Neuroanat.* **2010**, *4*, 13. [CrossRef] [PubMed]
4. Hensch, T.; Stryker, M. Columnar architecture sculpted by GABA circuits in developing cat visual cortex. *Science* **2004**, *303*, 1678–1681. [CrossRef] [PubMed]
5. Muir, D.R.; Cook, M. Anatomical constraints on lateral competition in columnar cortical architectures. *Neural Comput.* **2014**, *26*, 1624–1666. [CrossRef] [PubMed]
6. Douglas, R.J.; Martin, K.A.C.; Whitteridge, D. A canonical microcircuit for neocortex. *Neural Comput.* **1989**, *1*, 480–488. [CrossRef]

7. Hawkins, J.; Ahmad, S.; Dubinsky, D. *Hierarchical Temporal Memory including HTM Cortical Learning Algorithms*; Tech. Rep.; Numenta, Inc.: Palo Alto, CA, USA, 2011.
8. Cui, Y.; Ahmad, C.; Hawkins, J. The HTM spatial pooler—A neocortical algorithm for online sparse distributed coding. *bioRxiv* **2016**, bioRxiv:085035. Available online: https://doi.org/10.1101/085035 (accessed on 2 November 2016). [CrossRef]
9. Ahmad, S.; Hawkins, J. Properties of sparse distributed representations and their application to hierarchical temporal memory. *arXiv* **2015**, arXiv:1503.07469.
10. Ahmad, S.; Hawkins, J. How do neurons operate on sparse distributed representations? A mathematical theory of sparsity, neurons and active dendrites. *arXiv* **2016**, arXiv:1601.00720.
11. Cui, Y.; Ahmad, C.; Hawkins, J. Continuous online sequence learning with an unsupervised neural network model. *arXiv* **2015**, arXiv:1512.05463. [CrossRef]
12. Truong, S.N.; Pham, K.V.; Min, K.S. Spatial-pooling memristor crossbar converting sensory information to sparse distributed representation of cortical neurons. *IEEE Trans. Nanotechnol.* **2018**, *17*, 482–491. [CrossRef]
13. Nguyen, T.; Pham, K.; Min, K.S. Memristor-CMOS Hybrid Circuit for Temporal-Pooling of Sensory and Hippocampal Responses of Cortical Neurons. *Materials* **2019**, *12*, 875. [CrossRef] [PubMed]
14. Chua, L.O. Memristor-the missing circuit element. *IEEE Trans. Circuit Theory* **1971**, *18*, 507–519. [CrossRef]
15. Strukov, D.B.; Snider, G.S.; Stewart, D.R.; Williams, R.S. The missing memristor found. *Nature* **2008**, *453*, 80–83. [CrossRef] [PubMed]
16. Jo, S.H.; Chang, T.; Ebong, I.; Bhadviya, B.B.; Mazumder, P.; Lu, W. Nanoscale memristor device as synapse in neuromorphic systems. *Nano Lett.* **2010**, *10*, 1297–1301. [CrossRef] [PubMed]
17. Kügeler, C.; Meier, M.; Rosezin, R.; Gilles, S.; Waser, R. High-density 3D memory architecture based on the resistive switching effect. *Solid State Electron.* **2009**, *53*, 1287–1292. [CrossRef]
18. Shulaker, M.M.; Wu, T.F.; Pal, A.; Zhao, L.; Nishi, Y.; Saraswat, K.; Wong, H.-S.P.; Mitra, S. Monolithic 3D integration of logic and memory: Carbon nanotube FETs, resistive RAM, and silicon FETs. In Proceedings of the IEEE International Electron Devices Meeting, San Francisco, CA, USA, 15–17 December 2014; pp. 638–641.
19. Truong, S.N.; Shin, S.H.; Byeon, S.D.; Song, J.S.; Min, K.S. New twin crossbar architecture of binary memristors for low-power image recognition with discrete cosine transform. *IEEE Trans. Nanotechnol.* **2015**, *14*, 1104–1111. [CrossRef]
20. Truong, S.N.; Ham, S.J.; Min, K.S. Neuromorphic crossbar circuit with nanoscale filamentary-switching binary memristors for speech recognition. *Nanoscale Res. Lett.* **2014**, *9*, 1–9. [CrossRef]
21. Tunali, M.A.O. A survey of fault-tolerance algorithms for reconfigurable nano-crossbar arrays. *ACM Comput. Surv.* **2017**, *50*, 79:1–79:35. [CrossRef]
22. Chakraborty, I.; Roy, D.; Roy, K. Technology Aware Training in Memristive Neuromorphic Systems based on non-ideal Synaptic Crossbars. *IEEE Trans. Emerg. Top. Comput. Intell.* **2018**, *2*, 335–344. [CrossRef]
23. Truong, S.; Pham, K.; Yang, W.; Shin, S.; Pedrotti, K.; Min, K.S. New pulse amplitude modulation for fine tuning of memristor synapses. *Microelectron. J.* **2016**, *55*, 162–168. [CrossRef]
24. Pham, K.; Tran, S.; Nguyen, T.; Min, K.-S. Asymmetrical Training Scheme of Binary-Memristor-Crossbar-Based Neural Networks for Energy-Efficient Edge-Computing Nanoscale Systems. *Micromachines* **2019**, *10*, 141. [CrossRef] [PubMed]
25. *Virtuoso Spectre Circuit Simulator User Guide*; Cadence Design System Inc.: San Jose, CA, USA, 2011.
26. LeCun, Y.; Bottou, L.; Bengio, Y.; Haffner, P. Gradient-Based Learning Applied to Document Recognition. *Proc. IEEE* **1998**, *86*, 2278–2324. [CrossRef]
27. Deng, L. The MNIST database of handwritten digit images for machine learning research. *IEEE Signal Process. Mag.* **2012**, *29*, 141–142. [CrossRef]
28. Sun, X.; Ansari, N. EdgeIoT: Mobile Edge Computing for the Internet of Things. *IEEE Commun. Mag.* **2016**, *54*, 22–29. [CrossRef]
29. Gusev, M.; Dustdar, S. Going back to the roots ×2014; the evolution of edge computing, an IoT perspective. *IEEE Internet Comput.* **2018**, *22*, 5–15. [CrossRef]
30. Gopika, P.; Mario, D.F.; Tarik, T. Edge computing for the internet of things: A case study. *IEEE Internet Things* **2018**, *5*, 1275–1284.
31. Abunahla, H.; Mohammad, B.; Mahmoud, L.; Darweesh, M.; Alhawari, M.; Jaoude, M.; Hitt, G. Memsens: Memristor-based radiation sensor. *IEEE Sens. J.* **2018**, *18*, 3198–3205. [CrossRef]

32. Krestinskaya, O.; James, A.; Chua, L. Neuro-memristive Circuits for Edge Computing: A review. *arXiv* **2018**, arXiv:1807.00962.
33. Plastiras, G.; Terzi, M.; Kyrkou, C.; Theocharidcs, T. Edge intelligence: Challenges and opportunities of near-sensor machine learning applications. In Proceedings of the 2018 IEEE 29th International Conference on Application-specific Systems, Architectures and Processors (ASAP), Milan, Italy, 10–12 July 2018; pp. 1–7.

MDPI
St. Alban-Anlage 66
4052 Basel
Switzerland
Tel. +41 61 683 77 34
Fax +41 61 302 89 18
www.mdpi.com

Materials Editorial Office
E-mail: materials@mdpi.com
www.mdpi.com/journal/materials

CPSIA information can be obtained
at www.ICGtesting.com
Printed in the USA
BVHW020815280321
603588BV00009B/2327

9 783039 285761